PSYCHOLOGY: A Brief Overview

T. K. Landauer

BELL LABORATORIES
MURRAY HILL, N.J.

McGRAW-HILL BOOK COMPANY
New York St. Louis San Francisco
Düsseldorf Johannesburg Kuala Lumpur
London Mexico Montreal
New Delhi Panama Rio de Janeiro
Singapore Sydney Toronto

Library of Congress Cataloging
in Publication Data

Landauer, Thomas K.

   Psychology: a brief overview

    1. Psychology.   I. Title.

BF121.L25 1972   150   75-174618
ISBN 0-07-036113-4

For Katey and Debbie

1234567890MGMG798765432

This book was set in Patina by
University Graphics, Inc., and
printed and bound by McGregor
& Werner Graphics, Inc. The
designer was Ben Kann; the
drawings were done by Danmark
& Michaels, Inc. The editors were
Walter Maytham, John Hendry,
and Paula Henson. Peter D.
Guilmette supervised production.

Contents

FOUR
Adjustment and Psychopathology   *71*

NINE

TEN
Physiological Psychology   *272*

About the Author

T. K. Landauer studied anthropology and biology for a Bachelor of Arts degree from the University of Colorado in 1954. In 1960 he received a Ph.D. for his work in the Department of Social Relations at Harvard University.

Dr. Landauer has taught introductory, educational, physiological, experimental, and developmental psychology at the Harvard Graduate School of Education, Dartmouth College, Stanford University, and the University of Nairobi, Kenya. He spent one year at the Center for Advanced Study in the Behavioral Sciences, where he pursued his interest in biochemistry, and half a year in East Africa working on a culturally portable test of learning ability. He has done research (much of it published) on the biochemical basis of learning, conditioning in rats, child psychology, human memory, reaction time, physical growth, and thinking.

Currently he works at Bell Laboratories, the research and development division of the Bell System, where he does basic research into the processes of human learning and memory.

Preface

Introductory courses often pose a peculiar paradox. Because they introduce students to new realms of knowledge, to new ideas and insights, they should be tremendously exciting. Yet they are often tremendously dull.

Why so? The problem is certainly a complicated one, involving questions of university politics, professorial ambition or sloth, and issues of student unrest or rest. But perhaps the single most important factor in the frequent failure of introductory courses is the dilemma of breadth versus depth.

Much of the excitement of intellectual pursuit comes in mastery, in really understanding or being able to do something difficult that one couldn't before. But mastery of a topic requires a thorough grasp of its details and subtleties. How can such mastery be achieved in a first course in a new discipline? One solution would be to cover just one topic, but to cover it well. There is much to be said for such a solution, at least in some fields of knowledge.

On the other hand, an introductory course can serve important functions that do not lend themselves to such an approach. One of these is to show students what the field has to offer. How is a student to know whether he wants to pursue philosophy, physics, or psychology without some foretaste of what awaits him? To meet this need, introductory courses commonly *survey* a domain of knowledge, sampling as much of it as possible at a relatively unsophisticated level.

A survey course can also give the student a set of basic facts and principles—a starter kit of knowledge—that he can use in understanding and dealing with his world. Having had a course in economics, a student should feel cheated if he still knows nothing about GNP, and so still cannot read his newspaper intelligently.

So there are reasons, other than trying to see how much the student can swallow and spit back, for covering a lot of ground in an introductory course.

It is my impression that this dilemma has usually been solved by jumping on one side or the other of the seesaw. Most of the standard textbooks in psychology have undertaken to survey the field as exhaustively as possible, while some instructors have given up traditional textbooks entirely in favor of a selection of short works on selected aspects of the field.

A possible compromise solution is to use several original sources and monographs and also a broad-coverage textbook. Since most general textbooks in psychology run over 600 pages, the result of this approach is an extraordinarily difficult and tedious course.

It was to provide another way out of the depth-breadth dilemma that the present book was conceived. The basic idea was to produce a broad-coverage textbook that could supplement the intensive treatment of a few topics, but which would be short—on the order of 300 pages. I thought this could be done because I felt that traditional broad-coverage books are much longer than necessary for the purpose. Most of them have attempted to serve as comprehensive reference sources as well as introductory texts; to cover all areas of interest within psychology, whether much is known or not; to fairly represent all influential opinions, and to review the important research results on which current knowledge is based. I have heard Ph.D. candidates advised that they will certainly pass if they know everything in a good introductory text. Now, surely, I thought, a beginning student can get what he wants and needs from a less detailed treatment.

Psychology has matured to the point where many of its findings and explanations are, at least in broad outline, no longer much in debate. In my opinion, it is this core content to which the beginning student should be introduced by a general textbook.

Therefore, I have kept this book shorter than most (but not as short as I wanted to) by sticking mainly to assertions of fact and to principles upon which there is reasonable agreement in the field, and by summarizing them without citing the research literature. Actual studies are described only when they serve as clarifying examples. Unresolved issues and debates have been given very brief treatment or omitted entirely.

Trying to decide what is established fact and principle and what is still uncertain has required a certain amount of temerity (and gall). I am sure I have not succeeded in every case; readers will undoubtedly find areas in which I have erred. Nonetheless, if they find the separation of truth from conjecture reasonably adequate and the number of pages relatively small, I will have achieved my goal.

There are, of course, many topics in psychology that are extremely interesting but about which very little is known. The causes of behavior disorders is a good example. I have usually handled such topics in one of two ways. One way is to outline the problem and then state that nothing definite is known (you will find many such disclaimers). The other way, used sparingly, is to present my own tentative opinion, which has been carefully labeled as such, rather than describe several competing views.

For the rest, the sifting of the established from the uncertain has rested on my own judgment, guided by a few rules of thumb. Usually a conclusion is not stated if it would be based on only one research report or if there are substantial contradictory data. Usually an experimental finding is not reported unless there has been sufficient time for technical criticism to appear in the literature. Consequently, not much is said about research of the last decade. For more news from the frontiers of psychological knowledge the student will need supplementary sources.

To aid those who want more detail, more data, or more speculation and opinion, I have provided a list of readings at the end of each chapter. These range from textbook treatments more extensive than mine to a few original articles. Instructors will, of course, know of many more sources for interested students.

The coverage of the book is quite standard, topically speaking; the chapters deal with the traditional divisions of the field and use the traditional names for its subfields. The organization is somewhat unorthodox. The book starts with chapters on the behavior of human beings as individuals and as members of groups, next considers the mechanisms which generate individual behavior, and only then goes into the development of behavior and its physiological basis. This is farily close to the reverse order of most textbooks. Its justification is pedagogical. My experience has been that most students begin with an interest in the social and personal aspects of psychology and only develop interests in learning, perception, and the physiological bases as they become more curious about mechanisms. The order presented here tries to take advantage of this natural progression of interests. However, the chapters are sufficiently independent that they can be read in almost any order. Each chapter is followed by a summary of topics covered in it, arranged in a different order from that in the text discussion. I have done this intentionally, to give the reader a chance to think about the material in a way somewhat different from the way he did when reading the chapter. If he has really understood a body of knowledge he should be able to reorganize it—to crosscut the topical organization of what he has just read.

An instructor's manual is available. There is also a *Study Guide and Workbook*, by Robert S. Moyer, which reviews the text material and occasionally goes beyond it.

This textbook was a long time in preparation: I often felt the wisdom of Ben Franklin's remark when he apologized to a correspondent for having written such a long letter, begging that he had not had enough time to write a short one. During this lengthy task of writing a shorter book, I have had extensive help from many people. I am especially grateful for detailed critical readings of early chapter drafts by Rogers Elliott, Roger Burton, John Krauskopf, Charles Harris, Lynn Eldridge, Merrill Carlsmith, and Robert Moyer, all of whom not only told me about errors of fact and barriers to communication, but contributed examples, illustrations, and ways of explaining things. My copy editor, Judy Sternberg, did much more than that title requires—she made things not only more readable but more true.

I also had the invaluable help of a number of careful readings of the manuscript by students in various stages of their undergraduate and graduate careers. I gratefully acknowledge this kind of help from Norma Johnson and Walter Blair. Finally, there were three people, no one of whom I can thank enough, who served as editorial assistants and loyal supporters of the cause: Lynn Streeter, Norma Johnson, and Cynthia Landauer.

T. K. LANDAUER

ONE
The nature of psychology

"What was your trouble in Introductory Psychology?" asked the Dean.

"The course wasn't about psychology," replied the student.

It is a sad state of affairs when someone feels that a course is deceptively labeled; but for psychology, unfortunately, not a rare occurrence. The reason is not hard to find. Almost no one has had a course in psychology before college; therefore most people who enroll in the introductory course have acquired their "image" of the field from newspapers, magazines, television programs, and casual conversation. Such images are often greatly distorted since they are based only on applied, practical aspects of the field or, worse yet, on sensational fictions.

There are many common misleading uses of the word *psychology.* Here are a few examples: "My date is giving me a hard time. I'll have to use psychology on her." "The test was easy—I psyched it out." "His headaches are all psychological." Until recently the Yellow Pages in some city directories listed fortune tellers, mystics, and faith healers under the general title "Psychologist."

This book will not tell you very much about how to make friends, out-guess tests, interpret illness, or wage wars. One reason for this is that psychology really does not know very much about such things. But the primary reason is that there is much more to psychology, and much more that is central and basic, which the beginning student ought to hear about. So, be warned that this book will not teach you how to psychoanalyze your friends, succeed in business without really trying, or solve all your personal problems.

Nevertheless, you can expect to gain *some* personally useful knowledge from an introductory course in psychology. And, of course, much additional useful information is obtainable if you go on to learn about the specialized branches of the field.

DEFINITION OF PSYCHOLOGY

So much for what psychology is *not*; it is time to acquire some notion of what it *is*. The word *psychology* is derived from two Greek words meaning "the study of the mind." Unfortunately, *mind* is one of those words for which any two Greek philosophers had three different definitions. However, this definition of psychology can be made to fit what goes on in modern psychology if we mean by *mind* simply that which determines or controls the behavior of a living thing. Thus, *psychology is the study of the ways in which the behavior of living things is determined.*

Now we must define *behavior*. Behavior means, simply, what a living thing does. When we say that a student talked, raised his hand, or slept through a lecture, we describe his behavior. Many psychologists would be surprised to see all living things, plants as well as animals, included in a discussion of behavior. Yet several scientists have studied the behavior of plants (e.g., one-celled molds that bend toward light and have characteristic reaction times to light of different colors).

Naturally, this definition of behavior, like all others, is not entirely satisfactory. On one hand, the study of the behavior of living things is obviously part of a more general study of all aspects of living things, and this makes psychology technically a branch of biology. However, in many university organizations, and in many psychologists' eyes, psychology is a social, rather than a biological, science. On the other hand, calling psychology the study of that which controls behavior makes psychology sound much like neurophysiology, the field which specifically studies the nervous system. And it *should*, because there is a great amount of overlap between psychology and neurophysiology; but psychology is different in that it is broader. Psychology often considers the way behavior is controlled without looking inside the animal to see what its physical mechanisms are, much as one might describe the steering wheel of a car as that which, if rotated, causes the car to turn, without going into its mechanical principles.

Overlap between definitions of the field of psychology and those of other fields should not be cause for worry, because the fields themselves overlap. Many biologists, sociologists, anthropologists, neurophysiologists, and psychologists attend each other's conventions and read each other's articles. In short—pigeonholes are for pigeons.

RESEARCH IN PSYCHOLOGY: SOME EXAMPLES

At best, definitions of a field afford little understanding of its spirit and content. Real understanding comes only from studying the subject in depth, but a good beginning can be made by considering some well-chosen examples of its content.

(1) James McConnell and his collaborators (Zelman, Kabat, Jacobson, & McConnell, 1963) at the University of Michigan have trained planaria (small flatworms ordinarily found in ponds) to respond to a light. The animals were first exposed to a light followed by an electric shock; they soon learned to contract in response to the light alone in much the same manner as they normally did to the shock. This in itself is an intriguing finding. However, some of McConnell's students have gone on to perform an even more astounding feat. They took worms trained in this manner, ground them up, and fed them to other worms. A second group of worms was fed "untrained" worms. Then the two groups were compared in their tendency to respond to the light. Amazingly, the animals that had been fed a diet of "sophisticated" worms learned the contraction response much more quickly than those that had eaten naive worms. In fact, the ones that had eaten previously trained worms responded almost as well as if they had been trained themselves; whereas those that had eaten untrained worms showed no advantage. As might be expected, a hot debate followed announcement of these unexpected results. Other investigators found them difficult to repeat, and their proper interpretation is still in doubt.

(2) Professors Edward Bennett, Marian Diamond, David Krech, and Mark Rosenzweig (1964) at the University of California at Berkeley found that rats raised in a rich environment, that is, in cages containing toys and other young rats and open to the exciting world of the laboratory, have chemically different brains from rats raised in a more restricted environment. The brains of animals which in early life experienced a variety of sights and sounds had higher concentrations of the biochemical cholinesterase, which plays a role in the transmission of information between nerve fibers. They also had heavier, thicker cerebral cortices.

(3) Another psychologist, Harry Harlow (1958), working at the University of Wisconsin, has described a series of experiments in which he has raised young monkeys with artificial mothers of various kinds. One of his findings was that the young animals developed normal affectional responses to mothers made of terry cloth, but not to ones made of wire, while it made little difference whether or not the artificial mother provided milk. He inferred that the attachment of infants to their mothers was based on "contact comfort" rather than her provision of food.

(4) David McClelland (1961), at Harvard University, has investigated the origins of the kind of ambition which makes a nation prosper and expand. For example, he has published studies of the relation between the amount of achievement-related fantasies expressed in ancient Greek literature and the subsequent expansion of the trade area of ancient Greece. McClelland attributes both of these historical trends to a change in the child-rearing practices of the Greeks toward a greater emphasis on early independence. He suggests that when this kind of early-independence training broke down in the Greek ruling classes —perhaps as a result of the introduction of nursemaids—the foreign trade of Greece declined, as did the achievement imagery in its literature.

FIGURE 1-1

Young rats growing up in an enriched environment. Compared with litter mates raised in an impoverished environment, these animals developed heavier cerebral cortices. (From Bennett, Diamond, Krech, & Rosenzweig, 1964; copyright 1964 by the American Association for the Advancement of Science)

(5) John Whiting and Irvin Child (1953), at Harvard and Yale Universities, correlated the practices of adults in primitive societies around the world with the conditions under which children grow up in those societies. One of their most intriguing findings involves the antecedents of male initiation ceremonies. In these ceremonies, boys, upon reaching the age of puberty, are subjected to an extremely rigorous initiation rite in which they are circumcised without anesthesia, segregated from their friends and family, and subjected to painful and frightening hazing. About one-third of the primitive societies in the world practice such rites. The investigators found that these societies, almost without exception, are ones in which children grow up in a household without men. This usually occurs as a result of a polygynous marriage system in which the man keeps each of his several wives in a separate hut with her children, visiting them only occasionally, and rarely when there is a young infant about. In such societies, boys are often referred to by the same name as girls and women until the boys reach puberty and have been initiated. Moreover, in these societies the behavior of adult men is very distinct from that of women; for example, the men often live together in a "men's club" and share few activities with their

FIGURE 1–2
Infant monkeys prefer terry-cloth-
covered surrogate mothers to
wire ones that provide food but
no "contact comfort." (By
permission of the Wisconsin
Regional Primate Research
Center)

wives or families. Thus, in such societies a young boy tends to grow up as a girl, and then must make a sudden transition to the status of a man. Presumably it is this rapid transition which requires such extreme initiation rites.

(6) Elliot Aronson and Merrill Carlsmith (1963), working at Harvard University, studied methods of producing a "taboo" in young children by a method based on a theory about the way people resolve inconsistencies between their actions and their attitudes. The theory has it that if one commits himself to a course of action that is dissonant (inconsistent) with one of his attitudes, then he is likely to change his attitude to bring it into line with his behavior. Their experiment was as follows. They asked a child to rate a number of toys in order of desirability. They then told the child that he was *not* to play with the toy which he had rated his second favorite, and left the room. They told the child not to play with the toy in one of two ways—either by threatening fairly dire consequences of the transgression of their taboo, or simply by making a mild request. Now, according to the theory, if the child does not play with the toy because of a mild request, he should experience some dissonance and, as a result, change his attitude toward the toy, i.e., decide that he likes it less. On the other hand, if the child refrains from playing with the toy because he fears that the consequences would be worse than the pleasure, he has no great mental conflict to resolve and his attitude toward the toy should remain constant. This is essentially what Aronson and Carlsmith found, and it suggests that the best way to teach a child a taboo is to use the minimum threat which will serve to inhibit the performance of the undesirable act.

(7) John Wolpe (see Wolpe & Lazarus, 1966), a psychologist who treats people with mental problems, has described a series of cases in which he claims the successful application of a new therapy method for the treatment of phobias (intense, irrational fear reactions to particular objects or events). His method, which is based on the classical findings of the Russian psychologist I. Pavlov, consists of training his

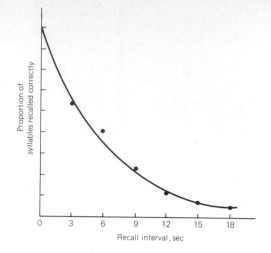

FIGURE 1-3
Recall of a single nonsense
syllable presented only once
declines very rapidly if the
subject is required to do mental
arithmetic during the retention
interval. (After Peterson &
Peterson, 1959)

Proportion of
syllables recalled correctly

Recall interval, sec

client to make a response to the phobic stimulus that is incompatible
with a fear reaction. He conditions the client to relax on command,
and then gradually to relax in the presence of thoughts or objects that
are progressively more like the phobic stimulus. For example, if a client
has a phobic reaction to a hypodermic syringe, the psychologist will
first get him to relax while thinking about purchasing a syringe that
is packaged in a box, then to think about opening the box, then about
having the syringe used on him, and so on in progressive steps until the
patient can tolerate an actual hypodermic injection. The psychologist
is careful at each step to allow the sufferer to learn to relax before
proceeding to a more lifelike and frightening approximation to the
phobic stimulus. Wolpe and his followers have reported much greater
success in the treatment of phobias than has previously been possible
with other forms of therapy.

(8) Lloyd Peterson and Margaret Peterson (1959) reported a series
of experiments conducted at the University of Indiana on the decay of
memories. They showed a college student a meaningless but pronounce-
able three-letter combination, or *nonsense syllable*. The student then
counted backward for a certain length of time—to prevent rehearsal—
until a signal told him to try to give the letter combination. Peterson and
Peterson found that the chances of a correct recall change in an orderly
fashion, so that a smooth curve can be plotted. Memory so measured
declines in a very rapid and orderly way over a period of about thirty
seconds of counting backward, reaching a halfway point after only eight
or ten seconds. Many important questions are raised by these results.
What causes memory loss over such brief periods? Clearly, a memory
doesn't always disappear in this way. How is it made to last? Many
psychologists are searching for the answers to such questions.

(9) Charles Stromeyer, at Bell Telephone Laboratories (Stromeyer
& Psotko, 1970), has been studying eidetic imagery, the ability to retain
an accurate, detailed visual image of a complex scene or pattern (some-

FIGURE 1-4
A test of eidetic imagery: try
to form an image of *a* and
superimpose it on *b* to form
a single pattern. What do
you see? Unless you have the
extremely rare ability of eidetic
imagery you will see only dots.
(Courtesy of J. Merritt and
C. F. Stromeyer)

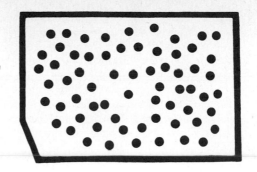

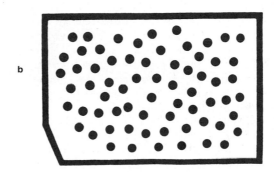

times popularly known as photographic memory). He and his coworkers
have developed several foolproof tests to distinguish people who actually
have this exceedingly rare ability from those who are only simulating
it. For example, a person with true eidetic imagery can stare at the
patterns in Figure 1-4 in succession, and by superimposing a remembered
image of the *a* pattern on the *b* pattern, *see* a single image which forms
a word.[1]

As was mentioned above, these are obviously only a few scattered
examples of recent work in psychology. They are probably sufficient,
however, to indicate how very broad the present field of psychology
is and that it contains some interests which one might not have expected.

THE FIELDS OF PSYCHOLOGY

We will approach the description of the fields of psychology by the
process of subdivision. Psychology may be divided into the academic
and the applied branches, each of which has subdivisions.

[1] Since Stromeyer is anxiously hunting for people with this ability (he has found *one* so far),
if you can put the two patterns together into a word—without cutting them out—he would
be delighted to hear from you. Correspondence can be addressed to him in care of Bell
Telephone Laboratories, Murray Hill, New Jersey, or to John Merritt in care of Department
of Psychology, Harvard University, Cambridge, Massachusetts.

Academic fields

Academic psychology refers to those psychological topics which are primarily investigated and taught, as compared with being primarily practiced or applied. Their study is motivated chiefly by curiosity about the ways in which men and other animals behave, although psychologists also hope that the knowledge gained from research will eventually prove useful. Several subjects of academic psychology are usually labeled *experimental*. Experimental psychology commonly is taken to include *physiological psychology*, the study of the bodily basis of behavior; *perception*, the study of how living things take in and interpret information about their environments; and *learning*, the study of the way in which the behavior of animals is altered by experience. The academic fields not usually included under experimental psychology include *personality*, the study of the behavioral characteristics of individuals; *social psychology*, the study of how one individual's behavior influences and is influenced by that of others; and *developmental psychology*, the study of how behavior changes with age. The reason for this traditional classification is that for a long time only physiological psychology, perception, and learning relied primarily on laboratory experimentation. But in recent years, all fields of academic psychology have come to rely more and more on controlled experiment, and so the distinction between experimental and "nonexperimental" fields has faded.

The divisions of psychology mentioned so far are only those which are generally considered to be its biggest subcategories. There are other ways of subdividing the field. For example, there are sizable numbers of psychologists who are interested in *motivation, mathematical psychology, cognition* (the study of thinking), *abnormal behavior, aesthetics*, and other specialized pursuits.

The reader will recognize a certain resemblance between the main categories listed above and the chapter headings of this book. Each chapter attempts to provide an overview of current knowledge in one of the major subfields of psychology. It therefore seems unnecessary to go into more detail at this point about these subfields.

Applied fields

Psychology can, of course, be applied to any number of practical problems. These applications may be thought of as the engineering branches of the basic science of behavior. The principal applied fields can be distinguished in terms of the problems with which they are concerned. They include *educational psychology, clinical psychology, counseling psychology, human engineering*, and *industrial psychology*.

Educational psychology, of which we will have a sample shortly, is concerned with questions of measurement, with questions of behavior and learning in the classroom, and with child development and mental health as they apply to problems encountered by teachers.

Clinical psychology is the application of psychological knowledge, methods, and techniques to the treatment of psychological disorders. The clinical psychologist works in mental hospitals and clinics as well as in private practice; he diagnoses mental illnesses by means of psychological tests and engages in therapy of a nonmedical variety. The clinical psychologist's activities are often very like those of a psychiatrist, and he often works in close collaboration with psychiatrists. There are, however, two major differences between psychiatrists and clinical psychologists. First, they have different training. While both undergo postdoctoral training in the treatment of mental disorders, their graduate school education is different. The clinical psychologist ordinarily holds a Ph.D. or other advanced degree in psychology, while the psychiatrist holds an M.D. Second, the psychiatrist, as a physician, is often involved in strictly medical procedures such as drug therapy, while the clinical psychologist is an expert in behavioral procedures of psychotherapy.

Counseling psychology is the use of psychological measuring methods and other techniques to help people solve personal problems of a more or less normal variety. For example, the vocational counselor uses a variety of tests to assess an individual's abilities and interests in order to help him find a career in which he is likely to find success and satisfaction. Counseling psychologists work in schools, industry, and social service agencies.

The field of *human factors engineering* involves application of psychological methods and knowledge, principally from the fields of perception, learning, and physiological psychology, to problems of engineering. Extensive psychological research is needed to design an instrument panel that will efficiently provide a mass of information to a human observer, or to design a complicated set of controls which can be operated with little error, or to write an instruction manual that will be generally understood. Such studies are carried out by engineering psychologists.

Industrial psychology includes a wide range of activities, from counseling and labor-relations work in industry to so-called *motivation research* in advertising. It involves primarily application of principles and methods from social psychology.

This book will have little more to say concerning the applied fields of psychology, not because they are uninteresting or unworthy, but because this is an introductory textbook. The applied fields are by their nature advanced fields which require special study. However, there are many good sources available for the interested student. Some are listed at the end of this chapter.

ORIGINS AND DEVELOPMENT OF PSYCHOLOGY

The question of how to account for the behavior of people and animals has troubled men for as long as men have been troubled by questions. Most of the great thinkers of history—the great philosophers, theologians, and scientists—have concerned themselves with problems of psychology. Aristotle, Descartes, and Locke had well-formed theories of psychology. The great nineteenth-century scientists Helmholtz and Darwin devoted much effort to problems of an essentially psychological

The nature
of psychology
9

FIGURE 1–5
The arrangement of the meter
in the bottom panel makes them
easier to use than those in the
top panel; an example of human
factors engineering. (After
Chapanis, Garner, & Morgan,
1949, p. 151).

Unpatterned dial display

Patterned dial display

nature. Helmholtz formulated a theory of visual sensation which is still very much alive, and which has recently been substantiated in some of its essential parts.

Nonetheless, despite the truly ancient interest in the problems of psychology on the part of the world's great thinkers, psychology was one of the last fields of natural philosophy to strike out for an independent existence of its own as an empirical science. The great early figures in the field, the men who would be called the fathers of psychology, did not appear until late in the nineteenth century. The first psychological laboratories were established in the 1870s by Wilhelm Wundt at Leipzig and William James at Harvard. Freud's influential thinking began around 1891. Pavlov reported his famous pioneering experiments on conditioned reflexes between 1903 and 1928. It is perhaps even more revealing of the youth of scientific psychology that Freud and Pavlov did not consider themselves primarily psychologists. Freud thought of himself as a physician; Pavlov considered himself a physiologist. Certainly neither was trained as a psychologist.

Perhaps one of the reasons why psychology was so late in creating an independent existence for itself was that it is a more complicated, more difficult field for empirical investigation than those fields which had begun their careers sooner. To this day, completely adequate methods of study have not been found for all the phenomena of interest to psychology. There is, however, another and more important reason for the lag of psychology. There is a certain amount of resistance to taking questions out of the realm of revelation and the jurisdiction of theology and into the realm of empirical investigation and the jurisdiction of science. Hundreds of years ago the question of whether the sun revolved around the earth or the earth around the sun was considered by some to be a theologically settled question which was not appropriate for scientific consideration. Not too long ago, the question of the origins of life and the historical origins of the human species was a topic thought by many to be unfit for scientific investigation. Perhaps it is still the case that questions involving the mind and "spirit" of man are suspected to be, if not illicit subjects for scientific inquiry, at least impossible ones to answer by objective methods. Perhaps man dislikes giving up the feeling of mystery and self-importance which goes with a mystical view of his nature. Perhaps it is simply a matter of rational conservatism not to give up old explanations until better ones have come forth. In any case, it was not until very recently that a wide acceptance of the possibility of an objective science of the mind existed.

THE DEVELOPMENT OF KNOWLEDGE IN GENERAL AND PSYCHOLOGY IN PARTICULAR

Fields of knowledge usually progress through a number of discernible sequential stages. The first stage is one of mystical or supernatural explanations. Man seems to have a need to explain things, and the behavior of himself and his fellows is no exception. Thus, concepts of nonobservable entities such as the "will" are postulated to explain the way in which people act. A second stage in the development of a field of intellectual inquiry is a proliferation of somewhat more sophisticated theories which are based on armchair logic coupled with a certain amount of unsystematic observation. The sometimes brilliant, sometimes farfetched, analyses of behavior offered over the centuries by the great and not-so-great philosophers were such. Then gradually, in most fields of knowledge, men grow dissatisfied with handed-down myths and with armchair theories. They insist on observing the phenomena which they are curious about, and they begin to take careful notes. A long third stage ensues in which observations are recorded, reported, shared, and revised.

Eventually, observations which are repeatable and reliable begin to pile up. Usually, more than simple note taking is required to make the observations yield the information which will assuage curiosity about causation. Experiments are needed. One needs to ask: What would happen if I changed something? During the development of a field of knowledge a tremendous number of such observations and experiments are made. That is not to say that this is all that goes on; theory and speculation are not kept in abeyance while facts are accumulated. However, there is, during this third stage, little real communication between the facts being accumulated and the theories being spun. This rapprochement is the fourth and final stage.

At some point the information collected begins to be sufficiently broad and deep that some genius can detect a pattern in it and can build a theory or model that organizes many disparate facts into a single principle. The fourth stage, then, is one of simplification. This is the ultimate aim of most fields of knowledge. If it were possible, a single, simple theory that generated all facts would be the ultimate goal and would end the search for scientific truth.

Psychology at present has advanced only into the middle of the third of these stages. A vast number of facts has been accumulated. Most of the early fictitious explanations have been given up. But few really good theories—ones that apply accurately to a wide range of facts—have been invented. This poses certain problems for the student. If good formulae and theories were available, as they are in physics, the student would need only learn a few very basic laws and some mathematical machinery to deal with many of the phenomena which he would encounter. He would not need to tax his memory too greatly to be in possession of a vast amount of precise knowledge. In psychology, the student's task is not so easy. He must simply plunge into learning what is known, which is quite a bit, without expecting much relief from simplifying theories.

Perhaps in closing this section a few words are in order on the question of what science and scientific methods are. Probably the most adequate way to describe science is by reference to its goals. Stated in a very rough and general way, the goal of science is to obtain reliable statements about the world. For this description to be accurate, the use of the word *reliable* must be very strict. A scientific statement must be capable of being *relied* upon to always be true—when put to observational test by any competent observer; when used to predict the occurrence of an event given circumstances under which the statement logically implies a prediction; or when used to control the environment if the statement implies that a certain course of action will produce a certain result.

There have been numerous attempts to describe how one goes about creating scientific statements. (Some general remarks on how to do psychological research are to be found in Chapter 11.) Many people who have observed the workings of science feel that its essence lies in the creation and testing of notions about what may be true. The scientist, on the basis of earlier information coupled with his own creative imagination, produces a conjecture as to what may be a generally true statement. He then proceeds to invent ways of testing his notion. If he or others test diligently enough, the initial statement will always be found wanting in some way and will have to be modified. The result of the scientist's effort, then, is a refinement of the statement to one which more closely approximates reality. And thus it goes in a never-ending cycle.

In a sense, however, all such descriptions of the activities of scientists are misleading. They do not really define what science is. Science is *not* a way of investigating; there are many ways of doing science. Science is, instead, a goal or set of goals. It is the goal of attaining truth under the strictest possible rules of evidence. If a scientist were to arrive at a theory about nature by dreaming it, his colleagues would not care so long as the statement stood the test of merciless scrutiny. If every question that could be put to nature resulted in confirmation of the dreamed theory, it would be just as scientific as if it had been discovered by years of toil in the laboratory. Science is not characterized by its method of creation, but by its tests of validity.

How, then, does one characterize a given field of intellectual inquiry as a *science?* In general usage, there are two ways. First, those fields in which a great body of verifiable knowledge about nature exists are called *sciences*. Botany, physics and astronomy are such. Second, those disciplines in which the rules of evidence of science are used in the accumulation of knowledge are usually called *sciences*, whether or not they have attained a large storehouse of exact knowledge.

What about psychology? On one hand, in most of its subdisciplines, the rules of evidence employed by one investigator to test the data and conclusions of another are very strict. And there are many verifiable findings about nature. However, there is not a really large body of precise scientific knowledge in the field. Certainly there is not yet the kind of advancement to general principles that characterizes physics and chemistry. Thus, whether one calls psychology a *science* or not may depend on how one likes to use the word. It really is not terribly important. Psychology is vigorously engaged in trying to obtain exact knowledge about behavior, and you may call it what you will.

PSYCHOLOGICAL MEASUREMENT: TESTING AND GRADING

To round out our introduction to psychology, and set the tone and level for what follows, we will dig a little deeper and more rigorously into one of its traditional problem areas—the measurement of people's psychological attributes. In all areas of psychology it is important to measure behavior in some quantitative fashion. Measurement is particularly useful in the applied field of educational psychology, in which the problem of evaluating scholastic achievement is a major, practical concern. It is an especially appropriate topic to serve as a final illustration of the nature of psychology, since it will at the same time introduce the reader to a deeper example of psychology and give him some knowledge of the language of measurement he will meet in later chapters.

The problem to be considered is how to assign grades to a large class. Let us assume that the instructor will give two examinations, a one-hour midterm examination and a two-hour final examination. Let us then consider what kind of examinations he should use, how he should go about combining the scores from the examinations to get a final grade, and how he should assign grades to final scores. (Whether he should give grades or examinations at all is an entirely separate and debatable question. Here we are only considering how to do it fairly and accurately.)

Constructing the test

First, what sort of examinations should he use? To answer this question, we must seriously consider what it is that the examination attempts to measure. This is not a simple problem. Among the things that cross one's mind as desirable to know about a student before assigning a grade are the following: How intelligent is he? How well does he express himself? How thoroughly has he thought through the implications of what he is talking about? How capable is he of combining information to produce solutions? How creative is he in producing novel answers? How well does he know the material covered in the course?

Now, the student's general intelligence is probably already known, for most students take IQ tests or very similar scholastic aptitude tests before starting college. Such intelligence estimates are fairly stable. If this were the sole content of each examination that the student received in each of his college courses, we would get the same answer over and over again. This is clearly not all that we are after.

A similar argument holds to some extent for many of the other possible goals listed above. That is, insofar as a trait which has to do with how the student performs in psychology classes is also relevant to other classes that he takes, and tends to remain fairly constant, there will be some question as to whether it is appropriate to measure it anew in each course. There would be limited value to a grade based on such an assessment, since it would not reflect a quantity which was specific to the course in question.

Such questions about tests and measurement, i.e., ones about whether the characteristic of the individual being assessed is really the characteristic one wishes to assess, are referred to as questions of *validity*.

There is another kind of question about a test which also must be asked. Say that we decide to assess only detailed, factual knowledge of the subject matter at hand. We give a test which asks the students to write an essay entitled, "What I Know about Psychology." Now presume that your test booklet is graded independently by two different instructors. Suppose that one decides that you deserve an A, whereas the other decides that you deserve a C. The test obviously was not a good one. More precisely, the test coupled with its grading system was not a good one. Here, however, the problem did not seem to be a matter of validity. We were trying to study a characteristic of the test taker which is clearly relevant to his grade. Nonetheless, we obtained a score that is not a very good estimate of his performance in the class. What was wrong

TABLE 1–1
Hypothetical exam scores

	Midterm	Rank	Final	Rank	Total	Rank
Adam	70	3	165	1	235	3
Joe	80	2	160	2	240	2
Eve	90	1	155	3	245	1
Average (mean)	80		160		240	
Range	20		10		10	

with it? What was wrong was that the score generated by the test was not independent of which reader the test taker happened to have for his exam. This aspect of the adequacy of a test is known as *reliability*. In this example, the reliability of the test was low.

Thus, what we require for the purposes of grading are tests that are both *reliable* and *valid*. Let us note an important relation between these two properties. Validity is the property of a test measuring what we desire to measure. Before it can measure what we desire it to, however, a test must be able to measure *something*. If a test is not *reliable*, it is not, in fact, measuring anything. Thus, a test must first be reliable before it can be valid.

Using test scores

Let us assume that the instructor has developed a set of appropriate tests. He will still have a serious problem—what to do with the scores after he gets them. How should scores from several tests be combined into one overall score? How should such an overall score be translated into a grade?

Consider first the problem of combining scores. In our hypothetical course, the instructor promises that he will count the one-hour midterm examination as one-third of the grade and the two-hour final examination as two-thirds. Now, how does he go about fulfilling this promise? One common approach is as follows: Make the one-hour midterm exam contain 100 questions, each worth one point. Make the two-hour final exam of 200 questions, each also worth 1 point. At the end of the term, simply add the points obtained on each of the exams together.

This seems, at first glance at least, to be a reasonable procedure. However, consider the following example. For simplicity, we take a class of only three people whose grades on a midterm and a final exam are shown in Table 1–1. A score comprising the sum of the scores on the two exams is shown in the right-hand column. Also shown is the rank order of the students for each exam and for the final summary score. Notice that on the final exam Adam was the highest in the class, and Eve was the lowest. This order was reversed on the midterm. Now note that on the total course grade Adam was the *lowest* in the class and Eve the *highest*. In fact, the rankings on the total course grade correspond exactly to the ranking on the midterm examination alone, and have not been influenced at all by the final. This seems rather peculiar in light of the instructor's promise that the final exam would count two-thirds and the midterm only one-third. How can it be that the student who does the best on the exam worth two-thirds does worse on the final grade than students who only do well on the exam worth one-third?

Examination of the table reveals some interesting properties of the numbers. The scores for the midterm are much more spread out than those for the final. In fact, there is so much variation among the midterm scores that they simply swamp the differences in the final. How could such wide discrepancies arise? One way in which they could arise is that there is a very large difference between how good the students are or how much they study for the midterm, but much less of a difference on the final. But such an occurrence would be very unlikely, particularly if the class is large. A much more likely source of difference in the spread on one examination from that on another is in the nature of the examinations themselves. To take an extreme example again, suppose that an examination is composed of 200 questions, of which 190 are so easy that everyone in the entire class gets them right, and only 10 are questions which actually discriminate between the good and poor students. This might have been the case on the final examination in the example given in Table 1–1. The *effective length* of such a test is not really 200 items, but only 10. If a second test has, instead, 20 items that differentiate better from worse students, as might have been the case in the midterm exam in the example, the amount which it contributes to the final ranking would be much greater.

What should the instructor do in such a situation to ensure a fair combining of scores? Ideally, of course, he should have constructed examinations which all had the same range of scores. This is nearly impossible to do in practice. An instructor cannot know precisely how difficult each of the questions will be. Some of them will always turn out to be too easy, and some too hard.

Alternatively, once the scores for the examination are in, the instructor can apply some correction factor to them which will equalize the contribution of each examination. This seems like a reasonable approach. But what kind of adjustment should the instructor make? Should he add some constant number to each student's score? Should he multiply each score by some constant number?

Adjusting the average for each examination by adding a constant to all the scores would not help, since this would not change the spread.[2] What is needed is an adjustment that will equalize the *variability* of the scores. Multiplying by a constant will have this effect. For example, if each score on one examination were multiplied by 2, the overall spread would be doubled.[3]

The next question, obviously, is what number should be the multiplier? To equalize the variability we need some standard measure of amount of variability in a set of scores. A simple one, which will serve adequately for present purposes, is the *range*, which is simply the differ-

[2] E.g., adding 2 to each of the set of numbers (2, 3, 4) yields a set of numbers (4, 5, 6) which are higher but no more spread out.

[3] E.g., 2 (2, 3, 4) = (4, 6, 8).

TABLE 1–2
Hypothetical exam scores transformed by dividing each by the range;
Total score obtained by adding weighted components

	Midterm	Rank	Final	Rank	2 X final	Midterm + 2 X final	Rank
Adam	$\dfrac{70}{20} = 3.5$	3	$\dfrac{165}{10} = 16.5$	1	33	36.5	1
Joe	$\dfrac{80}{20} = 4.0$	2	$\dfrac{160}{10} = 16.0$	2	32	36.0	2
Eve	$\dfrac{90}{20} = 4.5$	1	$\dfrac{155}{10} = 15.5$	3	31	35.5	3
Range	1			1	2	1	

ence between the largest score and the smallest. If we were to make the range for each examination in a series be equal, the contribution of each to a total score would be essentially the same. A simple way to do this is to divide each student's score by the range for the test. A little arithmetic will convince you that transformed scores obtained in this way will always have a range of exactly 1.[4] Transformed or "normalized" scores in one form or another constitute a common technique for solving problems such as the one we are considering.

Now if, as in our example, we want to weight the final exam twice as heavily as the midterm, all we need to do is multiply the normalized scores for the final by 2, while multiplying those on the midterm by 1, and then add. The ranges for the scores given in Table 1–1 are used in Table 1–2 along with weightings and additions to form a summary score for each student. Notice that now those students who did well on the final do well on the course totals. This is as it should be.

Many people, on first being introduced to this method of deriving a normalized score for a test, react by feeling that there is something illicit in the procedure. They feel that the original score expressed as a "percent correct" in some way really reflects the student's performance and ought to be used as the measure, come what may. Multiplying and dividing this score by mysterious numbers seems to be fiddling with the data. On the other hand, we are all accustomed to seeing measures of people's behavior, as well as many other things, expressed in percentages. Thus, a score in terms of percent-correct answers seems very natural and direct. However, a percentage is really no more natural than the normalized score which has just been described. Percent correct is also a transformation. Its purpose is to adjust for differences between tests in the number of items they contain. The use of a standard score based on variability simply takes this same procedure one step further and adjusts not only for length but also for the variability (effective length) of the test.

The problem with which we have been dealing is a common and fundamental one in psychology. If we wish to measure psychological

---

[4] E.g., the range of (2, 3, 4) is $4 - 2 = 2$. The range of (4, 6, 8) is $8 - 4 = 4$. Dividing each set by its range gives (1, 1.5, 2) and (1, 1.5, 2), each with a range of 1.0.

TABLE 1–3
Hypothetical distribution of exam scores and grades

Percent correct (1)	Grade (2)	Number of students who get this grade on first test (3)	Number of students who get this grade on second test (4)
96–100	A	0	10
85–95	B	10	20
70–84	C	20	40
60–69	D	40	20
50–59	E	20	10
0–49		10	0

characteristics, we must have measuring instruments. The measuring instruments must somehow be ones which measure the same way on one occasion as they do on the next. We have already discussed the problem of reliability—whether a measuring instrument will measure the same thing on two occasions or in the hands of two different investigators. We are also concerned that measurement of two related properties be made in the same units. We have seen one method that psychologists have found useful in dealing with this problem.

Other problems of measurement and of the establishment of equal units will be met in Chapter 5 when we consider the judgments which people make about physical qualities they perceive.

Assigning grades

Once the several scores from several tests have been added up into one final composite score, the problem arises as to how to assign a grade to the total score. Once again, this problem reflects a fundamental psychological issue. Fortunately, we have, in previous sections, developed some of the tools which we need to attack this problem.

One common approach would be to decide that a certain percentage correct, say 95 or above, was an A, and some lower percentage, say 90 to 95, a B, and so forth. The instructor might base his decision as to the division points on his own standards of excellence. That is, he might look over the test and make a judgment as to how well he thought a very good student who deserved an A should do, and so forth.

To see the problem in this method, consider the following fictitious occurrence. An instructor decides on a set of cutoff points to determine grades. He then gives the test and assigns grades and comes up with the distribution of grades among his 100 students that is shown in column 3 of Table 1–3. He is very disappointed with the performance of the students, so he gives another test the following day. This time the grades are distributed as shown in column 4. Do you conclude that the students improved in the interval? Or do you conclude that the tests were unequal? Obviously, if the class is very large, the chance of the average scholarship of its members changing radically in a short period of time is very small. On the other hand, it is not at all hard to imagine two tests that give very different results.

The point is that there can never be any really absolute standard of academic performance. All standards must be relative to what other students have done. What does this imply for a test in which the instructor decides beforehand that 95 percent or better will be an A? It means nothing more or less than that the instructor has committed himself to constructing an examination which will be exactly difficult enough that students who deserve A's will get 95 points or more. If precisely the same examination has been used many times before, this may be possible. If it is a new examination, it is a preposterous conceit.

The problem of grade assignment boils down then, in a sense, to one of discovering just how hard it was to get a certain total score in a particular examination or course. The proper way to answer this question is really quite straightforward. If 100 students have taken a course, the average score which they obtained is the score which we should expect from an average student. If the exam is difficult, the average will be low; if the exam is easy, the average will be high. Similarly, if there are a very large number of students, say 100 or more, then there is bound to be someone who does very well and someone who does very poorly. Thus, we can decide what an average, good, or poor performance is by seeing what average, good, and poor students accomplish.

A formal way of going about this is to construct a standard in terms of proportion of students. That is, it can be decided that an A is that performance which the upper 10 percent of students are capable of, B the performance of the next 25 percent, and so on. The method is based on the following fact. Given a large group of students, the chances are overwhelming that the top 10 percent will not be significantly better or significantly worse than would the top 10 percent in any other equally large group of students selected on the same basis. It presumes that the spread of abilities in a large group of students is a fairly constant quantity, and makes this quantity the basis of the unit of measurement.

Unfortunately, if the class is small, then the assumption of a constant spread of abilities may not hold. In fact, the confidence which we can put in the probability of any randomly selected group being like that of any other randomly selected group is subject to certain statistical laws. We will go into this in more detail in Chapter 11, but in general, confidence in the assumption of equality of groups is inversely proportional to the square root of the number of people in the groups. For practical purposes, when the number in the class is less than about 10, the assumption of equal abilities is quite bad. When the number exceeds about 50 or 100, the assumption becomes quite good.

We have seen, with respect to both the addition of scores and the assignment of grades, that in measuring psychological quantities we must often depend on the results which we obtain to determine the unit of measurement. The basic logic in both cases relies on the fact that the average behavior of a large group of people is much more constant and reliable than that of an individual. Whereas a single act of an individual can rarely be interpreted meaningfully by itself, judicious use of information about the performance of a large number of people can provide units of measurement and baselines in terms of which an individual's behavior can be evaluated with considerable precision. This general approach, with the methods which we have used to implement it, constitutes a theme which, with variations and embellishments, is found throughout the study of behavior.

PLAN OF THE BOOK

You now have an idea of what psychology is about. From here on we will plunge into the various fields of psychology. Each of the following chapters deals with one of the traditional academic fields of psychology. The chapter sequence is one of progression from the description of the overall behavior of man to the more and more detailed mechanisms underlying this behavior. The reasons for this arrangement are primarily pedagogical. The topics presented first are ones which deal with familiar items of behavior, with somewhat familiar concepts, and with people and social situations, rather than with animals, molecules, and formulae.

Thus, the second chapter deals with people as they interact with each other. The third chapter deals with the characteristics of individuals, the fourth with abnormalities of behavior. The discussion then moves on to those properties which are shared by all normal individuals, in chapters on perception, motivation, learning, and thinking. The concluding chapters consider development of behavior during a lifetime, and the physiological basis of behavior. Finally, there is an appendix on research methods and statistics designed to be read at any point at which it is needed.

TOPICS DISCUSSED IN CHAPTER 1[5]

1. The definition and nature of psychology as a field of study.

2. Subdivisions of the field.

3. The historical origins of psychology and its current level of maturity as a scientific discipline.

4. Some problems and methods involved in measuring and evaluating behavior, as exemplified by:
   a. Constructing course examinations
   b. Combining scores from two exams
   c. Assigning a course grade

SUGGESTED READINGS

1. Three general introductory textbooks with more extended treatments of the same material are:

---

[5] To help the student know whether he has understood and retained what he has read, at the end of each chapter there will be a list of topics covered. The student should try to reconstruct what he has learned about each, and then, in reviewing, pay heed to descrepancies between what is in the book and what was in his head.

Hilgard, E. R., & Atkinson, R. L. *Introduction to Psychology*. (5th ed.) New York: Harcourt Brace Jovanovich, 1971.

Krech, D., Crutchfield, R. S., & Livson, N. *Elements of Psychology*. (2nd ed.) New York: Alfred A. Knopf, 1969.

Morgan, C. T., & King, R. A. *Introduction to Psychology*. (4th ed.) New York: McGraw-Hill, 1971.

2. Some books about the history of psychology:

Boring, E. G. *A History of Experimental Psychology*. (2nd ed.) New York: Appleton-Century-Crofts, 1950.

Miller, G. A. *Psychology, the Science of Mental Life*. New York: Harper & Row, 1962.

3. Methods of psychological research:

Hyman, R. *Nature of Psychological Inquiry*. Englewood Cliffs, N.J.: Prentice-Hall, 1964.

Underwood, B. J. *Experimental Psychology*. (2nd ed.) New York: Meredith Corporation, 1966.

4. Books about applied fields not discussed later in this text:

Leavitt, H. J. *Managerial Psychology*. (2nd ed.) Chicago: University of Chicago Press, 1964.

McCormick, E. J. *Human Factors in Engineering*. (2nd ed.) New York: McGraw-Hill, 1964.

5. A pamphlet on psychology as a career, available from the American Psychological Association:

Ross, S., & Lockman, R. F. *A Career in Psychology*. Washington, D.C.: American Psychological Association, 1965.

6. Quantitative methods and measurement are developed in detail in:

Coombs, C. H., Dawes, R., & Tversky, A. *Mathematical Psychology: An Elementary Introduction*. Englewood Cliffs, N.J.: Prentice-Hall, 1970.

Lewis, D. *Quantitative Methods in Psychology*. New York: McGraw-Hill, 1960.

Wood, D. A. *Test Construction*. Columbus, Ohio: Charles E. Merrill, 1961.

7. A provocative article relevant to the nature and special problems of psychology:

Skinner, B. F. Freedom and the Control of Men. *American Scholar*, 1955 56, 47–65.

TWO
Social psychology

Among social animals such as man, behavior totally uncolored by the actions of others is virtually nonexistent. We depend upon each other for our livelihoods, our safety, and most of our important pleasures. Consider for a moment the sort of things that are likely to influence your behavior. What do you want to accomplish? What goals will you work to reach? What do you try to avoid? It turns out, doesn't it, that in almost every instance you work toward objectives that involve people.

The fact is that living as we do in a highly interdependent group, or society, we are influenced by others in the details of our behavior to a tremendous extent and in a wide variety of ways. Social interaction is the most readily apparent and familiar of all the determinants of behavior. It therefore makes an excellent starting point for our study of psychology.

In this chapter we will consider in some detail the processes and results of social interaction. The chapter is divided into three major sections. The first deals with *culture*, the second with *society*, and the third with *interpersonal interaction*. Let us first distinguish between these three aspects of social behavior.

Culture refers to features of behavior which are passed on from generation to generation and which typify a definable, geographically and historically connected group of people, despite the fact that the particular individuals who make up the group are continually changing.

An especially good example of culturally determined behavior is language. Language is a feature of behavior which is common to a group and outlasts the particular membership of the group. Thus, culture refers not to facts about how the ongoing activity of the group is being carried on at a particular historical moment, but rather to norms or features of behavior which have been adopted by a group of people and maintained by succeeding generations. We will discuss the range and variability of such shared aspects of behavior, the psychological mechanisms that bring them into being and reinforce their acceptance, and some of their effects on the individual.

Society refers to features of behavior which arise because people live together in more or less stable, interdependent groups—features such as cooperation, competition, and organization. Societal facts and principles concern the ways in which the behaviors of members of groups are interrelated. Under this title we will discuss the dynamics and functioning of groups, both large and small, and such topics as leadership and communication.

Interpersonal interaction refers to the individual aspects of social behavior—to the ways in which one person influences and is influenced by the behavior of another. In discussing interpersonal interactions we will deal with such questions as what brings people into interaction with one another, how one person perceives and is perceived by others, and the ways such interaction leads to changes in beliefs and feelings.

CULTURE: SHARED BEHAVIOR PATTERNS

The limitless variety of human behavior

One of the most important lessons to be learned from a study of different cultures is that different people behave very differently. Americans and Europeans rest by sitting in chairs—a position which many Japanese find downright uncomfortable, while their favored cross-legged squat is excruciating to most of us after about fifteen minutes (Figure 2–1). Westerners point with the index finger, the Kikuyu of Kenya do so with lips and chin. The young man in Figure 2–2 is indicating the whereabouts of a young lady. We read from left to right and from the top of the page to the bottom. Other people read from the bottom up, from right to left, or even up and then down. We think of our way as natural, and it has even been defended as more fitting to the "natural" motion of the eyes. The Chinese do not think so, nor do Hebrew readers. (Consider for a minute the possibility of turning your book upside down and reading from right to left and up the page from bottom to top. Why not? You could have learned this way just as easily if it were not for a set of quite arbitrary cultural norms.) Even in such a seemingly biologically determined behavior as copulation, human groups show vast customary differences. The most common position adopted by partners in sexual intercourse in Europe and America was thought to be totally indecent by the indigenous inhabitants of Alor, an island in Indonesia. Similarly, we view as inedible—even poisonous—the rotted remains of fish that

have been dead for several weeks, but to the palate of an Eskimo of Baffin Island this is ideal foodstuff. Similarly, many people view with positive horror the rotted milk[1] which we consume by the ton.

The marked consistency of behavior within any one culture

Perhaps even more striking than the tremendous diversity in behavior between different cultures are the relatively minute variations to be observed within any one.

The clearest example of the degree of intra-cultural consistency in behavior is in language. Language is not only an example of social behavior, but also its most effective tool. But for language to be of any use at all, there must be virtually complete agreement between speakers and listeners as to the meaning of the words of the language and the significance of its grammatical arrangements. Consequently, while there are probably an infinite number of possible sounds to use to stand for a given meaning, only one (or, in the case of synonyms, a few) actually is used in a given culture. Clearly the value of language depends on its consistent use by members of the same group. Somewhat less obvious, but more obviously arbitrary, are the ways we divide up musical tones. We use a scale of octaves divided into twelve named tones. On this scale elaborate rules of harmony have been constructed, and most of us find music that deviates from these rules "dissonant." Yet other cultures divide up sounds in entirely different ways, which they find pleasant and we often find unmusical. The value of music to people thus appears to rely on conformity to a set of arbitrary social conventions. The same thing is true, to some extent, of every aspect of culture.

The mechanisms of culture maintenance

SOCIALIZATION

How is intracultural consistency of behavior brought about? What ensures that you and I will, indeed, behave in ways that are the same or complementary? Obviously, all the processes of social interaction

[1] Cheese.

FIGURE 2–2
Many East Africans do not
point with the index finger,
but with the chin and lips.

which we are going to discuss in this chapter can and do play a part
in bringing one person's behavior into line with another's. But there
are some general processes which are particularly important with respect
to the sharing of culture. The first of these is the process by which
culture is passed from generation to generation—the teaching of culturally prescribed behavior. This process is called *socialization*.

Before reaching adulthood a person is taught a vast array of
cultural conventions. Consider an American. He is taught to obey his
father, but not strange adults. He is taught that he may have sexual
relations (if he is discreet) with, or marry, the girl next door, but not
his sister. He is taught to eat peas with a fork, hot dogs with his fingers,
and chicken one way or the other depending on the circumstances. He
learns to excrete only in the bathroom. He learns to be seen naked only
by members of the same sex, with the exception that his spouse may see
him naked, but only if there is no one else present. He learns what foods
and sounds to like, what accomplishments in others he should admire,
and what faults he should despise. He learns what are acceptable ways
of getting things for himself and of influencing other people, and what

Social
psychology
25

sorts of actions are improper or criminal. Above all, he learns a language and the abilities that language makes possible—to think, to reason, and to perform all the intellectual tasks involved in formal schooling.

Children learn culture by many means. They are instructed, rewarded, and punished by their parents. They spend many hours in imitative play. In fact, all the means of altering behavior and attitudes which will be discussed in later sections of this chapter, and in the chapters on learning and child development, are brought to bear in the process of socialization.

The period of socialization lasts from birth to death. But it is most intense during an early period that is more or less set aside especially for the purpose of teaching the child his culture. Schools, for example, are primarily a form of institutionalized socialization. Teachers are professional socializers hired to transmit the knowledge, behavior, and values of a complex society to its succeeding generations. In some societies the socialization period is demarcated clearly. Below a certain age, say puberty, the child is not expected to do any useful work and is forbidden to engage in certain adult behaviors such as marriage or hunting. In other societies, the line between the socialization period and adulthood is blurred—children gradually take on more and more of the responsibilities and prerogatives of adult membership in their society.

In modern Western society the period of socialization has been extended beyond that of any other present or historically known group. One reason is that our culture is fantastically rich in knowledge and in skills which a person must learn before becoming a fully functional member. In the good old days in Samoa one could get along reasonably well with a knowledge of how to weave pandanus leaf mats, cook mahi-mahi, and practice the intricacies of dance and love, all of which were learned through relatively informal instruction by the age of twelve or fifteen. Not so in modern America or Europe (or modern Samoa). In our highly industrialized, highly sophisticated society, there are few desirable roles in life available for those without at least a high school socialization.

GENERALIZED CONFORMITY

The social world tends to run more smoothly if friends and coworkers approve of each other's behavior. One way to ensure the respect and admiration of our fellows is to convince others that our ways of behaving are correct and should be valued and imitated by them. Another is for us to value and imitate theirs. In a situation which involves only two people, mutual approval can be accomplished by mutual accommodation—each giving a little. But in a situation involving one person joining many, the most feasible solution is usually for the one to adopt the manners of the many. Thus the immigrant from China does not expect to convert the whole of America to speaking Chinese.

It appears to be an important part of the process of transmission of culture for individuals to learn a broad habit of adapting their behavior to that of people around them. In every society in which the matter has been studied, adults are found to have such a strong general habit. For example, experimental studies indicate that college students in our society will often make quite drastic concessions in order to bring their behavior into conformity with a group. In a famous experiment by Asch (1956), college students were shown lines of various lengths and asked to tell which one was the same as a sample line held up by the experimenter. In each group of "subjects," all but one were confederates of the experimenter. At predetermined times, the confederates stated judgments of the line which were manifestly wrong. A sizable portion — 30 to 40 percent — of the uninformed subjects went along with these erroneous judgments. In similar experiments subjects have agreed that New York is 6,000 miles from San Francisco, that men are 8 to 9 inches taller than women on the average, and that in the United States male babies have a life expectancy of only twenty-five years. The habit of conformity is very strong in adults in our society.

Further experimental studies have shown that such conformity increases as the number of "others" in the group increases from two, to three, to four. Beyond a majority of four, however, the tendency to yield increases little as the majority gets bigger. The tendency to conform in such a situation is dramatically reduced if the erroneous judgments are not unanimous; a single fellow-dissenter makes nonconformity much easier for a subject. Conformity is also reduced if the subject identifies other group members as low in prestige or simply different in some important way from the subject. Rationally, people tend to conform more when it seems to them more likely that they might just possibly be wrong and the group right; thus when the problem is difficult or the subject is uncertain of the answer, when the group contains experts or has a history of being correct and/or agreeing with the subject, and when the subject himself has low general ability or self-esteem, the tendency to conform is stronger.

These various facts can be more or less summarized in three general reasons why people conform: first, because they don't want to be thought deviant — they want their behavior to fit into that of the group; second, because they want their judgments and opinions to be consistent with those of people whom they admire or to whom they feel similar; third, because they believe the group may actually be right.

An overly strong tendency to conform poses certain problems. One problem is that not all individuals will be equally satisfied by the same set of behavior patterns or by the same way of life. Another problem is one for the culture as a whole: Clearly, culture does not always profit from remaining static. It must change to adapt to new conditions, or to adapt better to old ones. If too great a degree of conformity exists, potentially useful innovations may be stifled.

Currently, there is a great deal of worry in some quarters as to whether our society overemphasizes conformity to the detriment of creativity and individual expression. Certainly the greater interrelatedness of people in modern times due to increased efficiency of communications has created greater opportunities for conformity. But whether we now behave in the same ways as our neighbors or friends to a greater extent than did our grandparents is empirically an unanswered question.

FIGURE 2–3

(a) To study conformity, groups of people were shown sets of lines like those at top, and each person was asked to say which comparison line was closest to the standard. On some trials, a majority—who were confederates of the experimenter—chose incorrect answers like line X as the best match to the standard. Many subjects went along with the "majority opinion."
(b) A subject (center), who didn't, shows the strain of disagreeing repeatedly with the majority. (From "Opinions and social pressure" by S. E. Asch. Copyright © 1955 by *Scientific american*, Inc. All rights reserved. Photographs by William Vandivert.)

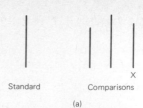

Standard   Comparisons

(a)

(b)

INTERACTION AND INFLUENCE

A general tendency to conform is not the only force which makes people in the same group similar. As will be discussed below, the processes by which people come to like one another are greatly promoted by frequent contact. In turn, the formation of beliefs and attitudes is influenced by whom one knows, likes, and talks to. To come full circle, one tends to have social contacts with people who are likely to share one's attitudes and beliefs. Thus if a group of people remain in frequent interaction for any length of time, they will tend to become more and more alike in their attitudes, beliefs, and values, more and more cohesive in their patterns of interaction, and more and more consistent in whom they like and dislike. The end result of this self-reinforcing cycle is ever-increasing similarity in the ways of behaving of the group members —in short, the creation of a culture.

INTER-GROUP HOSTILITY AND PREJUDICE

One of the less fortunate consequences of the fact of culture formation within interacting groups is the not-infrequent development of hostility toward out-group members as a counterpart of solidarity with in-group members. When a group of people develop a set of values, beliefs, and ways of behaving which they consider "right"—and which may be the only ones they know—there is always a possibility that the feeling of rightness will be extended to a feeling of wrongness toward other beliefs and values.

This natural and usually healthy tendency, when carried to an extreme, can be an important contributor to intergroup hostility and prejudice. One of the possible psychological effects of large cultural differences seems to be a sort of impersonalization of members of other cultures. What a "man" is, is defined by what people are like in *your* culture. (In many primitive tribes the only word meaning "human" or "man" is the name of the tribe.) People from other cultures are somewhat unlike one's notions of what a proper man is; they speak incomprehensible languages, they walk, express themselves, and gesticulate in strange ways; they may live in peculiar houses and eat funny foods. Thus it is easy to believe that they are not quite as human as we are and, therefore, not to be valued or respected as much. If you read the news account of an overseas airline crash, you can often detect an assumption that one American life is worth several of other nationalities'. Such devaluation of other people's human worth often makes it easier for people to justify wars, colonialism, and oppression.

Racial and religious prejudices also stem, at least in part, from a malfunction of normal, healthy cultural processes. If you are well socialized, you hold a set of values and beliefs quite strongly. There is a certain amount of rationality in prejudging that people who belong to cultural groups very different from yours, and therefore have different values and beliefs, may, on the average, be less attractive to you than members of your own group. For example, let us assume that you are an ardent animal lover and conservationist, by which we mean that you view animals as having important individuality which is to be treasured and protected. Would you expect to hit it off with a roommate who belongs to three different hunting clubs? Clearly a mild doubt would be realistic. But such an attitude would be very close to, if not indistinguishable from, what we usually call a prejudice—an opinion about a person based on his group membership rather than on knowing him.

Thus, the source of many rational and benign preferences for social contacts is, unfortunately, also an important contributory factor in the not-so-mild, socially nefarious kinds of prejudice. Particularly in America this source of prejudice poses a serious social problem. We pride ourselves on having a pluralistic society in which many different nationalities, religions, and races live side by side. It is one of our folk beliefs that the raison d'être of the United States is to provide freedom for diversity. But by necessity, if each group is free to practice and perpetuate its own culture, the members of each will have values and beliefs which differ from those of other groups. Each group's members will tend to view its particular brand of culture as better than that of others', and to prejudicially devalue people in other groups. This conflict between the American creed of toleration and appreciation of diversity and natural intergroup devaluative attitudes has been called "the American dilemma" (Myrdal, 1944).

All this is not to suggest that prejudice is either desirable or unavoidable, or that cultural differences are the whole reason behind the phenomena of prejudice. Not by any means. In the first place, with sufficient education, with sufficiently strong personal self-confidence and self-acceptance, most people learn the difficult art of appreciating other people's cultures and values as well as their own. It is well-known that prejudice usually decreases with increasing education. The development of hostility leading to aggression, the invention of disparaging myths about another group, and the denial of equal treatment and open association with members of other groups go far beyond the potential differences which arise from realistic cultural diversity. Rather, these more extreme manifestations often have their roots in pathological or near-pathological personality dynamics, or in real economic competition. However, even quite hostile attitudes and suppressive practices toward out-groups may become a part of a culture's tradition and be passed on from generation to generation of people who know no other way.

We will consider other aspects of prejudice later in this chapter in the section on attitudes.

SOCIETY: INTERDEPENDENT BEHAVIOR

The structure and processes of interacting groups

The ways in which one man's behavior is interrelated with that of other men range from war and international politics, to committee meetings of campus organizations, to a child passing the salt to his father at dinner. The interdependencies between people are the object of study of all the social sciences, including sociology, history, political science, economics and geography, and to a certain extent of the humanities as well. Social psychology is but one of many disciplines whose sphere of interest touches upon these problems.

The special interest of psychologists in social group phenomena is centered on the relation between the individual and the group, the group's influence on the individual's behavior, and the individual's contribution to the group product. We will begin by describing some general effects of being in a group on an individual's behavior; then discuss some principles concerning small, informal groups; and then consider briefly the similarities and special problems of larger and more formal organizations.

GROUP EFFECTS ON INDIVIDUAL BEHAVIOR

In our culture, at least, people tend to strive harder when in the presence of others. A classical observation by Triplett (1897) showed, for example, that the speed of bicycle racers averaged 20 percent more when a "pace" cycle was in view, than without it. This finding has since been repeated in a large variety of different situations and seems to hold whether or not the others present are competitors, and even when the presence of others is only imagined. This phenomenon is called *social facilitation*. There are limits to the benefits of company, however; as we will see below, the total output of a working group rarely increases in proportion to size. Other people can be distracting as well as motivating, shared responsibility may alter the incentive for effort, and the need for cooperation may produce problems and inefficiencies.

There are also qualitative ways in which people seem to behave differently when they are in groups than when they are alone. For example, both policemen and demonstrators, when there are large numbers of both in the same vicinity, often perform acts of violence that are in direct violation of their own codes of conduct and customary habits of behavior. While we cannot yet say exactly when and why such things happen, certain relevant observations have been made.

For example, one well-documented generalization (Wallach, Kogan, & Bem, 1962) is that people are willing to take greater risks when in groups than when alone. Research has failed to pinpoint a reason for this "risky-shift" phenomenon, but has found repeatedly, and in many contexts, that group discussion leads members to shift from more conservative strategies—about business decisions, gambling bets, diplomatic maneuvers, etc.—to more risky positions.

The antisocial behavior sometimes exhibited by people in mobs is probably also due, in part, to what has been called *responsibility diffusion* or *deindividuation*—the feeling of personal responsibility and the threat of retribution are diluted when many people are involved. Indeed, there is reason to believe that when people think they are anonymous, they are more willing to perform irresponsible acts.

Another aspect of the sometimes antisocial mood of multitudes is the appalling indifference with which large numbers of bystanders occasionally witness individuals in dire trouble. Once, in New York, one Andrew Mormille, aged seventeen, was stabbed in the stomach in view of eleven fellow passengers in a subway car. His assailants fled, leaving him bleeding badly. No one helped him, and he bled to death. Research (Latané & Darley, 1969) has shown that the presence of others actually inhibits an individual's tendency to help persons in distress. Alone, an individual will usually report a fire or help an accident victim, but if there are other people around, he usually will not. One possible line of explanation for such phenomena is the dilution of responsibility mentioned above. Another is a kind of snow-balling effect of conformity. When one person sees everyone else sitting on his or her hands for the first minute of the situation, he tends to follow suit, thereby setting a passive example for the others, and so forth.

Thus, in at least several respects, the way an individual acts, *qua* individual, can be altered simply by his being part of an assembly of people, even without considerations of the specific activities involved in coordinated group actions. Next we will discuss what happens when several people behave together as an interrelating group, rather than merely a collection of individuals.

DYNAMICS OF SMALL GROUPS

A very large amount of research has been done on small groups—groups like committees, clubs, work teams or discussion groups—whose members can all potentially interact, 1-to-1, with each other during short periods of time. The research has tried to describe their major activities in a way which can be related to the productivity of the group as a whole and the satisfaction with it of its members. A certain number of regularities have been observed.

Suppose one takes, as has been done innumerable times in psychological experiments, four people who have previously never met, places them in a small room, and gives them the task of discussing a case history of a girl named Mary Peebles who has been asked by her best friend to help her cheat on an examination. What sorts of interactions will the group engage in? What differentiations and specialization of activities will develop?

While there are, of course, large variations from one such group to another, certain generalizations are possible. First, the group will usually develop a leader. Participation in discussion groups is almost always very lopsided, two members doing more than half the talking, others virtually none (see Figure 2–4). During the first periods of group interactions comments of the other members of the group will gradually come to be more and more directed toward the most talkative persons. If after a single, short session of, say, twenty minutes, the group members are asked to rate each other as to who made the most constructive suggestions, who was the most influential or important, or more directly, who was the leader, these active participators will get most of the votes. They will also be rated as the most popular and probably the most likable members of the group.

With increasing time spent in interaction, things will change somewhat. The person who makes many suggestions will not necessarily continue to be popular or appreciated. Usually, his popularity will decrease while he will continue to be rated as the member who makes the most constructive suggestions. At the same time, another member of the group will be gaining in popularity. This second member will be found to make a relatively large number of supportive comments of the kind which could be classified as "shows solidarity," "gives orientation," "gives approval," and so forth. Soon this supportive person will be rated as the most liked and valued member.

Thus, after sufficient time most small groups come to have two different people filling two clearly different leadership roles. One acts to keep the members of the group satisifed, friendly toward one another, and peaceful and to keep the group working happily toward its goals. The other makes numerous suggestions, gives numerous opinions, agrees, disagrees, and in general engages in activities oriented toward the task of the group without much heed to their possible disrupting effect on group solidarity.

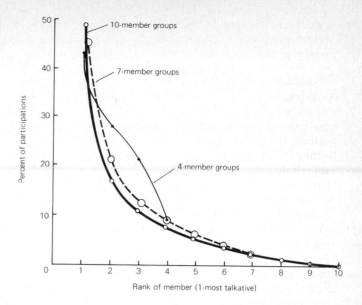

FIGURE 2–4
The distribution of participation of members of small discussion groups. Notice that the curves for the three different group sizes are very similar: In each case two members do over 60 percent of the talking. (After Stephan & Mishler, 1952)

To repeat, in self-structured interacting groups, there are usually not one, but two leaders. The first has been called the *socioemotional* leader, the second the *task* leader. It is a rare person who is capable of combining the two leadership functions.

LEADERSHIP
Leaders thus emerge in unstructured groups where no formal organization specifies who shall be leader. Leaders, of course, are also found in structured, deliberately organized groups. In most chartered organizations, the leadership roles are assigned to individuals whose position is signified by a title and other perquisites, and whose lines of influence on others in the group are to some extent formalized.

While the evidence is not overwhelmingly convincing, there appears to be fair consensus among experts as to certain general considerations and principles regarding leadership, and these will be summarized here. But keep in mind that there are many exceptions to any of the following statements, and many uncertainties of fact.

Ordinarily, in the formal structure of organizations there is no counterpart to the divided leadership of self-organizing groups. Rather, one person is specified as the leader—be he foreman, chairman, straw-boss, vice-president, colonel, Cardinal, or whatever. Often, of course, an individual other than the official leader takes over the second leadership role. Thus, while the president of the PTA may be an efficient, down-to-business woman, the vice-president may take over the role of keeping peace, making people happy, and making certain that minority opinions are heard.

Which of the two leadership roles should the official leader adopt? At first thought, it might seem apparent that the demands of the job of being president, boss, or sergeant settle the question in favor of

Social
psychology
33

task orientation rather than process orientation. The truth of the matter seems often to be largely the opposite. In leadership roles ranging from business management committees to production-line work groups—and even scientific laboratories—successful leaders seem most often to be those who are good at the socioemotional aspects of their job. Whatever the measure of success—the bricks laid by the men on his crew, the number and quality of new advertising gimmicks developed by his agency, or the number of demerits earned by his Marine outfit—the most effective leader is usually the one who is capable of producing a high degree of cohesiveness, inter-group mutual liking, and smooth interaction among his subordinates.

The reason seems to be that people will work well and even organize work among themselves well, provided only that their own interests and motivations are engaged by the task. There is abundant evidence that people work better if they are allowed to organize their own work patterns, that they strive harder and more effectively if they have taken part in establishing the goals toward which they work, and that they cooperate more effectively with fellow workers whom they like. The person doing a job is ordinarily better able to figure out how it should best be done than is anyone else, including the boss. Consequently, the most important thing for the leader is to make sure that workers or followers *want* to do a good job and have the environment in which it is possible and satisfying to do so.

Thus, despite a rather widespread and traditional feeling to the contrary, less supervision rather than more is often most beneficial to productivity. A famous example of this is given by Richards and Dobyns (1957). A group of nine women working in an insurance company were segregated in a cage (a wire-fenced enclosure) surrounded by high filing cabinets, which shielded them from view. There they spent the day filing checks and vouchers. They kept up with their work, despite the fact that they had a very jolly time playing games, eating officially illicit snacks, and chattering. Their supervisor left them alone because she could not see them in their cage. Then, for reasons of efficiency, the office was rearranged. The cage was moved out from behind the filing cabinets and into view. The chattering and eating decreased markedly under the now-present eye of the supervisor. The results? Not only did the contentment of the group members go down, but also their productivity. They got behind on their work as they had never done before, and their dissatisfaction showed itself in increased tardiness, absenteeism, and incompetence.

GROUP STRUCTURE AND EFFICIENCY

There are, of course, a number of different ways in which to organize a group, be it a committee for the homecoming beer blast or an army. It is known that groups made up of people who are similar to each other in background, attitudes, etc., work together better, and that groups become more effective with practice. But there are also bound to be certain differences in efficiency of meeting the goals of the group which result from differences in organization. Let us take, as examples, two of the most obviously relevant characteristics of group organization —size of the group and arrangement of its lines of communication.

Size of group

For groups of very many kinds, group productivity tends to be greater the larger the number of members, but it does not increase in proportion — each new member adds somewhat less than the one before. This is true whether we consider tug-of-war teams (Kohler, 1927) or creative groups. Take, for example, brainstorming groups used extensively in advertising to come up with ideas. Investigations have shown that the number and quality of ideas produced would usually be greater if each member worked by himself and the ideas were later pooled, than if they worked together in a brainstorming session (Taylor, Berry, & Block, 1958).

Group work does have some advantages: members can check each other's work, they can pool knowledge and skills, and most people seem to find pleasure and satisfaction in such situations. But as a group becomes larger, the opportunity for each member to contribute becomes less and less. Eventually this must mean that some members contribute, and perhaps profit, less than they could. The result is the common observation that groups too large for a given purpose are usually unwieldy. In fact, most research seems to show that for small face-to-face interacting groups, more than about eight to ten members is inefficient. This can hardly be classed as a general truth, however, and there are certainly cases in which very much larger groups function quite effectively. What is closer to a general truth is that the efficiency of a group is ordinarily greater the smaller its size, provided that it includes at least one representative of each of the major skills or resources which its task requires. Thus, a good general rule of thumb is to keep groups as small as possible within the limitation of having one expert in each of the needed specialties.

Communication patterns

Certain formal structures can be imposed on small, face-to-face groups, and it is interesting to see what the effects of these are on group activity. A common procedure for studying this problem is to allow a group to work on a problem without allowing members free access to each other. For example, the group members may be allowed to communicate only by passing notes, with the experimenter determining the paths along which notes can be passed. For example, if there are five people, he can arrange the situation such that certain ones can communicate only with certain others, as is shown in Figure 2–5. The two kinds of communication nets shown in the figure are called *circle* and *star*, respectively. Members can communicate with each other only as shown in the figure. The group may be given a problem such as the following: Each of the five members receives a set of five symbols out of a possible six. Among the five participants, there is one symbol which is shared by all of them, and their task is to discover which one it is. The traditional result for such simple problems is that the star arrangement leads to faster solutions and fewer errors than does the circle. The star can be described as a more centralized organization. Usually greater centralization makes a group more efficient on simple problems, ones in which all that is needed is to get the required information together. On the other hand, centralization does not lead to high morale or satisfaction; too many members are left out of the action. And for

FIGURE 2–5
Two experimental communication
nets are the circle and star;
arrows show who can
communicate to whom. For
some simple problems, the star
configuration is more efficient;
however, with practice the two
seem to differ very little.

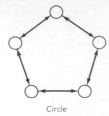

Circle

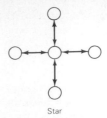

Star

complex problems, having all the members work hard and happily is sometimes very important. Thus, when the problem is very complex, the circle sometimes works faster (Shaw, 1954). In addition, which particular network works best depends on the amount of experience the group has had. After a good deal of practice, such that the members can develop their own patterns of interaction and organization, the experimenter-imposed network begins to matter less and factors such as the *de facto* organization of decision making, group morale, and cohesiveness matter more.

In general, at least with relatively new groups, the more inter-connection between the members, the more efficient the group processes are. If every member can communicate with every other, the group tends to work better both in efficiency and satisfaction than it would otherwise. The practical prescription, then, is to arrange organizations of people working on joint problems so as to maximize their communication links with each other. Try *not* to let chains of responsibility or command restrict communication to fewer channels than might be available. For example, circulate reports of committee or work group members to each other, rather than just to the chairman or supervisor.

NORMS, BELIEFS, AND VALUES

While the nominal products, or conscious result, of the activity of most groups and organizations are some tangible goods or services, or some activity which the group desires, such as a beach party, or an expression of views on how to teach Johnny to read, there are other indirect products of group interaction. As we have seen earlier, an interacting group tends to develop common values.

One of the mechanisms behind the phenomenon of convergence of values within a group is the tendency toward conformity. However, there is another reason. In being a member of a group, one tends to be exposed only, or at least more frequently, to the views of its other members than to the views of the population at large. One therefore gets a somewhat distorted view of reality. A person's standard of the range of opinions, his scale of comparison, is set by what he experiences—by his "social reality." Thus the member of a group or community in which prejudice against Negroes prevails sees and hears no expression of pro-Negro or tolerant sentiment. Assume that a person believes that Negroes are inferior and should be treated as such. There is only one practical way for him to test this belief—ask those whose opinions he values, i.e., the people he knows best. If these are all members of the group which shares his opinion, then all his tests of the proposition will meet with affirmation.

This process is often named *social comparison*. It is easy to underestimate how pervasive is the influence of the social-comparison process. The truth is that people almost never turn to actual research, either in books or experiment, to find out what is true. Instead they ask the opinions of friends. There are many important questions for which social comparison is the *only* way of getting an answer, e.g., can I run fast? Is he smart? Is this an appropriate dress? Is that a good place to learn to ski? Even when there are absolute answers, in most situations taking one's cue from others who are known to have similar ideas and values is both easy and pretty reliable. The result is that social comparison is the single most important source of beliefs and attitudes and is used pervasively, both consciously and unconsciously, sometimes to the exclusion of any other data.

The social comparison process is at once an aspect of group function—a matter of the effect of the group on its members—and a case of interpersonal interaction, the subject of our next section.

INTERPERSONAL INTERACTION

What sets off the topics to be discussed now is their focus on the individual. We will consider how an individual person comes into contact with and is induced to interact with other individuals, how he goes about this (from his point of view), and what the outcomes are for him in terms of changes in his attitudes and behavior.

Determinants of who interacts with whom and when
PROXIMITY AND LIKING

One of the most important determinants of who interacts with whom is geography. People who live close to one another and/or share centralized resources have a greater chance of interacting than do people who live at a distance. This sounds like, and in a certain sense is, a rather trivial observation. But the extent to which important interactions are a function of proximity alone is surprisingly large. A famous study of a graduate student housing development at MIT (Festinger, Schachter, & Back, 1950) is illustrative. Figure 2–6a and b shows the layout of the housing development and a typical apartment unit. The investigators asked the tenants to tell them the names of all their friends. (Such a plotting of friendships is called a *sociometric survey*.) Since all the residents were graduate students at MIT they were probably similar in many ways and thus reasonably compatible. Given this background, however, friendship among the couples was predicted best by the distance between their apartments. The single exception was that people who lived near the stairs and communal garbage cans were unexpectedly popular. In short, the best predictor of friendship, and a very good one, turned out to be simply the likelihood of people coming into each other's physical presence through sheer geographical accident. This is graphically illustrated in Figure 2–6c.

There is more to the mechanism by which proximity works than simply increased chance of meeting. The fact that the relations are called friendship implies that the people involved began to seek each other out. There is a sort of self-reinforcing cycle—being near makes

FIGURE 2–6a
The layout of units in the housing development employed in a study of proximity and liking.
FIGURE 2–6b
A typical unit.
FIGURE 2–6c
The percent of people living at various distances who were described as "friends." Choice of friends depended heavily on physical proximity.
(Reprinted from *Social pressures in informal groups* by Leon Festinger, Stanley Schachter, and Kurt Back with the permission of the publishers, Stanford University Press; copyright 1950 by Leon Festinger, Stanley Schachter, and Kurt Back)

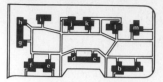 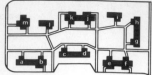

(a) "Westgate" housing development

(b) Typical unit in "Westgate"

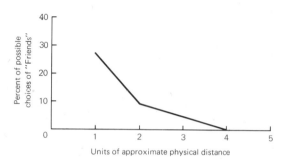

(c) Relation between physical distance and friendship in "Westgate"

people interact, and interaction provides the opportunity for many processes which lead to liking and to more interaction. What are these processes? Among them, we may list the discovery of mutual similarities (this was especially likely in the MIT studies since the subjects were so much alike); the gradual accretion of common and pleasant or simply shared experiences; the incremental influence on one another's beliefs and attitudes, which will increase similarity—thus liking . . . and interaction . . . and . . . .

We tend to like others who have the same tastes, interests, and values, although there are a few aspects of personality, such as dominance and submissiveness, in which people often get along better if they have complementary rather than identical needs (giving rise to the much over-stressed notion that opposites attract in human relations). We tend to like other people who say nice things about us, particularly if we believe they are sincere. There are also, of course, personal characteristics which make some people more generally likable than others. Culturally defined good looks is one example, and probably a stronger influence than we like to believe. Table 2–1 lists adjectives with which college students described likable people, ca. 1968. Note how important were sincerity and similar characteristics.

Simple familiarity also produces liking; faces and names that have been seen often are judged more pleasant in the absence of any

TABLE 2-1
Words that describe likable and unlikable people according to a large sample of college students

Highly likable	Highly dislikable
Sincere	Ill-mannered
Honest	Unfriendly
Understanding	Hostile
Loyal	Loud-mouthed
Truthful	Selfish
Trustworthy	Narrow-minded
Intelligent	Rude
Dependable	Conceited
Thoughtful	Greedy
Considerate	Insincere
Reliable	Unkind
Warm	Untrustworthy
Kind	Malicious
Friendly	Obnoxious
Happy	Untruthful
Unselfish	Dishonest
Humorous	Cruel
Responsible	Mean
Cheerful	Phony
Trustful	Liar

After Anderson, 1968.

other influences. But this principle can be overgeneralized, too. Prejudice, which often includes both biased, stereotyped beliefs about a group and antagonistic attitudes toward it, is not always completely erased by prolonged association. The erroneous beliefs usually disappear with acquaintance, as in shared work or neighborhoods, but the antagonistic feelings may persist. If one group views another as a threatening competitor, or even as an easily identifiable target or scapegoat for aggressions aroused by other frustrations, its members may continue to express hostility even after experience has destroyed the deprecatory myths.

THE DESIRE TO AFFILIATE
People vary considerably in the extent to which they desire to affiliate, and this desire changes with certain conditions. One of the primary situations that increases affiliation motivation is fear. Adults and children alike feel a greater need to affiliate with others when they are afraid. One of the best examples of the effect of fear on affiliation motivation is given by a series of experiments by Schachter (1959). In these experiments, college women volunteered for a study. When they arrived, each subject was individually ushered into a room filled with ominous gadgets and greeted by a serious looking man in a white coat. This man introduced himself as a research doctor and explained that

the subject was to participate in a study of intense and painful (although not harmful) electrical shock. He then asked her to wait while he got the experiment ready, and inquired whether she would like to wait alone or with other women who were also taking part in the study. As compared with control subjects who were not "frightened" in this way, the experimental subjects showed a strong preference for company while waiting. Further research has indicated that fear probably causes people to want to be specifically with other people who are afraid, not with just anyone. This suggests that an important value of affiliation in these cases may be the opportunity to compare one's feelings with others' to make use of social comparison to help determine how to feel and act. It is also likely that the presence of others in the same predicament reduces one's fear. By contrast, when people are embarrassed, they tend to prefer to be alone.

There are, of course, many other motives that lead people into interaction. For example, people like to be approved of by others. And there are many material and other rewards which can be gained only through interaction with others. But very frequently, as in the case of affiliating when afraid, people seek each other's company when they are unsure of themselves and need to know from others how to interpret and react to a situation.

The processes of interaction

Interaction between two persons can be analyzed into several partially distinct aspects. For example, each person must observe what the other person does and says; appreciate his relevant qualities; and infer his intentions, feelings, and so forth. As we shall see in Chapter 6, the use of information from the environment to judge what is "out there" is called *perception*. Thus, in interpersonal interaction we speak of *person perception*. Second, in interacting with another person, we constantly need to act in ways which will communicate to him what our intentions and feelings are, as well as communicate to him direct information through speech.

PERSON PERCEPTION

There are a number of things we can tell about someone else by observing him. We can tell that a man in a blue uniform with a nightstick is a policeman and likely to take offense if we double-park, or that a man behind a counter in a store is a salesman and likely to take our money. Such stereotyped clues to social roles are tremendously important in daily behavior, largely because it is very difficult to tell anything about how a person will behave without them. We all can tell whether another person is laughing, and therefore probably not sad; or whether he is crying, and therefore probably not glad. But we have very limited ability to judge other facial expressions. Try to guess the emotions being depicted in Figure 2–7. Ordinarily we can discriminate expressions of pleasant emotions like love and happiness from unpleasant ones like fear and anger, but research shows that finer discriminations are seldom better than guesses.

It is not obvious whether we can make really deep or subtle judg-

FIGURE 2-7

Examples of some posed facial expressions of emotions. (Try to identify the emotion intended by the actor before looking at the footnote.[2]) (From Hastorf, Osgood, & Ono, 1966)

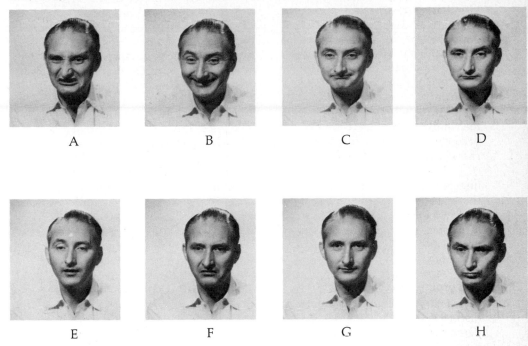

A   B   C   D

E   F   G   H

ments even of people we know well. Many people believe that they are very sensitive and can read the character of another person accurately. However, the evidence is overwhelming that no one is really very good at this. Experimenters have repeatedly found that their subjects could not do substantially better than chance at predicting, for example, which one of two friends had privately described himself as, say, unusually self-conscious. People cannot even tell very well who likes them. The author once asked a group of fraternity brothers and classmates to record which members of the group they liked and disliked, and then to guess who liked and disliked *them*. After taking into account the fact that most of them liked each other, the guesses were just as likely to be wrong as right.

Several reasons for the difficulty of making such judgments are known. One of the chief problems is that the words we ordinarily use to describe character are not well-defined. In describing someone's personality we might be tempted to say that he or she is very warm. However, it is not easy to specify exactly what we mean by *warm*. In fact, *warm* means rather different things to different people. Thus, if you say that Uncle Harry is a very warm person, I may retort, "You're out of your

[2] A-rage, B-glee, C-optimistic determination, D-complacency, E-passive adoration, F-mild repugnance, G-amusement, H-puzzlement.

mind, Uncle Harry is a cold fish." And yet we may both be right. What you may mean by *warm* is someone who talks a lot, and what I may mean by *warm* is someone who is generous. So our voluble, tightwad uncle may appear "warm" to you and "cold" to me.

A related question is just how many different dimensions or attributes or general traits of personality we are able to perceive, judge, and describe about other people. We have, in English, a very large number of words referring to personality attributes. For example, there are *warm, cold, intelligent, stupid, friendly, charming, obnoxious, talkative, quiet, sweet, passionate, brave,* and so forth. The use of such terms often tends to imply that people have general personality traits of these kinds, e.g., that some people are always more x (say, *cold*) than others, and that other people can make fine discriminations and judgments about who has what traits. It turns out that this implication is, by and large, false. In the first place, it has been found that almost all the broad descriptive judgments that one can make about another's personality, no matter how many words are used, can be reduced to three basic categorizations: good-bad, active-passive, and strong-weak. One method by which this rather striking conclusion has been reached is called the *semantic differential* (Osgood, 1952). A subject is given an extensive list of triads of words, e.g., *intelligent, clean, dirty,* and asked to rate the first in its closeness in meaning to the other two. It turns out that the way one word is rated with respect to any other two can be predicted with considerable accuracy from how each was rated relative to the three basic categories. It follows that when one person describes another, using words, where he places the person on the basic three dimensions predicts how he will rate him on any other attribute. It also follows, therefore, that a detailed description of any person by another which involves a very large number of different attributes presents a deceptive appearance of richness and precision of which the human judgmental process is incapable.

A closely related difficulty in person perception arises from the general tendency to think consistent thoughts. It is inconsistent to think a person both bad and good, so we tend to make him all one or the other. If we see a person as intelligent and we think that intelligence is good, then we are also likely to ascribe to that same person a variety of other attributes which we think are good. If we see him as inconsiderate, we will probably also judge him irritable, boastful, cold, and hypocritical (Bruner, Shapiro, & Tagiuri, 1958). This logical error is known as a *halo* (or *devil*) *effect*. The effect also holds for other dimensions than good-bad. There are many acts which we call by the same name—think of all the acts that might be called "dishonest." If we observe a person in one act, we have a strong tendency to think that he will perform others that have the same label. But often this is not so at all; the association between "honesty" in playing cards and "honesty" in self-appraisal is linguistic, not actual. Strong correlations between the frequency with which individuals do one kind of "honest" act and the frequency with which they do other kinds of "honest" acts, for example, have never been found in empirical studies. We will discuss this problem again in Chapter 3 (Personality) and Chapter 9 (Development).

All this is not to imply that people cannot judge each other at all.

They certainly can. Many detailed and important descriptions can be made of others' typical behavior with reasonable accuracy; for example, that he stutters, that she talks a lot, that he is shy with strange girls, that she studies hard. Even the general intelligence of another person can often be estimated with fair success by informal means. But for the vast majority of general personality traits, our perception of persons is actually far less accurate than we commonly assume.

Outcomes of interpersonal interaction

In interacting, people gain information about the ways in which other people see and evaluate the world, in addition to gaining information about each other as persons. As a result, a frequent and important result of interaction is a change in attitude about events and objects in the world (including other people).

ATTITUDES

The word *attitude* is used in social psychology in very much the same way as it is used in common speech. It refers to a person's feelings or way of thinking about another person, object, or event; or better, to his *potential actions or expressions of opinion* about them. Attitudes are usually distinguished from beliefs, which are also ways of thinking about social objects (as well as nonsocial objects), by the criterion that attitudes involve *affect*, that is, feelings or emotional values, as well as factual thoughts.

Consistency of attitudes

Attitudes do not ordinarily exist in people as separate fragments. Certain groups of attitudes and beliefs tend to be found together. A person who dislikes Catholics more often than not also dislikes Jews; someone who likes me more than likely likes my wife.

There are a number of different reasons for the consistency of attitudes. One reason is the influence of culture: certain sets of attitudes and beliefs tend to be found together simply because they are aspects of the same cultural heritage. A person who likes to eat snails in butter and garlic sauce usually drinks wine, not water, with his meals. There does not appear to be any logical or psychological necessity disposing one to like wine if he likes snails. But if one is born in France, one learns at his mother's knee to love certain things, among which are (1) snails and (2) wine. If one is born instead in Ratoon, Illinois, one grows up with a certain fondness for both (1) hamburgers (not too thick) and (2) milk shakes (very thick).

Often, sets of attitudes which by their aggregation appear to reflect underlying motives or quirks of personality, turn out on closer examination to be related only by fortuitous cultural association. A good example is the relation between attitudes toward government and toward Negroes in the United States. There is a syndrome (a related set of symptoms) of personality called *authoritarianism* (Frenkel-Brunswik & Sanford, 1945). People with authoritarian personalities are characterized by a set of beliefs and feelings about authority—its source in absolute standards of right and wrong, the importance of its exercise in the family and in other interpersonal settings, and so forth. As measured in the United States, authoritarianism is also associated with anti-Semitism and anti-Negro prejudice. But in South Africa the degree of anti-Negro attitudes held by white college students is totally uncorrelated with measured authoritarianism (Pettigrew, 1958). The explanation of this difference would seem to be that in the United States authoritarianism is generated within families practicing a subculture which includes prejudice against minorities, while the same subcultural correlations do not exist in South Africa.

A second but much-harder-to-document source of attitude consistency is personality. An example of a cohering set of attitudes with the markings of a deep personality difference is the set differentiating extreme liberals from extreme conservatives. (But be warned that there are also important similarities between these extreme groups, and that the liberal-conservative attitude dimension is probably anything but a simple continuum; few actual people fit all the characteristics of either ideal pole.) People who class themselves in these two categories appear to differ on a number of attitudes relevant to the conservative-liberal dimension. For example, on the average, self-declared conservatives agree and liberals disagree with the following statements: "Duties are more important than rights," "You can't change human nature," "The heart is as good a guide as the head," (McClosky, 1958). However, also associated with the conservative-liberal differences in attitude are average differences in certain personality variables that have no logical connection with the characteristic attitudes and beliefs. Extreme conservatives, as compared with liberals, are more often low on self-awareness, nonintellectual, low in dominance, low in feelings of social responsibility, low in self-confidence, high in feelings of rootlessness, high in feelings of alienation from society, high in general feelings of bewilderment, guilt, and hostility, high in contempt for weakness in others and in intolerance of human frailty, and high in need to defend their own egos from attack (all as measured with paper-and-pencil tests by McClosky).

These traits seem, intuitively at least, to define personality types which might be found in any cultural setting. That they may, indeed, be unrelated to culture-group background is suggested by McClosky's finding that conservative attitudes are not consistently correlated with political party affiliation, or voting, both of which are, of course, highly related to social-group membership.

A third source of consistency has been called *the need for cognitive consistency*. People usually strive for a certain amount of consistency in their thoughts, beliefs, feelings, and actions. That they do not always succeed cannot be gainsaid, but a general tendency to be consistent is apparent in us all. Cognitive consistency takes the form of consistency among and between attitudes and beliefs, and between these and actions. We will see many applications of this principle in what follows.

Attitude change

There is a wide variety of different influences and conditions which are important in attitude change. However, much of what is known can be summarized by considering the way in which new information

TABLE 2-2

Changes in party preferences during election campaigns

Year of survey	First poll	Last poll	Percentage of change
1940	May	November	8*
1948	June	August	8†
1948	August	October	3†
1960	August	November	7‡
1964	August	November	10‡

* Lazarsfeld, Berelson, & Gaudet (1948, pp. 65–66).
† Berelson, Lazarsfeld, & McPhee (1954, p. 23).
‡ Benham (1965)
From Freedman, Carlsmith, & Sears, 1970.

affects an individual and is incorporated into his existing set of attitudes and beliefs.

Information and other factors   Whenever a person is exposed to new information, there is a chance that one or more of his beliefs may be altered and as a result an attitude may be modified. On the other hand, people seem to be remarkably skillful at avoiding, rejecting, disbelieving, forgetting, or distorting new information which is at variance with their cherished beliefs and attitudes. For example, very few people change their minds as a result of political campaigns (see Table 2–2). Thus, while information is exceedingly important in determining what attitudes will change in what ways, other factors determine what information will be absorbed. Knowing what information a person is given tells something about the direction attitude change is likely to take, but not whether it will occur.

Some determining factors have been identified in laboratory research. The more prestigious the source of a counter-attitudinal communication, and the more expert and honest it appears, the more likely it is that attitudes will change. Usually a two-sided argument—one in which opposing views and facts are openly dealt with—works better than a one-sided argument, probably at least in part because a two-sided argument conveys an impression of honesty and expertise. A one-sided appeal sometimes works better when the audience is not very well-informed and already agrees with the communicator. Then giving the other side apparently can raise new doubts about both the issue and the communicator.

Still and all, perhaps the most impressive thing we know about attitude change is how little it occurs in real life, and how slowly. The Chinese Communists in Korea had complete control over the lives of thousands of captured American soldiers, yet intensive and prolonged brainwashing converted a mere handful. These attitudes ran deep, for they involved strong feelings, not just intellectual beliefs. Apparently the emotional aspect of attitudes is very persistent, requiring months or years of new experience to alter, as compared with the cognitive aspects which can sometimes be changed in minutes by a well-presented argument.

Cognitive consistency and attitude change Attitudes never change automatically with receipt of new information, but rather are modified as new information is rejected or incorporated into the individual's world. Many of the details of this process can be understood by considering the influence of the tendencies toward cognitive consistency referred to above.

As mentioned, one very important factor is the source of information. If your kid sister tells you that the use of cigarettes is dangerous and bad, you are unlikely to be influenced as much as if the same message comes from the Surgeon General. The cognitive consistency explanation is as follows: To be consistent in your beliefs, attitudes, and actions, you must do something to resolve the discrepancy between the knowledge that you smoke and the receipt of information that it is dangerous. One thing you can do is to stop smoking. But another is to decide that the source of unwelcome information is unreliable. It is easier to believe your sister stupid or misinformed than to give up your belief in the harmlessness of smoking. But by the same token, your prior belief is that the Surgeon General is neither stupid nor misinformed, so it may be easier to change your belief in smoking. In either case, whether you demote your sister's intelligence or change your attitude toward smoking, you will have maintained consistency in your cognitions. Maintenance of consistency demands that the more you respect the opinion of a spokesman, the more your attitudes will tend to shift in response to his persuasion.

Another way in which cognitive consistency enters into attitude change is in determining the total change that will result from change in one aspect of a given belief or attitude. Presume that you believe the following statements to be true: it is bad to endanger other people, and, fires endanger people in buildings. Now suppose that by quoting statistics I manage to persuade you that smoking in a classroom increases the likelihood of fires. Note that I make no statements concerning whether it is good or bad to smoke in classrooms. Nonetheless, to maintain consistency, if you are convinced of the fire hazard, you must adopt a negative attitude toward smoking in classrooms. The change in *belief* about smoking and fire hazard might come about immediately after my lecture on the subject. The *attitude* toward smoking might not change immediately, but given the change in belief and the prior set of attitudes specified, it would be quite likely to change within a few weeks as a result of "cognitive work" on your part. An especially interesting and typical case of delayed attitude change occurs when the information is transmitted by a negatively evaluated communicator. If someone you do not like tells you a fact that should change your attitude, e.g., your Army sergeant says that salt tablets are important on hot days, you may at first reject the new information, only to find yourself believing it several days or weeks later. Apparently the association of the information with the source tends to be forgotten, so that the information can be accepted later without dissonance.

Another and especially significant cognitive-consistency relation is that between actions on the one hand and beliefs and attitudes on the other. If a person is induced to behave, for example to make a decision or public commitment, in a way which is contrary to an attitude that he holds, then there will be a strong tendency for the attitude to change. A formal theory concerning the effects of postdecision shifts toward consistency has been proposed by Leon Festinger (1957). In this *theory of cognitive dissonance* each item of knowledge about past actions, each belief and each feeling toward an object or person, is called a cognitive *element*. The theory holds that a person will try to reduce to a minimum the number and strength of cognitive elements that are in opposition to each other. He can do this by changing beliefs or attitudes or actions, by distorting or denying new information, or by refusing ever to think about conflicting things at the same time.

The theory of cognitive dissonance, although it is intuitively "common sensible" in its basic point, makes some predictions that are not obvious. For instance, one striking experimental confirmation of the theory was as follows (Festinger & Carlsmith, 1959). A group of students was asked to do a tedious and boring task—repeatedly putting spools into boxes. After a certain amount of time at this humdrum activity, each student was asked to act as assistant to the experimenter in introducing the task to the next subject. Some of the "assistants" were offered $1 for their help, while others were offered $20. In either case they were to tell the new subjects that the experiment was fascinating. Thus, subjects had committed themselves publicly by stating that the task was fascinating, when they actually thought it anything *but*. They could reduce this dissonance in at least two ways. One way was to say to themselves that the pay was so great that they were willing to perjure themselves; the other was to decide that, after all, the task *was* pretty interesting. Obviously it was easier to do the former for those offered a lot—$20—than for those offered a little—$1. Thus, the subjects who were offered the small amount changed their attitude in favor of the opinion they expressed to a much greater extent than those offered more to say the same thing.

This is not to say that being rewarded—achieving some desired result—for expressing an opinion does *not* shift one's attitude toward the opinion. There is ample evidence that it *does*. What it does say, however, is that you are more likely to shift your opinion if the inducement to commit yourself is just barely enough than if the inducement is an overwhelming one.

A related general consequence of this theory that has been corroborated by many experiments has to do with the effect of induced compliance. We often hear that one cannot legislate attitudes. The theory says otherwise. Consider a prejudiced person who has somehow been induced to act as if he likes Negroes. In order to reduce the dissonance between the knowledge of this activity and a prior negative attitude toward Negroes, he is quite likely to reduce the negative attitude. In such situations as forced integration in the Armed Forces, the attitudes of previously prejudiced people have been found to shift quite markedly in the positive direction.

In summary, while the processes of inter-personal influence are far from being well understood, many variables which affect whether a given piece of information will be incorporated or whether an attempt to influence will work have been identified. In particular, the principles of cognitive consistency have been found to be very valuable in understanding the attitudinal outcomes of interaction.

TOPICS DISCUSSED IN CHAPTER 2

1. Intercultural variation versus intracultural homogeneity of behavior.

2. Socialization.

3. Conformity.

4. Social comparison processes.

5. Some sources of prejudice.

6. Emergence of roles in small interacting groups.

7. Group efficiency and satisfaction.

8. Who interacts with whom.

9. Liking and affiliation.

10. Person perception.

11. Attitude change.

12. Cognitive consistency.

SUGGESTED READINGS

1. A good, not too long textbook on social psychology is:

Freedman, J. L., Carlsmith, J. M., & Sears, D. O. *Social Psychology*. Englewood Cliffs, N.J.: Prentice-Hall, 1970.

2. Some interesting, readable monographs in the field are:

Festinger, L., Riecken, H. W., & Schachter, S. *When Prophecy Fails*. Minneapolis: University of Minnesota Press, 1956, which chronicles the history of a group that predicted the end of the world, relating the goings-on to the theory of cognitive dissonance, and

Schachter, S. *The Psychology of Affiliation*. Stanford, Calif.: Stanford University Press, 1959.

3. *A selection of original journal articles includes:*

Bandura, A., Ross, D., & Ross, S. A. Transmission of agression through imitation of aggressive models. *Journal of Abnormal and Social Psychology*, 1961, 63, 575–582.

Dunnette, M. D., Campbell, J., & Jaastad, K. The effects of group participation on brainstorming effectiveness for two industrial samples. *Journal of Applied Psychology*, 1963, 47, 30–37.

Latané, B., & Darley, J. M. Bystander "apathy." *American Scientist*, 1969, 57, 244–268.

Schein, E. H. The Chinese indoctrination program for prisoners of war. *Psychiatry*, 1956, 19, 149–172.

Stein, D. D., Hardyck, J. A., & Smith, M. B. Race and belief: An open and shut case. *Journal of Personality and Social Psychology*, 1965, 1, 281–289.

THREE
Personality and assessment

What do we mean by the word *personality?* In common parlance we use it to refer to what a person is like, how he acts, what his habits or traits—distinguishing qualities—of character are; whether he is honest or deceitful, intelligent or dull, outgoing or shy, generally happy or usually sad. We often say that an acquaintance has a "pleasing personality." We mean that he is not morose, that he is usually friendly and kind and generous to us, that he appreciates the same kind of humor that we do, and that he talks in a way that is not boring. The use of the term *personality* in psychology is not really very different from its common use. It means *the characteristics of behavior which are enduring attributes of a given individual.* We previously defined culture as those behavorial characteristics typical of a group of people. Similarly, personality consists of the behavioral characteristics typical of an individual. Whenever we describe what a person is like—his primary needs, motives, and values; his temperament, interests, habits, and abilities—we are describing personality.

This will do as a basic and very general definition of personality, and is what will be implied by the word in this book. However, many psychologists who interest themselves in personality go further. They define personality as the enduring and interrelated underlying processes and structures, the "inner essence," that gives rise to the outwardly visible acts and traits of a person. This makes of personality an inferred *cause* of an individual's behavior, as opposed to simply its observable regularities. The two kinds of definition are, for our purpose, nearly equivalent. In either case, in studying personality we would want to describe people's characteristics and then try to understand what lies behind them.

The central questions on which we will focus in studying personality are (1) how to account for the total behavior and experience of an individual and (2) how to account for the differences between one person and another. These concerns will necessarily lead to questions, interesting in their own right, of how the various facets of a person's nature are integrated, and by what processes. We will also be interested in how a personality comes into being, although discussion of many aspects of the genesis of personality will be postponed to the chapter on development.

PERSONALITY TRAITS AND THEIR ASSESSMENT

Our first problem in studying personality is to be able to observe it. Suppose you are writing a letter home and wish to describe the personality of your roommate. What sort of words would you use? Upon what would you base your statements? If it is your first week with your roommate you are likely to write something such as "My new roommate seems nice, but rather quiet." You are unable to be more specific because you have not had enough opportunity to observe. Such characteristics, or traits, as studiousness, constant drunkenness, or chronic inability to make decisions have not yet manifested themselves in your presence. Later on, after you have gotten to know each other better, you may say something like "My roommate is nice enough, but he's rather cold and we don't have a lot to talk about." Or, "My roommate turns out to be a real swinger after all." If you are like most people, your description will never become much more detailed than this.

In informal descriptions of personality, there is a great deal of error. As we noted in Chapter 2, people's judgments of each other are not very reliable, being colored to an extreme by the attitudes and biases of the observer. One's close friends usually have a different estimation of one's personality than do one's enemies.

Clearly, then, the serious study of personality demands that we try to find some way of describing the behavioral characteristics of people in an objective and reliable fashion. We must try to develop a way of arriving at descriptions that are at the same time (1) sufficiently detailed and rich to be of some use and (2) sufficiently reliable that more than one person can agree on a given description. A good deal of effort has gone into the development of methods for obtaining such descriptions, with mixed results. Some kinds of personality traits, or variables, have succumbed over the years to reasonably accurate assessment, while others have resisted. In what follows there will be examples of some of the most accurately measurable personality descriptors and of some of the least accurate as well. While this chapter cannot present anything like a complete catalog of the presently available means for assessing and describing personality, it will provide examples of the range of methods which are used and the range of traits which psychologists have striven to describe.

In describing tests and measures of personality, we will focus on those traits which are probably the most significant aspects of personality and which have, therefore, been studied most intensively. What follows, then, is not simply a list of available tests, but is, at the same time, a description and discussion of the important attributes of behavior that characterize persons.

Intelligence and ability

INTELLIGENCE

Of all the traits we can and do use to classify people, perhaps the one most often used in everyday life, and in psychology as well, is *intelligence*. Everyone, especially those of us who are in one way or another concerned with education—as students or teachers—constantly classifies friends and acquaintances in terms of how "smart" they are. Intelligence, therefore, is an important part of personality as defined here.

The reason intelligence is such a popular descriptor is that "intelligence" is actually an estimation of a person's general all-around ability to succeed at the kinds of tasks which our society and especially our schools value. Since Western society is highly competitive and achievement-oriented, such an estimate is very pertinent to our dealings with and feelings about people.

The objective measurement of intelligence was one of the first major accomplishments of modern psychology. In 1905, Alfred Binet, in answer to a request by the French government, developed a method of predicting school success and lack thereof in young children. The test he developed, which was later modified and translated into English as the Stanford-Binet Intelligence Test, was the prototype instrument for measurement of human intellectual capacities. The Stanford-Binet test consists of a series of problems, graded according to difficulty, which average children of successively older ages can "pass." While the history of this particular test is complicated, the general procedure by which it was developed is as follows. By trial and error, questions were found which on the average could be answered correctly by children of one age but not by children of a younger age (for example, by an average six-year-old but not by an average five-year-old). Many such questions were tried on literally thousands of children—children of all kinds, from all social and economic walks of life, and from all parts of the United States. Only those questions the correct answering of which turned out to be associated with increasing age were included. This is a most important point. One might imagine that in the construction of an intelligence test questions would be selected which seem to experienced educators or psychologists to reflect basic intelligence. However, this is not really the main criterion. Rather, the criterion is whether the question or problem is correlated with increasing sophistication and knowledge. Table 3–1 gives some sample items from the Stanford-Binet test. No matter how unintellectual or even silly a question may appear, if people who pass it are, on the average, older than those who do not pass it, that question is a good candidate for an intelligence test. It turns out, also, that items on intelligence tests are very predictive of success in school. This is not too surprising since one important characteristic of older children, on the average, is that they have progressed farther in school.

Personality
and
assessment
51

TABLE 3-1
Some sample items from the Stanford-Binet intelligence test.* These items can be passed, on the average, by children of the ages indicated.

Age	Type of item	Example or description
2	Three-hole form board	Places form (e.g., circle) in correct hole.
	Block-building: tower	Builds a four-block tower from model after demonstration.
3	Block-building: bridge	Builds a bridge consisting of the side blocks and one top block from model after demonstration.
4	Identifying parts of the body	Points out hair, mouth, etc., on large paper doll.
	Naming objects from memory	One of three objects (e.g., toy, dog, or shoe) is covered after child has seen them; child then names covered object from memory.
	Picture identification	Points to correct pictures of objects on a card when asked, "Show me what we cook on," or "What do we carry when it is raining?"
7	Similarities	Answers such questions as: "In what way are coal and wood alike? Ship and automobile?"
	Copying a diamond	Copies a diamond in the record booklet.
8	Vocabulary	Defines eight words from a list.
9	Verbal absurdities	Must say what is foolish about stories similar to: "I saw a well-dressed young man who was walking down the street with his hands in his pockets and twirling a brand new cane."
	Digit reversal	Must repeat four digits backward.
Average adult	Vocabulary	Defines twenty words from a list.
	Proverbs	Explains in own words the meaning of two or more common proverbs.
	Orientation	Must answer questions similar to: "Which direction would you have to face so your left hand would be toward the south?"

*From Terman & Merrill, 1960.

The original Stanford-Binet method of scoring is as follows. The tester determines the highest level of question which the child is able to pass. This level is called the child's *mental age*—commonly abbreviated MA. MA represents the average age of children who can solve the problems that the tested child can. A given child may score well above his own real chronological age (CA), i.e., may have a mental age in excess of his chronological age, or he may be able to answer only those questions typically answerable by children much younger than he. By taking the ratio of mental age to chronological age (MA/CA), a single number is formed which represents the child's mental age relative to his real, or chronological, age. This number, multiplied by 100 (to eliminate fractions), is called the *intelligence quotient*, or IQ. For example, a child with an MA of 6 and a CA of 4 has an IQ of 6/4 × 100 = 150. This measure, the IQ, has, of course, an average of 100 (a mental age divided by the same chronological age times 100) for the American population on which it was standardized. In a random sample of 1,000 American children, IQ will range from about 55 to about 145 (it has an approximately normal distribution with a standard deviation of 15—see Chapter 11). An idea of the ability levels described is given by the fact that the average IQs of high school and college graduates are about 110 and 120, respectively, and of Ph.D.s about 130.

There have been a large number of other intelligence tests developed since the Stanford-Binet, and there are many different tests in use at the present time. Some of them are specialized for certain parts of the population: for example, the Wechsler Intelligence Scale for Children (usually abbreviated WISC), the Army General Classification Test, and the Scholastic Aptitude Tests. But the basic approach of most is quite similar. In general, IQ tests consist of a large number of problems. One's score is the number of problems answered correctly, multiplied by some factor which results in a standard score with a mean of 100 and a range similar to that of the Stanford-Binet. Such scores (and formulas for IQ) are derived by using the techniques introduced in Chapter 1. The questions, as with the Stanford-Binet, are chosen by trial-and-error research to correlate with age, school success or, in some instances, other types of intellectual success. In addition, most intelligence tests have been purposely constructed in such a way that their results agree closely with those of the Stanford-Binet.

One of the principal refinements of intelligence testing has been an attempt to differentiate between several different aspects of intelligence. A great deal of methodologically sophisticated and mathematically complicated research—and a considerable amount of controversy—has gone into investigating just how many different kinds of intelligence there are. Some investigators have maintained, and some evidence has suggested, that there are many specialized intellectual abilities, for instance, spatial reasoning, mathematical ability, and verbal skills. While there are tests available which make a large number of such distinctions, the most commonly used tests currently distinguish only two subtypes of intellectual ability—mathematical and verbal. For example, the intelligence test commonly taken by college and university applicants provides separate scores for verbal and mathematical aptitudes. The reason for this is that some people can obtain high scores on a "mathematical" test but only moderate or even low scores on a "verbal" test, and vice versa. This is not to say that the two abilities are unrelated—they are in fact fairly closely related—and individuals with widely differing scores in the two abilities are the exception. However, just such a lack of correspondence between these two abilities does occur often enough to make it worthwhile to measure them independently. (It is noteworthy that verbal ability is more closely related to overall success in college than is mathematical ability.) For even more specialized abilities, such as spatial reasoning, the profit from separate measurement is less, because the number of individuals who will score high in a given special ability but low in others becomes smaller and smaller as the abilities become more and more specific.

Despite differences between tests, the measurement of intelligence is always a measurement of a characteristic of an individual that is related to his ability to do well in school (usually described by a *correlation coefficient* of about .50 [see Chapter 11], which means that about one-fourth of the variation between children in school grades can be predicted from IQ scores; this is pretty good, as such things go). This ability to predict academic success is the basic validity criterion against which intelligence tests have been evaluated and with which they are associated. Scores on intelligence tests, that is, measured IQs are, of course, indicative or predictive of many other things—for instance, success in business or even in the Army. However, it is important to realize that IQ is basically a measure of abilities related to academic tasks.

APTITUDE, ABILITY, AND ACHIEVEMENT

In addition to general intellectual ability, or intelligence, success obviously requires the ability to perform the particular tasks required by a job. Several kinds of tests have been used to assess ability and predict whether an individual will be able to acquire the necessary skills to make him competent. Tests which assess the level of skill or knowledge that a person has attained are called *achievement* tests. School exams are one common example. On the other hand, tests which are designed to *predict* how able a person will be to take advantage of training and acquire skills and abilities are called *aptitude* tests. There are aptitude tests for the study of medicine, law, and languages, and for overall or general scholastic success. Some of the methods used in constructing achievement tests were discussed in Chapter 1. The main difference in the construction of an aptitude test is that some standardization method must be used to assure validity. Ordinarily, this is a fairly straightforward matter, for a test of aptitude in learning French the criterion is whether a high-scoring person does well in French studies; the criterion for general scholastic aptitude tests is whether high scorers usually do well in college. The intelligence test is a very general form of aptitude test.

Other tests of personality

We have seen that intelligence tests are an excellent example—probably the single best example—of the way in which instruments for measurement of personality are constructed. A critical element of the process is to find a standard against which to test the efficacy of the components to be put into the final instrument. In the case of the intelligence test, the criterion for validity was an association with age and with progress in school and/or success in other intellectual tasks. With other personality traits the identification of such a clear criterion has not been as easy. But there have been some notable successes.

One famous successful example comes from the development during World War II of tests to select pilots for the Army Air Force (Dubois, 1947). Here the criterion which was most useful was whether the test could predict successful completion of pilot training. Pilot training is quite costly in both money and man-hours. Initially a very large proportion of the candidates, around 75 percent, had to be dropped from the program before they became pilots. The psychologists began by trying to construct tests which would, they felt, find the robust "he-men" they viewed as potentially successful pilots. At first the tests met with little success. Gradually, however, the psychologists began trying all kinds of test questions, relaxing their attempt to second-guess what type of questions would be associated with success in pilot training. They included items that sounded frankly silly, such as "Do you prefer showers to baths?" (Guess what the right answer is.) They retained those items which succeeded in predicting who would finish pilot training and who would not. The final test bore little relation to the psychologists' initial guesses about what kinds of questions would tap the proper characteristics of pilots. What the test finally *did* do, however, was to predict who was likely to be a successful candidate. When only candidates scoring in the upper quarter on this test were accepted, the number of those washed out was reduced from 75 to around 35 percent, saving hundreds of thousands of dollars and a great deal of human effort and anguish.

The same general method of test construction, with certain variations and refinements, has been applied to the development of personality tests measuring a wide variety of different behavioral characteristics. Let us review briefly what some of these characteristics are. In each case notice particularly the kind of criterion against which the validity of the test was established.

MOTIVES

One of the most general and important dimensions of difference between personalities that has been measured is *motivation* (the general concept of motivation is discussed further in Chapter 6). By a *motive* we mean a tendency to strive for certain goals. If we can describe what things or happenings a person works toward, what things are important to him and will serve to reward his efforts, we know a great deal about him. We know what kinds of things he is likely to do and what courses of action he is likely to pursue. It is the very fact that a person who is motivated in certain ways tends to act in ways that reflect this motivation that allows us to measure motives.

One well-known measure of motivation assesses *achievement motivation*—the desire to compete successfully with a standard of excellence. People who strive to overcome obstacles are said to be *achievement-motivated*. Their lives are marked by achievement-oriented efforts. In addition, if the motive is strong, their daydreams and the very way in which they express themselves are colored by this orientation toward achievement.

One measuring instrument for determining a score for need for achievement (*n* Ach) relies on stories which the test taker, or subject, tells about a series of somewhat ambiguous pictures (McClelland, Atkinson, Clark, & Lowell, 1953). For instance, the person being assessed might be handed a picture of a boy playing a trumpet, and then be asked to invent a story about the boy: what has led to the present situation, what is going on, and what the outcome will be. The story is then scored according to a definite set of rules in terms of how many word images or actions in the story are related to overcoming obstacles.

The method of scoring was developed by noting differences between stories invented under differing conditions. One group of subjects had just completed a relaxed, noncompetitive, creative task. Another group had just completed a test which was to be graded and compared with results from a competing group. The second group was *achievement-aroused;* the first was not. A number of reliable and repeatable differences were found between stories told by achievement-aroused people and those not thus aroused. The *n* Ach score is essentially a tally of such elements in a given set of stories.

The *n* Ach score has been found to be related to real-life behavior in ways which would be expected if the score indeed represents a desire to successfully overcome obstacles. For instance, successful businessmen —entrepeneurs—tend to score high. Children who prefer to take moderate level risks in games, who try something just a little harder than what they have previously been able to do, on the average have higher *n* Ach scores than do children choosing other levels of risk. The *n* Ach scoring method can also be applied to published materials such as poems, stories, and children's books. In this case the amount of achievement imagery has sometimes been taken as a measure of the achievement motivation both of the author and of the readers with whom it is popular. The level of achievement imagery in literature increased markedly about a generation before the great expansion of trade and industry in ancient Greece, and decreased shortly before the decline of these indices of national vigor (see McClelland, 1961). One interpretation of these data is that the achievements of a society rest on high motivation to achieve on the part of its members.

There are a number of other measures of motivation which rely on scoring procedures similar to those used to estimate *n* Ach. For example, the needs for power, for affiliation with others, and for sex have all been measured by analogous means.

In a less formal way, the same sort of method, i.e., that of having people tell stories about ambiguous pictures, has been used in the clinical assessment of the personalities of people with mental problems. In this case the tester relies on his own intuitions and experience to make judgments of very personal kinds of motivation for which formal scoring schemes have not been validated. There is, of course, considerable danger of error in such a method since even a psychologist's intuition about the meaning of a given response is likely to be wrong almost as often as it is right. However, in the hands of experienced psychologists these thematic apperceptions tests (TAT) are often thought to be of value when there is no better method available for the purpose.

The *n* Ach scores and the other uses of thematic apperception tests are cases of a general type known as *projective* tests. A projective test is one in which a person's interpretation of an ambiguous situation is used to reveal his personal ways of seeing the world and, thus, his needs and feelings. The term *projective* comes from the psychoanalytic hypothesis that one tends to "project" onto the world his own characteristics. One way of showing that this must be true, at least to some extent, is to point out that we can interpret the world only in terms of what we already know about; we can describe only the kinds of situations or plots for which we have the necessary words and knowledge.

There are several other projective tests in use, of which perhaps the most famous is the Rorschach test. In this test, a person is shown a series of more or less random inkblot shapes and asked to tell what they look like. The Rorschach test is used quite widely in the evaluation of mental patients. Unfortunately, attempts to validate objective scoring systems have met with little success, and interpretation of the Rorschach remains a highly subjective and unreliable matter.

Motives can also be measured by *objective*—as compared with projective—tests. For example, a person's need for approval by his fellows is tapped by the Marlowe-Crowne scale of social desirability (SD). This scale consists of a large number of statements that may or may not be true of a given individual. The taker of the test is asked to indicate which ones are true of him. The statements are concerned with socially desirable actions, for instance, "I always get my car checked before a long trip." The point is not so much that people with strong motives for approval actually conform to socially approved behavior more than the average person, but rather that such people will try to present themselves on the test as doing so. In general, people who give themselves high scores on this test comply more in conformity experiments (such as the one described in Chapter 2). They also tend to be influenced more by being rewarded by approval, as compared with people who score low on the SD scale (Crowne & Marlowe, 1964).

VALUES AND INTERESTS

A person's values, like his motives, have to do with what goals and ends he counts as important. There is, in fact, a considerable overlap between the concept of a motive and the concept of a value. However, *values* refer directly to those things which a person *says* are good or bad, rather than necessarily to those toward which his efforts are expended. In other words, a person may express strong religious values and yet not devote his life to them.

The most widely known scale of values is one constructed by Allport, Vernon, and Lindzey (1960). In the Allport-Vernon-Lindzey Scale, the person is asked to check a large number of comparative statements of value like the following:

Do you think that a good president should be mostly concerned with:
  (a) helping the underprivileged
  (b) improving the economy
  (c) fostering more ethical principles in government
  (d) gaining the respect of other nations

From a variety of such items in the test, various value orientations of the test taker can be discerned. The values for which scores are obtained are *theoretical, economic, aesthetic, social, political,* and *religious*. In the course of its construction and validation, this test was administered to a number of distinct occupational groups, such as businessmen, artists, and scientists. For each group the average pattern of high and low scores on the various value scales in the test was found. Such a pattern is called a *profile* (see Figure 3–1). The patterns, by and large, seemed appropriate—for instance, businessmen tended to have high economic and political values, and relatively low aesthetic value scores. By contrast,

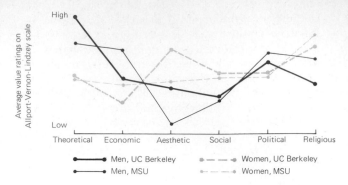

FIGURE 3–1
Value profiles for a sample of men and women from Michigan State University and the University of California at Berkeley. (After Warren & Heist, 1960; copyright 1960 by the American Association for the Advancement of Science)

artists tended to have high aesthetic values. Figure 3–1 shows the profile for several different college groups.

Closely related to values are personality characteristics called *interests*. While values have to do with what one considers generally good and bad, interests have to do with what one finds personally attractive, enjoyable, and absorbing. Interests may be formally distinguished from motives in that they involve preferred activities or means rather than sought goals; but the distinction is sometimes difficult to maintain. At any rate such distinctions are unimportant for our present purposes; the terms are being used here only as rough categorizations of personality traits, not as fundamental entities (the relation among activities, goals, rewards, and motives will be discussed in a deeper way in Chapter 6).

People vary widely in what interests them. Many scales to measure interests have been constructed. For the most part they have been intended for use in vocational counseling. If a counseling psychologist is to give good career advice, he must have a good idea of what sorts of occupational activities would appeal to a person. Scales which measure interests usually consist of sets of paired statements describing two activities that appeal less or more to different people. The test taker checks which one he thinks he would prefer. By pairing such statements in many different combinations a score is obtained that gives the relative degree of appeal of the activities involved in a number of different types of vocational pursuits.

In the construction of such a test, two criteria may be used. First, the activities chosen may be actual day-to-day components of the vocations represented. The statements used to detect interest in scientific activities, for instance, might be about things that scientists actually do. This means that in constructing such a test, the psychologist would first make a detailed and accurate study of the day-to-day activities of people in various vocations. A second and more important criterion is that such a test actually predict whether the person taking it will in fact enjoy the vocation which the test results say he will. One method used to assure this is to standardize the test on representative samples of successful members of various professions, assuming that they are indeed interested in and like their work. Thus, a group of established lawyers are assumed, on the average at least, to have an interest in law. Items which they endorse are selected for a law-interest scale.

Interest scales in current use do moderately well in predicting satisfaction with a given career. However, one point should be remembered. The results of such a test do not specify a particular profession or career as the single best choice for an individual. Rather, they specify general *kinds* of activities which are *usually* of interest to the person. It is then up to the individual, with some help from his counselor, to consider vocations in which those activities are common. The fact that such tests do not make specific prescriptions is not a failing; on the contrary, it reflects a fact about the nature of personality and life. People and careers are not so rigidly constructed that any one person is fitted for only one specific calling. Rather, people tend to have quite general preferences for certain kinds of activities, and these preferences can be satisfied in a variety of different vocations.

INTROVERSION-EXTROVERSION

A characteristic of people that many psychologists have long felt to be a very important dimension of personality and behavior was first described by Jung (1923) in his concept of *introversion-extroversion*. As everyone knows, the introvert is one whose values and activities revolve around solitary, reflective behavior, while the extrovert is an outgoing person who obtains his satisfactions from social interactions. There are several measures of introversion-extroversion which consist of "paper-and-pencil scales." These are inventories in which a person describes his own preferred activities; they closely resemble other scales of values and interest. However, introversion-extroversion seems to crosscut most other dimensions of value and interest (i.e., both the introvert and the extrovert can be interested in music and value things economic).

The several existing scales of introversion-extroversion do not correlate well with each other, which raises some question as to whether this is really a unified, measurable personality trait. If there were a single, well-defined characteristic of introversion, attempts to measure it in several ways should give similar results (unless *all* the measures are bad, an alternative which cannot be completely ruled out). This same problem exists for many of the measures of value and interest we have mentioned; for others it has simply not arisen because only one method of measurement has been tried. The best tests are those—like the objective *n* Ach scoring system, the Marlowe-Crowne scale of need for approval, and some of the personality inventories to be discussed later—which have been shown to be related to many other measurements of what should, in concept, be the same personality trait.

PERSONALITY INVENTORIES

There are a number of personality tests which attempt to give a general description of a person's overall characteristics. These tests have been developed by trying out a great many questions of a paper-and-pencil variety, and then subjecting the results to statistical analyses that determine which of the questions tend to be answered alike. Several factors of personality, or at least groups of questions that hang together, are thereby isolated and purified. In the better tests of this kind, the various factors are related to outside validity criteria. For instance, if there is a scale for schizophrenic tendencies, then known schizophrenics are studied and only those questions kept which significantly differentiate them from the normal population. Some of these scales are highly sophisticated instruments. They contain questions to find out whether the test taker is faking, whether he has an overall tendency to answer yes to all questions, and whether he is simply answering in a random and inconsistent manner. These questions are incorporated in so-called "validity" scales, which can be used to reject the results of the test for a given individual.

Perhaps the best known of the personality inventories is the Minnesota Multiphasic Personality Inventory, or MMPI. The MMPI has scales that measure factors related primarily to abnormal tendencies, plus several validity scales. The scales of the MMPI and some sample items, plus a rationale for their ability to measure the trait in question, are listed in Table 3–2.

Interviews

Most of the assessment methods which we have discussed so far employ paper-and-pencil tests. Many psychologists believe that there is an inherent limitation to the accuracy and validity of paper-and-pencil tests, since they sample only a severely limited range of the test taker's behavior, and one that is somewhat removed from the situations in which his personality usually operates. Indeed, the results of this type of test for predicting behavior have been, with the exception of the intelligence tests, rather disappointing. The correlations between test results and actual behavior as observed tend to be in the range of .2 to .3, which means that only about 5 to 10 percent of the variations between the behavior of one person and another can be accounted for by predictions from the tests.

At least partly in an effort to improve the relation between assessment methods and real-life behavior, a number of other methods have been tried.

INTERVIEWS

Perhaps one of the oldest and most obvious methods for obtaining information about a person's characteristics is to talk to him. Interviews may be structured—they may follow a preset schedule of questions and "probes"—or they may be more or less unstructured and simply attempt to get the subject to tell as much about himself as he will. The long-term discussions used in some kinds of psychotherapy represent the most intensive use of the interview as a means of learning about a personality. Methods of objective analysis of interview material are fairly cumbersome, however, and the results are usually not impressive. Despite a tenaciously held common belief to the contrary, interviews are very seldom of appreciable value in personality assessment. Even when intensive interviews are added to a set of more objective assessment techniques, they do not produce improvement in overall results. Human impressions

TABLE 3-2
Scales of the Minnesota Multiphasic Personality Inventory, and some sample items*

Scales		Sample items	Probable reason why the item measures what it is supposed to
VALIDITY SCALES			
L	Lie	I gossip a little at times.	Almost everybody gossips.
F	Validity	I have nightmares every few nights.	Surprisingly enough, few real psychotics or neurotics check it.
K	Correction	At periods my mind seems to work more slowly than usual.	True of everyone to some extent; the difference between a person who endorses it and one who doesn't is most likely the latter's general tendency to disagree with statements.
PERSONALITY SCALES			
Hs	Hypochondriasis	I have a great deal of stomach trouble.	A typical symptom.
D	Depression	In am easily awakened by noise.	A typical symptom.
Hy	Hysteria	I frequently notice my hand shakes when I try to do something.	A typical symptom.
Pd	Psychopathic deviate	I have not lived the right kind of life.	A typical symptom.
Mf	Masculinity-feminity	I like "Alice in Wonderland" by Lewis Carroll.	Girls like it more than boys.
Pa	Paranoia	I feel uneasy indoors.	A typical symptom.
Pt	Psychasthenia	I have a habit of counting things that are not important, such as bulbs on electric signs.	A typical symptom.
Sc	Schizophrenia	I dislike having people about me.	A typical symptom.
Ma	Hypomania	When I get bored I like to stir up some excitement.	A typical symptom.
Si	Social Introversion	I shrink from facing a crisis or difficulty.	A typical symptom.

* After Dahlstrom & Welsh, 1960.

are simply not good instruments for the measurement of personality (the simple and sad fact is that people really are not good judges of character; they just think they are—see Chapter 2).

Some ethical issues in personality testing

Since personality testing, by its nature, is a very personal matter, precautions must be exercised to ensure the ethical use, interpretation, and application of these tests. First, they should be administered only by a competent professional who is fully aware of their limitations and the caution with which their results must be interpreted. Second, experimental forms of tests should be used only in settings where there is complete guarantee of the anonymity of the test takers, since it is all too easy to make an unfounded interpretation of results which may mean absolutely nothing. Third, it must always be realized that taking a test involves disclosing information about oneself. Therefore, the issue of whether the invasion of privacy involved is justified by the reasons for testing must be considered carefully in each instance. Clearly there are occasions in which it is completely appropriate to divulge as much of your personal beliefs and qualities as possible, for instance when you are seeking help from a counselor or therapist who believes he can help you only if he has such knowledge, and whose ethical standards are above reproach. On the other hand, there are instances where the use of personality inventories is somewhat more questionable. For example, if you were required to take a test for latent homosexual tendencies in order to get a job in the State Department, a real legal and moral question could be raised.

Many knotty questions can arise in this regard, and there is no simple rule to cover all occasions. The gains and costs must be considered in each case. It should not be forgotten that there are real gains in terms of personal liberty which may be brought about by the use of personality tests. In particular they allow the assignment of jobs to people on the basis of ability rather than on more specious and undemocratic bases. A particularly good example comes from one of the earliest applications of aptitude testing, as reported by Brayfield (1965). Until well into the present century certain banking firms refused to employ women because it was thought that women lacked the kinds of skills which would be necessary for executive positions in banks. However, as part of a program of developing tests to determine aptitudes for various positions in banks, it was found that predicted banking abilities were actually more prominent in women than in men. As a result, women have become more and more commonly employed in banks.

Consistency and validity in personality assessment

As the above examples amply demonstrate, it appears to be possible to devise a test or assessment method to measure with varying degrees of accuracy, usually low, almost any posited facet of personality. Although they are the exception rather than the rule, some of the tests in existence today are of considerable utility. The prime example is, of course, the intelligence test; certain others, notably some of the aptitude and interest tests, have proved their worth in practical applications. It must be remembered, however, that a test can be useful for some purposes even if its reliability or validity is fairly low. If the turnover rate in a given job or the failure rate in a training program can be reduced by as much as 10 percent, a testing program may be worthwhile, at least to an employer. However, as a scientific matter, such a level of prediction is rather unsatisfactory. While the combination of many weak and unstable relations between variables can often yield important hints about nature, it can also be very misleading.

Unfortunately, for most personality tests the correlations between test results and other, objectively observed behavior are, as we have said before, quite low. It is easy to excuse this by saying that the proper methods of testing have not yet been developed. On the other hand, nearly a half-century of intense effort by highly competent people has gone into attempts to develop accurate personality assessment methods. The general techniques used have paid off quite quickly in a few areas, most impressively in the intelligence tests. Thus it appears that the problem is not in the tests but in the nature of personality. Tests are usually based on an assumption that there are generalized characteristics of people that will manifest themselves in a variety of settings and a variety of ways. If, instead, personality actually consists primarily of a huge conglomeration of unrelated tendencies to behave in very specific ways in specific circumstances, then such tests are doomed to failure. Although it seems too early for a final judgment on the matter, we must consider this possibility seriously.

ORGANIZATION AND DYNAMICS OF PERSONALITY

So far we have treated personality only in fragments. We have considered this and that isolated trait or characteristic which an individual may have. Is a person's character really only a hodgepodge of assorted traits thrown together any which way? Or is it an intricately organized and interrelated system? One form of this question is a distinction between *trait* and *type* theories of personality. So-called *trait* theories are theories that specify all the different traits that people can have and then treat a given personality as a particular combination of traits. So-called *type* theories assume that there are a limited number of types of personality, that traits cannot be combined in an arbitrary fashion, but that a person who has one trait will have a number of others. For example, people who are stingy should also be neat, reticent, and conservative, and have a number of other characteristics, because they belong to a type which might be labeled *anal retentive* (for reasons which we will go into later). The truth certainly lies somewhere between the two extremes. Traits are not totally independent; some of them tend to go together in the same individual. On the other hand, traits are not always found in the same combinations—one person may be stingy but talkative while another is generous and talkative.

A good deal of investigation has gone into determining just how much association there is among various traits. One way to go about this is to assess a large variety of personality traits in a group of people, and then compare them by statistical analysis. There are ways, one of the most popular of which is called *factor analysis* (Cattell, 1950), to determine mathematically whether clusters of traits tend to be found together. Investigations of this sort usually find a certain amount of clustering. And there are a number of personality scales which are constructed on the basis of these clusterings of traits. On the other hand, the clusterings are usually fairly weak. The correlations between different traits are not high, so that one can always find individuals who have entirely different combinations of traits from that of the average. Moreover, the clusterings found from one statistical analysis usually differ from those from another statistical analysis, and the clustering found with one group of subjects is often different from that found with another group of subjects, or even with the same group of subjects measured at a later time.

It would thus appear that there are few hard-and-fast connections between one trait and another. This would not necessarily mean that for a given individual two traits are never intimately related. While, on the average, people who are stingy may be no more likely to be shy than people who are not stingy, one particular person's shyness might well be related to his fear of exposing his stinginess, for example. This kind of connection would be demonstrated if one could show that changing the person's basic stinginess would result in the loss of his shyness. At the present time, unfortunately, there is almost no objective evidence to suggest what would happen in such a case, and only limited anecdotal support for such "dynamic" interrelations between traits within a given individual.

The problem of the interrelatedness of traits within an individual is encountered in attempts to treat certain psychological disorders. It has long been known that certain undesirable habits, such as nail biting and stuttering, and some phobias, such as fear of snakes, can often be alleviated by hypnosis. Recently it has been shown that such problems can often be cured by conditioning methods (to be described in Chapters 4 and 7). However, some psychologists and psychiatrists believe that such symptomatic treatment may not work in the long run because the habits are only symptoms of underlying disorders, and that if the symptom is removed, the cause will manifest itself in some other way. For instance, they believe that if a person is made to stop stuttering by hypnotic or conditioning techniques, he will only turn to some other unfortunate habit, e.g., nail biting. There are, however, many other psychologists and psychiatrists who believe that this is not so; that symptoms can be treated individually and that their connections, if they exist, with other parts of the personality are not binding or necessary; that one part can be changed without necessarily involving other parts. This issue is unsettled as of this writing. There is no scientifically acceptable evidence to substantiate the existence of the symptom substitution postulated by the "underlying cause" camp.

Origins of traits and the relations between them
CULTURAL FACTORS

Although associations between traits are not usually very strong, some do exist. Certainly there are many good reasons for expecting certain traits to be found together. One obvious reason is that every person grows up in a particular subculture, and all the people in a given subculture will have several traits in common. Members of a different subculture will tend to have a different set of traits in common. Thus, a member of a given group—a family, a community, an occupational group, or a social class—will be marked by several traits. If one measures at the same time people from a number of different subcultures, certain traits will tend to be correlated. Thus, if people in Glencoe, Illinois, are both stingy and modest as a cultural fact, and people in Glendale, California, are both generous and immodest, then when one measures students at the University of Colorado who come from either Glencoe or Glendale, it will appear that the trait of modesty is found primarily in people who are also stingy. Such a reason for the association of traits has been fairly well established in the case of social classes. People in a given social class share a large number of characteristics. This is simply a result of learning a similar set of ways of behaving through similar child-rearing practices and from adults and peers with similar behavior patterns.

BIOLOGICAL FACTORS

Another source of association between traits is heredity. More than one trait may follow from an inborn biological characteristic of the individual. There is a great deal of evidence that predisposition toward certain kinds of behavior is inherited. An increasing number of forms of mental retardation have been clearly traced to genetic sources. For instance, the disorder called *mongolism*, which will be discussed in more detail in the next chapter, is the result of an imperfection in the chromosomes. This imperfection leads to a whole set of behavioral symptoms rather than just one. The victim is not only mentally retarded, but appears to have certain other behavioral characteristics, such as being more tractable and less aggressive than other retardates. There is also a heavy genetic contribution to normal differences in intelligence—the correlation of intelligence between identical twins is much greater than it is between fraternal twins. This and other sources of evidence have led to an estimate that up to 70 or 80 percent of differences in intelligence between people who grow up in roughly similar circumstances is usually attributable to inheritance (see Hunt, 1961). On the same kinds of evidence, traits measured by personality scales such as the MMPI also seem to have inherited aspects. Now, although there is no direct evidence, it seems unlikely that one inherits specific characteristics such as high intelligence. More probably a given genetic background produces an individual who is apt to differ from others in a number of ways. This would lead to association between traits: those individuals who have a particular genetic background would have several different traits which would not necessarily be found together in an individual of another genetic background.

COGNITIVE FACTORS

As discussed in Chapter 2, there is a strong general tendency for people to try to avoid inconsistency, or dissonance, among their beliefs, attitudes, and actions. This should in principle, and probably does in fact, produce a certain amount of integration of personality traits. Thus a man who believes himself honest in his business dealings may want to think of himself as honest in other respects as well. If he finds himself in a clandestine love affair, he may experience a great deal of uncomfortable dissonance over his conflicting self-descriptions. One way for him to resolve such dissonance is to change his behavior and become consistently honest. This kind of resolution obviously would contribute to a tying together of personality traits which are related to one another by sharing the same description, i.e., those which people believe logically (or psychologically) to imply one another. Similarly, having been forced to change his behavior by the circumstances of his life, a person would tend to change any attitudes that were now inconsistent, and then perhaps other related behaviors, and so forth. Having lost an inherited fortune and being forced to work as a laborer, a man might be expected to change hobbies, tastes, political attitudes, etc., to bring them into line with his new role in life. However, the effectiveness of the need for cognitive consistency in integrating personality should not be overestimated. Apparently there are ways of reducing dissonance other than by actually becoming consistent—for example, by isolating, in thought, the spheres of life in which potential conflicts exist, giving them different labels and never thinking about them at the same time, or never thinking about one of them at all. The man in our first example might redefine honesty as applying only to finance, or acquire a strong belief that "all's fair in love and war." More is said about the ways people avoid painful cognitive (and interpersonal) conflict in the discussion of *defense mechanisms* in the section on adjustment in Chapter 4.

DYNAMIC FACTORS

Underlying forces and processes which are thought to organize and systematize behavior are called *dynamic processes*. Such dynamic processes, or underlying forces, include motives, unconscious wishes and fears, and habitual mental processes used to deal with conflicts. Various manifestations of the same underlying process should tend to go together and thus provide another source of correlation between personality traits. Most major theories of personality dynamics have their origin in Freudian theory, which will be discussed in the next section. Suffice it for now to say that attempts have been made to see whether appropriate clusters of personality attributes which correspond to the formulations of Freudian theory are actually found in people, and that the success of such investigations has been mixed at best.

Nonetheless, it is interesting and important for the student to get an idea of how a theory of personality might relate the various characteristics of a person to each other and to the influential events in his life. There are many theories of personality dynamics, some of which will be briefly summarized in the next chapter; but for present purposes we need consider only one good example.

PERSONALITY DYNAMICS AND PSYCHOANALYTIC THEORY

The most thoroughly developed personality theory is the psychoanalytic theory of Freud. But before we consider it, a word of orientation is in order. There is a continuing and deep controversy over the scientific status of psychoanalytic theory. Psychoanalysis is by no means an accepted body of fact or principle. Opinion as to its validity runs the gamut from thorough, almost religious conviction through skepticism to outright and vigorous disbelief. Although the theory will be discussed in this book in several places, it is not offered as truth, or even as probability, but rather as an existing and influential, but unproved, body of ideas. Freudian ideas have become deeply entrenched in our society, in its literature and literary criticism, and in its daily language and thought. Since these ideas deal with the substance of psychology, the student should become acquainted with them and become capable of critically evaluating them. Thus in the case of psychoanalysis, for reasons of historical and cultural importance, we make an exception to our usual rule of considering only those theories which are fairly well agreed upon among psychologists and for which a great deal of positive scientific evidence exists.

Freud was a Viennese physician who treated patients with nervous and mental disorders in the early twentieth century. On finding that many symptoms made no sense in terms of neurology, Freud turned to more subtle, nonmedical means to find the roots of abnormal behavior. The principal method that Freud came to use, which he called *psychoanalysis*, was essentially a matter of inducing the patient to think and speak freely, without attempting to edit his own words, or even to make sense. He would, for instance, have the patient "free associate," that is, say anything that came into his mind. Much was made of subtle forms of expression, such as gestures and inadvertent remarks. Freud and his followers believed that every act, no matter how seemingly trivial, is dictated by the inner workings of the mind. Therefore, they thought, particularly important clues to what is going on "underneath" could be gained by paying attention to dreams, to slips of the tongue, to manners of expression. Freud used all these kinds of evidence to piece together conjectures about what was going on in the patient's mind below the level of conscious awareness.

Freud came to believe that dynamic forces in the unconscious were always the source of the manifest disorders which he was trying to treat. One of Freud's earliest cases is a good example. A woman came to him with a paralysis in one arm. The anatomical extent of the paralysis was totally unrelated to the distribution of nerves in the arm, and thus inexplicable on neurological grounds. After much probing and reconstruction, the patient, with Freud's help, remembered—correctly or incorrectly—that she had been seduced by her father in her early childhood. Freud soon advanced the idea that all such hysterical reactions were related, if not to actual incestual seduction, at least to a subconscious belief that such seduction had occurred. Freud postulated that such a belief is the result of an intense wish for such a seduction, a wish that is impermissible in conscious thought and thus severely repressed. He proposed that it is the severe repression of the wish, and the attempt to deal with the anxiety provoked by having such a wish, which leads through unconscious processes to neurotic symptoms. In this case the hysterical paralysis prevented the patient from ministering to her father, and thus, symbolically, from attempting to seduce him.

The notion of unconscious dynamic processes is the cornerstone of psychoanalytic theory. But there is another fundamental idea—that of instinctual drives. According to Freud, the subconscious is occupied by wars between drives, and between drives and reality. Freud thought that there are a small number of basic drives, or tensions, with which an infant is born. The most important of these for the dynamics of personality is the drive related to sex and sensual pleasures. This drive or instinct Freud called *libido*. It should be noted, however, that by sex Freud understood not only activities involving procreation and the genital organs, but all forms of pleasure and excitement that result from stimulation of the body. Thus, in Freudian terms, an infant is a creature with a great deal of interest in sex. He likes to be cuddled, to be patted and rubbed, and to be in contact with warm, soft objects—all of these desires being defined as sexual. It should also be noted that Freud did not believe in sex as the *only* instinctual drive. He recognized other drives such as those relating to hunger and to elimination. There are, however, two reasons why sexual instincts occupied such an important place in his theory. First, sexual drives are exceedingly intense. Second, and perhaps more important, sexual instincts are severely limited in their expression in our society (even the most liberated still don't fuck in public the way monkeys do, while they do eat and even urinate with far less inhibition), and were even more so in the Viennese society of the early 1900s in which Freud's theory was born.[1]

Psychosexual stages

According to Freudian theory, the infant develops through a series of more or less fixed stages defined in terms of the objects and manner of expression of his libidinal urges. First is the *oral* stage, during which the infant derives his greatest pleasures from the stimulation of his mouth and lips, primarily through sucking. Next is the *anal* stage, during which the focus of pleasurable sensation shifts to the anus and to pleasures derived from defecation. Soon after this, in the normal developmental sequence, the child begins to form a genuine sexual attachment to his parent of the opposite sex. The case is clearly stated concerning male children only, however. The boy is believed to have a strong unconscious desire for sexual relations with his mother. This stage, in reference to the Greek myth in which a son has sexual intercourse with his mother, is called the *oedipal* stage. Normally, so the theory runs, the desire of a boy to sleep with his mother is met with severe sanctions from the outside world, particularly from the father, and the boy represses the desire and enters a period of latent sexuality. The so-called *period of latency* is thought to run from the ages of about six to twelve. Emergence from latency depends on the boy identifying with his father; that is, coming to believe that the way in which he can obtain the gratification he desires is to be like the individual who has access to those gratifications. This final or *genital* stage is characterized by the development of normal adult interests and roles, including heterosexual relationships. This, in outline, is the presumably normal progression when no untoward influences have interfered with it. (It must be stated emphatically that what is presented here is only a very sketchy and, therefore, not wholly accurate representation of psychoanalytic theory.)

Fixation

Rather than passing smoothly from one stage to another, many children, perhaps most, are thought to encounter influences which distort the

[1] If you were a little shocked by finding *fuck* in a textbook, the point should be clear; we're still not completely liberated.

course of development. These hypothesized processes of overinvolvement are called *fixations*. By this is meant that the child occupies a given stage longer and/or with more emotional involvement than he should, and, as a result, as an adult continues to express libido in ways representative of that stage. Two kinds of fixation were postulated by Freud. The first is *positive fixation*, which is said to result from an overly intense or overly prolonged gratification of libidinal urges through the mode of a particular stage. For instance, a positive fixation at the oral level would, according to theory, result from overindulgence of sucking—prolonged breast feeding might be a cause. The second kind is *negative fixation* which results, according to theory, from a very brief, severe, or harsh treatment of such gratifications. Given either of these situations, the theory predicts that an overemphasis on the mode of gratification, e.g., on oral activities, will remain as a particularly important part of the person's personality.

Fixation at a given stage is presumed to manifest itself in different ways. According to Freudian theory, some anal characters are compulsively neat, while others are incorrigibly sloppy. In the former case the person is said to be *anal retentive*—that is, dealing with his abnormal preoccupation with excretion by adopting an extraordinary desire *not* to do things that are like excreting, such as making messes or throwing things away. The latter, the *anal expulsive*, is said to take the opposite course, and exult subconsciously in doing things that are like excreting.

To postulate that an underlying concern with the anus leads to a personality ruled by desires for neatness seems like a wild analogy. This is no accident. It was Freud's view that the subconscious mind works precisely by such wild and irrational analogies. The representation in consciousness and in dreams of underlying desires is often, according to this theory, by crude puns and by any manner of highly personal and exotic associations. In fact, the only way of discovering the connections between underlying motives and fixations and the personality characteristics which are their symptoms is considered to be by a long and detailed probing of the unconscious.

Particularly relevant to our discussion is the fact that psychoanalytic theory expects not just one, but a large number of related symptoms to spring from any underlying fixation. Thus the dynamics of subconscious life postulated by the Freudians provide another potential mechanism for the integration of otherwise disparate facets of personality.

However, at this point it must be repeated that a good deal of research into the correlations between one adult trait and another, and between childhood experiences and later personality characteristics, has not, by and large, produced results which strongly support the psychoanalytic or any other theory of underlying personality function (see Chapters 4 and 9 for further discussion). In the main, proponents of such theories base their faith on having found the theories to provide intuitively satisfying descriptions and explanations in individual cases. This is, of course, a useful function of a set of ideas. But is not a scientifically adequate criterion of truth since, as almost all theories of personality recognize, people are often capable of great feats of misperception, distortion of memory, and self-deception when they interpret their own and others' thoughts and feelings.

In this discussion we have been concerned with possible inner functions of personality, and with the way in which traits or factors of a single individual might be related to and affect each other. In the next chapter we will take up the ways in which a person adapts or fails to adapt his behavior to the demands of the world he lives in.

TOPICS DISCUSSED IN CHAPTER 3

1. The description and measurement of personality traits.

2. Intelligence tests, their nature, their criteria of validity.

3. Motives, including achievement and social approval.

4. Values and interests.

5. Extroversion-introversion.

6. Measurement of aptitudes and abilities.

7. Attitudes as personality traits.

8. Personality inventories.

9. Interviews.

10. The utility and ethics of personality tests.

11. The question of whether personality traits are highly interrelated and integrated; social, biological, and cognitive factors.

12. Dynamics of personality; Freudian theory.

SUGGESTED READINGS

1. *An elementary and readable book on psychological testing is:*

Cronbach, L. J. *Essentials of psychological testing.* (2nd ed.) New York: Harper, 1960.

2. *An essay on the history of and important issues in intelligence testing:*

Tuddenham, R. D. The nature and measurement of intelligence. In L. Postman (Ed.), *Psychology in the making.* New York: Alfred A. Knopf, 1962.

3. *One of the better places to find out more about Freud:*

Freud, S. *An outline of psychoanalysis.* New York: Norton, 1963. (Paperback; originally published in 1940).

FOUR
Adjustment and psychopathology

ADJUSTMENT
The factors of adjustment: desiderata, skills, and circumstance
Conflict
Theories of the adjustment process
PSYCHOPATHOLOGY
Description and classification of behavior disorders
Causes of psychopathology
Therapies for psychopathology
Evaluation of the effectiveness of psychotherapies

In this chapter we will discuss some of the ways in which people succeed and fail in conducting and experiencing their lives. We will be concerned, first, with a general description of the interaction of an individual with his environment—with the two-way relation between his personality and the physical and social world in which he operates. This process, when successful, is called *adjustment*, our first topic. When unsuccessful, the result is *phychopathology* (abnormal or disordered behavior), our second topic. Under psychopathology we will describe some of the categories and characteristics of maladjusted behavior, then consider what little is known about their causes, and finally take up the matter of therapies directed to their amelioration.

The student should be aware that in some parts of this chapter we will be, scientifically, on thin ice. However, we will try to post adequate warning signs.

ADJUSTMENT

Indeed, we start with a topic which requires a warning flag. Psychological adjustment is a field in which there is little professional agreement and, despite substantial and interesting efforts, not many really reliable and relevant data. In accordance with the hard-core focus of this text, such a topic might well be omitted. But adjustment is one of the topics of greatest interest in the whole area of psychology. It is a place where psychology touches life most intimately; and it needs to be discussed. Nonetheless, there seems no need here to detail the names of all the principal expositors and their many conflicting opinions. Rather, with due notice hereby given of its highly personal, opinion-flavored, deterministically biased nature, what follows is largely one psychologist's—the author's— current view of the problem of adjustment.[1]

We often speak of a person as being well-adjusted or poorly adjusted. By *well-adjusted* we mean that he is able to perform the functions demanded by his position in life and the situations in which he finds himself and do so with a minimum of strain and a maximum of satisfaction. There are a number of possible criteria for deciding whether a person is well-adjusted—for example, whether he is happy, content, free from obvious symptoms of unmanaged stress, acceptable to his peers, and successful by social criteria such as, in some societies, status and wealth.

While *adjustment* has sometimes been taken to imply fitting into someone else's value structure, it need not, and is not so intended here. The kind of adjustment involved in making the parts of an engine work together is closer to the intended meaning. If we think of adjustment in this way, the core of the question is how well a personality functions in terms of its own goals. Thus a person can usually be considered well-adjusted to the extent that he is satisfied with himself. Such a definition includes most of the criteria just listed, even those involving the judgment of others, since a person can ordinarily meet his own goals only if he meets those of his peers and of society at large. Nonetheless, there obviously can be conflicts between personal and social criteria of adjustment. On the one hand, an outstandingly creative and strong person might develop a new and better life style which nevertheless is damned by his community because it violates tradition. On the other hand, a person for whom the welfare of others is of no concern might pursue all his own goals through ruthless antisocial behavior. In such cases most of us would have little difficulty choosing which, the person or the society, was disordered. But there are many situations in which the choice is not so easy. Is a person maladjusted who, out of sincere religious conviction, refuses to allow his child to be vaccinated for smallpox? Unfortunately we can only raise, and not answer, such questions here. The fact is that there are really two ways of judging adjustment, from the viewpoint of the individual and from the viewpoint of society, and the two are not always concordant. Since the psychological processes we wish to discuss in this section involve primarily *personal* criteria of adjustment, we will make these our main focus, postponing the question of *social* adjustment until a little later.

The factors of adjustment: desiderata, skills, and circumstance

We may think of the process of adjustment as involving the interaction of desiderata, skills, and circumstance. By *desiderata* we mean what the person wants, what are his basic, derived, and day-to-day needs, what he

[1] A few other controversial topics will be given similar sermon-style treatment later in the book; they will, like this one, by preceded by warning flags. Some instructors and students may wish to omit these sections.

likes, what pleases him, and in what he finds satisfaction and value. By *skills* we mean all those capabilities, aptitudes, achievements, and strength of character with which he can deal with his problems and attain satisfaction. By *circumstance* we mean the situations in which he finds himself by virtue of his associations, his culture, and the happenstance of his life.

DESIDERATA

A certain number of biologically given drives or need-states are shared by all animals. All animals need water, food, and air. In addition, there appear to be a number of biologically given pleasures, that is, stimulations or activities which are pleasurable and for which all animals will work (see Chapters 6 and 7). Included among these are elimination, sleep, sex, and certain pleasant sights, smells, and tastes. There are also, of course, biologically given unpleasant states, such as fear and pain.

In addition to these biologically given drives and pleasures, all animals seem to be capable of learning new motives. The primary example of this is the class of learned fears. Places that have been associated with pain, and actions that have led to bad results come, themselves, to be feared, and avoidance or escape from such places or actions comes, itself, to be a desideratum. Similarly, stimuli which are associated with pleasant events tend, themselves, to become pleasant. The mechanisms and principles governing the learning of such acquired rewards and pleasures will be considered in more detail in the chapters on motivation and learning.

It is interesting to consider what sorts of motives or needs most adults in our society have. A number of psychologists have proposed lists of important needs. It will suffice here to give one of the most widely respected of such lists, that of Murray (1938). This list should not be treated as a definitive or comprehensive statement of the needs that all people have, but merely as a catalog of the important kinds of needs possessed in varying degrees by most people. Presumably, a specification of the strength of each of these needs for a given person would constitute a pretty complete description of what motivates his actions. Murray's list is given in Table 4–1. Such a list does not, of course, include very special, idiosyncratic needs and tastes—like a love of trout fishing—which can be very important aspects of a given person's behavior.

It should also be realized that needs are not static. Changes in needs and values occur by a number of processes, some of which have already been discussed; others will be discussed in later parts of this book. Things which are familiar tend to become liked. Things that are associated with pleasurable events tend to become, themselves, desirable. If one suffers for something or commits oneself to it, the process of post-decision dissonance reduction (see Chapter 2) tends to result in its acquiring added attraction. Thus, the events of life and the results of a person's own actions tend constantly to modify desiderata.

TABLE 4-1
Summary of Murray's list of important personal needs

Need	Desires and effects
Abasement	To submit passively to external force; to become resigned to fate; to admit inferiority and wrongdoing; to blame oneself; to seek and enjoy misfortune.
Achievement	To accomplish something difficult; to master or organize things, people, ideas, rapidly and independently; to excel oneself and rival and surpass others.
Affiliation	To draw near and enjoyably cooperate with a friend; to win affection; to remain loyal to a friend.
Aggression	To overcome opposition forcefully; to revenge an injury; to punish another.
Autonomy	To be independent and free to act according to impulse; to resist coercion and restriction; to defy conventions.
Counteraction	To make up for failure by trying again; to overcome weaknesses; to search for obstacles to overcome; to maintain self-respect on a high level.
Deference	To admire and support a superior; to emulate an exemplar; to conform to custom.
Defendance	To defend the self against criticism or blame; to conceal or justify failure.
Dominance	To control one's environment; to influence the behavior and attitudes of others.
Exhibition	To make an impression; to be seen and heard by others.
Harmavoidance	To avoid pain, danger, illness, and death.
Infavoidance	To avoid humiliation; to refrain from action because of fear of failure.
Nurturance	To give sympathy and support to a helpless other; to assist someone in danger.
Order	To put things in order; to achieve cleanliness, balance, precision.
Play	To act for "fun" without further purpose.
Rejection	To separate oneself from a disliked other; to exclude an inferior person.
Sentience	To seek and enjoy sensuous impressions.
Sex	To form and further an erotic relationship; to have sexual intercourse.
Succorance	To have one's needs gratified by a sympathetic other; to always have a supporter.
Understanding	To ask or answer general questions; to be interested in theory; to emphasize logic and reason.

After Murray, 1938.

SKILLS

Skills required for adjustment are, of course, just those skills that are required to live successfully in the world. The skills of intellect, of motor response, of speech, and of language are important instruments in achieving one's goals and gratifying one's desires. Clearly, occupational skills that allow a person to gain security, luxury, recognition, or a sense of accomplishment are often intimately related to whether he is going to be satisfied with his life.

That skills are modifiable probably needs no elaboration. The reason for school, or for training or for experience, is to acquire new skills. A normal person usually becomes ever more competent at his job, ever more adept in his relations with other people, and ever better at doing those things which bring him pleasure.

Some of the most important skills for successful adjustment are those involved in interpersonal relations. This is because the majority of important needs for most people can be fulfilled only through the agency of other people. Being able to interact with other people so that they fulfill your needs and you fulfill theirs is, consequently, an exceedingly important adjustive skill.

There are other skills that relate simply to how a person lives with *himself*. There are such skills as flexibility, frustration-tolerance, patience, and perseverance. It is not usual to speak of these characteristics as skills, but that is what they are. Clearly they are not innate qualities in most young children, but become more and more developed as a person becomes increasingly mature. And clearly they are skills of the utmost importance in adjustment.

CIRCUMSTANCE

By *circumstance* is meant the environment and the happenstance of one's time and place on earth. Circumstance has a great deal to do with whether a person is satisfied with his life and with himself. In some circumstances it is comparatively easy to be well-adjusted, while in others it is virtually impossible. While this assertion may seem a truism, it is easy both to underestimate and to overestimate the contribution of existing situations to an individual's life. An accurate analysis of their true importance is necessary to understanding the adjustment process. Durkheim (1897) early observed that suicide rates varied widely between one European country and another; and the incidence of many behavior disorders varies greatly between different social classes. Thus, where and when one is born seems to have a great deal to do with his overall chance of adjustive success. On the other hand, certain differences in environment have less effect on some kinds of success than is commonly supposed. For example, it has proved very hard to show, when all other factors are taken into account, that going to one college or to another changes one's chance of doing well on Graduate Record Exams (see Table 4–2) or of eventually getting a Ph.D. (Astin, 1962). Wars, depressions, maiming auto accidents, and painful diseases would seem to pose serious threats to adjustment. But whether such things, on the average and in the long run, have good, bad, or indifferent effects on adjustment we just don't know. Which statement, if either, is true: "A hard life tends to make a person bitter," or "Adversity leads to strength"? A potential field of psychology, one devoted to ascertaining, empirically, what kinds of events tend to make people happy or unhappy and why, remains as of this writing virtually untouched.

Perhaps even more important than what, on the average, are adjustively desirable and undesirable circumstances is the question of how circumstances interact with the particular skills and desiderata of a given individual. Being drafted or winning $100,000 in a lottery may have different consequences depending on whether a person is physically and socially adept or financially wise, highly treasures personal freedom

TABLE 4-2
Relations between graduate record examination scores and two factors:
(a) the abilities and characteristics of students on entering college
(input) and (b) what college they attended (environment)

	GRE area test		
	Social science	Humanities	Natural science
Proportion of variance attributable to*			
(a) Input (student talent) independent of environment	.317	.380	.426
(b) Environment (which college) independent of input	.033	.056	.034

After Astin, 1968.

*Essentially this measures how well one can predict the outcome (GRE scores) from what is already known. The table thus shows that knowing what college students attended does not help much to predict GRE scores.

or sports cars. It is a complex problem. And clearly one can often change one's circumstances—move, change jobs, go to school, join the Army, get married or divorced, go to the movies, buy a new car, take drugs or a vacation. Indeed, such are the main ways in which we ordinarily attempt to improve our adjustment. But whether and to what extent actions of these kinds can really help, as compared with changing our skills or needs, it is impossible to say. Does it really matter *whom* you marry, or does marital satisfaction depend primarily on your skill in creating a satisfactory relationship, on your possession of easily satisfied needs, or on your ability to readjust your desiderata to accommodate the skills and needs of your spouse? And don't all these considerations depend to some extent on other circumstances—your income, the weather, disease, and disaster—over which you may or may not have control? It may even be, when all is said and done, that being happy or sad is a characteristic of a person, which, like the color of his eyes, is largely uninfluenced by circumstances. It's a fearfully complex problem, and one for which psychology has found no firm answers. We have only become sophisticated about the difficulties. But perhaps just knowing that a problem is very complex makes it easier to grapple with—or ignore.

We have summarized various factors involved in the process of adjustment. And we have stressed that adjustment depends not only on having reasonable aims, competent skills, and good luck, but even more on the way in which these factors interact. One very important aspect of the adjustive process is what happens when some of the influences are working at cross purposes with each other—an aspect to which we now turn.

Conflict

When two or more desiderata require mutually incompatible actions in the same situation, *conflict* exists. A good example of conflict is found in the reactions of neophyte sport parachutists to their first jump. People who want to go in for parachuting as sport, if they have any sense at all, are in a certain amount of conflict. On the one hand, they want the

FIGURE 4–1
Approach-avoidance conflict.
When an event has both
attractive and repellent features,
the individual is in conflict, and
what he does depends on the
relative strength of the approach
and avoidance tendencies. In
some circumstances the degree
of approach tendency varies
with the saliency of the event
according to a different function
from that which describes the
relation for avoidance. For
example, sport parachute-jumping
may arouse much more fear on
the day of the scheduled jump
than a week before, while the
expectation of its fun stays about
the same. As depicted here, the
person would approach the goal
of parachuting until the last day,
and then begin to avoid. (After
Epstein & Fenz, 1965)

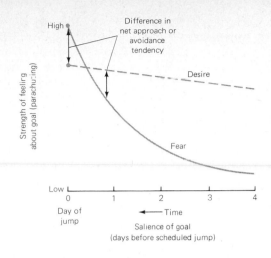

excitement, thrill, and camaraderie of jumping. On the other hand, they
are afraid of death or injury.

There is a well-formulated theory about the nature of conflicts,
which originated in the work of Lewin (1935) and of Miller (1944). In
this theory, several kinds of conflict are distinguished: *approach-approach* conflict, in which two positive goals are in opposition; *avoidance-
avoidance* conflict, in which one has to choose between two evils; and
approach-avoidance conflict in which the same act has both attractive
and repellent consequences. Sport parachute jumping is an instance of
an approach-avoidance conflict. So, often, is whether to get married.
Whether to be drafted or join the Navy can be an avoidance-avoidance
conflict. Choosing a meal from a menu is (usually) an approach-approach conflict.

The theory as formulated by Miller asserts that the tendency to
approach a given object or activity usually increases as that object or
activity gets more and more visible or salient. Similarly, the fear of an
unpleasant consequence increases as the situation becomes more and
more reminiscent of the fearful event. However, under certain circumstances the fear increases more rapidly than does desire as the person
gets nearer and nearer to the goal. For example, in the case of parachuting, the fear of death may be relatively weak until just before the jump,
while the desire for the thrill may be felt almost as strongly several weeks
before as at the time of the jump itself. Figure 4–1 shows the relative
amounts of fear and pleasure that neophyte sport parachutists in one
study reported experiencing as the time of jump approached (Epstein
& Fenz, 1965).

There are several important aspects of conflict with regard to adjustment. Conflict leads to vacillating behavior, to difficulty and delay
in making decisions, and to constant flux and uncertainty as to what

Adjustment
and psycho-
pathology
77

actions will maximize satisfaction. In addition, the very state of conflict itself is unpleasant, painful, even dangerous. Animals and people will often strive to escape from conflict—even an approach-approach conflict. And, as will be more fully described in Chapter 7, prolonged conflict can sometimes lead to serious physical disorders, the most common of which is ulcers.

DEFENSE MECHANISMS

Conflicts in human existence can be of many sorts—between a person's own incompatible desires and values, between his goals and the restraints of society, between contradictory behavior, beliefs, and attitudes.

People adopt many methods for dealing with their conflicts. Some of the more common strategies are described as so-called *defense mechanisms*. Originally conceived by the followers of Freud as defenses specifically against anxieties which they believed to arise from the conflict between instinctual desires and conscience, these descriptions of coping behavior have been expanded, modified, and applied by others to conflicts of all kinds.

The following is a list of some major defense mechanisms. These should not be viewed as causes of behavior, or as concrete entities, but simply as naturalistic descriptions of some behaviors often used by people as a means of dealing with the conflicts of life. Also note that at this point we begin to come close to problems of behavioral disorder. Failure to find adequate ways of dealing with conflict is an important aspect of maladjustment. In addition, as will be pointed out, defense mechanisms can sometimes be overused and themselves become problem behaviors for an individual.

Perhaps the most basic and pervasive of all the defense mechanisms is *repression*. Repression is the banishing of a thought, wish, or memory from consciousness. If it makes one uncomfortable to think about death, learning not to think about it, e.g., by immediately thinking about something else, may help.

Repression, like all the defense mechanisms to be discussed, can be carried too far. If instead of merely repressing the biologically natural but socially unacceptable sexual desire for one's brothers, sisters and parents, a person represses *all* sexual desire, the result is maladjustment. It is believed that a frequent cause of frigidity may lie in prolonged and severe sanctions against almost all forms of sex for unmarried girls in some parts of our society. Given a need to repress any sexual desires for sixteen years or so, it becomes difficult to express them at all.

In *isolation*, an object which is ordinarily part and parcel of a larger whole is placed in a category by itself so as to allow the person to feel differently toward it than toward the rest of the category to which it naturally belongs. For example, one may believe quite firmly that murder and killing are universal evils, but still be willing to eat the meat of slaughtered steers. Inventing special names for meat—"beef" and "pork" rather than "cow" and "pig"—may help to keep the object in a separate category from those objects which we think it is wrong to kill. Probably this is a healthy application of the mechanism of isolation.

However, when the same means is used to make us able to kill foreigners in a war while maintaining that murder is wrong in our own country, the issue becomes less clear.

Displacement is the shifting of a strong desire away from the original object toward a substitute. For example, if a man is terribly angry at his boss but is unable to express this anger, even to himself, he may take it out on a tennis or golf ball if he is psychologically healthy, on his secretary, wife, or children if he is an ordinary man, or on himself in suicide if he is mentally disturbed. Generally, the defensive property of this mechanism lies in the expression of the same emotional feeling toward a safer object—safer in the sense that it is one toward which a particular feeling can be felt with less anxiety.

Similarly, the energy which would ordinarily be put into a desired activity may be channeled into a different activity. This is called *substitution*. Engaging in substitute activities when thwarted in a particular line is certainly a useful way of dealing with conflict. While people often learn to love a substitute activity, there is reason to believe that desires cannot always be fulfilled by substitute activities, and so the individual runs a danger of never gaining real satisfactions.

In *reaction formation* the person transforms his feeling for an object into the opposite feeling. Hatred toward the father is transformed into overenthusiastic displays of affection toward him. The apparent function of reaction formation is to hide anxiety-producing feelings by smothering them in outward or conscious expressions with which the true feeling is incompatible.

In *projection* the true feeling is recognized, but the person doing the feeling is disguised in consciousness. The boy who accuses his girlfriend of being afraid to ride the roller coaster may be projecting his own unexpressible fear by imputing it to her. We all constantly assume that other people have values, attitudes, and feelings like our own. Usually this does help us to understand what is going on inside another person, since most of us are fairly similar to one another. However, when this mechanism gets out of hand the results can be most unfortunate. If a person has a deep distrust and hostility toward others which he does not recognize consciously but projects as suspicion that others distrust and hate him, the seeds of trouble exist.

Rationalization consists of creating an emotion-free reason for an action or way of feeling to disguise an unacceptable motivation for the same action or feeling. Freeing one's thoughts of emotional content is, of course, often a tremendously useful tool in producing objective consideration and discussion, and insofar as rationalization and intellectualization serve this end, they are socially and personally adaptive modes of operating. But they, too, can be overdone. For example, by inventing elaborate theories of child-rearing a cruel father might hide from himself the fact that he was expressing hostility toward his children.

In general then, the defense mechanisms may be seen as modes of resolving, or at least dealing with, conflicts arising from a tendency to engage in some kind of behavior (or thought) which is blocked either by its social or personal unacceptability or by its impracticality. Coping with life requires means of dealing with such frustrations and conflicts. However, frustrations and conflicts are real. Defense mechanisms cannot solve all conflicts and do not always lead to gratification of desires. When they do not they can themselves become impediments to adjustment. A person who becomes a full-time rationalizer or a full-time projector is in trouble. A person who constantly denies reality will, by necessity, be maladjusted. A person who washes his hands all day as a displacement of a need to expiate guilt will have trouble going about his daily life. Instances could be added indefinitely. The point is that a healthy person's energies should be devoted to more constructive ends than the constant evasion or disguise of conflict.

Theories of the adjustment process

How then should a person manage himself so as to avoid conflict and anxiety and attain gratification? How can one optimize one's existence? The answers to such questions obviously depend on what problems are faced and what skills, strengths, and goals are most relevant and important. These will often be very idiosyncratic since each person is different and leads a different life. But perhaps something useful can be said in general about the essential problems we all face, and about the nature of good solutions to these problems.

There have been any number of attempts to delineate the fundamental problems which characterize the human condition and to set forth prescriptions for the best ways to deal with them. The best of such discussions has yet to attain the status of an evidence-based, scientific theory of personality functioning. But viewed as psychologically sophisticated philosophies of living, many of them offer original, provocative, and sometimes compelling ideas. One authority (Maddi, 1968) classifies such theories of personality into three types according to the nature of the fundamental problems and goals of living which they postulate. He calls the three types *conflict theories*, *fulfillment theories*, and *consistency theories*.

The first type, the conflict theories, are exemplified by Freudian psychoanalysis and its followers. These theories assert that man is heir to certain inevitable and inescapable conflicts. Freud saw the basic antipathy as between the expression of universal instinctual drives and the necessary constraints imposed by society. One part of a person, Freud said, wants constantly and with no restraints to gratify urges for sex, elimination, gluttony, even murder; while another, representing social mores and parental strictures, says, "No, you cannot," and enforces its regulations with threats of punishment and guilt. Psychoanalytic theories view the opposing forces as unalterable, and hence offer no hope of complete escape from conflict. The best one can do, they imply, is to learn to compromise and cope, largely by the use of defense mechanisms, with minimum though substantial anxiety and guilt, and with minimum though substantial frustration of important emotional impulses.

Maddi's second type, the fulfillment theories, assume that the major factors to be dealt with in life are either consistent with one another or are modifiable; thus it is possible to achieve one's truly important goals. These theories usually postulate one factor or set of factors that is given and immutable. This may consist either of a person's individual, genetically determined characteristics, or of a set of ideal goals, values, achievements, and activities which are thought to constitute universal desiderata. Thus Rogers (1961) and Maslow (1962) assert that each individual is born with a set of inherent potentialities, and that the core problem of living is to *actualize* these potentialities. While physical and social reality may at times pose obstacles, full development and expression of one's potentialities is assumed to lead to a way of life which either is naturally consistent with these realities or can adequately deal with them. Other fulfillment theorists, such as White (1959) and Allport (1961), emphasize the overcoming of all obstacles, even those consisting of one's own characteristics, in striving toward an ideal human existence.

Maddi's third and final type, consistency theories, postulate no defined, universal set of factors or problems, but merely assert that life has a lot of unpleasant surprises, dissonance, and conflict, and that people try to adjust their actions and attitudes to keep such inconsistencies within desirable limits. Maddi himself believes that people prefer to have *some* rather than *no* inconsistencies at all in their lives— that they like a certain amount of surprise and arousal (see Chapter 6). Such a preference should lead to exploration, change, and psychological growth.

This has been an extremely sketchy summary of only a few of the currently influential theories of personality, and has mentioned only those aspects which are particularly relevant to our discussion of adjustment and conflict. For more details the student is referred to the surveys by Maddi and by Hall and Lindzey (1957), and to the original works listed at the end of this chapter. At this point we conclude our descriptions of factors and processes by which normal and successful people adjust, and turn our attention to what happens when adjustment fails.

PSYCHOPATHOLOGY

Pathological behavior is behavior that is seriously maladjusted— behavior that leads to a failure to obtain desiderata such as contentment, freedom from pain and anxiety, and adaptation to the demands of society. A person is said to be mentally or psychologically unhealthy when, because of peculiarities in his behavior, he himself suffers or is unable to function adequately as a member of society. Perhaps the simplest way, then, to classify behavior as pathological is to call pathological any unusual behavior that causes grave difficulties for either the person himself or for those around him. Psychopathology is an extremely serious personal, medical, and social problem. It has been estimated that one out of every 10 to 12 persons born in the United States will at some time be admitted to a mental hospital. And largely because the recovery rate in serious behavior disorders is so low, approximately half of all hospital beds in the United States are occupied by mental patients.

There are two general ways in which a person's behavior can become sufficiently maladaptive to warrant classification as pathological. One way is for normal variations to become extreme. We all have peculiarities and oddities in our behavior. Usually, such variations constitute desirable individuality. But sometimes individuality becomes so extreme as to become troublesome. When a person's bizarre behavior begins to interfere with his work or enjoyment of life, or to alienate and antagonize his neighbors, then it begins to become pathological.

The second source of pathological behavior is specific and distinct pathogenic factors to which most people are never exposed. Certain diseases or malfunctions of the body, and certain extreme environmental stresses can lead to strange and/or maladjustive behavior.

An important thing to realize is that in every aspect of behavior there are all shades of normality and abnormality. There are seldom clear, precise demarcation lines between the normal and the abnormal. Nonetheless it may be that, because of the existence of abnormalities caused by specific pathogenic processes, there are many more individuals with very extreme characteristics than there would be by chance alone. Perhaps this matter of the distribution of abnormalities can be most clearly seen in the case of intelligence. Intelligence, as measured by standard IQ scores, varies all the way from zero to nearly 200. Now, if intelligence were randomly distributed, we would expect it to follow an ordinary normal distribution—the familiar bell-shaped curve. To a large extent it does, as can be seen in Figure 4–2. In such a normal distribution one expects a few unfortunate people whose intelligence falls, simply by the fortuitous combination of the myriad factors that influence everyone's intelligence, into the lowest level. But, as you can also see in this figure, there is an extra hump in the lowest region of the curve. This hump means that there are more people with very low IQs than there would be if the distribution were truly normal. The reason for this is that the distribution of intellectual abilities is made up of the sum of two parts. One part is a normal distribution of ordinary individual variation. The other consists of a group of individuals with very low IQs due to specific pathogenic processes. In the case of intelligence, some of these specific processes have been identified as genetic and prenatal accidents. An analogous situation undoubtedly holds for most other behavioral traits. That is, first there is a general, normal distribution of the trait—be it fear, superstitious behavior, dreams, visions, or what-have-you. There are a few people with no fears, no superstitious behaviors, etc., many with a moderate number, and a few with very many. But there is also usually an additional hump in the distribution, representing those individuals who have very many strong fears (or some other condition) because of some specific (even if unknown) cause.

Essentially any habit or aspect of behavior can become a problem if it is used too much, too little, or in the wrong way. Bathing too much, or not at all, driving too fast or too slow, balancing your checkbook constantly or never, thinking only good thoughts or only morose ones,

FIGURE 4–2
Hypothetical distribution of intelligence quotients in a large population. The solid curve shows a symmetrical normal distribution of general intelligence. The dashed curve shows what the actual distribution of measured intelligence looks like. The asymmetrical region of the curve at the lower end of the IQ scale is explained by the existence of a smaller, abnormal group of individuals with very low intelligence quotients—as shown by the dotted curve. (After Dingman & Tarjan, 1960; reprinted by permission from the *American journal of mental deficiency.* Copyright 1960, American Association on Mental Deficiency)

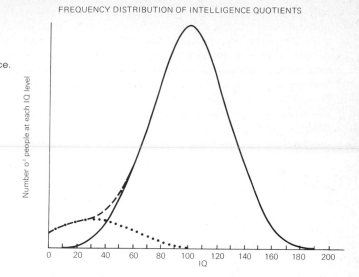

all can be pathological behavior. As a result, there are a very large, if not infinite, number of different ways in which behavior can go awry. Let us now consider how one might describe and classify behavioral disorders.

Description and classification of behavior disorders

The main problem in classifying behavior disorders is precisely that so very many things can and do go wrong with behavior. We will return to elaborate on this statement after a few introductory comments. In the study of medicine, disorders are frequently classified into distinct entities called *diseases*. The definition of a physical disease usually depends on one or more of the following three criteria: First, defined diseases usually have a fairly consistent combination and progression of symptoms. Thus, mumps has characteristic glandular swellings, a fever, and so forth. Having diagnosed the disorder—that is, having given the disease the name which best applies to it—the physician is able to make a reasonably accurate prediction of what will happen next. Second, a disorder may be defined by its cause, if one is known. While most diseases probably do not result from a single factor—even viruses and bacteria need a susceptible host in order to induce illness—there is often at least one causative factor which is a necessary condition. Thus, tuberculosis does not exist in the absence of the tuberculosis bacillus. Third, a physical disorder may be classified according to the treatment which is called for. Having made a diagnosis, the physician usually has also pretty much determined what the therapy should be. Indeed, this is the principal reason for making a diagnosis.

In behavior disorders, however, none of these three criteria is very useful. In the majority of cases, as we shall see, there is no well-defined set of symptoms which are always found together, and the course of a behavior problem is seldom predictable. Second, there are only a few

Adjustment and psycho-pathology

behavior disorders for which a specific cause is known. Third, as we shall also see, the art and science of treating behavioral disorders is not well advanced, and only rarely is there much connection between traditional diagnosis and choice of treatment. What all this adds up to is that there are few clearly definable disease entities in the area of behavior disorder. Indeed, many authorities in the area believe that the concept of disease is not appropriate at all. Instead, they feel that pathological behavior should be described and classified in a way entirely different from that used for physical disorders. What this way should be is a matter that is still in doubt, although some promising suggestions have been made (see Franks, 1969).

One such suggestion will be outlined here a little later. But first, we will consider some of the more traditional and widely used classification schemes. These categories are not intended as definitions of discrete diseases, although many of them were originally conceived of as such, but they do offer a set of terms with which to describe the nature and range of commonly occurring adjustive failures.

The broadest classification of pathological behavior which is in common use, and is fairly well agreed upon by most people in the field, is one which is based on essentially social criteria. People cause concern to their community in different ways, and require different kinds of social response. The four main categories so defined are: *mental retardation*, *neurosis* including psychosomatic disorders, *character disorder*, and *psychosis*.

Mental retardation, of course, refers to intellectual disability. Neuroses are abnormalities in any other aspect of personal or social behavior which cause discomfort to the individual or annoyance to others, but are not severe enough to make him incapable or unwilling to assume responsibility for himself or to require his isolation from society. Character disorders refer to chronic failure to keep behavior within socially acceptable limits. The psychoses are those forms of behavioral aberrations that are severe enough to keep the person from functioning in a normal community environment.

We will take up these four major classifications in order, and describe the general symptoms that fall under each. However, it should be made clear from the outset that few people suffering from psychopathological conditions have symptoms which fit neatly into any one classification. For example, it is frequently impossible to tell whether a person is simply mentally retarded or is psychotic as well. If a child does not speak, it may be that he has not learned to do so, or that he is so asocial that he will not do so, though he can; and it is often extremely difficult to make what is called a *differential diagnosis* between (in this case) retardation and psychosis.

MENTAL RETARDATION

Mental retardation is most easily defined in terms of deviation from the normal in measured intelligence. While intelligence as measured by standard IQ tests does not give the whole story of a person's adaptive capabilities, even in the intellectual sphere, it is the best approximation

TABLE 4–3
Mental retardation categories of the American Association on Mental Deficiency

Word description of retardation in measured intelligence	Range in standard deviation value	Corresponding range in IQ scores for tests with SD of 15
Borderline	−1.01 to −2.00	70–84
Mild	−1.01 to −3.00	55–69
Moderate	−3.01 to −4.00	40–54
Severe	−4.00 to −5.00	25–39
Profound	−5.00	<25

After Heber, 1961.

available and is used by most workers in the field. The present standard descriptive terminology for different degrees of mental retardation is that of the American Association on Mental Deficiency (AAMD), as shown in Table 4–3.

Although estimates vary considerably, it is clear that at least three percent of the people in the United States suffer from mental retardation of sufficient severity to be classified as a psychopathological disorder. One out of thirty is unable to get through the primary grades of school, and is thus incapable of full participation in our society.

In addition to the classification by degree of intellectual deficit, it is also possible to subdivide mental retardation into a number of very specific syndromes (sets or clusters of symptoms), such as mongolism and cretinism. Mental retardation, in contrast to most other kinds of psychopathology is often a symptom of one of a number of well-defined "diseases." Some of these more specific types of disorder will be discussed later in this chapter, in the section on causes of psychopathology.

NEUROSES

The *neuroses*, or *psychoneuroses*, are serious failures to adjust. They usually involve failure to deal adequately with anxiety. This can mean either being overwhelmed by anxiety or developing behavior patterns to deal with anxiety that are themselves maladaptive. The neuroses can be classified into five subtypes: anxiety reactions, phobias, obsessive-compulsive reactions, and psychosomatic disorders.

Anxiety reactions, probably the most common neurotic condition, are emotional overreactions. A person in an anxiety state is extremely excitable, extremely irritable, or constantly worried and fearful. Usually he has accompanying bodily symptoms—nausea, sweating, palpitations of the heart. This reaction consists not of occasional periods of worry over rational or partly rational problems, such as the normal person has, but prolonged periods of extreme, diffuse, and uncalled-for nervousness and apprehension.

Phobias are intense fear or anxiety reactions to particular objects, situations, or classes of stimuli. A common phobia is an intense fear of snakes. To the person who has a snake phobia, a snake is not simply an object of distaste, but one of real terror. Such an intense fear constitutes a neurosis insofar as it causes difficulty or discomfort in a person's life.

Obsessive-compulsive reactions are characterized by repeated stereotyped behaviors. The classic literary example is of the person who constantly rubs his hands as if washing them. Or the person may actually wash his hands hundreds of times a day; or he may assiduously avoid touching doorknobs; or he may never go out of the house without a raincoat; or he may be unable to get a certain thought out of his head.

Psychosomatic disorders are bodily malfunctions which have psychological origins. As everyone knows, uclers are caused not by what you have been eating but by what has been eating you. There is, of course, a considerable danger in deciding that a disease is due to psychological causes simply because a physical cause cannot be found. Nevertheless, there is evidence that for a number of diseases a contributing (if not the major) cause is prolonged or severe emotional conflict. Fitting in this category, in addition to ulcers, are asthma, migraine headaches, and probably several others.

These, then, are the commonly used categories of neurotic reactions. They describe some of the symptoms of the less severe psychopathologies. Two general points should be noted. First, all the symptoms of the neuroses can be found in normal people. We all have occasional unproductive preoccupations, occasional attacks of free-floating anxiety, occasional irrational fears, and occasional nervous stomachs or headaches. The difference between the normal person and the neurotic is that the neurotic's symptoms are so severe that they cause him extreme discomfort and make him seriously maladjusted. Second, as noted before, these categories rarely describe real people. Most neurotics have mixtures of these symptoms, or have symptoms which lie between the categories and cannot be easily fitted into one or another. Thus, a given person may have a phobia and also show anxiety reactions. Another may have obsessive-compulsive habits and also suffer from ulcers, and so forth. The categories are descriptive labels for kinds of behavior, not— by and large—for particular people.

CHARACTER DISORDERS

Character disorder is a term applied to a variety of different kinds of antisocial behavior, including alcoholism, drug addiction, and delinquency. The common element is socially deviant behavior that is a long-lasting characteristic of the person. One particularly interesting form of character disorder is called *antisocial reaction* or *psychopathic personality*. The psychopath fails to regulate his behavior with regard to the long-term effects it will have on his life. He acts as if he has no conscience, no guilt, and very little appreciation of the relations between present actions and possible undesirable outcomes. While he is often capable, intelligent, and pleasant, he is perfectly willing to use socially unacceptable means, like lying, stealing, or violence, in pursuit of his own pleasure. He is unable to stand frustration or postpone gratification, and seems virtually unconcerned about social sanctions or any other consequences of his behavior. Such people are obviously extraordinarily dangerous to have loose in a civilized society.

TABLE 4-4
Analysis of symptoms in 500 consecutive admissions to a mental hospital

Symptoms	Incidence per 100 patients
Behavior: bizarre, peculiar, annoying	98.8
Behavior: detrimental or dangerous to self	74.0
Behavior: detrimental or dangerous to others	17.6
EMOTIONAL-SOCIAL DISTURBANCES	88.0
Depression	33.2
Irritability	27.4
Apprehension	19.6
Incongruity	18.8
Suspiciousness	17.2
Suicidal trends	15.6
Destructive-Assaultive	14.8
Apathy	14.8
Amoral conduct	7.0
THOUGHT DISTURBANCES	87.6
Delusions	45.6
Confusions	42.6
Hallucinations	27.8
Ideas of reference	14.6
Obsessions	3.2
SPEECH ABNORMALITIES	56.0
Incoherent	30.2
Retarded-Mute	13.8
Other peculiarities	17.0
MEMORY DEFECTS	44.6
Disorientation	37.6
Losses-Confabulation	35.4
PSYCHOMOTOR DISTURBANCES	40.0
Hyperactivity	20.0
Mannerisms-Stereotypies	13.6
Hypoactivity	6.2

After Page & Page, 1941.

PSYCHOSES

Some behavioral abnormalities are so severe that they render a person incapable of managing his own life. The sufferer is unable or unwilling to care for himself, and may behave in such a bizarre way that his family, friends, and neighbors are unable and unwilling to deal with him. Such severe disorders are called *psychoses*. The best way to describe psychosis is to state the symptoms which psychotic people display. Table 4-4 gives an analysis of the symptoms described for 500 consecutive admissions to one mental hospital. The most striking thing about this list is the tremendous overlap in symptoms. Almost everyone admitted to a mental hospital shows bizarre, peculiar, or annoying behavior. Likewise almost everyone admitted to a mental hosptial shows emotional, social, and thought disturbances. Almost half show speech abnormalities, memory defects, and psychomotor disturbances. Thus, psychotics usually have not one but many and varied symptoms. This fact is important background for the description of kinds of psychosis that follows. A term such as *schizophrenia* describes a set of symptoms that may or may not describe an individual. An individual psychotic person is always characterized by his own individual set of symptoms and maladjustments.

The psychoses are often divided into the *organic types*, which are associated with a definite disease process or deterioration of the brain, and the *functional types* for which no physical cause is apparent. The organic psychoses may be due to senility or to syphilis or other diseases in which the infection involves the brain or to prolonged overuse of alcohol or other poisons. No more will be said about organic types here.

The so-called *functional psychoses* are the ones which we hear most about. They are often classified into a number of descriptive sub-categories. Several of these subcategories are briefly discussed below.

Schizophrenia is by far the most commonly diagnosed and broadest category of psychosis. The term is used to refer to a wide variety of symptoms, including peculiar distortions of feelings, emotions, percep-tions, and actions. Schizophrenia is often said to be characterized by loss of touch with the realities of the social world. The schizophrenic fre-quently fails to relate in the most simple and rudimentary ways to people around him. A schizophrenic patient is often indifferent, apathetic, and generally "can't be bothered about anything." He may be subject to hallucinations or indulge in bizarre behaviors—laugh and giggle, make odd faces, and say strange, irrelevant things. Speech is often jumbled. Sometimes there is extreme withdrawal. Frequent symptoms are nega-tivism and muteness. At times a schizophrenic may adopt stereotyped behaviors or postures—he may turn rigid and immovable, or show waxy flexibility, allowing his limbs to be placed in any position without resistance.

A second type of functional psychosis is *paranoia*. Paranoia refers to a systematic set of delusions, usually of both grandeur and per-secution. The paranoid may believe that he is a very important scientist who is being pursued by a band of foreign spies who want to steal his secret. He may be able to give details with times and places and inter-pretations of real events that fit cogently and logically into his de-lusional world. If he gets a stomach ache, he may take it as proof that his enemies have poisoned him. Usually, however, a paranoid's delu-sional system is limited to certain areas of his life, and he is otherwise able to function quite adequately. But his extreme delusions and sus-picions and the chance that he may turn on his imagined attackers make a paranoid very difficult to tolerate in a normal social environment.

The *affective disorders*, a third type of functional psychosis, are characterized by excesses in emotional mood. The person may be manic, that is, in a state of great elation and activity, or depressed, sad, and slow in thought and action. In extreme manic states, psychotics sometimes engage in unrestrained and violent or otherwise dangerous behavior. In extremes of depression, they may become suicidal or withdraw into physical immobility. Often, but not always, a person who is subject to one of these states is also subject to the other, the two occurring at different times, interspersed with periods of relative calm.

Such are some general descriptive titles often used to describe the symptoms of psychotic individuals. Three general remarks about these categories are in order. First, it is rare for a psychotic patient to display such symptoms continuously. An individual who has hallucinations or depressions usually does not have them all the time. Even severely afflicted psychotics in mental hospitals usually have periods of lucidity and apparent normality. Second, to repeat what was said above, most patients have mixtures of symptoms, and may have symptoms falling into more than one, or lying between two or more, of the classifications. Third, again to repeat, the diagnosis of mental illnesses is not yet on as firm and reliable a basis as is the diagnosis of obviously physical diseases such as pneumonia or diabetes. There are no definitive laboratory tests, x-rays, or comparable criteria for determining the nature of a psychosis. Indeed, an astonishingly large proportion of those admitted to mental hospitals have their diagnoses changed within the year following their admission.

Because of these inadequacies in the traditional classification schemes, several psychologists have recently proposed entirely different ways of approaching the description of behavioral disorders. Kanfer and Saslow (1969), for example, propose that the attempt to classify behavior problems into discrete groups of diseases be abandoned entirely, and that, instead, those who deal with psychopathology develop a system for describing the particular problems and peculiarities of each individual case. In the system tentatively proposed by Kanfer and Saslow themselves, the diagnostician analyzes the problems of the patient in several ways. First is an initial description of the patient's characteristic behavior, the things which he does to excess, the things which he fails to do but should, and the things he does well. Second is a description of the situations in which the patient has troubles, the people or groups of people among whom his difficulties occur, and the consequences that his maladjustive behavior has for himself and others. Third is an examination of the person's motivations to see what kinds of goals he has which lead him into and reinforce his maladjustive behaviors. Fourth, the analyst tries to trace the history of the patient's problems, to see when his maladjustive behavior began to occur, under what physical and social circumstances, and in reaction to what events. He looks for biological determinants as well. Finally, the person's ability to control his own behavior is analyzed. As we have mentioned before, few people exhibit abnormal behavior under all conditions, and it is important to know the extent and conditions under which self-control can be exercised. All these factors are important in obtaining a detailed description of exactly how a person behaves and in what respect his behavior is working against his or society's advantage.

The basic idea behind Kanfer and Saslow's proposal, then, is to describe thoroughly the problem behaviors of an individual and the events and situations which instigate and mitigate them, rather than trying to force them into artificial categories. This seems to make a great deal of sense. It may turn out that personality is primarily a conglomerate of only weakly connected characteristics, or that the cause of a good portion of pathological behavior lies in the learning of specific bad habits, or that the appropriate therapy for disordered behavior is frequently the correction of particular problem behavior. In light of current understanding, all of these are real possibilities. If any one or more is true, then a frankly descriptive rather than classificatory technique of diagnosis is likely to be the most useful. However, only time and more knowledge will tell.

Causes of psychopathology

By and large, the causes of pathological behavior are as yet unknown. For a few specific types of organic disorders, especially some forms of mental retardation, the underlying etiology has been discovered. But for most, while a great deal of research has been done and some progress made, no real understanding exists. We will summarize what is known and some of the more popular unproved hypotheses about causes, according to some of the major classifications described earlier—always keeping in mind that different categories do not necessarily reflect different causes.

CAUSES OF MENTAL RETARDATION
Congenital and inherited anomalies
There are several forms of mental retardation which are clearly the result of disease processes, accidents, or inherited malformations or malfunctions of the nervous system. Among these are some of the most severe forms of birth defects, such as *hydrocephaly*, a head enlarged greatly out of proportion by excess fluids; *anencephaly*, a tiny "pinhead"; and many more. Cerebral palsy can also be included in this category. While the exact cause of these gross anomalies is not known, it is known that they originate in fetal development and are probably due to either accidents or diseases occurring in the womb.

Another class of congenital anomaly consists of disorders caused by defective chromosomes. Chromosomes are the carriers of inheritance in the egg and sperm cells which are responsible for the direction and specification of all growth. They may be thought of as the blueprints on which the structure of the body is built. Normal humans have forty-eight chromosomes, twenty-four coming from the mother and twenty-four coming from the father. There are several severe disorders that are known to be associated with the presence of an extra chromosome, or with some defect in one or more chromosomes. Perhaps the most common of these, and also one of the most common forms of severe mental retardation, accounting for about 10 percent of all institutionalized retardates, is the affliction known as *mongolism*. The mongoloid individual is stunted in growth, has broad cheekbones and oddly shaped eyes which give him a somewhat Mongoloid appearance (although, of course, there is nothing about this disorder that remotely associates it with the Mongoloid race; mongolism is more properly called *Downe's Syndrome*). Downe's Syndrome always includes mental retardation in some degree, ranging from moderate to very severe.

Metabolic disorders

Metabolism refers to the utilization of nutrients to manufacture the components of cells and tissues in the body and in the production of energy. When certain complex chemical processes in the body break down, grave difficulties can result. In the disorder known as *phenylketonuria* (PKU), a component part of most proteins—phenylallinine—is not properly processed in the body. Instead, it is processed into a poison that causes severe damage to a developing nervous system. Luckily, this metabolic failure can be diagnosed easily and early. If it is discovered within the first few days or weeks of an infant's life that he is suffering from PKU, he can be put on a special synthetic diet which includes no phenylallinine. As a result, the body will not produce the poisonous substance and if the diet is maintained until after the brain is fully developed, the severe mental retardation will be avoided. Some states now require that all infants be tested for PKU.

Several other metabolic disorders are known, and undoubtedly many more will be discovered. The study of genetically caused metabolic defects is one of the most promising areas of research in the field of retardation and mental illness in general.

Accident and disease

Mental retardation can be caused by direct damage to the brain. While damage to the brain can occur any time in life, noticeable effects on mental abilities have been observed primarily in the case of injuries before or during birth. A particularly important instance of damage to the brain at birth is that which results from a lack of oxygen, a condition called *anoxia*. The brain has a very large demand for oxygen. If it is deprived for more than three or four minutes serious damage can result. One of the everpresent dangers of the birth process is asphyxiation, which can result either from physical obstruction of breathing or from a failure of the infant's own breathing apparatus to start functioning properly at birth. A breathing failure can result from overdoses of certain anesthetics. Infants who have suffered moderate to severe anoxia run a very large risk of some degree of mental retardation.

Similarly, there are many diseases which can lead to damage to the brain and mental retardation. These include not only such severe and well-known ones as encephalitis, tuberculosis, and syphilis, but also such generally innocuous diseases as measles.

While there are many specific known etiologies for mental retardation, nevertheless in a large proportion of all cases no physical cause can be found. It is hard to know in a particular case of retardation whether there is some undetectable damage to the nervous system. Thus, mild cases are sometimes classified as showing "minimal neurological deficit." On the other hand, there is reason to believe that many mild cases of mental retardation may be due to an inadequate environment. Children raised in intellectually deficient surroundings, where there is little opportunity to use language, tend to have lower IQs than those raised in very stimulating environments. There is evidence that nursery-school training can sometimes produce a striking gain in the IQ of children growing up in educationally deficient environments. (Unfortunately the gain seems to disappear during the first few years of school.) Thus, mild retardation of unknown cause is often ascribed to "cultural-familial" sources. By this phrase is meant that it is judged likely that the retardate simply comes from a subcultural group or family in which language and other intellectual skills are underdeveloped.

CAUSES OF NEUROSES
Neuroses are generally thought to be functional disorders, that is, not due to any physical malformation or malfunction. The explanations for them which have been advanced have almost all stressed the psychological history, particularly the early social experience, of the individual.

Most theories of the adjustment process, including those mentioned earlier in this chapter, assume that the major cause of neurosis is a failure to solve those problems of existence which the given theory postulates as central. Each of these theories implies that if a person does not learn its prescribed means of overcoming conflict and anxiety, then he may develop ineffectual and maladjustive habits instead, and will probably suffer imperfectly controlled anxiety.

Let us see how this is presumed to work in detail for one theory, taking psychoanalysis as the example.

Psychoanalytic theory of neurosis
Recall that psychoanalytic theory presumes the major adjustive problem to involve a conflict between desires and social reality. The theory further asserts that very high levels of anxiety can be aroused if an overly strong desire must be repressed. The existence of overly strong desires is attributed largely to fixations (see Chapter 3) at some stage of development. For instance, the theory predicts that a person who, when an infant, was severely frustrated at weaning, will grow up with an extraordinarily great need for oral activities such as eating, talking, and smoking. An extremely strong desire to suckle cannot easily and openly be expressed by an adult, of course, and the thought of the adverse consequences (shame, punishment) for such expression leads to anxiety. Unmanaged, such anxiety can constitute neurosis. Perhaps more important, though, according to psychoanalytic theories, is how the person deals with the conflict and anxiety. As described earlier, normal adults have well-developed systems of defense mechanisms. These defense mechanisms can sometimes keep anxiety within tolerable limits, even when the conflicts are quite strong. However, if a person has never learned adequate defense mechanisms, or if those he has break down, the result is presumed to be neurotic anxiety. By the same token, the aberrant behaviors often associated with neuroses are hypothesized

to be manifestations of overused defense mechanisms. For example, a snake phobia might be considered a displaced fear of a penis. A compulsive obsession with neatness might be considered a reaction formation against a strong, unexpressible desire to play with feces. Some of the explanations of this type offered by psychoanalysts have been even more fanciful. But the basic idea that a behavior first used as a harmless way of dodging conflict can, by overuse, become an annoying symptom, nevertheless seems quite reasonable.

Neurosis as a result of improper learning experiences

There is a competing though not entirely dissimilar view that does not rely on elaborate unconscious processes. This view, held by an increasing number of psychologists, is that many behavior disorders, especially among those classified as neuroses, result simply from the learning of bad habits. Either from his parents, or from peers, or from the fortuitous happenings of life, an individual may acquire ineffectual ways of behaving. He may learn extreme, unreasonable fears. He may pick up odd habits of speech or conduct which make him unpleasant to be around. He may not learn acceptable ways of expressing or dealing with his emotions. He may fail to learn adequate means of obtaining gratification or managing conflict.

The learning hypothesis is especially clear in the case of phobias. A phobia is an intense fear reaction to a certain object or event. It is possible to produce extreme fear reactions in laboratory animals by the methods of *conditioning* which will be discussed in Chapter 7. Strong fears may be caused in humans, too, by the association of a traumatic occurrence with a particular event or stimulus. Whether or not this is the whole story in any or all cases of phobia is hard to say. However, some recent developments in therapy, to be discussed later in this chapter, lend considerable credibility to this view.

CAUSES OF PSYCHOSES

For some of the so-called "organic" psychoses there are known bodily defects. In *senile psychosis* there is a general deterioration of the brain. In *general paresis* there is specific damage to the central nervous system due to the syphilis germ. There are also certain cases of psychosis which can be traced directly either to short-term or long-term effects of toxic substances. Perhaps the best-known example is alcoholism. Chronic alcoholism may eventually lead to delirium tremens and other psychotic manifestations. Certain drugs can produce psychotic episodes, and, occasionally, severe and enduring psychosis even when taken only once or a few times. LSD is one such drug.

Of the causes of the so-called "functional" psychoses, such as schizophrenia and manic-depressive psychosis, much less can be said with any confidence. It is known that there is a considerable hereditary component in some of these disorders, notably schizophrenia. As Table 4–5 shows, the incidence of schizophrenia in twins gives good evidence of this. If one of two identical twins is schizophrenic, the other is very likely to be so too, whereas this is not the case with nonidentical twins.

It is likely that other forms of maladjustment, perhaps even mild

TABLE 4–5
Concordance rates for schizophrenia found in studies of twins

Investigator	Number of pairs		Concordance rate,* %	
	Dizygotic	Monozygotic	Dizygotic	Monozygotic
Luxenburger (1928)	48	17	2	59 (67)
Rosanoff et al. (1934)	101	41	10	61
Kallmann (1946)	517	174	10 (15)	69 (86)
Slater (1953)	115	41	11 (14)	68 (76)

*Concordance rate is the percentage of cases in which, if one member of a pair has the characteristic, the other one will too.

*Figures in parentheses indicate rate after correction for the chance that a co-twin, normal at the time of observation, may develop the disease later. (Monozygotic=identical twin.)

From Kety, 1959.

neuroses, have some hereditary basis. On the other hand, it seems unlikely that heredity is the whole story in any psychosis or neurosis. In all probability, heredity bestows a heightened susceptibility which only in combination with environmental factors leads to disorder. It is possible that psychotic symptoms may be brought on by physical causes such as metabolic dysfunctions, allergy-like reactions, toxic substances in the blood stream, and even viruses. Many suggestive discoveries have been reported which make one or another such notion plausible. But to date none of these promising leads has been confirmed. There is presently no single necessary or sufficient cause or set of causes on which to pin the blame for most psychoses.

Any number of theories of the experiential origin of psychoses have been advanced. They include theories based on psychoanalytic ideas, others that focus on traumatic conditioning, and still others that stress peculiar conflicts in early home environment. To date there is no solid evidence in support of any one theory. This should be emphasized. Indeed, it is extraordinarily difficult to obtain the kind of evidence which would prove that a particular kind of experience leads to a behavioral disorder. Since most neurotic and psychotic symptoms cannot be mimicked in animals, the avenue of research into causes of disorders that is used in most medical investigation is ruled out. This leaves observation of naturally occurring relations between presumed causes and effects as the best available method. But this method has serious deficiencies. Let us take an example. One theory that has received attention recently is that schizophrenia is generated by mothers who make extremely strong and contradictory emotional demands on children, first urging them to be affectionate, then punishing them for expressing affection. In order to prove such a theory, one would have to compare a number of children whose parents treat them this way with equivalent children whose parents are more normal in their actions. But even if the aberrantly treated children showed higher incidence of schizophrenia, one could not conclude that the parental treatment was the cause: such strangely acting parents might well harbor predispositions to psychopathology and pass them on genetically to their offspring.

Such problems have so far thwarted our efforts to pinpoint the causes of behavioral disorders. Nevertheless, from time to time in the press you will read claims for discoveries of causes of schizophrenia or other psychotic reactions. While it is certainly to be hoped that the future will hold some legitimate claims, all the multitude of those which have appeared in the past have turned out to be chimerical. Such claims must, unfortunately, continue to be viewed with scientific skepticism.

Therapies for psychopathology

Let us first make it clear that there exist few well-established cures or palliatives for psychopathological conditions. There are a multitude of different kinds of treatment available, but many of them stand primarily on the recommendation of their practitioners rather than on objective evidence that they actually help patients materially in overcoming their problems. We will consider some of the major varieties of treatment, again organizing the discussion according to broad categories of disorder.

TREATMENT OF MENTAL RETARDATION

There exists an opportunity to prevent many cases of mental retardation by seeing to it that, at birth, deliveries are made with the right kind of anesthesias and by trying to avoid accidental traumatic damage to the head; by striving for early diagnosis of metabolic disorders such as PKU; by preventing diseases such as German measles during pregnancy, and common measles during childhood. But for the organically caused forms of mental retardation, once they have appeared there is no known cure. However, even for severe organic mental retardation, and more particularly for mild forms, special training is often extremely beneficial. Most moderately retarded individuals experience their major difficulties in life in their school years. Life outside the schoolroom can make surprisingly light demands on intellectual abilities. The vast majority of mildly retarded individuals, who have a terrible time getting through school, are absorbed into their communities as normally functioning adults. Even severely retarded individuals are able to learn to some extent. Mildly retarded ones can acquire most of the skills and knowledge of normal adults if they are given sufficient extra attention and training. New and more effective methods of training are coming into use, many of them based on the principles of learning to be described in Chapters 7 and 8. And, of course, efforts are being made to remedy the social conditions which generate intellectual deprivation in early life and to provide compensatory enriched experiences for deprived children. All of these are hopeful and important ways of treating this form of psychopathology.

TREATMENT OF NEUROSES AND PSYCHOSOMATIC DISORDERS

Current approaches to treating neuroses can be divided into *chemical*, or *drug*, *therapies* on the one hand and *psychotherapies* on the other.

Chemical therapies

The chemical therapies in present use are, by and large, empirical — that is, they are treatments which have been reported to help, without anyone knowing exactly why. Among the drug treatments, perhaps the most notable are the tranquilizers. Both mild and severe anxiety reactions can be attenuated to some extent with drugs such as *chlorpromazine*. A highly apprehensive, agitated person usually becomes calmer and more comfortable after its administration. It is not unreasonable to suppose that this artificial calm may in turn make it easier for the patient to find new ways of adjusting, if only because his behavior is likely to be less alarming or obnoxious to other people.

Although not yet as successful as the tranquilizers, there are also drugs that are sometimes effective in alleviating depressions. It is well to keep in mind, however, that all the psychologically active drugs have at least occasional undesirable side effects, and that few have been in use long enough for their long-term effects to be well known.

Psychotherapies

The psychotherapies are those techniques which rely on the therapist interacting with the patient, listening, discussing, suggesting, persuading, teaching, and training. They have been called "talk" therapies, although a good deal more than talk sometimes goes on. There is a very wide variety of different psychotherapies practiced, ranging from psychoanalysis to speech training. They can be subdivided into two main groups: the *insight therapies*, which stress self-understanding, and the *behavior therapies*, which stress modification of actions.

Insight therapies   Many psychiatrists and psychologists believe that a neurotic patient can deal more effectively with his problems if he understands their nature and origins. Where and how the therapist and patient go about looking for the underlying reasons for maladjustment varies according to the theory of personality held by the therapist. If he believes, with Freud, that neurotic problems are due to repressed instinctual urges and deep unconscious fixations, then he will try to find ways of exploring the patient's subconscious mind. On the other hand if, with Rogers, he believes that adjustment problems are fundamentally related to weaknesses in self-esteem, then he may attempt to find ways of getting the patient to make his own progress without too much reliance on the therapist. In *psychoanalysis* the therapist uses free association, dream analysis, and discussion of the patient's thoughts, feelings, and memories in an attempt to help the individual bring to light the presumed conflicts underlying the symptoms. It is assumed that such insight is instrumental in alleviating neurotic problems. There are other theoretically important aspects to psychoanalytic therapy, including emotional relationships between patient and therapist. We will not go into these details here, but simply stress that the method relies on the patient's acquiring a new understanding of himself through prolonged conversations with the therapist. In *nondirective counseling*, which originated with Rogers, the therapist encourages and draws out the client while avoiding, insofar as he can, the imposition of his own interpretations. The hope is that by talking and thinking about his problems the client can arrive at a better understanding of them, and acquire more confidence in his knowledge of himself and more ability to deal with his own psychological processes. Similar assumptions lie behind *group therapy* in which a number of people "talk out" their problems together, usually along with a therapist.

The main objection to the insight therapies is that insight and understanding have never been shown to actually change people's neurotic behavior. While many people who undergo such therapy find the new understandings quite gratifying, there is really no scientifically adequate evidence that neurotic symptoms lessen as a result. One might guess that people whose major problems are conflicts of thought and feeling and who are disturbed by feeling that they do not understand themselves would be most likely to profit from insight therapies.

In addition to the effect of understanding, however, it is thought that conversational therapies may sometimes serve the function of training the individual in social skills. Unfortunately, the situations in which psychotherapies usually take place are far removed from those in which neurotic symptoms cause trouble. Consequently learning to get along with a therapist may not help a person very much in getting along with his family or workmates.

There are methods that make more direct attempts to modify problem behavior as such. These are usually called *behavior therapies*.

Behavior therapies   When a neurotic patient comes to a psychologist he usually complains either of specific problem behavior or of acute anxiety. Behavior therapists try to rid the patient of his problem behavior or reduce his anxieties without necessarily searching for causes. As psychology has progressed, more and more ways of altering behavior have emerged from laboratory and field research. Quite a number of these laboratory-discovered techniques have been adapted for use in therapy. The techniques which have been tried include the following.

Systematic desensitization: Relaxation is in many respects the opposite of anxiety. Most people can be taught, by instruction and practice, how to relax in a secure and comforting situation. After having learned how to relax in the best of circumstances, a patient can often be taught to relax under more trying conditions. One way to do this is called *systematic desensitization* or *counterconditioning*. In this method, the therapist, after first teaching the patient to relax in the absence of any threatening object or situation, produces a situation which is very slightly fearful, allowing the patient to learn to relax in its presence. Then he produces a somewhat more fear-provoking situation, and so forth. Many of the reported successful cases using this method have involved the treatment of phobias. Let us take an example. Rachman (1959) had a woman patient who was terrified of hypodermic injections, tampons, and sexual intercourse. As is now common practice in this kind of therapy, Rachman first established a hierarchy of fears for the patient, i.e., he found out those things which she feared most, next most, and so on down to not at all. Rachman had the patient imagine one of the events which she found only slightly frightening—purchasing a box of tampons. This aroused only mild anxiety, and after a little practice the patient was able to relax while vividly imagining such a scene. Then they moved on to more frightening images. Little by little the patient was able to relax while thinking of things that had previously been more and more anxiety-provoking. Eventually she could even think calmly of a hypodermic needle being used to give her an injection. Moreover, once she was able to undergo hypodermic injections she told the therapist that she had lost most of the other apparently related fears; she was able to use tampons and to have sexual intercourse without alarm.

Systematic desensitization has been used to treat a variety of different kinds of phobias—of snakes, high places, spiders—and there have been reports of apparent success in cases of frigidity, impotence, test anxiety, fear of public speaking, and several other conditions involving neurotic anxiety.

Aversion therapy: A second technique involves punishing a patient for performing behaviors which he wishes to rid himself of. Many reports of complete or partial success with this kind of therapy have involved sexual deviance. For example, a group of men with sexual fetishes for female clothing—they became sexually aroused by wearing such things as corsets, panties, and brassieres—were treated by Marks and Gelder (1967). The treatment consisted of having the patient imagine using the garment in his deviant manner, or actually do so, and then administering a painful electric shock. Figure 4–3 shows what happened to the patient's attitudes toward these articles of clothing as treatment progressed. The results were mixed. The treatment obviously had a considerable effect on attitudes, but there were marked limitations. Applying shock after use of one of the objects did not have any appreciable effect on attitudes toward the others; they all had to be treated separately. Moreover, after discontinuation of the treatment the original attitudes began to return.

This form of treatment has also been used with homosexuals who wish to change their behavior, and with alcoholics. These techniques hold both promise and problems. Not least of the problems is an ethical one; it is to be hoped that more humane methods can be found.

Reward therapies: A more humane method of behavior modification is to reward the patient for desirable responses rather than punish him for undesirable ones. This method has been used in a number of settings. Perhaps the most widespread application is to produce increases in self-sufficient and social behavior in severely withdrawn hospitalized psychotic patients, a matter on which we will comment again in the next section. However, such methods have also been used for other purposes—for example, to alter the behavior of children in classroom situations. If attention is withheld from an obstreperous child until he is quiet instead of rowdy, this will frequently cause a desirable change in the relative frequency of the two behaviors.

Modeling therapy: People, particularly children, frequently learn things by observing and copying the behavior of others. This sort of

FIGURE 4-3
Results of the use of aversion therapy for treatment of sexual fetishism and transvestitism. Men who were sexually aroused by female garments were given electric shocks while having fantasies about the garments. Their attitudes toward these objects changed over the course of treatment, but the effects were limited to the shocked item and largely disappeared after the treatment was discontinued. (After Marks & Gelder, 1967)

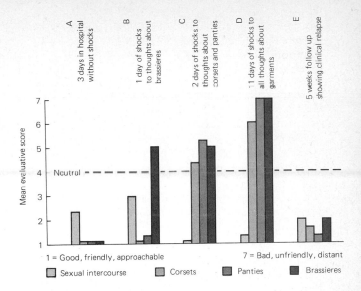

A 3 days in hospital without shocks
B 1 day of shocks to thoughts about brassieres
C 2 days of shocks about corsets and panties
D 11 days of shocks to all thoughts about garments
E 5 weeks follow up showing clinical relapse

Mean evaluative score

Neutral

1 = Good, friendly, approachable   7 = Bad, unfriendly, distant

■ Sexual intercourse   ■ Corsets   ■ Panties   ■ Brassieres

social learning has been called *modeling*. Bandura and others have used this technique to modify phobias. For example, children who were terrified of dogs watched adults and other children interact with dogs in increasingly intimate ways over a series of sessions. This, in a controlled experimental situation, produced significant improvement (Bandura, Grusec, & Menlove, 1967).

These various techniques can be applied in several different settings, varying in closeness to real life. In the examples we have used, the therapist has treated reactions to either imagined or artificially rigged situations. Such therapy, to be effective, must somehow carry over into the outside world in which the patient operates. This could be a serious drawback. To get around this problem, therapists sometimes suggest ways in which the patient can learn new behaviors in situations outside the psychologist's office, for example, by changing his living arrangements or trying a new job, hobby, or schedule of visits to his mother. Some therapists actually go out with the patient into his normal life situations and try to arrange new learning sequences. Some are even beginning to take the sensible, but rather heretical, view that behavior problems may sometimes be the fault of the circumstances in which the person finds himself rather than of his personality. They may actually try to find ways to help the patient alter his stressful environment rather than placing all the emphasis on changing his habitual ways of responding to it.

We have mentioned only a sample of the techniques that have been used in behavior therapy and only a few of the conditions they have been used to treat. There is no reason why many other techniques — for example, the attitude-changing effects of cognitive dissonance — could not also be used in therapy. The whole field of behavior modification is so new that many promising possibilities have simply not yet been tried.

One of the reasons why these methods are so new is that for a long time it was assumed that the direct modification of a symptom would do no good in the long run because the patient would just substitute other bad habits. The idea was that a symptom like stuttering was not the disorder itself, but only a surface manifestation of some underlying problem. If this were the case, it was reasoned, a person who was induced to stop stuttering might start biting his nails instead. While this hypothesis seems quite reasonable, and was sufficiently compelling to inhibit research in behavior modification for many years, there was never any direct evidence of its validity. Encouragingly, recent follow-up studies of behavior therapy have failed to find evidence of symptom substitution.

We have devoted so much space to behavior therapy techniques not only because they are new and exciting, but also because they are essentially psychological in outlook; they make use of many principles which have been developed and studied in the psychological laboratory. In later chapters we will have occasion to refer to the examples given here and to elaborate further the bases of these techniques. Another reason that behavior therapy has been emphasized here is that it is probable, although not certain, that these methods actually work better than do other kinds of psychotherapy. Let us now consider how one evaluates psychotherapies and what the outcome has been of such evaluations.

Evaluation of the effectiveness of psychotherapies

It is not easy to determine whether a particular psychotherapy for neurosis works or doesn't work. There are several difficulties. First, a large proportion of neurotic complaints go away spontaneously. It has been estimated that about 60 percent of people with disabling neuroses, with or without treatment, go back to work within about two years. Since so many people recover from neurotic disorders on their own, it is very hard to tell what caused any particular recovery. Indeed, most studies of recovery rates of large groups of people undergoing insight therapies have come up with figures in the vicinity of 60 percent. Second, for many neuroses it is very unclear what the criterion of recovery should be. Neuroses are defined by experiential discomfort and by social maladjustment, conditions which are difficult to quantify. It is obviously less than adequate to rely on the therapist's opinion that a patient has recovered, or on a patient's own report. For example, in one well-controlled study (Paul, 1966) a group of patients undergoing treatment was compared to several control groups, including one that was just given nonspecific attention but no actual therapy. All patients in every condition stated afterward that they were much improved. What can this mean? One thing it clearly means is that such reports do not get us very far in determining the effectiveness of psychotherapies. These difficulties have tended to dampen the enthusiasm of therapists for research into the efficacy of their methods.

At least two conditions must be met to establish the effectiveness of a therapy. First, there must be a reasonably large number of patients, randomly assigned to be either treated by the therapy or not. It is best if the nontreatment, control group members are seen by the therapist every once in a while, but not specifically treated. The reason is that mere attention may itself lead to a certain amount of improvement, particularly self-described improvement, as just noted. Second, the change in the patient from before treatment to after treatment must be evaluated in some objective manner, and by people who do not know what treatment the patient was undergoing and are therefore not biased.

Very few studies of therapeutic effectiveness have met these criteria. The study by Paul (1968) is probably the most outstanding example of one that has. In that study, students with intense public-speaking anxieties who were treated by systematic desensitization were compared with groups of students having the same complaint who were randomly assigned either to a traditional insight therapy technique or to one of several control groups. Paul obtained clear results that the behavior therapy was effective, and more effective than the traditional therapy, which was not reliably better than a control in which the therapist simply paid attention to the students on a regular schedule. There have been a few other reasonably well-controlled studies showing that behavior therapy in some forms and for some uses, notably for the treatment of phobias and anxiety about specific activities, is indeed of positive value. However, a great deal more work of this kind will be required before any firm statements can be made about the general value of this or any other psychotherapy.

TREATMENT OF PSYCHOSIS

With respect to the psychoses, the situation is much more discouraging than for the neuroses. Some forms of severe psychosis can be treated, if not successfully at least to some benefit, by *electro-shock therapy*. In this rather drastic technique the malfunctioning brain is literally jolted out of its unfortunate pattern. Electricity is passed through the head between the ears, causing a convulsion, a literal brainstorm. Apparently the disorganized function of the brain in certain severe psychoses is broken up, at least temporarily, by this severe interference.

A more humane and effective treatment of psychosis has been the use of *tranquilizing drugs*. Many of these have had dramatic effects in reducing the severity of symptoms in psychotic individuals. There has been a marked decrease in the number of people who stay for long periods of time in mental hospitals, probably as a result of the widespread use of these drugs. While the available drugs do not appear to effect complete cures, they often render fit to get along in society people who would otherwise have to be isolated.

Most kinds of psychotherapy, although sometimes used with psychotic patients, are not commonly thought to be beneficial for the large majority of cases. The demonstrated value of insight therapies for psychoses is even less impressive than for neuroses. Psychoanalysis, for example, is rarely even attempted with psychotics. Behavior therapies, in the form of explicit reward schedules for socially acceptable behavior by otherwise unmanageable mental hospital patients, have been tried with some success. One way in which this is done is in the establishment of so-called *token economies*. Patients are rewarded with tokens for performing certain kinds of behavior. The tokens can be exchanged for candy, cigarettes, grounds passes, trips, or, sometimes, money. By making the tokens contingent on desirable behavior, such as talking or eating, psychologists have been able to bring even extremely withdrawn and antisocial patients to a more cooperative and self-sufficient state. While such methods do not yet purport to cure, the ameliorative benefits they provide are such that their use is spreading rapidly.

We are still a long way from having established cures for most psychopathologies, but there are signs of progress on many fronts. And there is a constant and growing research effort into psychopathology. The problem is a major one for society and a tragic one for individuals. We can only hope that important advances will be made in the near future.

TOPICS DISCUSSED IN CHAPTER 4

1. Adjustment as the interaction of desiderata, skills, and circumstance
2. Conflict
3. Mechanisms by which people defend against conflict and anxiety
4. Some theories of the adjustive process that stress conflict, fulfillment, or consistency as basic problems
5. The nature and classification of behavior disorders:
   a. mental retardation
   b. neuroses and psychosomatic disorders
   c. character disorders
   d. psychoses
6. The known and unknown causes of psychopathology
7. Therapies for behavior disorders:
   a. chemical and physical treatments
   b. insight therapies
   c. behavior therapies
   d. evaluation of the effect of psychotherapy

SUGGESTED READINGS

1. *In the area of adjustment, conflict, and defense, some interesting books which go much farther in several directions are:*

Dollard, J., Doob, L. W., Miller, N. E., Mowrer, O. H., & Sears, R. R. *Frustration and aggression.* New Haven, Conn.: Yale University Press, 1939, an account of a theory that thwarting goal-directed behavior arouses aggression.

Freud, A. *The ego and the mechanisms of defense.* London: Hogarth, 1937, which is the classic work on defenses.

Sarnoff, I. *Personality dynamics and development.* New York: Wiley, 1962, gives a thorough review.

2. *A book on personal adjustment is:*

Lindgren, H. C. *Psychology of personal adjustment.* New York: American Book, 1964.

3. *Theories of personality are described in:*

Hall, C. S., & Lindzey, G. *Theories of personality.* New York: Wiley, 1957, and

Maddi, S. R. *Personality theories: a comparative analysis.* Homewood, Ill.: Dorsey, 1968.

4. *Some fascinating descriptions of individual personalities can be found in:*

Allport, G. W. *Letters from Jenny.* New York: Harcourt, Brace & World, 1965.

White, R. W. *Lives in progress: a study of the natural growth of personality.* (2nd ed.) New York: Holt, 1966.

5. *Primary source works on some of the principal theories of personality include:*

Allport, G. W. *Pattern and growth in personality.* New York: Holt, 1961.

Freud, S. *An outline of psychoanalysis.* New York: Norton, 1963. (Paperback, originally published in 1940.)

Rogers, C. R. *On becoming a person.* Boston: Houghton Mifflin, 1961.

6. *For general and case descriptions of behavior disorders, read:*

White, R. W. *The abnormal personality.* (3rd ed.) New York: Ronald Press, 1964.

Ullman, L. P., & Krasner, L. *A psychological approach to abnormal behavior.* Englewood Cliffs, N. J.: Prentice-Hall, 1969.

7. *The following book makes a powerful, nontechnical case for social responsibility in the prevention of retardation:*

Hurley, R. *Poverty and mental retardation: a causal relationship.* New York: Random House, 1969.

8. *Summaries and reviews of various aspects of behavioral therapy can be found in:*

Franks, C. M. *Behavior therapy: appraisal and status.* New York: McGraw-Hill, 1969.

Ullman, L. P., & Krasner, L. (Eds.) *Case studies in behavior modification.* New York: Holt, 1965.

9. *And these journal reports of therapy cases are instructive and far from dull:*

Davison, G. C. Elimination of a sadistic fantasy by a client-controlled counterconditioning technique: A case study. *Journal of Abnormal and Social Psychology*, 1968, **73**, 84–90.

Lazarus, A. A. The treatment of chronic frigidity by systematic desensitization. *Journal of Nervous and Mental Diseases*, 1963, **136**, 272–278.

Rachman, S. The treatment of anxiety and phobic reactions by systematic desensitization psychotherapy. *Journal of Abnormal and Social Psychology*, 1959, **58**, 259–263.

10. *Perhaps the best evidence of effectiveness of a psychotherapy is contained in:*

Paul, G. L. A two-year follow-up of systematic desensitization in therapy groups. *Journal of Abnormal Psychology*, 1968, **73**, 119–130.

FIVE

Sensation and perception

Living things, in general, have the ability to adjust to the demands of a constantly changing environment—to make their actions appropriate to the current state of the world around them. The ability is most highly developed in man. In order to adjust to reality, a person must be able to detect the existence and characteristics of objects and happenings. He must be sensitive to physical events which contain clues to the nature of the world outside himself, and from these clues must be able to make the proper inferences. The receipt and interpretation of information about external reality (and to some extent internal reality as well) constitute *perception*.

We may distinguish two rather different reasons for being curious about perception in animals and man: the subjective and the objective. On the one hand, a very great part of our subjective experience of life depends on sensory intercourse with the world around us. The evidence on which we act in dealing with the world comes first and foremost from perception; and so do our experiences of pleasure and pain: from the raw experience of a brilliant color, to the thrilled recognition of a beloved face, or to the common comfort of a soft pillow. The richness of experience, its clarity, and its detail are among the most important ingredients of life as viewed by an individual. The overwhelming subjective importance of perception must also be cause for curiosity about its nature and mechanisms. How do we see bright color? How do we feel hardness? How do we recognize a face, a letter, a printed or spoken word? What are the properties of the physical world which give rise to experience?

The second way of approaching the problem of perception is to stand off and consider man and other animals as nature's current crop of life forms. In what ways and by what mechanisms do these organisms obtain and utilize information about their environment? The objects and events of the physical world have a vast array of properties and features by which they might possibly make themselves known. Which of these are used by the organisms we know, and which are not? We can wonder about perception as a phenomenon of nature completely external to ourselves and our own lives, simply as an object of scientific inquiry.

These two sets of reasons for being curious about perception are, of course, very much intertwined. Our egocentric curiosity about the foundation of personal experience cannot be satisfied without an over-all view of the place in nature of our perceptual capabilities; and the natural functions of perception cannot be fully understood without concern for their place in the private worlds of the living creatures in which they occur. The discussion that follows will be motivated by both sorts of interests. The description of the facts and underlying mechanisms of perception, as they are known at present, should high-light both our amazing perceptual abilities and our often unsuspected limitations.

The study of perception is concerned with the relation between the properties of the physical world and an animal's appreciation of them. The physical world contains many, many times more information than any animal is capable of using. The range of perceptual appreciation of the world is extremely narrow compared with the range of variation existing in it. By contrast, however, within the range to which we do respond, our sensitivities are often quite exquisite. For example, we hear only a limited range of pitch, while the atmosphere around us teems with sounds at frequencies to which we are totally unresponsive; but within the range of sounds to which our hearing apparatus is best suited, we are about as sensitive as is physically possible. This contrast between marvelous sensitivity within a narrow range and general insensitivity elsewhere is widely characteristic of our senses. It is as if nature, over the course of evolution, had discovered that there were but a handful of kinds of signals from the environment which animals should know about, but that these should be known extremely well. Perhaps more impressive than our sensitivity is our extensive ability to analyze and make inferences from complex combinations of the stimuli to which we are sensitive. We not only can detect black against white, but can also infer that the pattern before us is the word *psychology*, and we can do so whether the word is written large or small, with capital letters or lower case, at a slant, with embellishments, in dim light or bright, as a white pattern against black, or as a green pattern against yellow. This ability to find stable properties in incredibly variable and complicated stimulus patterns has an adaptive value that cannot be overestimated.

This chapter will first survey the domains of perceptual sensitivity —the senses and their corresponding physical stimuli. It will then go on to consider the analysis of combinations of stimuli, and finally broaden the discussion to include the imposition of meaning onto stimulus patterns by the processes of judgment, recognition, and choice.

SENSITIVITY

Let us survey the various sensory domains and describe briefly the physical events to which our sensory experiences correspond. Before we do so, however, it is necessary to deal with the problem of how to measure such sensitivity. We will make use of two common measures of sensitivity: the smallest amount of the physical stimulus which reliably leads to sensation, and the smallest change in the physical stimulus which is reliably perceived as a change.

The first of these—the smallest amount reliably detected— is called the *absolute threshold*. The second—the smallest change reliably perceived—is called the *difference threshold*. How are such thresholds ascertained? Let us consider first the absolute threshold. Assume that you wish to find out what is the smallest intensity of a small spot of light that a human observer can detect. One way of finding out would be to start with no light and then by very small steps increase the amount of light on a spot until an observer declares that he sees something. This is called the *method of limits*. It has a distinct drawback in that the measured threshold will depend on the size of the steps by which the light intensity is increased.

There is another and better way of measuring an absolute threshold, the *method of constant stimuli*. This consists of presenting in random order a number of different stimulus intensities that span the range in which the threshold must lie. For example, you might present a series of thirty different levels of illumination, each ten times, and in random order. For each one you would ask the observer to state whether or not he sees the spot of light. You could then plot the proportion of the times when the spot is reported as a function of the intensity of the light. This would give a function like that in Figure 5–1. The most important thing to note about this graph, and about absolute thresholds, is that there is no sharp cut-off point between intensities at which the stimulus is seen and others at which it is not seen. In a way, there is no such thing as an absolute threshold. Rather, as the stimulus increases in magnitude, the probability that a subject will report seeing it increases gradually. When the intensity is very low, the observer almost never reports seeing it; when the intensity is high, he almost always does. At medium levels, he sometimes says he sees it and sometimes does not. Ordinarily, a threshold is defined as the point at which 50 percent of the judgments are positive and 50 percent are negative. This is what we meant earlier by referring to the threshold as the point at which the stimulus was "reliably" detected.

There is, however, a fundamental problem involved in these methods of threshold measurement, and that is that the measured threshold will depend to some extent on the subject's expectations that the stim-

FIGURE 5–1

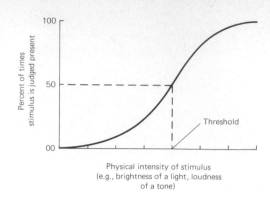

A generalized graph of the relation between the physical intensity of a stimulus and the probability that an observer will report its presence. Such a relation holds for all perceivable stimuli: brightness of light, loudness of tones, etc. Note that there is no distinct level below which the stimulus is never reported, or above which it always is. Rather, the probability of report increases gradually as the physical stimulus becomes more intense. The *threshold* is defined as the physical magnitude which is reported as perceived 50 percent of the time.

ulus will appear. If there actually is a stimulus on all trials and the subject knows this, he may tend always to report that the stimulus was indeed there. Therefore it is always good practice in such measurements to use "catch" trials in which one does not actually present the positive stimulus. Observers will quite often give "false alarms"—that is, say that they saw the stimulus although it wasn't presented—on such catch trials.

There are methods by which the effect of an observer's expectation and bias can be measured and taken into account. We will discuss some of these later. However, if we just want to compare different sense modalities and get a rough idea of what thresholds are like, it is sufficient simply to keep expectations fairly constant from one experiment to another. In the measurement of thresholds this has usually been done, first, by the use of highly trained observers who try to maintain a constant criterion and, second, by the use of a small proportion of catch trials. The thresholds which will be described for the various sensory domains were obtained in this way.

Light and vision

Light consists of waves of electromagnetic energy.[1] It is but one of many familiar forms of propagated electromagnetic energy; others are radio waves, radar, infrared heat, ultraviolet light, x-rays, and cosmic rays. Electromagnetic energy is capable of traveling through wire, other materials, or empty space at speeds up to 186,000 miles per second. Waves of electromagnetic energy may be thought of as analogous to spreading waves caused by a stone dropping into a puddle of water. The various kinds of electromagnetic radiations differ from one another in their wave lengths—the distance between the crest of one wave and that of the next. The properties of a particular kind of radiation, such as its ability to penetrate various materials or to be absorbed by different types of re-

[1] According to modern physics, light has both wave and a quantal properties: in some respects it is best described as continuously oscillating energy, and in some respects it is best described as a collection(s) of discrete packets called *photons*.

FIGURE 5–2 The wave lengths of common forms of electromagnetic energy. Note what a small part of the range we are sensitive to.

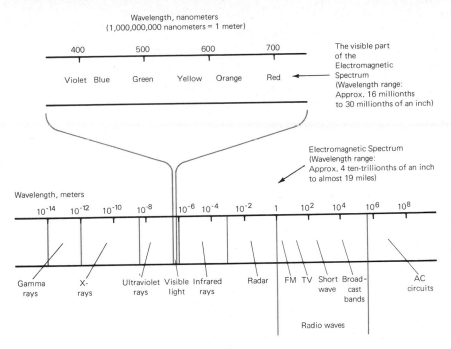

ceivers, depend on its wave length. What we know as light is nothing more nor less than a particular very narrow range of wave lengths of electromagnetic energy that are able to be absorbed by and cause changes in certain chemical substances in our eyes. Light differs from other electromagnetic waves in no other important way. The range of wave lengths to which our eyes are sensitive—that is, which we see as light—is an exceedingly small portion of the total available spectrum of wave lengths. As Figure 5–2 shows, the entire visible spectrum is contained between the wave lengths of about 400 to 700 nanometers. A nanometer is one billionth of a meter (formerly referred to as a milli-micron). By contrast, the full range of electromagnetic radiation is approximately one thousand million million million times as wide.

What adaptive advantages would account for the evolution of eyes sensitive to this particular tiny segment of the available wave lengths? No one can say for sure, but several tentative answers can be put forward. One is that the kinds of molecules that are common in biological environments are of a size which makes them most likely to be able to absorb (utilize) the wave lengths which constitute visible light. Another line of explanation is that certain other wave lengths have distinct disadvantages. Those in the ultraviolet range, for example, are absorbed by water; but we, and our eyes, are made mostly of water, and therefore need to use a radiation which will penetrate it. Similarly, it is an advantage to use the electromagnetic radiations that we do use for vision be-

FIGURE 5–3.
The anatomy of the eye.

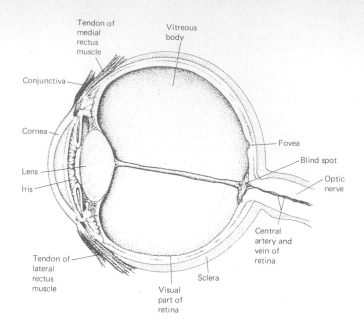

cause they tend to bounce off objects that are solid enough to hurt if we bump into them. Compared with x-rays, which can go through many things that we cannot, or compared with very long wave-length radiations that are partially reflected by air—which we would prefer to see through—visible light is pretty reasonable in the things which it passes through and is reflected by. In other words, visible light affords information that is particularly useful to us. It is not ideal in all respects, however. Consider the fact that visible light goes through glass while most animals would rather not. (Although one can argue that it is handy that we have some hard substances we can see through.) Another advantage of visible light is that it is abundant on the surface of the earth, at least during daylight hours, because the sun emits a large amount of energy in this region of the spectrum and this energy is able to penetrate the atmosphere of the earth. However, other forms of energy might well be more useful at times when sunlight is unavailable; radar and infrared energies, for example, can now be artificially utilized at night and in bad weather.

So far we have discussed light only as a form of energy to which we are sensitive. Obviously this is not the whole story. We do much more with light than simply tell whether it is there or not. Light-energy in the world is, in fact, a vast and intricate hodgepodge. Most of the light by which we see comes from the sun, but before reaching us it is diffused by the atmosphere and reflected millions of times in millions of directions. It encounters objects in the world in a helter-skelter way, being absorbed or partially absorbed by some objects, reflected by others. Indeed, the light that reaches a single point on the outer surface of the eye has come from all over the visible world in front of us. Some will have come from a leaf of a tree on the left, some from the top of a tele-

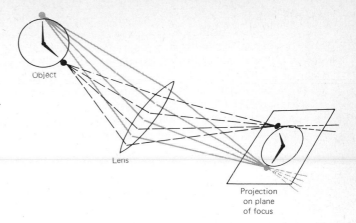

FIGURE 5–4
A properly shaped lens can bend light so that energy coming from one point in the world to any point on the lens converges at a common point somewhere behind the lens, thus forming an image of the object from which the light has been reflected.

Object

Lens

Projection
on plane
of focus

phone pole to the right, some from the surface of the pavement below. In fact, a single point on the surface of the eye is struck by light that has bounced off every object that can be connected to that point by a straight line. If a sensitive photocell were located at the front of the eyeball, it would record merely the sum of light-energies from all over the world in front of us—a complete blur.

What good to us is such a massive confusion of energies? Or, more properly, how do we make use of the light that strikes our eyes in order to make inferences about the objects off which it has bounced? What makes it possible to process visual information is that light rays are bent when they go from one transparent medium to another, e.g., from air to glass or from air to water. As is shown in Figure 5–4, light rays coming from the same point in the outside world and striking a lens at two different places can be bent by the lens in such a way that they converge at a single point on the other side of the lens. All the light available at that point behind the lens, then, has come from a single place in the outside world. Notice, however, that the light rays from a single outside point will converge at one and only one distance behind the lens. What that distance is depends on characteristics of the lens: what it is made of and what its shape is.

Now we are ready to understand how the eye works. The eye has a lens which can be made thicker and thinner, thereby changing the angle by which light bends on going through it and thereby changing the point of convergence behind the lens (actually most of the bending is done at the cornea, but only the lens changes shape). By changing the lens in this way, we change the distance of the points in the environment on which we are focusing. To *focus* is to make all the light that comes from a single point fall on a single point on the *retina*, the sensitive portion of the back of the eye. By thickening the lens we make objects that are closer to us come into focus, and by stretching it and making it thinner we make objects that are farther away come into focus.

When we have a section of the world in focus, the retina (see Figure 5–3) has on it a point-for-point image of the part of the world at which we are looking. What is this "image"? It would be a mistake to think of it as "what we see." As we will show below, before we "see" anything we process this retinal image extensively; what we see is more like a map made on the basis of measurements taken at the retina than it is like a photograph of the light patterns on the retina itself. But more of that later. What does exist on the retina is a pattern of light with a point-to-point correspondence with points in the environment. The reason why there is variation in the light on various points of the retina is that there is variation in the way in which light is absorbed and reflected from the corresponding objects in the world. Some objects reflect a lot of light; some reflect little and absorb the rest. Some objects primarily reflect light of certain wave lengths, that is, light of certain colors, and absorb light of other wave lengths. A leaf reflects a large amount of green light, while absorbing most of the light in other parts of the spectrum. The leaf as a whole, however, reflects much less light than is transmitted through the air from the sky directly around the leaf. Consequently the area of the retina receiving light from points around the leaf receives more than does the area receiving light reflected from the leaf itself. Thus, there is a pattern of differences in the amount of light received, and in the wave lengths of the light received, which corresponds to differences in the physical structure and size of the objects from which light is reflected to the eye.

We use these differences in the kind and amount of light reflected from objects to infer the objects' size and nature. This is a complex, difficult inference, of course, since the properties of the light and of the image on the retina are in no sense in direct correspondence to the properties of the world in which we are interested. It is a long step between the light that is falling on the retina and the knowledge that the object from which it is coming is solid. It is even a considerable problem to decide how large the object is, since the amount of retinal area which light reflecting from an object will cover depends not only on how big the object is but also how close it is—the closer the object the bigger the retinal image.[2] Figure 5–5 illustrates the simple geometry involved in the projection of visual patterns in the environment onto the retina.

Vision is ordinarily clearest for images falling on a small portion of the middle of the retina, the *fovea*. This part of the eye contains a very much denser concentration of the cells which are sensitive to light, and is therefore much more sensitive to small variations from one point to another. The surrounding area, or periphery, of the retina is also capable of important perceptual functions, of course, but will not allow as fine a differentiation as will the fovea.

[2] The inferences that a human perceiver makes in using physical energy to arrive at knowlege of the world are mostly unconscious and automatic. The person does not do conscious mental calculations to determine the size of a seen object. Yet, what his nervous system must do is the logical equivalent of such calculations (in Chapter 10 we will discuss how some of this is actually done). The visual and other perceptual systems take raw data received by sense organs and combine, manipulate, and compare, producing, essentially, conclusions about aspects of environment which are of potential importance. This processing of information is logically inductive and this is why it is referred to as *inference*. The term does tend to suggest conscious thought, but that is not the meaning intended here. Just as one can think of a computer drawing inferences from data without imagining it to be consciously cogitating, so one can see that the nervous system is able to derive the implications of information, i.e., make inferences, without consciousness.

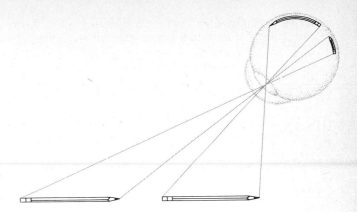

FIGURE 5-5
Geometry of retinal projection:
closer objects produce larger
images on the retina.

VISUAL SENSITIVITY

How sensitive is the eye? It is very sensitive. On a very clear, dark night a single candle 30 miles away would be reported as present about half the time (Galanter, 1962). At this absolute threshold, the amount of light entering the eye is only about 100 photons (a photon is the smallest package of physical light-energy). What makes this even more impressive are the following considerations: First, only about 10 percent of that light gets through to be absorbed at the retina of the eye. Next, it requires the stimulation of a number of cells in the retina, not just one, in order for any message to go up to the brain and for a sensation to be reported by an individual. This means that the individual receptor cells are almost certainly capable of the absolute physical maximum sensitivity, that is, they can respond to a single photon of light. In short, the eye is almost as sensitive as it could possibly be.

However, we have so far been talking about sensitivity to white light. White light consists of a mixture of different wave lengths (just what mixture will be discussed later). If one studies perceptual sensitivity to the different visible wave lengths separately, one finds different degrees of sensitivity to different parts of the spectrum. A curve showing visual sensitivity to various wave lengths of light is shown in Figure 5-7.

An interesting point arises in connection with Figure 5-7. If I asked you how much illumination was provided by an electric light bulb, how would you answer? You might use some kind of meter to measure the amount of physical energy coming out of the bulb. But would this measurement be of much value? What if a large portion of the electromagnetic energy coming from the bulb was at wave lengths to which the human eye was insensitive? You might conclude from your measurement that the bulb was shedding a great deal of light—which would be true enough in a physical sense but totally misleading for purposes of household utility. The question of the amount of illumination, in terms useful to humans, is a psychological question pure and simple. What we are interested in is how much good the electromagnetic emanations do for a human observer trying to detect characteristics of the environment around him, that is, how much *vision* a bulb gives rise to, not how much electromagnetic energy. To get a reasonable measure of the amount of useful illumination from a source like a light bulb, psychologists have

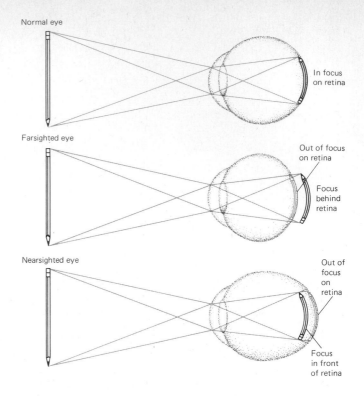

FIGURE 5–6
In nearsighted and farsighted eyes, the points of convergence are in front of or behind the retina—the sensitive surface—because the eyeballs are not spherical.

Normal eye

In focus on retina

Farsighted eye

Out of focus on retina

Focus behind retina

Nearsighted eye

Out of focus on retina

Focus in front of retina

developed a measure of *luminosity*. They arrive at this by measuring at every possible wave length the electromagnetic energy coming from the source, multiplying the energy at each wave length by the average sensitivity for that wave length, and then summing.

Sensitivity varies also with the state of adaptation of the eye and with the part of the retina involved. The eye is much more sensitive to light after it has been in the dark for long periods. Figure 5–8 shows a so-called *dark-adaptation curve* which gives the threshold for a light as a function of the amount of time which the observer has spent in the dark immediately beforehand. There is a corresponding light-adaptation curve, which depicts that as one comes out into the light after a long period of darkness, the sensitivity of the eye rather quickly decreases.

There are at least two different mechanisms by which the eye adapts to the dark. One of them is retraction of the iris to allow more light to come in. Another and more important factor is a complex biochemical change that occurs in the cells of the retina.

The absolute threshold for a spot of light is, of course, only one of many aspects of sensitivity. We can also ask about spatial sensitivity—for example how far apart must two sources of light be before we can tell them apart? This aspect of sensitivity is called *visual acuity*. In general, two lines or points must be at least 1/60 of a degree apart (the angle is measured at the lens) in order for us to see them as separate 50 percent of the time. However, this is true only for the center of the fovea. Further out on the retina, acuity decreases rapidly: at only 1/2 degree from the center of the fovea acuity has decreased by 50 percent. In the peripheral

FIGURE 5–7

Graph showing sensitivity of the eye to light of different wave lengths. The upper curve (cones) is for the perception of the color of light focused on the fovea; the lower curve (rods) Is for perception of achromatic light focused outside the fovea. (Rods and cones are the two types of receptor cells found in the retina; the cones are responsible for color vision, while the rods —as you can see from this graph—are more sensitive to light, but they do not give information as to color; cones are found primarily in the fovea, rods elsewhere.)

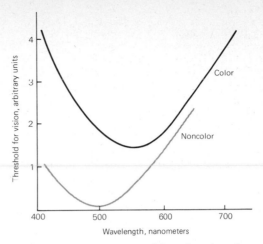

regions of the eye acuity is very bad indeed. Perception of fine detail and clear, sharp images are possible only in the fovea.

We can also ask about temporal resolution. How close together in time can two successive flashes of light be and still be seen as separate? This question is related to how accurately we can perceive rapid changes in the world. One traditional approach to this problem has been to study vision of a repeatedly flashing light. For example, an ordinary incandescent light bulb goes on and off 60 times per second, but we do not see the fluctuations. How slow would the physical fluctuations have to be before we would see them? The rate at which a flickering light is seen 50 percent of the time as flickering is called the *critical flicker frequence,* or CFF. The CFF varies with light intensity. With very weak lights it may be as low as 15 cycles per second, and with very bright light as high as 40 cycles per second.

Finally, we may ask about our sensitivity to differences in wave length. We see different wave lengths—ranging from 400 to 800 nanometers—as having different colors, the colors of the spectrum. As we will see later, the physiological basis of color perception rests on three[3] different receptor processes, the full range of color being produced by a combining of these three. And it is a fact that all the colors visible to us can be created by mixing three different lights; many different sets of three will do, so long as the lights are appropriately chosen (for example, no one of the three can be simply a mixture of the other two). Despite what you may previously have been led to believe, they do *not* need to be any one particular set, such as green, blue, and red. We distinguish color in three dimensions: hue, which corresponds to wave-length differences; brightness, which corresponds to the amount of energy in the wave length in question; and saturation, which corresponds to the "purity" of the wave length's mixture. (Saturation is experienced as greyness at one extreme and pure color at the other.) Our ability to distinguish along all these dimensions is sufficient that it would be possible to construct 350,000 different color samples, each one of which could be reliably distinguished from every other one.

[3] At least; it is not yet certain, but there may be more.

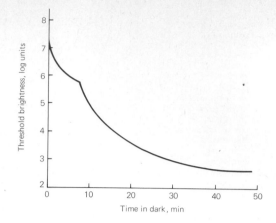

FIGURE 5-8
The eye becomes very much more sensitive to light— thousands of times more sensitive—after a period of time in the dark.

It is interesting to consider that the spectrum of light waves to which we are sensitive is a continuous one, ranging in wave length from about 400 to 800 nanometers. There are no sharp boundary lines; light waves of all possible lengths exist and strike our eyes. But we do not see a continuum of colors. We see instead distinct, discrete colors, and, as shown in Figure 5–9, these do not even seem to fall in any qualitatively continuous order. The reason for this is that our eyes are not simply measuring instruments which record physical quantities. They are instead biological organs by which we can discriminate differences in the environment and from them infer some of its qualities.

Sound and hearing

Sound, like light, consists of waves of spreading physical energy. How-ever, the energy in sound is mechanical rather than electromagnetic. Molecules in the air, or other media, are alternately pressed closer to-gether and pulled apart by a vibrating object, the region of compression spreading out in all directions. Sound waves travel at a rate of about 700 miles per hour in ordinary air at sea level pressures. Our ears are constructed in such a way that they allow detection of the presence of such waves and the differentiation of varying frequencies. The frequency of a series of waves refers to the number of crests that pass a stationary point in a given period of time. The unit of measurement of sound fre-quency is cycles per second, called *hertz* (Hz). If 1,000 regions of compres-sion (and rarefaction) pass a point every second, there is a sound of 1,000 Hz.

The perceptual use of sound energy is quite different from the use of light energy. We do not ordinarily use sound to help us determine the size or shape of objects. (It could be so used, in ways very analogous to those used for creating images with light, but for certain physical rea-sons sound would be very much less useful for this purpose than is light.) Instead of inferring from the patterns of sound energy which reach our ears the shape of the objects which gave rise to the sounds, we primarily extract from sound only its temporal patterns of loudness and frequency. These patterns contain important information for an organism that is able to interpret them. One reason for this is that the kind of vibratory

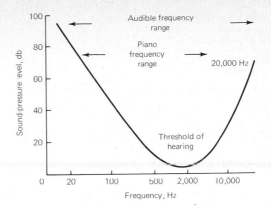

FIGURE 5–10
The absolute threshold of hearing for pure tones of different frequencies.

patterns set up in the air depends on the kind of objects involved and what happened to them. For example, when a tree falls to the ground, the trunk—a resilient, massive object—produces sound waves of great intensity but low frequency; whereas wind rustling the small leaves of a birch tends to produce high frequency sounds. The sounds produced by an object doing something characteristic of it can form a sort of "fingerprint" of what happened. Notice again the important fact that sounds stand in no simple 1-to-1 relation to the events that produce them, but rather are by-products of the events which a clever receiver can use to make certain limited inferences.

As with light, the range of frequencies which exist in nature is very much broader than the range of sound to which the human ear is sensitive. We hear frequencies ranging from about 20 to 20,000 Hz. Other animals can hear wider ranges, e.g., bats can probably hear frequencies as high as 150,000 Hz, but no animal has unlimited range. The range in which sensitivity is sufficient to be really useful is even smaller—for humans the region is approximately 1,000 to 4,000 Hz. Figure 5–10 shows our relative sensitivity in terms of absolute threshold to sounds at various frequencies.

Differences in frequencies of sound waves are experienced by us as differences in pitch. However, pitch and physical frequency are not identical. For one thing, perceived pitch does not rise in direct correspondence to frequency. The successive octaves of musical tones sound approximately equally spaced, although they differ by a factor of two in physical frequency. Moreover, the relation between sound and frequency is not even a regular one; the amount by which frequency must be increased to get what sounds like an equal increase in pitch is different for low tones than for high tones. And two notes exactly an octave apart sound more similar than do two slightly more closely placed frequencies. Also, differences in frequency which we can detect are exceedingly small. A trained musician can tell the difference between two tones that differ by only a few cycles per second—tones of, say, 1,500 and 1,502 Hz. In the perception of speech we ordinarily make distinctions based on differences in the timing of changes in pitch which are astonishingly fine; a difference in 1/20 of a second in the onset of a particular frequency may make the difference between hearing one word and hearing another (for example, *do* and *to*).

Sensation and perception
117

Smell and taste: the chemical senses

At every breath we bring into our lungs a complex mixture of gases consisting not only of the major components of oxygen, nitrogen, and carbon dioxide, but also of a broad array of other substances in minute quantities. Most of these other gases have been given off by animals, plants and objects in our environment. To a considerable extent the gaseous chemical substances given off by things are special to them, and thus offer a rich source of information. For example, the smell of pine pitch, if properly analyzed, could tell a person that he was near a tree.

Similarly, whenever you put something in your mouth, a whole host of chemicals in varying quantities is dissolved from the object into the saliva. These dissolved substances, once again, offer potential clues as to the nature of the world. We detect chemical substances only if they are diffused in the air we breathe or dissolved in a fluid which bathes the tongue. Substances in solid form have no taste or smell as such. (Would it not be useful to be able to sense the chemical constituency of a rock or piece of wood without having to chew it up or dissolve it?) We are not sensitive to all chemicals (consider water and air), but for those to which we are sensitive our absolute thresholds are often quite low. For example, under ideal conditions a single drop of perfume diffused in an amount of air about equal to the volume of an average classroom is sufficient for detection half of the time. Similarly, a single teaspoon of sugar dissolved in two gallons of water reaches the absolute threshold for taste. Sensitivities to chemical substances vary tremendously. Some substances can be smelled or tasted in very, very tiny quantities, while others are needed in larger—although still tiny—amounts.

In contrast to the great sensitivity of our chemical sense, the order we impose on our tasting and smelling experiences by the words which we commonly use to talk about them is quite crude. English has no adequate vocabulary for describing either smells or tastes. Tastes we can broadly classify as sour, bitter, or sweet; smells as putrid, sweet, acrid, etc. But compared to the ones we use for pitch and for visual characteristics these descriptions are extremely vague.

Heat, pressure, and pain: the skin senses

Still another class of senses is that which involves some sort of contact between the environment and a surface—external or internal—of the body. Sensations of physical pressure or exchange of heat with the environment are the result of perhaps our most direct intercourse with the world around us. If one sees, hears, or smells a tree, one knows that it is near and that some maneuvers should be implemented to avoid it, or some caution exercised in case the maneuver fails. But when one actually *feels* a tree, the time has come to stop forward motion completely and instantly. And if, perchance, the feeling is not only of pressure but also of pain, the implication may be that it is not merely time to stop but also time to run away.

The physical stimulus which gives rise to the sensation of touch is an actual displacement of the skin. A distinction is usually made between touch and deep-pressure sensations. Touch sensations are the source of perceptions of things rubbing lightly on the skin, for example, when the fingertips explore a small object. Deep-pressure sensations are the source of perception of actual distortions of the body surface, for example, when the buttocks are indented by a chair.

The physical stimulus that gives rise to sensations of temperature is not absolute temperature, but rapid changes in the temperature of the skin. Heat and cold are probably not separate sensations but, rather, involve the same physiological mechanisms, and, indeed, are sometimes indistinguishable from each other as sensations. A hot object may sometimes be felt as cold, and an intensely cold object, e.g., a piece of dry ice, may be felt as hot. In general, sensations of hot and cold are highly relative. If you soak one hand in hot water and the other in cold water for five minutes and then place them both in water of intermediate temperature, one will feel hot, the other cold. Such relativism is, of course, a very general phenomenon in perception, but it is perhaps most striking in sensations of hot and cold.

Reliable detection of a difference in temperature requires a considerable change of temperature on the surface of the skin. Sensitivity to light touch, on the other hand, is quite acute, particularly in specialized parts of the body such as the fingertips. Galanter (1962) estimates that under ideal conditions a person would feel the wing of a bee falling on his cheek from a distance of one centimeter.

Other senses

There are, of course, events to which we are sensitive other than those so far described. We know what position our arms, legs, fingers, and eyes are in, even in the dark. We know, at least roughly, whether we are upright or reclining, even if strapped into a padded dentist's chair. The physical stimulus which gives rise to sensations of gravitational position is movement of the fluid in a specialized organ of the middle ear, the vestibular apparatus.

We also know, roughly, whether we are hungry, excited or calm. All these kinds of knowledge about ourselves are based on sensory mechanisms of one sort or another. We will not discuss them in more detail here. But it would be unfortunate to leave the topic of sensation without noting that these very personal and important experiences are of the same nature as our exterior perceptions of the world, and like them, involve selective sensitivity to certain kinds of energies or aspects of events which we use to make inferences that influence our conduct. We have not evolved any sensitivities to the current status of our liver function, probably because there is no gross behavior we could engage in that would aid or hinder this bodily process. On the other hand, we have quite sensitive abilities to monitor the state of distension of our bladders—which is probably an evolutionary adaptation to the fact that there are overt acts required of us to assist the kidney in the proper discharge of its duties. Similarly, the vestibular apparatus in our inner ears, which allows us to sense direction with respect to gravity, is extremely useful in walking, running, and swinging from one limb of a tree to another. The balance sense is remarkably sensitive. By contrast, although we can tell positions of our limbs in the dark or with our eyes closed, we are not very good at it. Close your eyes and try to bring together rapidly the index fingers of your left and right hands. It is interesting to speculate on nature's probable reasons for giving us exquisite sensitivities to some aspects of the environment and crude ones, or none, to other aspects. By the same token, it is fascinating to contemplate the overwhelming influence which this fact has on our experiential lives. Those sources of information to which we are sensitive are those about which we have clear and strong experiences, and from which can come intense pleasures and pains. If we are to derive joy from experience, nature has decreed that we cannot do it by concentrating our attention on the workings of the liver. We are constrained to enjoy ourselves among a limited range of stimuli.

ANALYSIS AND INFERENCE

We have seen that we are sensitive to certain potentially useful sources of information about the world. The fact that we can detect only some features of the world and not others by itself helps us to keep the information which we gain about the world highly concentrated in utility and low in nonessentials. We ignore most of the information available to us. Failure to use all the available information does not end here; as we will see, it happens throughout the perceptual process.

We are anything but passive registrars of the information we do let in. We are, instead, data processors and analysts. The way we receive visual or auditory information, for example, is not at all analogous to the recording of light patterns on a photographic plate, or sound energies on a recording tape. A much closer analogy is in the activities of a weatherman who takes data from weather stations throughout the world and from them makes a forecast of the local weather for tomorrow. In this analogy, perception corresponds not to the data acquired and written down about temperature readings here and there, but to the forecast itself. The oft-noted errors in forecasting makes the analogy even more apt. Our experiences—perceptions of the world—are not simply composites of sensation: they are our inferences as to what the world is like, based on extensive and sophisticated analyses.

Stimulus to rudimentary percept

Let us take, as an example, perception of the brightness of a small, brief spot of light. Suppose that a small flashlight bulb is illuminated for a few hundreths of a second in the dark at a great distance. What one sees, of course, is a flash of light. Now consider what happens if the length of the flash or its intensity is increased. In physical terms the total amount of energy that is emitted by the light bulb is a product of the intensity and the time during which it stays on. For brief flashes we preceive *only* the total amount of light. We cannot distinguish between short, bright flashes and longer dim flashes, so long as the total amount of light is constant. This is true, however, only for flashes of a duration of less than 1/10 second. Apparently, the perceptual apparatus we have evolved determines, for brief lights, only how much light was there and nothing else. This relation is called the *Bunsen Roscoe law*. It is illustrated in Figure 5–11.

What if in a dark room you were to see a very small light go on and off and then very soon afterward another small light go on and off

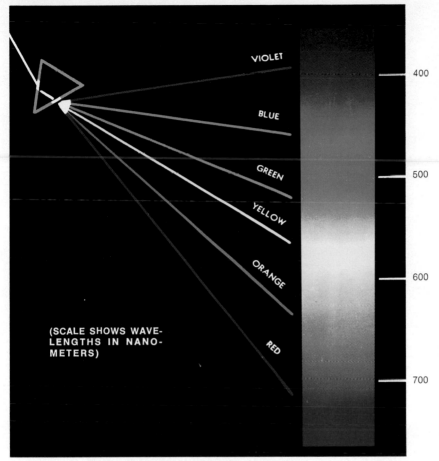

Figure 5.9 The visible spectrum. The colors are in the order produced by sunlight coming through a prism. See also Figure 5.2 on page 109.

Figure 5.12 A color afterimage. Stare at the colored dot for one minute; then stare at the empty box.

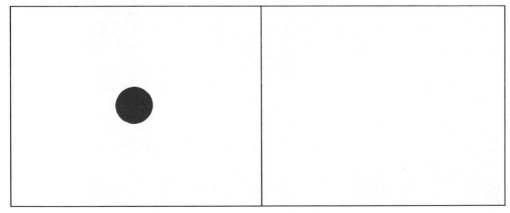

(a)

Figure 5.13 Simultaneous contrast effects. In (a), the arrows and the outside border are a continuously uniform gray, but the gray looks darker against the lighter background. The contrast effect would also appear if the yellow background were white and the blue were black, but the colors afford another simultaneous contrast effect as well: *induction* of complementary colors. The blue induces a bluish hue in the gray arrow in the yellow surround, and vice versa. .

Induction is particularly striking in (b), where the gray of the ring is uniform throughout. Is seeing still believing? If so, try placing a pencil or your finger along the line where the two colors meet in (a) and (b). (Courtesy of Inmont Corp.)

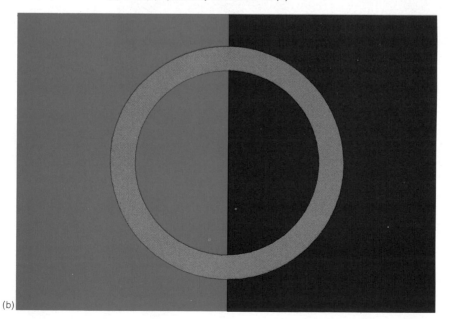

(b)

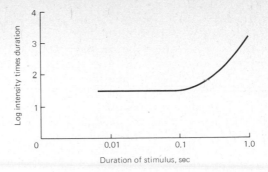

FIGURE 5-11

Absolute threshold for perception of a small spot of light, in terms of the total energy (intensity × duration) as a function of the duration of the stimulus. Notice that below about 0.1 seconds, threshold is the same no matter what the duration, so long as the total energy is constant. This relation is called the Bunsen Roscoe law. (After Long, 1951)

nearby? You might reasonably infer that a single continuously illuminated light had moved from one position to another. In fact, as long as both the distance and the time between the two lights are sufficiently small, perception does not differentiate between the successive illumination of two neighboring lights and the motion of a single, continuously illuminated light from one point to another. This apparent motion—or *phi phenomenon* as it is technically known—is the basis for movies and television. In these media, depicted objects do not move steadily from one point to another, but rather jump rapidly from one position to a slightly different position to another slightly different position, etc. However, our perception of them is exactly the same as it would be for a smoothly moving object. It is as if it simply does not matter to us whether an object is moving smoothly or in rapid discrete jumps; we make the same unconscious interpretation of the world in either case; our experience of the event is identical.

Nothing that we perceive is a 1-to-1 reflection of the physical energies which impinge upon us; all percepts bear the stamp of the peculiar mechanisms by which information is processed in perception. Should any further proof of this be needed, it is to be found in the fact that we often see things that are not actually there. An easily demonstrated example is the *visual afterimage*. If you stare steadily at the red spot in Figure 5-12 for one minute and then stare at the adjacent blank white area, you will see a color which is perfectly real in your perception but which does not correspond to any reality in the physical stimulus. You might think that this phenomenon is simply an imperfection in the perceptual mechanism, a malfunction occurring under unusual circumstances. But colored afterimages are but part of a broader set of phenomena, the *color contrast effects*, which have an important role in normal color perception. Virtually never do we see pure colored light; rather, we are exposed to a world of contrasting hues. Our perception of the hue of an object is based not only on the wave lengths of light that it reflects, but equally on the contrast between that light and light reflected by surrounding objects. A tree appears green either in bright sunlight or in artificial light, yet the actual wave lengths of light involved are quite markedly different. To see the green as green despite such variations, we rely on the fact that the relative greenness of a leaf as compared to trunks of trees remains the same. The visual system is specifically adapted to determine the color of objects from their relative rather than absolute wave lengths. This is why when you put on dark glasses, you still see the world in fairly natural hues.

A very general feature of perception is that it is concerned primarily with changes and contrasts, not with steady states. That this is a very basic and primitive fact of animal life can be seen from a knowledge of the workings of the frog's eye. The frog apparently *sees* only small moving objects (flies), large moving objects (predators), and very large areas of contrast between light and dark (sky and water). His eye receives patterned light and focuses it onto a retina in much the same way as ours does, but the frog's visual system ignores almost all the information in that visual display, and makes use of only those aspects which are critical to his survival and which will not overload the capacity of his tiny brain. Although our brains are much larger and we seem to be capable of putting to use much more of the detail from the world around us, we too make use of only that fraction of the information impinging upon us that is important to our adaptation.

Humans, as well as frogs and probably all other animals, are much more apt to notice a moving object than a still one. Look out at a sea of faces in an auditorium, and your attention will be caught by someone who is waving his arm. A hunter intently watching a bushy slope may completely fail to spot a deer until it moves.

Another form of visual change is spatial contrast. Line drawings that give only outlines can often communicate the perceptual essence of an object or person to us almost as well as a photograph that contains all the nuances of shading. The fact is that we are much more sensitive to and make special use of the edges of objects—the places where there are sharp discontinuities between one area and another. It is changes in stimulation, either in motion or in simultaneous contrast, which are most important in perception. Indeed, our eyes are always in motion; even during a "steady" gaze the eye drifts involuntarily. There are also small oscillations known as tremors. An image that does not move on the retina is not seen. For example, there are blood vessels laced over the surface of your retina. Do you see them? If a visual pattern, such as an alphabetic letter, is presented to the eye in such a way that its position on the retina does not change at all—this can be done through a system of mirrors, one of which is attached to a contact lens which moves with the eye—the object will disappear completely. If the letter is removed for a brief interval and then replaced, it is seen again for a short while, then disappears again. We are sensitive primarily to changes.

Another aspect of this relativity in perception is the phenomenon of *adaptation*. Perhaps the most familiar form is dark adaptation. It is important to be adjusted, in visual reactions, to the level of light available at a given time.

There are also adaptation phenomena with respect to other sensory modalities. We have already referred to the color contrast phenomena of afterimages (Figure 5–12), and to *simultaneous color contrast*, which is illustrated in Figure 5–13. And we have mentioned adaptation in heat sensitivity. There are also adaptation and contrast phenomena in taste; for example, what tastes salty depends on the level of salt to which one is accustomed. The phenomenon is exceedingly general. No matter whether one tries to taste for the strength of coffee flavor, to tell the weight of a sack of potatoes, to judge the loudness of a rock-and-roll band, or to evaluate the beauty of a woman's face, all one's judgments will vary enormously as a function of the prior adaptation level.

Being sensitive only (or mostly) to changes is one way in which an animal can markedly reduce the amount of information it needs to deal with. Once a thing has been perceived and behavior has been appropriately adjusted, that thing can usually be safely ignored until it changes in some further way.

An even more direct way of admitting only relevant information is found in the phenomenon of *selective attention*. Perhaps the most familiar human example is the so-called *cocktail party phenomenon*. If you are in a room with a large number of people all talking at once, you are faced with the problem of too much simultaneous information. You can't possibly listen to all the conversations at once. But you are able to concentrate your attention on the conversation in which you are engaged. And, what is more striking, you can suddenly catch a fragment of conversation behind you, and, while looking at someone who is speaking to you, begin to follow the other conversation instead. This is a very dramatic and useful ability. And it is another way in which we make sensory data analyzable by reducing it.

Higher-order characteristics of percepts

The object of perception, of course, is to gain information about the nature of objects and events in the world. Not only must the information that is received be reduced to a manageable amount, but also it must somehow be combined and organized so that conclusions can be drawn from it. We want to know where things are, what their shape is, what they are, where they are going, and what they seem to be trying to do. Let us examine briefly some examples of the way in which sensory input can give rise to higher-order abstractions.

Take, for example, the question of how we determine the distance of an object. Consider first the way in which this is accomplished visually. There are many cues in the retinal image which are sometimes, but not always, correlated with the distance of objects. One of these is *size*. Recall that, in general, the farther away an object is, the smaller is the retinal pattern that corresponds to it. Thus, using the size of the retinal pattern as a cue, one can infer the distance of a familiar object whose real size is known. Other cues for depth perception are contrast, parallax, interposition, texture density, and stereoscopic effects.

Contrast as a distance cue arises from the fact that distant objects transmit to us less light than do close objects, and consequently they appear somewhat more hazy. This is because the atmosphere absorbs some of the light. The atmosphere also scatters light, and absorbs its wave lengths differentially, thus, for example, making distant objects appear bluish.

Parallax refers to the fact that when one moves, the movement of the retinal image of a distant object is less than that of a close object. Fixate your finger and move it laterally in front of one eye, first a few

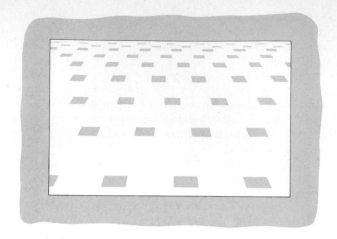

inches away, then at arm's length. Note the relation between your finger and the objects in the background behind it as it moves. The distant objects appear to move more rapidly relative to your finger when it is close. This is an important cue to its distance from you.

Interposition refers to the fact that a portion of an object that is behind some other object cannot be seen. If you can see only a part of one person and the whole of another, the second may be standing in front of the first.

Texture density is illustrated in Figure 5–14. The textures of things which are distant look much finer than those of objects which are closer.

Stereoscopic effects occur in visual systems having two eyes that can look at the same object at the same time. The image of an object which is presented to one eye is not identical to that presented to the other eye. Again hold up a finger in front of your face and look at it first with one eye and then with the other. There is a difference between the two images. Now look at your finger with both eyes. The two images fuse—you do not see the two separate images, although the "pictures" on your two retinae are obviously different. The visual system is arranged in such a way that it produces a single percept from the two disparate images and, moreover, yields from their differences an added dimension of the percept which we experience as depth. While stereoscopic effects are important cues for depth, particularly in judgment of relative depth of fairly close objects, they are not the only, or in everyday life the most significant, indicators of distance. This is clearly demonstrated by the fact that one-eyed individuals function in an essentially normal manner. The other cues are ordinarily sufficient.

Another interesting aspect of the process of perceptual analysis is that certain relations or patterns are perceived as the same despite the difference in their absolute values. For example, a melody is perceived as the same melody no matter in which octave or key it is played. As long as certain relations between the notes are maintained, the experience of the melody is maintained. This kind of phenomenon occurs also in visual perception of meaningful patterns. If you look at a letter of the alphabet, a *T* for example, you will see it as a *T* no matter whether it is a very tiny letter in a textbook or a huge letter on a wide movie screen, and no matter whether it is upright, tilted to the left or right, or even upside down. For a person to see something as a *T* it is not the absolute pattern of a particular set of lines in a particular place that is critical but, rather, something about the relation between the lines. The basic process by which this is accomplished is unknown. No one even knows how it *could* be done; attempts to construct electronic or computer systems that perform such feats have so far been unsuccessful. It is clear that what is involved is an extremely powerful analysis of the incoming information.

Constancies

One of the most important tasks for a perceiving individual is maintaining the constancy of objects. In order to behave adaptively we must recognize an object as the same object despite changes in its orientation, its distance, the amount of light which is falling on it, and so forth; the lion must still look like a lion, not a pussycat, as he walks away into the dark jungle. A lump of coal in bright sunlight reflects more light than does a piece of white paper in a dimly lit room. And yet the lump of coal must be seen as black in both instances and the white paper as white. The preserved integrity of objects and their characteristics, despite changes in the absolute values of the physical stimuli by which we know them, is called psychological or perceptual *constancy*.

While there are constancies in our perception of almost every aspect of the world, including color, size, and distance, some of the clearest examples are to be found in the perception of shape and brightness. We have already referred to one of the most compelling instances of *brightness constancy*, the fact that grey objects are perceived as grey almost independently of the amount of light reflected. Once again this is an example of the relativity of perceptual processes. In this case the relativity gives rise to a constancy. We judge grey not by the absolute value of the light it reflects but by the contrast between that light and the light reflected by other objects. Probably much the same thing applies, although in a more complicated way, to the other constancies.

Shape constancy can be appreciated very clearly when one considers the perception of rectangles. Look at a rectangular object somewhere about you—a book, a door frame, or a window. We never have any problems in recognizing that they are rectangles and not, say, irregular trapezoids. However, if you consider the shape of the images projected onto the retina, you will realize that almost never is an image rectangular. The retinal image of a rectangle is almost always a trapezoid in which the distant side is shorter than the near side and the remaining two sides are not parallel. These are the familiar facts of perspective which are represented in realistic drawings. That we do easily tell a rectangle from a lopsided trapezoid in any position must mean that we unconsciously make the necessary "calculations" to determine that the distortions are exactly what would be expected if the object being seen were indeed a rectangle.

FIGURE 5–15
Which line looks longer?
Measure them. This is known
as the Muller-Lyer illusion.

The same observation holds for the other constancies. We see red
as red, no matter what the light, in an immediate way which does not
involve saying to oneself, "That looks not quite red, but it must be because the light falling on it is green." Such inferences are, of course,
completely unconscious; they are made by the automatic processing of
the perceptual analyzing systems. The point bears repeating that when we
say perceptual "inference" we are not talking about conscious reasoning, but about the inferential or interpretive results of perceptual processing.

Illusions

One of the most compelling demonstrations that perception consists
of inferences or predictions about the world, rather than direct reflec-
tions of it, is that the predictions are sometimes quite wrong. Look at
Figure 5–15. Compare the center portions of the lines. Which looks
longer? Now measure them.

When contrast effects in brightness (Figure 5–13a) or size (Figure
5–16a) occur in "abnormal" or "unusual" arrangements, they can give
rise to illusions. Figures 5–16b through e show several other famous illusions.

In general, illusions are created by the arrangement of normally
valid cues in such a manner that they lead to an invalid unconscious
inference. The existence of such illusions is compelling evidence that
perception yields only inferences about features of the world rather than
a direct report, since we do not see the lines, angles, and brightness as
they actually are. Illusions are also compelling evidence for the completely automatic, mechanistic, and unconscious nature of such inferences, since we are so surprised to discover our errors.

Organization and reorganization

Objects with no strong physical relation to each other are nonetheless
seen as having a certain amount of geometrical organization. Two lines
close together are seen as a more or less unified pair. A row of dots is
seen as a line, not simply as unrelated dots. Another form of perceptual organization that is clearly imposed on the physical stimulus by the
observer is the *figure-ground* relation. A famous illustration of a figure-

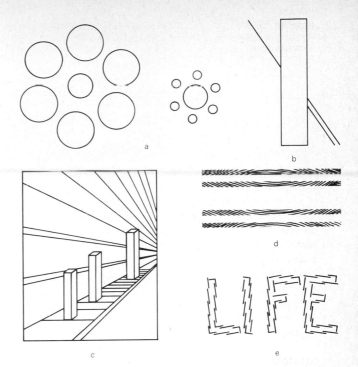

FIGURE 5-16
Some visual illusions. In *b* which oblique line on the right is the prolongation of the one on the left? *d* is from actual photos of end grain of boards.

a

b

c

d

e

ground relation in shown in Figure 5–17. As one looks at this picture, two perceptions alternate rapidly: the white portion can be seen as a vase or the black portion can be seen as two faces. Obviously it is not the physical stimulus that is changing, but how we see it.

If one accepts that perception consists of a complex process of data analysis, abstraction, and unconscious inference about real objects and events, then it is natural to ask whether this complicated system can be modified through experience. For example, if you wear glasses that distort the visual scene in some bizarre way—such as by turning everything upside down or into a mirror image—what happens? When you first reach for something, you miss, but by trial and error you soon learn to reach properly. What has happened? Did you find out where things really are by reaching out and touching them? Did you then use this tactile-kinesthetic information to correct your visual processing, so that the world actually *looks* normal again, despite the optical distortion? In fact, just the opposite often happens. When prism glasses displace the image of a person's hand several inches to the right of where it really is, he begins to feel that that's where it really is. The change appears to be in the kinesthetic system, not in the visual one. If the person shuts his eyes, eliminating visual stimulation, and is asked to point at his adapted hand with the other one (which he has never seen through prisms), he will point several inches too far right. One experiment by Harris and Harris (see Rock & Harris, 1967) revealed an even more striking effect. After wearing reversing glasses that made his hand appear

FIGURE 5–17
An illustration of the figure-
ground relation.

to move left-to-right when it was really moving right-to-left, the subject often wrote letters backward when blindfolded, yet felt that he was
writing them correctly. In other situations, however, it is not so clear
that what changes is the kinesthetic perception of the positions of the
limbs, head, or eyes; real reorganization in the processing of visual information may sometimes occur. What is certain is that the human system as a whole can succeed in reestablishing normal behavior even when
the various senses are providing conflicting information.

A related question is to what extent perceptual processes are built
into organisms by virtue of birth, and to what extent they are acquired
through experience. Clearly, a percept of the identity of a meaningful
object, such as "a book," is necessarily based on prior experience. Moreover, some quite fundamental qualities of perception are influenced
by experience. For example, the illusion shown in Figure 5–18 is apparently seen much more readily by people who live in houses with square
walls, floors, windows, and so forth, than it is by people who live in
round huts and who do not have such things as windows or builders'
squares. On the other hand, even such people who rarely see rectangular
objects do see this illusion—it is only that they do not see it as readily
or as strongly. This illustrates both that very strongly unconscious
perceptual phenomena are to some extent influenced by the meanings
of the objects seen—meanings acquired over a lifetime of experience—
and also that many perceptions do not depend on experience. It has
become increasingly clear that there is no simple answer to the question
whether perceptual skills are either learned or innate. Rather one must
ask to what extent they are present at birth, and to what extent they
result from physical development or experience. Some details of this
interesting problem will be discussed in the chapter on developmental
psychology.

JUDGMENT, CHOICE, AND RECOGNITION

In this section we will consider three related questions about the results
of the process of perception. The first of these concerns the relation
between physical measurements of stimuli observed and the experience
of the observer. We will discuss the surprisingly regular transformation
made by an observer in going from physical energy to experienced

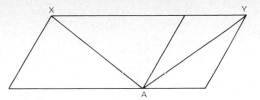

qualities and quantities. The second question concerns the way in which the judgment or inference of what has or has not been seen depends on the biases of the observer and on his expectations as to the likelihood of different events. The third question is how a person imbues perceptions with meaning, that is, relates what he is seeing now to what he has learned about such events in the past.

Psychophysics

In a dark room turn on one 25-watt light bulb. Now turn on another 25-watt light bulb. Does the brightness of the room increase as much as you go from one bulb to two as it did from no bulbs to one? Clearly it does not. And yet the amount of light energy has doubled. The experienced brightness increases as the physical energy increases, but not proportionately. In general a given amount of increase in a physical stimulus gives rise to relatively less increase in the corresponding psychological experience. If human observers are shown lights with a variety of brightnesses, and are asked to assign a number to each representing how bright it appears, a function such as that shown in Figure 5–19 is generated. The ordinate (vertical axis) of this graph is the magnitude of the reported psychological experience; the abscissa (horizontal axis) is the magnitude of the event in physical energy units. This particular curve is represented by the equation:

$$\text{brightness} = k \times (\text{light intensity})^{.33}$$

The equation is simply a concise way of saying that if one light is physically eight times as intense as another, it will appear two times as bright, regardless of what physical intensity you start with: 200 watts looks twice as bright as 25 watts does, 600 watts looks twice as bright as 75 watts does, and so on. In other words, a given ratio of physical magnitudes always gives rise to the same ratio of psychological magnitudes.

This ratio principle, expressed by psychophysical equations similar to the one above, turns out to hold for judgments of such diverse things as the strength of flavor of coffee, the intensity of pain from electric shock or heat, the size of a circle of light, the weight of an iron pipe being lifted, the sweetness of a sugar solution, the pitch of a musical tone, the loudness of a motor—in short for almost everything about which one can make a dimensional quantitative judgment.

The general mathematical function relating physical and psy-

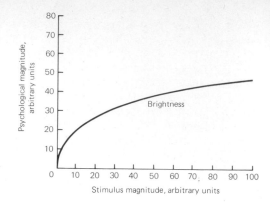

FIGURE 5-19
Psychophysical function for
brightness. (After Stevens, 1961)

Psychological magnitude, arbitrary units

Brightness

Stimulus magnitude, arbitrary units

chological events is called the *psychophysical law*. This law (sometimes called the *Stevens power law*) is:

$$S = kI^n$$

S stands for the sensation; *I* stands for the intensity of the physical stimulus measured in physical units; *k* is simply a constant that adjusts the units of measurement; the exponent, *n*, is a constant which depends on what stimulus dimension is being judged (0.3 for judgments of loudness or brightness, 1.2 for pitch, and so forth). An equation like this is called a *power function*, since the intensity in physical units must be raised to the power *n* to yield the psychological magnitude. If *n* were one-half, for example, the formula would be read as: the psychological magnitude is proportional to the square root of the physical magnitude. But no matter what the power, the formula always implies that equal ratios of magnitudes in the physical dimension give rise to equal ratios of magnitudes in psychological experience.

The underlying relation expressed by the psychophysical law is made use of in many engineering applications. For instance, the unit used to measure sound, the *decibel*, is one whose basis is not physical intensity but rather the logarithm of the physical intensity. The logarithmic scale was derived from an earlier form of the psychophysical law, Fechner's law, which stated that the psychological experience Ψ was proportional to the logarithm of the physical magnitude.

The psychophysical law gives a good account of the relation between physical energies and experience, particularly when the psychophysical judgments are made in appropriate ways. These consist either of direct assignment of a number to the intensity or magnitude of an experience—which is called *magnitude estimation*—or of procedures known as *fractionation* or *doubling*. In these latter procedures an observer is given a reference stimulus, say a tone of a certain loudness, and then allowed to adjust a second stimulus until it appears either half as intense (fractionation) or twice as intense (doubling) as the reference stimulus. Fractionation, doubling, and magnitude-estimation methods give equivalent results, all yielding a very good fit to the psychophysical law. There are other ways of making psychophysical judgments. Also, there are some sensory attributes that do not yield such a good fit to the psychophysical law, but the deviations are small enough that we need not consider them here.

The relation expressed by the psychophysical law appears to hold not only for simple sensory experiences, but also for more abstract judgments such as the utility of money. The psychological difference between $10,000 and $10,001 (what economists call its marginal utility) is not as great as the psychological difference between $1 and $2. A saving of a few cents on a tube of toothpaste may be quite noticeable, but a saving of a few cents on an automobile will be psychologically insignificant, although the "physical" magnitude is the same. Similarly, tax of $500 on an income of $1,000 seems exorbitant, while the same $500 tax on an income of $20,000 does not. Unless the psychophysical law for tax rates has an exponent of exactly 1, the painfulness of a tax will not match the *percentage* of income which it represents. Our present income-tax laws suggest that to create as much of a burden for a man earning $30,000 as for one earning $10,000, the tax for the former must be a much larger percentage of his income. This is equivalent to a psychophysical function with an exponent of less than 1.

Signal detection

As we have already mentioned, a person's report that he sees or does not see a given event reflects not only his sensory abilities, but also his bias to detect or not detect the event. We would like to have a deeper understanding of the way in which a person combines sensitivity and expectations or motivations in arriving at inferences about what is going on in the world. A rather elegant theory has recently been proposed to describe this process. It is a little difficult to describe rigorously, but is important enough that some idea of its basic elements is essential to understanding the psychology of perception.

Let us begin with an informal, more-or-less intuitive description of this *signal-detection theory*. Let us say that you are trying to decide whether a badly reproduced photograph in a newspaper is a picture of your cousin Jake. Photographs vary tremendously in the extent to which they capture the familiar aspects of a person's face. One hundred photographs of your cousin would differ greatly in how much evidence they provided that they really were pictures of Jake. In other words, you expect, in looking at a photograph, that the evidence will sometimes be quite good and sometimes be quite bad. Now let us consider the task of trying to separate 100 photographs, badly reproduced but actually pictures of your cousin, from 100 similar photographs of someone else. The 100 photographs of your cousin would include some which were obviously him, a large number that might or might not be him, and an additional small number that didn't look like him at all. Of the 100 photographs of someone else, there would be some that were obviously not Jake, a large number that were probably not Jake but might be, and a few that looked just like him. We depict this situation in Figure 5–20a. Here we show two frequency distributions. The ordinate in such a diagram shows the relative frequency of each of the events indicated on the

FIGURE 5-20
Two overlapping normal distributions. In the explanation of signal detection theory given in the text, the solid curve on the right represents a distribution of positive instances (actual pictures of Jake), while the dashed curve on the left represents negative instances (pictures of other people). Signal detection theory is based on the idea that there is always a distribution of values for real signals and a distribution of values for false signals — noise — and that the detection problem consists of deciding which distribution any one event comes from.

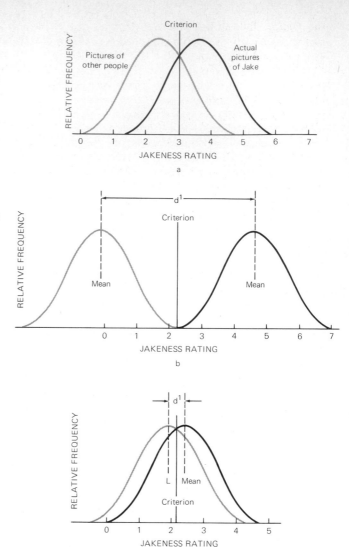

abscissa. (For an explanation of how to interpret a frequency distribution see Chapter 11.) Now let us assume that you put all the pictures into a box and pulled out one of them at random. How would you decide whether it was or was not of Jake? Essentially you would try to decide which of the piles it had come from. You could do this formally by giving the picture a rating between 0 and 7 on Jakeness, consulting the graph, and asking how likely it was that it came from the Jake pile and how likely it was that it came from the non-Jake pile. Suppose in addition that you adopted a strategy of deciding it was a picture of Jake if the rating you gave it was greater that 4. We can see from the figure that almost none of the non-Jake pictures exceeds such a rating. Consequently if you refused to believe it was Jake unless it had at least a 4 rating you would almost never make errors of commission, that is, you would almost never say a picture that was not of Jake *was* a picture of Jake. On the other hand, a fair number of pictures from the actual Jake pile have ratings of less than 4. Consequently you would be quite likely to reject a picture that had come from that pile. What if you moved your criterion to the left and said that you would declare any picture with a rating higher than 2 to be a picture of Jake? You can easily see that this would result in fewer errors in which pictures were judged not to be of Jake when they were, but more errors in which pictures were judged to be of Jake when they were not.

A wide variety of situations in which an event is to be detected can be represented in this way. Telling whether one heard a given tone, or saw a light go on, or if a particular word occurred in a passage can all be described as a receiver trying to judge whether the actual event really was or was not the one he was looking or listening for. An important assumption of the theory is that non-events often give rise to experiences indistinguishable from those caused by the real thing. Thus, over an imperfect intercom, a person listening for a particular signal will, although that signal doesn't occur, nevertheless hear various noises, some of which may sound like the signal. By analogy to this situation, the non-events which can be confused with a signal are called *noise* even, for example, when they consist of background lights in a visual detection problem. Thus, in general, signal detection theory is concerned with a decision whether an event was signal or merely noise.

According to this theory, the detection of a signal will depend on two things. First, it will depend on what the distributions of possible signals and noise are like. If, in our example, all the pictures of Jake were unmistakably Jake and all the pictures of other people were unmistakably not Jake, a situation illustrated in Figure 5–20b, then one would have only to set a criterion somewhere between the two distributions and no mistake would ever be made. On the other hand, if the quality of photography was so poor that the pictures of Jake had a distribution very much like that of the pictures of other people, as is shown in Figure 5–20c, then there would be no place where one could put a criterion that would give much more than 50 percent accuracy. Thus the first factor in the detection problem is the distance between the two distributions (which is usually taken as the distance between their means and called d'). If the distributions are far apart (d' large) as they are in Figure 5–20b, the detection can be made with great accuracy, while if they are close together (d' small) as they are in Figure 5–20c, it cannot be.

The second factor influencing detection outcomes is the place at which the criterion is set (usually called β). If the criterion is not set at exactly the place that best separates the two distributions, accuracy will suffer. This is easily seen when one considers what would happen if the criterion was very far toward one extreme or the other. In that case the judgment would almost always be the same no matter which picture you actually drew. Where the criterion is set will determine the frequency of each of the two possible kinds of error. If a stringent criterion is set, the signal will seldom be judged present when it is absent, but will often be judged absent when it is actually present. If the criterion is lax, the opposite will result, i.e., there will be many errors of commission (false alarms), but few of omission. The setting of a criterion can be influenced by many things. If, in our example, the newspaper was one from a foreign country in which Jake had never been, then it would be expedient to set one's criterion very stringently (far to the right), and accept as a true picture of Jake only one that was utterly conclusive in its resemblance. On the other hand, if the picture was taken from a newspaper published in his locality, and Jake was a common subject for the newspaper's photographers, then it would make more sense to place the criterion leniently (far to the left), so that in guessing that any picture looking even remotely like Jake *was* a picture of him, one would stand a good chance of being right.

Signal-detection theory is a formal mathematical expression of these kinds of ideas. It was first developed for electronic engineering problems. In its application to perception, the theory presumes that all perceptual input is subject to a great deal of variability. (One reason is that nervous transmission in the body is not perfect.) Consequently, even on occasions when there actually is a signal the experience is not always the same. Moreover, on those occasions when one is looking for a signal and it does not occur, there is also a variety of different experiences. Thus some experiences when the signal is actually there may be the same as some experiences when it is not (as happens, for example, if the observer is blinking when a brief visual signal occurs). The theory states that an observer judges the presence or absence of a given sensory event by determining whether his present experience exceeds a cut-off point, or criterion, (β). Sensitivity, in this theory, depends on the difference between the kinds of experiences the observer has with and without the signal. If the distribution of experiences with the signal is very different from the distribution of experiences without it, then the system is very sensitive. The role of the response criterion can easily be seen. If it is important to detect a signal when it is there (for example, if the signal indicates an approaching enemy aircraft), but unimportant whether there are false alarms, then the criterion can be set leniently. On the other hand, if it is exceedingly unlikely that a signal will actually occur, an observer can increase his average accuracy by setting the criterion strictly and guessing that it is not there unless the evidence is very strong.

Given a set of data on judgments actually made by a human observer, it is possible to use this theory to describe his mode of operation with considerable precision. Perceptual performance is described by the two factors, the sensitivity—d^1—and the criterion—β—of the observer. The theory thus makes it possible to compare true sensitivities in different situations, independent of observer bias.

Recognition

From what we have just seen, it is apparent that memory of the kind of events that should be interpreted as signal rather than noise may serve as the baseline for detection judgments. Reference to the remembered implication of sensory events becomes of even more import when we consider the perception of such things as familiar faces, letters and numerals, or words. Clearly, in recognizing a word, for example, we do not see it simply as a set of funny-looking lines and patterns on a page. Rather, with familiar words we immediately perceive a word as a word. Since this ability to perceive whole words as meaningful units of language is obviously acquired through long commerce with the world—it is not a thing which young children can do—perception in this instance must require a comparison of the stimulus input to some stored record of previous inputs. Thus, in reading a word one is in essence inferring from a complicated visual pattern the presence of a thing which one has seen many times before and which has often been associated with a certain meaning.

We are now getting into a realm in which perception and memory are indistinguishable. Perception of words, recognition of faces, and so forth, while having the same introspective immediacy as the perception of noises and lights, clearly are examples of retrieval of information from memory. This is an area which we will discuss further in Chapter 8—although not very much further since precious little is known. For the time being it is sufficient to note that the product of the process of perception is a consciousness of an object, meaningful occurrence, or pattern in the world—an abstract result of a great deal of sophisticated processing, analysis, and unconscious inference.

TOPICS DISCUSSED IN CHAPTER 5

1. The definition and nature of thresholds.

2. The nature and range of physical energies to which we respond, and why it makes adaptive sense for us to respond to what we respond to.

3. The degree to which we are sensitive to various kinds of stimulation; by light, sound, etc.

4. Some of the means by which physical energy is converted to sensation; with emphasis on certain exemplary aspects of vision and hearing.

5. That sensory input is analyzed and interpreted to produce unconscious inferences about potentially important aspects of the environment:
(a) in perceiving brightness, duration, movement, color, and distance
(b) in detecting change rather than continuity
(c) in attending selectively
(d) in maintaining the perceptual constancy of objects despite changes in the information we receive about them
(e) in making incorrect inferences (illusions)

6. The relation between the physical magnitude of stimulation and the magnitude of the corresponding psychological experience; the psychophysical law.

7. The theory of signal detection, and the separate roles of sensitivity and response criterion in deciding whether something happened.

SUGGESTED READINGS

There are a number of solid and readable books on sensation and perception. Here are some.

1. *On sensory and perceptual processes in general:*

Mueller, C. G. *Sensory psychology.* Englewood Cliffs, N.J.: Prentice-Hall, 1965, is a particularly clear and authoritative introduction.

Hochberg, J. E. *Perception.* Englewood Cliffs, N.J.: Prentice-Hall, 1964, presents a lot of information about perception in a succinct fashion.

Cornsweet, T. *Visual perception.* New York: Academic Press, 1970, is an informative and interesting treatment of the science of sight.

Gregory, R. I. *Eye and brain.* New York: McGraw-Hill, 1966, has, among other good things, some fascinating illustrations of perceptual phenomena and some exciting ways of making them comprehensible.

2. *For a deeper and more rigorous treatment of signal detection theory, a good source is:*

Coombs, C. H., Dawes, R. & Tversky, A. *Mathematical psychology: an elementary introduction.* Englewood Cliffs, N.J.: Prentice-Hall, 1970.

SIX
Motivation, emotion, and consciousness

In the last chapter we discussed the means by which information about the world is gained. We now want to turn our attention to action and experience, to what it is that determines what a person will do and feel. Let us be clear at the outset that behavior is largely a product of what we have previously learned to do in a given situation. Nonetheless, there is a variety of factors determining how we act and feel on any one occasion which are not directly matters of learning, but of "the way we are built," of our inherited structure, of our momentary needs, desires, and fears, and of turmoils and changes in our internal states. We will start by considering those forms of behavior and experience which seem most primitive: those having to do with unlearned patterns of reaction, need, and feelings. We will then discuss ways in which behavior is modified by temporary shifts in needs and internal states. Finally we will turn our attention to some of the ways in which behavior is related to goals, values, and incentives.

First a word about the meaning and proper use of the term *motive*. In common parlance, and sometimes in psychological writings, people use this word to mean simply "why it is that people do something." Unfortunately this practice can lead to a tendency to give a name to a bit of behavior and presume to have explained it by so doing. There is the famous story of a mother who takes her child to a psychologist to complain that he is wetting his bed. After much deep and impressive deliberation, the psychologist says, "Madam, your child has enuresis." The lady says, "Oh, is that what's wrong!" and goes away delighted to have had the problem explained to her with such erudition. Now, of course, *enuresis* means incontinence, an inability to keep from urinating at inappropriate times. The psychologist has simply given a fancier name to the behavior which he was asked to explain. We must vigorously avoid this kind of trap in dealing with behavior.

In this chapter we will be talking about motives. At times we will use this term in almost the manner we have just decried. That is, we will describe a certain kind of behavior and assign to it the name of a motive. But we will use such names only as shorthand descriptions, not as explanations. Thus when we say that an animal is hungry, we mean nothing more than that he is in a state of food deprivation that can be expected to lead him to perform a variety of actions which, in general, lead to food and are terminated by the receipt of food. Similarly, if we say that a man has a strong need or drive for sex, we do not intend to imply that anything about his behavior has been explained by such a statement, but imply merely that a large and perhaps varied set of behaviors related to sex is carried out with high frequency by the individual in question.

What we eventually want to do is *explain* tendencies to behave in a certain way, not merely describe them. The explanations that we seek lie in the mechanisms and sources which generate behavior. We wish to know what factors tend to produce the kinds of behavior summarized by such labels as *hunger, sexual desire,* and *anger.* We will look for these in the control of behavior by reflexes and ready-made responses that have been built into animals and men by their long evolutionary history. We will look for them in the influences of the state in which the animal finds himself—whether he is low on food, has a high hormone level of one kind or another in his bloodstream, has been aroused by exciting stimuli, is awake or asleep, and so forth. We will look for them in desired states—the ones which tend to terminate behavior and to be associated with pleasure and healthy states of being. We will consider, in turn, innate or instinctual behavior patterns, state-determined behavior and experience, and the process of maintenance of adaptive equilibria called *homeostasis.*

INNATE BEHAVIOR PATTERNS

One of the ways in which animals can be adapted to the requirements of their environments is to be built that way—to come equipped by heredity with behavior patterns that allow them to react in appropriate ways to the demands of life. The aspects of life for which hereditary behavior patterns are appropriate are, by and large, those which make the same demands on all members of a given species. For example, swallowing when a pleasant-tasting food is being masticated, spitting when stimulated by a noxious flavor, or moving the eyes so that both focus on the same point of light are things that all humans must do. It makes sense, then, for such primitive reactions to be "wired in." There are, in fact, a great many reaction patterns in all animals, including man, which are there by virtue of genetic constitution.

It is interesting to note in passing that for a long time in psychology there was a rather strong bias against the explanation of behavior, particularly human behavior, on the basis of inherited characteristics. A part of this bias stemmed from a mistaken egalitarian premise that if all men are born equal it must mean that all men are born without behavioral tendencies, and their characteristics filled in by experience and learning. In part, the bias toward environmentalism was based on a feeling that complicated behavior could not be inherited because it was incomprehensible how a complicated nervous system could be wired up ahead of time. This argument is fallacious, however. Clearly the nervous system *does* carry out its functions and therefore it is clearly wired up *sometime*. It is no more obvious how this wiring up could be done through experience than how it could be done through genetics. In either case the fact that it is accomplished is an awesome mystery.

An important qualification has to be kept in mind as we discuss innate behavior patterns. There is probably never any such thing as a purely instinctive behavior pattern. Put very simply, animals begin experiencing as soon as they are born and continue to experience throughout their lives. It is manifestly impossible to observe any response—unless perhaps in the first few moments of life—which has not been colored by experience. Thus any piece of behavior is a compound of predispositions given by heredity, and embellishments and revisions added by environment. Such questions as whether a given behavior is inherited or learned cannot possibly be answered with a simple yes or no. On the other hand, it is possible to say to what extent and in what way some kinds of behavior are influenced by inheritance or by experience.

How would one go about finding out what influence heredity has on a given behavior? There are several ways. For one, if we observe that all animals of a given species, say all humans, have a certain behavior pattern which is fixed and invariable, then it is very likely that it is a result of their common genetic endowment. It is possible that a common set of ways of behaving could come from a common set of experiences. But if we look at people whose experiences differ widely, all the people in the world, for instance, and we find them acting in the same way, then we can be reasonably sure that the item of behavior in question is strongly influenced by heredity. Thus, upright posture and a bipedal gait seem clearly genetic. Another way is to study the effect of ancestry. If we find that a certain kind of behavior tends to be associated in identical twins—that is, if one of a pair of twins shows it the other does too—whereas it is not associated in fraternal twins or in ordinary siblings, we are prompted to infer that the item of behavior is heavily influenced by genetics. We saw such a case in the discussion of schizophrenia in Chapter 2. There are, of course, pitfalls in this approach. Identical twins are likely also to share similar environments. However, even this problem can be partially overcome by studying twins who were raised apart and comparing them with twins who were raised together.

One can also study the influence of genetics on behavior experimentally. If you were to take a large number of fruitflies, *Drosophila melanogaster*, commonly used in laboratory experiments in genetics,

Fruitflies, in this hypothetical
apparatus, enter at the end
marked "start." If they fly up,
they are allowed to reproduce;
if they fly down, they are not.
After many generations of this
kind of selection, offspring would
include mostly up-flying flies.

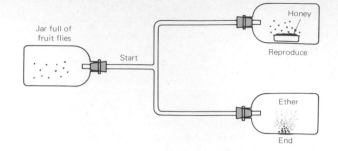

and breed them selectively for a trait in which they initially vary, you
could produce a line of fruitflies with an average behavior-character-
istic different from that of the original group. Such an experiment might
proceed as follows: You put fruitflies into an apparatus such as the one
shown in Figure 6–1 at the end marked "Start." At the junction, some
flies fly up and some fly down. Next, at the end of the lower path you
put a bottle filled with ether, which kills fruitflies. Now you allow several hundred flies to enter at the starting place and fly in whichever
direction, up or down, they wish. Say half of the flies fly up and half fly
down. This indicates that in the normal population of laboratory fruitflies half of them are up-fliers and half of them are down-fliers. Next,
you allow the ones that flew up to intermix and produce a new generation of fruitflies; while those that flew down sacrifice their lives to
science. Thus the only flies that are allowed to breed are those that have
already demonstrated a natural tendency to fly up. If there are genes
which control tendencies to such behavior in the fruitfly, you will have
produced a group of flies characterized by the possession of genes which
lead to up-flying—at least on the average. Therefore, you will expect
a second generation of such flies to have a much higher concentration
of such genes, and a greater tendency to fly up. Thus, if you take the
offspring of the up-flying flies and introduce them into the start end of
the tubes, you will expect not the original 50 percent, but perhaps 60
or 70 percent to fly upward. Again, you could allow only the up-flying
flies to interbreed. By doing this for several generations you would gradually produce a group of flies in which there is a higher and higher proportion of up-fliers.

This procedure would be a laboratory analog of the process of
natural evolution. Those animals that are best at surviving *and reproduc-
ing* in the environment in which they find themselves will tend to reproduce more of their own kind. After several generations more like them
will be found. The basic logic is simply that if a given kind of individual
produces more offspring, and offspring tend to be like their parents,
there will be more of those kinds of individuals in the world. Essentially
the very experiment just described has been done under careful laboratory control, as have a number of similar experiments selecting for other
characteristics of fruitflies, e.g., their tendency to fly toward light (see
Hirsch & Boudreau, 1958).

In addition, many similar experiments have been done with rats, mice, and other laboratory animals. There is a long list of behavioral characteristics which have been shown to be influenceable by artificial selection. Maze-learning ability, preference for particular temperatures, preference for particular salt or sugar concentrations, anxiety in a strange situation, susceptibility to seizures, and amenability to being trained to be friendly or ferocious are only a few examples. And it is common knowledge that various species of domesticated dogs and other animals have been bred to have desirable behavioral characteristics—for example, being easily trainable as hunters, or riding horses. Although there is no certain evidence, nor could there be, one would have to guess from the data on hand that almost any characteristic of behavior of an animal could be influenced by selective breeding.

It is worth noting at this point that the genetic determination of most behavioral traits so far studied by psychologists is quite complicated. While eye color in fruitflies (and sometimes in man) is determined by the possession of a single gene, inherited tendencies to learn mazes rapidly or to be intelligent are ordinarily polygenic—that is, they result from combinations of many different genes. In most cases we do not know what the actual route is between genetic differences and behavioral differences, but there are usually many possibilities. Genes can determine behavioral tendencies through a primary effect on endocrine gland function. For example, too much thyroid hormone produces hyperactive, irritable behavior while too little usually leads to mental and physical laziness. Of course, genetic differences also influence the growth and structure of the nervous system, and differences in the nervous system are obviously important to behavior. Perhaps the best understood genetic effect on behavior involves the mentally retarded state of phenylketonuria described in Chapter 4. In phenylketonuria a specific genetic failure results in the absence of an important enzyme whose lack leads to poisoning of the nervous system.

Certain general kinds of traits of animals seem to be given to them almost exclusively by inheritance and either cannot be affected by experience or, more likely, are usually not altered by the ordinary experiences which an animal has. Among these are certain behavior patterns which very young animals manifest. A young rat when placed on an inclined plane will crawl uphill. Moreover, he will choose to crawl uphill at a particular angle with respect to gravity. If the slope of the plane does not coincide with his preferred angle he will compensate by traversing the slope as he crawls up. Many species of young birds respond to special kinds of stimuli for feeding. For instance, a mother herring gull has a beak with a particular circular red marking. To this stimulus baby herring gulls respond by opening their mouths so that the mother can place food therein. The beak must be the right shape, and the spot the right color or the infant will not open up. Older animals often show similar specific reactions to so-called *releaser* stimuli in respect to important aspects of their adaptive behavior.

If we trace in a very rough way the phylogenetic progression of behavioral characteristics with which animal species have been endowed, we find gradually increasing complexity both in the stimuli to which animals react and in the behaviors with which they deal with the environment. The amoeba, a very primitive single-celled organism, comes equipped with rudimentary abilities to discriminate things in its world and to respond appropriately. If an amoeba comes in contact with a particle that it senses chemically to be a food—that is, something which if incorporated into the amoeba would be metabolically usable—it extends a pseudopod and wraps itself around the object. On the other hand, if the chemical sensitivity of its outer membrane detects a particle of dangerous material, the amoeba changes shape so as to draw away from the undesirable area of the world. Thus the amoeba has, essentially, two reactions to the world—to approach and to avoid.

We will see that the basic dichotomy between approach and avoidance remains throughout the progression of philogeny, but the manners of executing the actual acts of approach and escape become very much more sophisticated, as do the perceptual analyses on which the decisions about what response to make are based. However, what we are concerned with here is that these important perceptual abilities and responses can be given to the animal by birth. The complexity of perception and response which can be based on genetic inheritance increases markedly as more advanced animals are considered. The frog either approaches or avoids by either sticking out his tongue to catch a fly when one is close enough or by jumping into a pond when danger appears. However, the perceptual analysis involved is very sophisticated. The retina of the frog sends messages over the optic nerve to the brain only under certain circumstances. If there is a very small spot of dark moving rapidly up and down, a signal which is generated by a fly, the frog sticks out his tongue to catch a meal. The perceptual analysis required to respond only to a fast-moving object is a case of performing calculus. The retina of the frog must calculate the fact that the spot is moving and at an appropriate rate in order to be able to respond only if a fly-like object is in view. In other words, the frog has a sophisticated perceptual analyzer, the results of which he uses to decide among a very primitive set of alternative reactions.

Still more advanced animals also show complex response patterns which are clearly theirs by inheritance. One of the best examples is the communicative activity of honeybees. Honeybees live, of course, in a hive. Sometimes, when a single bee has been away from the hive foraging for juicy flowers from which to gather nectar and then returns to the hive, an astonishing thing happens. A whole swarm of other bees will leave in a beeline for the flower found by the original scout. How do they know where to go? The matter was studied in a brilliant set of seminaturalistic observations by the Austrian biologist, von Frisch (1954).[1] He replaced one side of a hive with a piece of glass so that he could watch. A returning scout often danced around in a sort of figure eight, as illustrated in Figure 6–2. The middle or zigzag portion of the figure, in which the bee wags its hindquarters vigorously, bears an angular re-

[1] There were, for a time, some doubts about the accuracy of von Frisch's conclusions, but these now seem to have been cleared up (see Gould, Henery, & MacLeod, 1970).

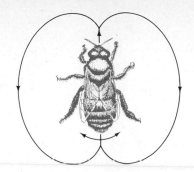

lation to the vertical dimension of the hive which is exactly the same as the angle formed by the sun, the hive, and the flower. Moreover, the rate at which the bee dances is inversely proportional to the logarithm of the distance of the flower. Here, then, we have an example of a very sophisticated response pattern which is given not by experience but by genetic endowment.

In summary, there is no reason why the most complicated kinds of perceiving and reacting cannot be based on genetic inheritance. There is no known limit to the complexities which can be passed on from generation to generation through the blueprint of the genes. Indeed, the complexity of the biochemistry and organization of the bodies of large animals is so staggering that we have no choice but to believe in an almost unlimited possibility for genetic specification. It is not the complexity of the behavior of advanced animals that requires learning, but the needed flexibility. We will return to these issues later.

What about humans? How much of human behavior is genetically determined? We find it hard to believe that much of it is, because the behavior we observe from day to day is so heavily encrusted with the effects of prior experience. This does not mean, however, that behind even the most highly learned behavior do not lie innate and necessary basic reaction patterns. For instance, there are those who believe, with considerable justification, that there is something in the inherited behavior pattern of humans which allows us to speak whereas no other animal can do so.

Certainly humans have a large number of reflex responses which are important to our welfare and clearly not the product of experience. We swallow, we blink, we withdraw our hands from hot objects. There are many tastes and smells which all humans, but not all other animals, find pleasant or noxious. It appears likely that the kinds of sounds, motions, and ways of being held that soothe a human baby are also given by heredity. There are undoubtedly many additional varieties of genetic influence on human behavior awaiting discovery.

STATE-DETERMINED BEHAVIOR AND EXPERIENCE

The same animal, even in the same situation, does not always behave the same way. A person will exhibit different patterns of behavior depending on whether he is tired, hungry, excited, angry, or contented.

Motivation,
emotion, and
consciousness
143

And, obviously, people act differently when they are asleep from how they act when they are awake. Exposed on different occasions to exactly the same events, a person will react in a way that depends on his level of excitement. And much behavior is determined by cycles of one sort or another, by the levels of hormones and other substances in the bloodstream, and by states induced by, for example, hypnosis or drugs.

Cycles

One of the more important cycles that affects behavior, as well as fundamental physiological functions, is the day-night or *diurnal* cycle. All animals and plants show pronounced variation in bodily functions over an approximately twenty-four hour period. Hormone levels, pulse rate, brain rhythms, and many important cellular chemical processes vary from high to low at fixed periods in each twenty-four hours. A flower opens its petals at certain times of day and not others. A hamster given an activity wheel will run at certain times of the day and rest at others. Ordinarily such cycles seem to be controlled by the light-dark cycle of the day. However the situation is not quite that simple. If a hamster is kept under a normal light-dark regime and then the lights are turned off permanently, the cycle does not cease. Rather, there continue to be distinct periods of activity and inactivity which recur approximately every 23 to 24 hours. These cycles eventually get out of phase with the light and dark in the world outside, but they do not disappear. If, after several months, the hamster is again put on a normal twenty-four hour light-dark cycle, the timing of the ups and downs becomes once again coordinated with the light-dark cycle in the world. Thus, it appears that the light-dark cycle does not directly influence the activity-inactivity cycle, but simply acts as a timing device which sets the point at which the animal's own internal cycle begins each day. Many biologists have spoken of such cycles as being controlled by an "internal clock." The internal clock appears to be of tremendous importance in the physiological economy of an animal. It is hypothesized that many of the physiological processes by which life is sustained must be coordinated in time. When a certain biochemical has been manufactured, certain others must be available for combination. Many different processes of the body must work together in the smooth running of the biochemical factory which the tissues constitute.

That human behavior is strongly influenced by the existence of an internal clock is attested to in many ways. For example, long distance jet travelers experience great difficulty in adjusting to new diurnal cycles. The difficulty is more severe than simply a lack of sleep. A person may feel quite uncomfortable for days, until his bodily cycles have come into pace with the new dark-light cycle. The time of day at which a person is accustomed to eat also seems to be strongly conditioned by the internal clock. If you are used to eating lunch at noon and for some reason or another don't, you will feel very hungry at about that time, even hungrier at 12:30 or 1:00 P.M., but then, remarkably, you will stop feeling so hungry by about 2:00 or 3:00 P.M. Your body certainly has not lost any need for food in the additional hour of fasting. An explanation is that habitual practice produces a cyclicality in the body's demand for food—a cyclicality controlled by the internal clock rather than by a state of depletion in the stomach, tissues, or blood. We have no idea how many aspects of behavior are influenced by diurnal cycles, but it is not unlikely that our behavior varies cyclically in many, many respects of which we are unaware.

Arousal

We all experience times when we are exceedingly alert and energetic, and other times when we are calm and lazy. When you are sitting comfortably in a chair looking out of the window and drowsing, your body and brain are operating at a slow pace. If at such a time an exciting event occurs, your whole state of being can change quite radically. The state of arousal can be measured in terms of changes in physiology and changes in nervous system activity. When you are very strongly aroused, as when under the necessity to flee a threatening situation, your body is sent into a state of "general alarm" (Selye, 1956). In this state the pulse beats faster, the blood circulation to the muscles increases at the expense of internal organs, breathing increases, and pupils dilate. A host of interrelated changes in physiology occur which shift the emphasis of the body's activities from those of maintaining and building tissue to those of protecting the whole organism.

The brain at rest shows different electrical activity from the brain excited. If electrical potentials are recorded from the surface of the scalp by very sensitive instruments, small changes which are called *brain waves* (or *electroencephalographic activity*) can be observed. If a person is awake but relaxed, the predominant component of the electrical activity is a ten-per-second cycle called an *alpha wave*. If the person becomes mentally active, for example if he begins to think about a difficult problem, the alpha waves disappear and are replaced by a jumble of desynchronized activity. (See Figure 6–3.) It is as if the various parts of the brain suddenly become involved in the processing of information, but are not synchronized with one another. At the other extreme, when a person is asleep, slower, more highly synchronized electrical activity is observed. The various "depths" of sleep can be detected in this way.

There is a primitive part of the brain, called the *reticular formation*, which is intimately involved in arousal-level changes. This part of the brain is situated in the region where the spinal cord connects to the lower parts of the brain. All entering neural pathways from the sense organs have side routes, or *collaterals*, which go through the reticular formation. The reticular formation, in turn, is connected in a diffuse way to the higher cortical centers. When an animal is at rest, the reticular formation is fairly quiescent. However, when exciting things happen in the environment—when the sensory apparatus is bombarded by stimulation—then the reticular formation becomes active and in turn activates the rest of the brain. It is this activation of the higher brain by the reticular formation that is seen as desynchronization in electroencephalographic records. The reticular formation also acts downward from the brain to excite those changes in bodily function already referred to which

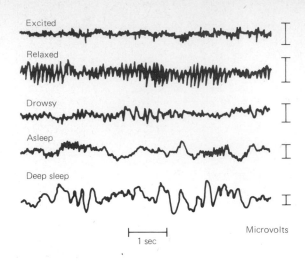

FIGURE 6-3
Electroencephalograms showing the brainwaves generated at various levels of arousal—general excitation, relaxation, drowsiness, light sleep, and deep sleep. Note the 10-cycles-per-second "alpha rhythm" in the relaxed state and that it disappears during excitation. (After Penfield & Erickson, 1941.)

accompany alarm and excitement—the so-called *"flight-fight"* reaction.

The reticular formation itself is actuated by certain salient outside stimuli, particularly noises, painful stimulation, and feelings of stretch in the muscles during walking or other exercise. It can also be stimulated artificially. If a low level of electric current is passed into the reticular formation of a sleeping cat or monkey, the animal awakens. If the reticular formation is electrically stimulated in an awake animal engaged in a difficult task, he will act suddenly more alert. A monkey experiencing difficulty with a very fine discrimination can sometimes be induced by stimulation of his recticular formation to perform more adequately (Fuster, 1958). The effect is very much like that of drinking a cup of coffee. Indeed, many of the effects of reticular-system activation can be produced by excitatory drugs such as caffeine, and it is quite likely that many such drugs achieve their arousing influence by acting on the reticular formation. If the reticular system is stimulated too strongly, disorganization of behavior results. Excessive behavioral arousal, too, can disrupt rather than facilitate ongoing behavior. Being too hungry or too anxious can, like drinking too much coffee, make it very difficult to carry out intricate response patterns smoothly.

In general, the level of arousal can be viewed as an adjustment of the animal to the current demands of his life. If he is about to go to sleep, all systems are set at idle; if he is about to be attacked, they are put into ready alert. That the adjustment is not always optimal is simply because animals aren't perfect. We sometimes see visual illusions, and we sometimes get too excited for our own good.

Emotion

Emergency situations evoke strong physiological responses, including the pumping of hormones into the bloodstream, shifts in blood flow and breathing, and changes in the activity of the nervous system. The experiencing person perceives both the physiological changes and the events which give rise to them. If a bus suddenly bears down on you, your experience is compounded of perceptions of the situation and perceptions of your responses to it. You judge the situation as dangerous; your body reacts simultaneously in most of the ways just outlined; and you perceive changes in your internal functions. This compound of perceptions is experienced as an emotion; in this case the emotion is fear. Similarly, if you are severely thwarted—as when you have tried over and over again to hit a golf ball out of the rough—you interpret the situation as one of frustration; your body responds with a set of mobilizing actions; and you experience the emotion of anger. The emotional experiences themselves serve as cues and activators of further responses. When you feel afraid you tend to run. When you feel angry you tend to strike out and try to injure someone or something. Emotions are, thus, part of the process of adjusting the system to current requirements.

Emotional arousal can vary from extremely mild to very intense. The so-called *affective states* of pleasure and displeasure are relatively mild degrees of emotion; anger and terror are relatively intense. In addition, an emotional experience can be classified as pleasant or unpleasant. Many attempts have been made to classify emotions in more detail than this, but none has succeeded well enough to be accepted widely by psychologists. The fact seems to be that emotional experiences are exceedingly complicated, perhaps as complicated as the situations which give rise to them.

A good deal of effort has gone into trying to distinguish the different emotions from each other on the basis of differences in the concomitant physiological changes. So far few differences have been found. All strong emotions include most of the mobilization and arousal features of physiological activation. Fear and anger can be partially distinguished on the basis of patterns of physiological activity: by and large the physiological changes produced by fear are like those produced by the hormone adrenalin, while those produced by anger bear more resemblances to the effects of another hormone, noradrenalin. Nonetheless, all intense emotional states—ranging from fear to love—share many of the same physiological changes. Indeed, even in the case of anger and fear there are more similarities than differences.

Many of the physiological concomitants of emotion can be mimicked by the injection of adrenalin into the blood. How does a person interpret these artificial changes? It turns out that his interpretation depends on the environment around him. If there is nothing in particular going on, other than the injection, he reports that he feels excited and aroused, "as if" he were feeling angry or afraid, but that he does not *really* feel that way. On the other hand, when the situation is one that would ordinarily induce anger or euphoria, then an injection of adrenalin makes a person feel angrier or happier than he otherwise would (Schachter & Singer, 1962). Apparently, many of the perceptual interpretations of the internal changes accompanying emotions are in terms of the intensity of the emotion being experienced, not its quality.

If, then, the various emotions and feelings are not easily distinguished from each other by their physiological components, what does allow us to tell whether we are angry or sad, frightened or in love? A clue to the situation may lie in observations such as those on the effect of adrenalin described above. A person apparently evaluates the emotional or affective significance of a situation in a primarily perceptual or cognitive manner. On the basis of the evidence of what has happened and what is happening you decide that a situation is dangerous, provocative, or romantic. Or you decide that the person with whom you are interacting is obnoxious, threatening, or lovable. You can make such perceptual judgments without a great deal of affect—almost objectively. But you can also make them under conditions that are strongly arousing. If you judge the situation to be one of affection and romance, and you are at the same time physiologically aroused, you are likely to label your strong emotional feeling "love." Similarly, if you judge the situation to be very threatening, and you find yourself in a state of intense excitement, you experience the total event as a strong emotional feeling of fear. It should be stressed that this view of the nature of emotional experiences is only one reasonable inference from present, insufficient data. It may yet turn out that there are subtle internal cues that distinguish one emotional state from another, particularly in the case of prolonged states such as cronic anxiety or love, which have not been adequately studied. Nonetheless, it is fairly well established that most of the important components which give the emotions their experiential power—the strong feelings of arousal, the palpitations of the heart, the trembling of the fingers, the blushing or blanching, and the queer sensations in the pit of the stomach —are by and large common to all the emotions, rather than being attributes peculiar to one or another. In other words, you cannot tell whether you are suddenly in love by the fact that you feel weak in the knees; that might mean that you are afraid or just hungry! But you can tell that you are having a strong emotion of some kind by such feelings, and coupling these with your perception of the nature of your circumstances, you have a very real and very distinct emotional experience.

Can we identify the emotional experience which another person is undergoing? Obviously, we can usually tell whether another person is having a pleasant or an unpleasant experience. And in fact people are good at telling whether another person, say an actor, is expressing joy, contentment, fear, rage, or revulsion (but not much more—see Chapter Two). How much of this perceptual ability is based on innate forms of expression for the various emotions is hard to tell. Probably some of it is. The famous biologist Darwin (1872) observed many stereotyped emotional expressions in lower animals which seem to be inherited ways of signaling to other members of the species. In all probability, laughter is a universal sign of a positive affective state in humans—the result of release of tension, or of being tickled or in some other way pleased. Crying, too, probably occurs in circumstances which are much the same in all human societies, for example in sorrow and bereavement. On the other hand, the degree to which the same experience gives rise to laughing or crying varies immensely from one person to another, and from one culture to another. In our culture men and women do not cry for the same reasons. Probably a considerable part of our ability to tell another person's feelings is based on conventions of communication. The meaning of some facial expressions, such as widening of the eyes or sticking out the tongue, is based on conventions much like those which underlie the use of words. Our society has tacitly agreed that a certain kind of furrowing of the brow or lifting of an eyebrow has a certain meaning. Other societies may use these symbols to mean other things or may not use them at all. In Chinese literature, widening of the eyes expresses anger, not fear as in English usage. To a Kikuyu a protruding lower lip means disgust, not sadness as it does to Europeans.

Dreaming

One of the most fascinating states of being—an entirely different form of experience from the rest of life—is the state of dreaming. Dreaming occurs during one of two major kinds of sleep. When a person is sleeping, there are times during which his musculature is extremely relaxed but the electrical activity of his brain is very pronounced. There are other times during sleep when the situation is reversed—the muscles are not so relaxed, and ordinary reflexes can be elicited easily, but the brain's activity is very slow. During the former type of sleep, the eyeballs are often observed to oscillate very rapidly. This type of sleep has been called *rapid eye movement* (REM) or *paradoxical* sleep. If a person is awakened during REM sleep, he will almost always report that he was dreaming (Dement & Kleitman, 1957). Dreams probably do not occur in non-REM sleep.

REM sleep and dreaming occupy about 20 to 30 percent of the sleep time of an average adult, i.e., about two hours, and occur primarily in the last third of the night. It is likely that everyone dreams, but some people do not recall their dreams the next day. It has been suggested that REM sleep is necessary in some way to the well-being of animals and man. An adult deprived of REM sleep by being awakened whenever it occurs will show apparent discomfort, and will enter REM more rapidly when allowed to go back to sleep (Dement, 1960). The amount of REM sleep per night is higher in young infants than in adults, and even higher in premature infants. It also occurs in lower animals. Exactly what the function of this kind of sleep is cannot be specified at the moment, but it has been established that when an animal is deprived of REM sleep over long periods he becomes quite abnormal in ways which resemble heightened levels of hunger, sexuality, and anxiety.

The content of dreams has long fascinated men. When dreaming we engage in much freer, more imaginative forms of thought than we are capable of while awake. The experiences which we have while asleep are often extraordinarily interesting and sometimes emotionally strong. A dream lasts anywhere from a minute or so to well over an hour. (There is an old belief that dreams are instantaneous, cramming hours or days of experience into seconds, but modern research shows otherwise.) What determines the subject matter of dreams? To some extent a dream can reflect concurrent events. For example, personal names spoken to a dreamer during REM sleep are sometimes incorporated into the dream. Sometimes, in addition to the rapid oscillations which almost always accompany the dreaming state, there are orderly eyeball movements which reflect the actual content of the dream. If a person is dreaming of a tennis game, his eyes may move back and forth as if following the ball. And certainly dreams also incorporate many experiences of the previous day. It is believed that dreams sometimes also reflect wishes of the dreamer which he may not have expressed in other ways; analyzing dreams in an attempt to discover subconscious desires is one of the principal methods of Freudian psychoanalysis. While something can certainly be learned about an individual in this way, in the context of a great deal of other information, there is no generally valid method of interpreting dreams, and there is most definitely no 1-to-1 correspondence between particular dream-contents and characteristics of the dreamer.

Hormones

Hormones are the secretions of the endocrine glands. These glands empty their products directly into the bloodstream, from whence they influence the various tissues of the body. Hormones are another important factor in the continual adjustment of an organism to changes in the world and his relations to it. They help to arouse, regulate, and control the extensive modification in levels and kinds of functioning which an animal must continually make. We have already discussed the influence of some hormones—the emergency secretions of the adrenal gland, adrenalin and noradrenalin. These substances come from the medulla, or inner part, of the adrenal glands. The outer part, or cortex, of the adrenal glands secretes other hormones—also involved in emergency reactions—called the *adrenal-cortical* hormones, which include cortisone and hydrocortisone. Other important endocrine glands are the gonads or sex glands (the testes in the male and the ovaries in the female) and the pituitary gland. The pituitary gland is located at the base of the skull and is the master or control gland for the endocrine system. The secretions of the pituitary are responsible for the growth and level of production of hormones of all the other endocrine glands in the body.

Perhaps the most interesting, best understood, and most dramatic of the relations between hormones and behavior are those which have to do with mating and reproduction. Sexual behavior depends on an intricate relation between perceptual and sensory factors and factors of internal state, many of which are directly related to hormone levels.

Sexual activity does not occur if the organism is not physiologically ready. The sexual receptivity of female lower mammals depends almost entirely on cyclical variations in hormone secretions from the ovaries, which are in turn influenced by secretions from the pituitary gland. The female rat, for example, goes through a repetitive four-day cycle that not only involves changes in the anatomy and physiology of the vagina and other sexual apparatus, but also involves psychological readiness to mate—receptivity, inducibility of the reflex arching of the back which must occur before the male is able to effect copulation, and certain nonsexual aspects of behavior. General activity in the female rat rises and falls in the same four-day cycle as does her sexual receptivity.

If a female rat is castrated, that is if her ovaries are removed, the sexual cycle disappears and all activity falls to a constant low level. All the features normally occurring at the high points in the cycle can be restored by an injection of the hormones usually secreted by the ovaries. Thus the hormone level is clearly a controlling factor in sexual matters. On the other hand, a female rat does not show the signs of readiness for copulation in a vacuum. She must be stimulated by the sight of a sexually agressive male, or by artificial stimuli which contain essential components of normally sexually arousing stimuli. For instance, stimulating the vagina of a rat in heat with the finger will evoke a full lordosis—back-arching response—which is part of the reception of the coital act normally induced by a mounting male.

There is huge variation between different sexes and species in the role played by hormones in sexual behavior. This should be emphasized. The highly cyclical receptivity of the rat, the guinea pig, and many other lower mammals, and of birds, reptiles, and fish is much weakened in primates and almost nonexistent in man. Most primate females show a certain amount of receptivity throughout their sexual cycles, but often, nonetheless, show a pronounced period of relatively greater excitability.

Similarly, the effects of castration and hormonal-replacement therapy or of hormone injections into the intact animal vary from species to species. In general, the effects of hormones become less with higher species, while the influence of sensory and social factors becomes greater. Male rats and guinea pigs show variations in sexual activity as a result of injections of testosterone, the male hormone secreted by the testes. A large dose of testosterone arouses heightened sexual activity. On the other hand, castration does not immediately or completely abolish sexual activity. There is, in fact, no immediate effect at all. However, with the amount of time involved varying greatly from one individual to the next, sexual activity gradually decreases. Eventually, ejaculation becomes impossible, but sex play, mounting, and incomplete copulation may continue for an indefinite period. Replacement therapy—injection of extraneous testosterone—results in complete reappearance of the sexual activity normal to the animal. Rats who are comparatively active sexually before castration return to relatively high levels of activity compared to rats who were less active before castration. There is, apparently, a normal level of activity given by neural structures.

The time at which castration occurs has an influence on its effect. Early castration results in a greater deficit in sexual behavior than castration later in life. In many cases, whether or not the animal has had sexual experience before castration may have an effect on the amount of activity he shows afterwards. Thus, whether an animal will engage in sexual activity depends on the situation—the availability of a receptive partner, particular sensory stimulation such as sights, smell, and touch, and pre-existing states of experience, neural organization, and hormone level.

In humans, both male and female, the role of hormonal factors has taken a distinct second place to social and experiential factors. Castration, for instance, has very little effect on sexual motivation of either men or women. Castration before puberty probably reduces the sexual motivation of either sex, but castration after puberty usually has very minor effects, if any. Similarly, therapy with fairly large doses of sex hormones has little effect on sexual activity in normal individuals.

Another very interesting feature of human sexual activity is the constant receptivity of the female. Unlike the lower mammals that experience receptivity only during a period of fertility, the human female tends to be receptive during the whole of the sexual cycle, a condition which exists to a lesser degree among the lower primates—the monkeys and apes. Insofar as there is any period of greater sexual interest in the human female it appears to be at a time of low fertility rather than high. It is thought that the human female may be the only mammalian female to experience an orgasm during copulation, and this seems consistent with a pattern of more constant sexual interest. However, whatever the truth of such speculations may be, it is certainly the case that sexual activity in the human is more intimately related to social and experiential factors than to the biological cycles of the reproductive system.

Drugs

There are drugs that potentiate or interfere with normal neural and behavioral activity, others that mimic changes in hormonal cycles, and still others that produce unique and profoundly abnormal psychological states.

For example, there are drugs which suppress hunger—so-called *anorexic agents*. For the most part, it is not known whether such agents work directly on the "hunger" centers of the brain or act elsewhere to make the recipient feel a bit sick and thus lessen his appetite. Nonetheless, many of the motivational features of the state of hunger can be controlled by drugs. There are drugs which potentiate behavior based on fear. If a rat has learned to jump a barrier to escape from an electric shock, he will do so more readily if the shock is intense or if he is made more frightened in some other way. He will also respond more readily when he is under the influence of an amphetamine drug such as dexedrine. Amphetamines appear to potentiate the state of fear. On the other hand, the tranquilizing drugs such as chlorpromazine can, under some circumstances, produce states opposite from fear. Thus, if a rat is jumping a hurdle to avoid a shock of which he is afraid, his performance may be slowed down by administration of a tranquilizer.

There are drugs which influence the state of cortical arousal, and the degree of wakefulness. The amphetamines in general produce wakefulness, the so-called *narcotics* make an animal more sleepy. The drug-induced states are not identical to those of normal intense wakefulness or drowsiness, but they mimic them in many respects. However, many drugs have effects which are different from and greater than the simple mimicking of natural variations in internal environment. Some narcotics, for example, produce euphoric experiences which are not obviously present when one is simply drowsy from lack of sleep.

Drugs are sometimes used intentionally to produce experiential states different from ordinary experience. The legal drug alcohol (ethanol) and the illegal drug marijuana (cannabis) are often used because the taker finds the unusual states which they induce pleasant. Alcohol induces, in various people, states of lessened anxiety, lowered social inhibition, or simply a mild and somewhat euphoric relaxation. Marijuana is reported to produce relaxation, heightened consciousness of sensory events, and sometimes, in high doses, mild hallucinations.

There are stronger drugs which produce markedly abnormal psychological states sometimes accompanied by bizarre behavior. Among these are the stronger hallucinogenic drugs such as mescaline and LSD. These drugs are called *psychotomimetic* because some of their behavioral effects resemble those seen in certain psychoses. For instance, the intense hallucinations and loss of touch with reality caused by LSD are similar in many ways to states seen in schizophrenia. In addition, bizarre, maladaptive, and dangerous behaviors sometimes occur under the influence of LSD, just as they sometimes do in schizophrenia. However, the two states are almost certainly not identical, and it is even doubtful that the underlying biochemical mechanisms are similar.

The question of the safety and value of the use of exotic drugs should be considered. It is well known that most if not all narcotics are physiologically addictive. What physiological addiction means is that some metabolic process of the body becomes dependent on the presence of the drug, so that if the drug is withdrawn the chemical machinery of the body is thrown into serious disorder. The result is a set of very violent physical *withdrawal symptoms* which are medically serious in addition to being extremely unpleasant. No such physiological addiction appears to exist in the case of marijuana. It is probably too early to tell whether there is any physiological addiction to hallucinogenic drugs such as LSD and mescaline.

There is a class of drugs, which includes alcohol, caffeine, and nicotine, which while probably not physiologically addicting nevertheless under certain circumstances can be *habit forming*. These drugs produce psychological and physiological states that a person may not only find pleasant or useful, but which he may become dependent upon in a very strong way. If you are able to function only when under the influence of large amounts of caffeine, you may become very strongly dependent on coffee and find it extremely hard to give it up. If your feeling of well-being becomes habitually dependent on smoking, you may find it difficult to stop, even if you know that the habit entails a great risk of consequences as dire as a slow and painful death from cancer or emphysema. Alcoholism is an acquired psychological dependence on the state induced by alcoholic consumption. Prolonged overdoses of alcohol not only can interfere with normal behavior in very maladaptive ways, but also can cause cirrhosis, a severe liver disease. Thus, to say that a drug is not physiologically addictive does not by any means imply that is safe.

Hypnosis

Still another kind of altered state of being which affects behavior in a very radical way is the state induced by hypnosis. Although hypnosis has been the subject of investigation for many years and much of the magical aura which used to surround it has been removed, its essential features and conditions are still only poorly understood. In essence, the hypnotic state consists of a pronounced relaxation of many of the activities by which a person usually makes sure of the validity of his perceptions and actions. The subject accepts suggestions of the hypnotist in a more uncritical way than he would in the normal state. The normal person engages in a great deal of "reality testing." He does not accept any one source of perception without checking against other information which he has at hand. The hypnotized subject seems to put into abeyance much of this skepticism.

The usual technique of producing hypnosis consists of having the subject concentrate very hard on a small visual area, and providing him with monotonous, repetitive auditory stimulation and suggestions that he is going to be hypnotized. How this procedure has its effect is simply unknown at present.

There is a good deal of difference among people in the depth to which they can be hypnotized, and in the ease with which they can be hypnotized at all. And the same person will vary in hypnotizability from one occasion to the next. Frequently, people who at first cannot be hypnotized at all do become hypnotizable after many tries.

Unfortunately, very little can be said at the present about the nature of hypnotizable versus relatively unhypnotizable people. Children around the ages of 6 to 10 are comparatively more hypnotizable than older people. But aside from this there are few strong correlates of hypnotizability.

There are many common misconceptions about hypnosis. It is not true, although often said, that hypnosis is a form of sleep. The electrical activity of the brain in hypnosis is unlike any of the accepted stages of sleep, and in other respects, too, the hypnotized person is not asleep. He is relaxed in the sense that he has relaxed some of his usual skeptical activities, but he is not relaxed in the neurological sense. Further, the things which a person will do under hypnosis are not unlimited, and are related to how willing and cooperative an hypnotic subject he is. Generally, the things which a person is most unwilling to do in the waking state are the things which are most difficult to get him to do under hypnosis. And many if not all of the rather surprising things which a person can do under hypnosis will be performed by a person in a normal state if he is offered sufficient incentive for so doing. No definite line can be drawn between those things which a person will and will not do under hypnosis.

Hypnosis does not grant any magical powers. For example, the use of hypnosis for what is called *age-regression*, making a hypnotized person assume an age from his past by suggesting to him that he is, say, three years old, certainly does not make him *actually* three years old. What is more likely to happen is that he will try very, very hard and without embarrassment or self-censorship to act as much like a three-year-old as he can. But he will still act more like an adult trying hard to be a three-year-old than like an actual three-year-old. However, it would be incorrect to assume that the hypnotic state and the normal state are exactly the same. Clearly there is something very different going on when extreme suggestibility and abandonment of reality-testing occur.

HOMEOSTASIS

The main business of a living organism is to keep itself alive. In order to stay alive, an animal must keep the nutrients in its blood—sugar, amino acids, and the like—at a proper level. If blood sugar gets too low the animal becomes weak and unable to function, and may die. If blood sugar is too high, unhealthy fat deposits ensue. Similarly the amount of water in the tissues must be kept at an appropriate level. Indeed, there is a whole host of physiological conditions which must be maintained within narrow ranges for survival. The means by which living things maintain adaptive levels of the things they need are called *homeostatic mechanisms*. The resulting state of balance is called *homeostasis*. A large amount of the activity of animals can be seen to be intimately involved with homeostasis.

A particularly good example of homeostasis is the maintenance, in warm-blooded animals, of a constant body temperature. The nervous system of warm-blooded animals fails to function properly if the internal temperature of the body goes below a certain point, and unconsciousness results. On the other hand, if the internal temperature rises too high, convulsions may result. Temperature must be maintained within a very small range. The way in which this is effected is quite similar to the way in which a thermostat controls the temperature of a house. In a modern centrally heated house, whenever the temperature gets too low an electric switch run by a thermometer activates a furnace. When the temperature gets too high, the same gadget turns the furnace off. The house temperature oscillates between a minimum at which the furnace is activated and a maximum at which the furnace is turned off. In the temperature control of the body, the detection of blood temperature is carried on in the brain, and the principal means for raising and lowering body temperature are muscular activity and sweating. The temperature range which is maintained is adaptive to the organism. Its metabolic processes and neural functions are adequate at these temperatures. Temperatures outside of the maintained range would be both maladaptive and uncomfortable.

Almost all the processes of life share this necessity of being kept within certain limits. The amount of food, water, oxygen, carbon dioxide, waste products, proteins, vitamins and minerals, and many other substances in the bloodstream must be kept at a concentration which is neither too high nor too low. In order to do this an animal must have available error signals which tell him when any of these concentrations is at an undesirable level. And he must have available response mechanisms, both of a purely physiological variety and of sophisticated behavioral kinds, which will enable him to bring his system back into equilibrium whenever any of these levels fluctuates out of bounds. Moreover, the homeostatic principle of adaptation carries over into many less obviously physiological domains. The amount of information which an animal must have about his surroundings is an example. In order to be safe, he must know the location of his enemies, the cliffs that he might tumble over, the rafters that he could bang his head on, and the nettle bushes that might sting him. If an animal is in doubt about his environment, he will set out to learn more about it. This is sometimes called *curiosity* or *need for exploration*. But he will not continue to explore forever. There is no need to know the minutest details and the smallest changes in the immediately surrounding world. There is some reasonable level of familiarity and knowledge which will do, and for which the expenditure of energy and time is worthwhile. Thus, even such a thing as the amount of environmental information possessed at a given time can be seen as a product of a homeostatic balance.

It is dangerous to attribute to homeostatic processes a causative role in behavior. An animal does not really eat "in order to keep his blood sugar level within bounds." At the least, to say that he does is to beg the question of the mechanism by which he is able to do so, and that is the really important and interesting question. To say that there is a homeostatic process involving the control of blood sugar level is to describe a fact—a quite impressive fact—about what animals and men actually do. They actually maintain a whole host of important functions within narrow limits in a most exquisitely refined and adaptive way. How they go about this is another and fundamental question.

Part of the story of homeostasis lies in the existence of appropriate error signals. For blood sugar level, for instance, there is a distinct hunger signal, both neurological and experiential, which indicates that the level has dropped below the allowable range. Similarly, the experience of thirst is an error signal concerning the amount of fluid in the tissues of the body.

In terms of overt behavior patterns, the signals which indicate that a homeostatic level is in danger are often *trigger stimuli*. These trigger stimuli initiate patterns of actions which result in reinstatement of homeostasis. For instance, hunger leads to foraging in cows, to hunting in mountain lions, and to opening the refrigerator in humans. These actions in turn lead to increases in blood sugar. When these increases in the blood sugar level are sufficient or more than sufficient, another signal or stimulus acts as a *terminator* of the action pattern. Having swallowed enough water or beer an animal or man stops drinking.

In general, there is a constant fluctuation in homeostatic levels. There is first a gradual and continuing decrease, then, usually triggered by some error signal, a set of actions to increase the level, another stimulus or signal that the level has been brought up far enough, and then again begins a gradual decrease. The existence of a suboptimal level in any requirement for adaptation is called a *need*. Needs wax and wane. With fulfillment of the need comes *satiation*. With deprivation, the need arises once more.

A need state very often is the condition for a certain kind of behavior—a simple reflex or instinctive response, or a complicated learned behavior. A *reflexive* knee jerk is triggered by a blow to the patellar tendon. The actual trigger stimulus is a stretching of that tendon which in nature would indicate that the leg was giving in to gravity and the person in danger of falling. The knee jerk relieves the tension on the patellar tendon by returning the leg to its extended state.

The *instinctive* reactions are exemplified in the grey wasp's building of a nest. If the wasp, having built a nest, finds a hole in the side, she immediately sets to work to fill the hole and continues until there is no hole left. If, as she goes along, one keeps removing the new work, the wasp will keep working forever. The trigger stimulus which starts the behavior pattern is a hole in the nest. The terminator stimulus that ends the pattern is a whole nest.

Complex learned behavior patterns often become attached to the need states in which they were learned. If you learned to open the refrigerator when you were hungry, then you will tend to open the refrigerator only when you are hungry and not at other times. The way in which such learning occurs will be analyzed and described in succeeding chapters. For the moment, suffice it to say that behavior sequences which have been learned do not occur constantly; they occur only when the appropriate stimuli to which the responses have been learned are present. By and large such stimuli are ones which indicate that certain behaviors are particularly adaptive in the situation. A need, or, as it is sometimes called, a *drive state*, is one of the most effective stimuli for execution of learned behavior, since a drive, almost by definition, determines what is adaptive behavior at a given time. For example, the feeling of hunger specifies that activities that lead to food are, at the moment, particularly important.

We speak often of goals in human behavior. To a great extent goals may be seen as the terminators of behavior sequences, that is as the stimuli which say, "You have done enough." (If your goal is a Ph.D., when you get one you stop going to school.) A goal is that condition which says that the homeostatic process has achieved its end, things are again in balance. We may thus think of needs and goals as the two end points of a cyclical homeostatic adaptation. A *need* arises when a level is below the desired range, and can lead to the execution of appropriate behaviors to bring the level back into that range; and the goal can be seen as the signal that things are once again in order. In Chapter 10 we will discuss the physiological mechanisms by which hunger and thirst operate to turn behavior on and off. Behavior which is turned on and off by needs and by goals is seen as purposive. The animal is said to have the "purpose" of keeping his blood sugar level just right, or the "purpose" of raising a family. Such a purpose is inferred from the fact that when the blood sugar level is low or the nest is empty, behaviors are initiated which lead to raising the blood sugar or filling the nest, and that when the blood sugar level is high or the nest full, these behaviors cease. This is what we mean by purpose.

Pleasure

Trigger stimuli, which initiate behavior designed to restore homeostatic balance, and goal stimuli, which terminate such behavior, can be entirely unconscious. We are usually unaware of varying our rate of breathing in order to compensate for changes in carbon dioxide production when we walk after a period of sitting. Very often, however, trigger stimuli are experienced as unpleasant. For example, the stimuli which lead to flight or withdrawal are experienced as the unpleasant emotion of fear. By the same token, stimuli which are associated with reinstatement of optimal states are frequently experienced as pleasant—for example the taste of food when one is hungry. It would probably be a mistake, however, to equate displeasure with trigger stimuli, or pleasure with need reduction. Bitter tastes, like that of quinine, are unpleasant without being directly associated with a state of homeostatic unbalance. Nature appears to have provided us with certain natural aversions, probably to act as warning signals that protect us from eating or touching things that might be dangerous. Likewise, some trigger stimuli, such as sexual foreplay, are experienced as pleasant. It is probably generally true that return toward homeostatic balance, if consciously experienced, is pleasant, and deviation from such balance is unpleasant. But not all pleasant or unpleasant sensations are directly associated with homeostatic shifts.

However, even when one considers stimuli that are pleasant without being accompanied by immediate improvement in homeostatic balance, such as those leading to sexual arousal, it is clear that their positive evaluation is usually adaptive for the individual or the species. Many of the events that are pleasant or rewarding for a given species can be related to obvious features of its modes of adaptation—for example, predator species probably take more pleasure in exploration than do their prey—but there are, also, known instances of artificial stimuli producing pleasure, as judged by positive choice in lower animals and by report in humans, in which the connection to an adaptive advantage is less direct. For example, a saccharine solution is preferred to plain water by rats, and is reported to be pleasantly sweet by humans, although it has no appreciable nutritive value. It can be shown that the degree of a rat's preference for a sweet solution is directly correlated with the extent to which it stimulates a neurological response of the sweetness detector organs in the tongue. It is a reasonable inference that our own experience of pleasure on exposure to sweet things is similarly a direct correlate of their ability to stimulate a particular kind of neural activity. In other words, it is not the reduction of a need in this case, but the stimulation itself that is pleasant.

Apparently, evolution has resulted in direct perceptual appreciation of some substances not only as sweet, but also as pleasant and desirable. One can easily discern the survival value for a species of a liking for sweet things, since they are usually nutritive. A similar situation seems to be the case for some potentially harmful stimuli: we experience intense heat and pressure as unpleasant at levels much lower than those needed to produce actual physical harm.

When the neural responses ordinarily associated with pleasant stimulation are artificially excited, pleasant experiences may be evoked. The effect of saccharin has already been mentioned. Electrical stimulation of certain parts of the brain acts as a powerful reward for behavior of lower mammals, and by inference (and according to a few reports of similarly stimulated humans) is probably intensely pleasurable. It seems likely that certain euphoric drugs also produce pleasurable experiences in a direct, physiologically unnatural, way.

The sensations which yield pleasure are not all innate, of course. We all have many acquired tastes—events that we have come to enjoy through experience. There are probably several ways by which initially neutral, or even mildly unpleasant, things can become hedonically positive. Perhaps the most important is habituation. If a healthy rat is fed for a long time on one of two different-tasting, but nutritionally equivalent feeds, he will prefer, if given the choice, the one he is used to. In a similar way most children and many adults prefer food prepared in the way it is prepared in their homes: steak rare or well done, for example, or bacon crisp or flabby. There is the story of the bride whose morning biscuits, despite weeks of effort and experimentation, always failed to please her husband until one day she burned them badly, upon which he shouted delightedly "Ah, now that's the way my mother made them!"

Foods or other stimulating events that have been associated with unpleasant consequences often become aversive. Most people can tell stories similar to the one about the origin of my own dislike for cinnamon in a very bad experience with a cinnamon-flavored punch at my first college party. There is reason to believe that food aversions of this sort are very easily learned (more in Chapter 7); certainly it would be of adaptive advantage to eschew chewables that are followed by violent spasms and nausea, at least until careful testing has established their safety (Garcia, Ervin, & Koelling, 1966). By the same token, flavors, sights, and sounds that are associated with pleasant outcomes may themselves become pleasant by conditioning mechanisms (to be discussed later). In addition, the mechanisms of cognitive consistency (outlined in Chapter 2) may often lead to the evaluation of a particular kind of perceptual event as desirable because an individual has taken decisions which would be inconsistent otherwise. For example, in one experiment people who were induced to eat grasshoppers by gentle persuasive methods tended, on the average, to like grasshoppers more afterward (Smith, 1961). They had to be consistent, runs the theory.

HUMAN "MOTIVES"

Up to now, what we have said about motives has borne only indirect relation to what we commonly mean by the word *motive*. Partly this is because the word is commonly used in the kind of vague and sloppy explanations of behavior which psychology is trying to replace. As was mentioned earlier the word *motivation* is often equated with "the moving force" or cause of behavior. In that sense of the word, this whole book is about motivation. But we wish to be much more detailed and exact about the causes of behavior, and to discuss perception and judgment, the conditioning and learning of habits, the effects of social interaction and of thought, and many other causes of behavior separately and in depth.

Nevertheless, there are features of the common usages of the term *motive* that refer to interesting and important aspects of behavior which should be discussed. The discussion will, however, have to be somewhat conjectural and informal, since there is not yet good agreement on the best ways to conceptualize these matters. One approach is to try to see what is usually meant by a motive in descriptions of human behavior.

Consider what is meant by a motive in a murder case. The inspector thinks that the butler may have strangled the duke, but says he, "What is the motive?" What is being asked? A satisfactory answer could take at least three forms. One might be a statement such as "The butler was defending himself from a homicidal attack by the crazy duke," or "He has hated the duke for seducing all the chambermaids." The question being answered is "Under what circumstances would an ordinary person from our culture be likely to behave in that way?" *Motive* used in this sense refers to what we have been calling *trigger stimuli*. They are events or states that can be expected to lead to certain kinds of behavior.

A second kind of answer to such a question would be "He took the duke's 20-carat diamond ring," or "The duke's death allowed him to retire on a pension to Bloomsbury," or the like. In this case, the answer refers us to the terminal stimulus or reward that followed the behavior. We then infer, perhaps, that the behavior would not have occurred without the presence of this incentive. The behavior is thus "explained" insofar at least as the presence of incentives is an important determiner of such behavior for average individuals.

A third form which the answer might take is "The butler is a long-time homicidal maniac," or "He was under the influence of a powerful drug," or the like. In this case the behavior is not explained in terms of conditions that would lead an average or normal man to perform it. Rather, the *unusualness* of the behavior is explained, at least partially, by known unusual characteristics of the performer. Notice that this is hardly a complete explanation, since not even homicidal psychopaths kill every person with whom they come in contact, even when they are drunk. A complete understanding of the act would require us to be able to explain just why this particular person performed this particular act at this particular time. We could feel that the act was adequately explained only if we were sure that given the information we now possess we could have predicted the act before it occurred. Clearly we are seldom able to do any such thing.

Notice also that these three aspects of motivation are closely related. The sorts of situations which incite to violence are not the same for all people. If I went around calling everyone I met a "son of a bitch" only some of them would hit me. Even though this is the kind of trigger which often leads to aggressive behavior in our culture, its actual effect depends greatly on the characteristics—habitual responses—of the person to whom it is addressed. A similar argument applies, of course, to the effect of incentives. For example, a large monetary bribe may be thought of as a "motive" for perjury, but such an incentive will not work with everyone. Conversely, the kinds of habitual responses a person has will depend in large part on the kinds of things that act as rewards and initiating stimuli for him. If he is easily intrigued by the smell of foods and unusually rewarded by pleasant tastes, he will very likely be a gourmet and spend a lot of time eating.

Because of the interrelation of triggers, habits, and rewards, it is usually impossible to tell which came first or is the "cause" when behavior is observed in a natural setting. We observe that a person spends a lot of time eating, reading cookbooks, and squirreling away money toward an evening at Maxim's. We cannot tell whether he is particularly sensitive to food stimuli, especially rewarded by hunger-reduction, a habitual food-lover by virtue of his early environment, or some combination of these things. In fact, given (a) that one usually learns to like and be rewarded by the outcomes of his behavior [by cognitive consistency mechanisms (Chapter 2), and by conditioning (Chapter 7)]; and (b) that one learns to react to triggers with behavior that leads to rewarding outcomes; and (c) that one tends to make habitual those reactions that are often triggered and often rewarded; triggers, habits, and desired rewards are usually incapable of being disentangled. As a result, when we describe a person's behavior, we frequently fail to distinguish between the various aspects of a motive, but tacitly assume that they go hand in hand. Whether they always do is another question.

A good demonstration that at least one measurable adult human "motive" does contain these three related but separate aspects has been provided by a series of studies of *approval motivation* by Crowne and Marlowe (1964). Their test, described in Chapter 3, determines whether a person tends to describe himself as a socially desirable person. From what we have been saying, it would be expected that a person who wants to be seen as socially desirable would also tend to be more than normally susceptible to stimuli which induce social or compliant behavior, and more than normally influenced by rewards of social approval. This is what Crowne and Marlowe have been able to show. In one study, they found that people scoring high on the approval-motive scale tended to conform to group pressures significantly more in the Asch experiment (see Chapter 2) situation than did people scoring low on the scale. That is, when faced with a group of people who said an obviously longer line was shorter than another, high scorers on the approval-motivation test were more likely to go along with the majority than were low scorers. In another experiment, subjects in a rigged conversation were rewarded for referring to themselves. The reward was an approving nod from the experimenter. People high in measured approval-motivation increased the frequency with which they made self-references more than did people low on the measure. Thus those who demonstrate high approval-motivation in their self-descriptive behavior also appear to be more sensitive to trigger stimuli for social approval–seeking behavior and to be more influenced by social approval as a reward or incentive.

Many psychologists who are interested in the "real-life" behavior of people, particularly adults, have chosen to ignore the complexities of tracing the interrelations among the various facets of motives and, instead, deal only with the major attributes of characteristic behavior which emerge. For example, rather than being concerned with the precise stimuli leading to and rewards following each act, a psychologist may notice that a given person is frequently observed to engage in acts that are initiated by a competitive challenge, characterized by hard work and striving, or followed by obvious success or failure. The psychologist either establishes empirically or assumes that these various aspects of achievement behavior are closely interrelated—part and parcel of the same trait of personality. Then, rather than attempting to separate them, he concerns himself with the origins and consequences of the whole package. Thus, the psychologist interested in achievement behavior may first try to identify achievement-oriented people by any or all of these criteria, and then proceed to study what kind of genetics, early environment, or child training may be associated with this trait, or to determine whether people with this trait are more or less likely than others to succeed in school or in business.

Very often these "packages" are labeled *motives*. A person who is often observed in achievement-related activities is said to be *achievement-motivated*. A person who does many things evoked by social demands and calculated to win approval is said to have a high *need for approval*. It is not clear whether this sort of "motive" is the same in all respects as the more physiologically based motives such as hunger, thirst, etc. However, in both uses the term *motive* points toward a state of being in which a certain complex of related stimulus-conditions, terminal stimuli, and habits are to the fore.

Some motives of this kind are obviously acquired—that is, learned by the individual. The money motive is certainly learned; and, almost as certainly, so are motives for achievement, approval, and the like. Others may not be, or at least not wholly so. For example, a generalized tendency to be stimulated by a new environment and to explore and master it may, just possibly, be shared in greater or lesser degree by all mammals. The differences between individuals in the amount of such "competence" motivation may mostly follow from differences in their early experiences; but then again, at least some differences along these lines may be due to heredity. Such questions have hardly begun to be asked, much less answered.

Many so-called *motives* were discussed in the chapter on personality in relation to individual differences or characteristics, since motives in the present sense are nearly synonymous with traits of personality. There we saw that motives or character traits describe only weak tendencies of certain people *usually* to behave *somewhat more* in one particular fashion than in another. This weakness of personality traits fits our common sense about motivation: even the most extreme gourmet sometimes prefers to do something other than eat.

Despite the somewhat elusive nature of motives and other personality traits, it has proved possible in a few instances to trace the kinds of early experience which tend to produce people with relatively strong motivation of a certain kind, and to discover some of the consequences of being a person with a high level of certain kinds of motives.

Perhaps the best example of known antecedents of high motivation is in regard to the need for achievement, measured by TAT scoring according to the method of McClelland described in Chapter 3. People high in achievement motivation (n Ach), more often than chance would have it, grow up in families where an unusual amount of stress is placed on early independence training. In such families, children are generally taught and allowed to do things that require a certain amount of responsibility—for example going to school alone, running errands to stores a few blocks away, crossing streets, and staying alone at home—at an earlier age than is the norm. Mothers of such children, and probably fathers as well, tend to apply sanctions—rewards, praise, and criticism—contingently on the child's performance. They encourage their children to try to do things by themselves, reward them when they succeed, and reprimand them when they fail (Rosen & d'Andrade, 1959). Parents of children with low achievement-motivation are more likely to help them whenever they are stumped and to give their support or condemnation with little regard to whether the child is actually trying and succeeding or not.

A good example of a motive whose consequences have been traced is generalized anxiety. As was described in Chapter 3, people with a high level of nonspecific anxiety often exhibit a number of symptoms—frequently sweaty palms, vague fears, and the like—which can be at least crudely measured by a self-report questionnaire, the Taylor Manifest Anxiety scale (Taylor, 1953). Since general anxiety is, in part, a state of arousal, anxious people could be expected to show some of the same characteristics associated with arousing drugs or reticular activation. Arousal usually facilitates the learning and performance of uncomplicated tasks, but interferes with intricate and highly coordinated activities. Accordingly, people who score high on this anxiety scale have been found to be more susceptible to certain kinds of simple conditioning procedures and to learn simple tasks more rapidly than people who score low on the scale. On the other hand, high scorers tend to do more poorly on complex tasks requiring calm concentration, just as one might expect.

Finally, we may ask what happens when several different motives interact. What is a person like, and how may he be expected to behave if he is known to have strong motivation for both achievement and approval or if he is both very anxious and very approval-oriented? While some psychoanalytic thinking and a few other theories of personality (see Chapter 4) have been concerned with such questions, no really adequate solution has been proposed. Similarly, certain philosophically minded psychologists (Maslow, 1962; Fromm, 1941; Rogers, 1961; Allport, 1955) have tried to describe the combination of motives which constitutes the ideal person and leads to the ideal life. Unfortunately, the basis of such attempts to date has been primarily anecdotal evidence and speculation. Scientifically valid advice on how to optimize the quality of life is, sadly, not yet available.

TOPICS DISCUSSED IN CHAPTER 6

1. The proper use of the term *motive*.

2. Genetic and evolutionary determination of behavioral tendencies.

3. State-determined behavior; arousal, cycles, hormones, drugs.

4. The interaction of perception, arousal, and reaction in emotions.

5. Convention and instinct in the expression of emotions.

6. The two kinds of sleep, and their association with dreaming and neural and muscular activity.

7. The relations between hormones, experience, and sexual activity.

8. The nature of hypnosis.

9. Homeostasis; and the relation between needs, activities, and goals.

10. The basis of pleasure and displeasure.

11. Human motives; the interaction of trigger stimuli, habits, and incentives. The origins of achievement motivation.

SUGGESTED READINGS

1. *The standard reference text is:*

Cofer, C. H., & Appley, M. H. *Motivation, theory and research.* New York: Wiley, 1964.

2. *Some very interesting monographs on various aspects of motivation include:*

Darwin, C. *Expression of the emotions in man and animals.* Chicago: University of Chicago Press, 1965 (paperback; originally published in 1872).

Lorenz, K. *On aggression.* New York: Harcourt, Brace & World, 1966.

Crowne, D. P., & Marlowe, D. *The approval motive.* New York: Wiley, 1964.

SEVEN
Conditioning and learning

In the last chapter we discussed the way in which the behavior of the members of a species becomes adapted to the requirements of their environment through the process of natural selection and evolution. Evolutionary changes take many generations, but many critical environmental changes happen during the life span of a single animal, sometimes within months, days, or even minutes. Fortunately, animals have evolved with means of changing their ways of behaving in comparably short periods. Such changes in the individual animal are called *learning*. Learning may be defined formally as *a change in the behavioral tendencies of an animal resulting from experience*. The phrase *behavioral tendencies* means the typical or average way in which an individual behaves in a given situation.

In this chapter we will discuss three processes by which learning occurs. It should be made clear that these three learning processes are not necessarily different in terms of the underlying physiological or psychological mechanisms involved. For all we know at the present time, all learning may take place by the same reorganization of the nervous system, and all learning may eventually be related to a single underlying series of psychological events. However, no unifying description that fits all kinds of learning has yet been found. Rather, several different procedures have been discovered which lead to changes in behavior patterns, and accordingly it is possible to classify different types of learning in terms of the sorts of events involved. The three kinds of learning which we will discuss in this chapter are *imprinting*, *classical conditioning*, and *operant conditioning*. In each case we will outline the experiences which an animal must have in order for his typical behavior to be modified, and then describe some of the variables that determine how quickly learning progresses, some of the primary features of behavior learned through that process, and some of the aspects of life in which such learning is particularly significant.

IMPRINTING

A newly hatched duck or gosling will follow almost any moving object it sees. But after a few days it begins to follow its own mother and nothing else. The sight of a female duck being followed by a string of young is a familiar one.

   The famous Austrian biologist, Konrad Lorenz (1937), discovered that under some special circumstances the newly hatched goslings with which he was working would follow *him* around the barnyard instead of the mother goose. (see Figure 7–1). The process can be mimicked and studied in the laboratory. Figure 7–2 shows the experimental set-up used by Hess (1959) to study this phenomenon in ducks. A model of a mother duck was made to move in front of the infant. If the infant's initial exposure to the model occurred in the right way and at the right time, the infant developed a "following response" to the model. Figure 7–2 also shows the relation between the time at which the procedure was carried out and the strength of the following response. Imprinting of following -in the species of duck studied by Hess was much more effective if it occurred between about the sixteenth and twentieth hour of life than if it occurred either earlier or later. This is a general feature of the process of imprinting: it occurs best at a particular time in the life span of the individual, usually very early.

   This time is often called a *critical period*. In the case of ducks following a mother object, a partial explanation of the critical period is found in certain correlated developmental events in the duckling's life. Before about eight or ten hours of age, a duckling is unable to follow well because his motor coordination is insufficient. But after the age of about twenty-four hours a duckling begins to be afraid of strange animals and objects. Thus before the critical period the duckling cannot make the responses which facilitate imprinting, while after the critical period he has some tendencies which interfere with imprinting.

   The sorts of behavior patterns that are acquired through imprinting tend to be associated with the early identification of an animal with its family, parents, or species. Following responses are part of the proper behavior of a young duck toward its mother. Imprinting also appears in the learning of songs by some species of birds. When a young bullfinch is shifted from the nest of its biological parents to that of a slightly different subspecies, it grows up singing the songs of its foster parents rather than those of its real parents. Moreover, whatever songs it learns first, it sings for the rest of its life. The song was *imprinted*. Thus again, the learning is of whatever the animal does first, in this case, that remains its pattern for life.

FIGURE 7–1
Ducklings following K. Lorenz, as if he were their mother—an example of imprinting.
(Photograph by Thomas McAvoy, LIFE magazine, 1955, 39(8), © Time, Inc.)

Whether humans learn any behavior by imprinting is an open question. Certainly some things are learned better and more permanently if they are learned early. In fact there is an old law, Jost's law (1897), which states just this—that things learned earlier are forgotten less

Conditioning
and learning
167

FIGURE 7-2

(a) Ducklings will learn to follow a mechanical model that is moved in front of them.
(b) This imprinting happens most effectively during an early critical period. (c) The
critical period for imprinting lies between the time the duckling becomes able to follow
and the onset of fear. (From Hess, 1959.)

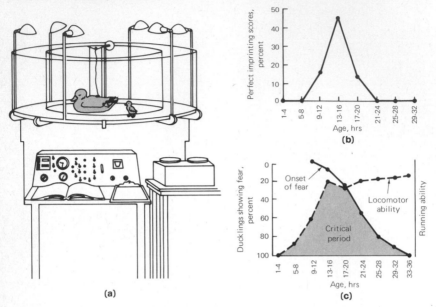

quickly and performed more strongly than things learned later. However,
it is impossible to say whether the learning of a first language, for instance, which seems to conform to Jost's law, is actually true imprinting.
To take another possible case, the smiling response of a baby to his
mother's face shows many of the characteristics of imprinting. The
particular face which a child takes as "mother" is learned between his
first and sixth month. Before one month he smiles at no one. Between
three and six months (on the average) a baby begins to smile at any
pair of eyes and wide mouth. After about six months of age, however,
he begins to be afraid of strange faces and to cry or at least not smile
when he sees faces other than those with which he is familiar. Whether
the process present in the imprinting of following in ducks is different
from the process underlying the development of the smiling response
in infant humans cannot really be said. It is certainly possible that the
two events are fundamentally alike.

Classical conditioning

Around the turn of the century the famous Russian physiologist, Ivan
Pavlov, had become interested in the digestive secretion of saliva. He
studied the salivary response of dogs to food or other substances placed
in their mouths (1927). In Pavlov's typical experiment the dog was put
in a restraining harness, a metronome was turned on, and meat powder

was injected into the dog's mouth. As the dog salivated the saliva ran, drop by drop, through a tube sewn in its cheek into a graduated cylinder. With the aid of the metronome, the reaction time and rate of salivation were measured. Pavlov noticed that dogs on which he had experimented many times sometimes began to salivate when he started the metronome —before meat powder was put in their mouths. Being a brilliant and perceptive scientist, Pavlov recognized the importance of this observation. He had discovered a means by which nature modifies an inborn reflex response.

The kind of learning which Pavlov discovered is now referred to as *classical conditioning*. In classical conditioning an initially ineffective stimulus acquires some of the capabilities of a stimulus that can already evoke a response from the animal. In the Pavlov experiment outlined above, the initially ineffective or neutral stimulus was the ticking of a metronome, and the already adequate stimulus for salivation was meat powder on the tongue. The neutral stimulus became a substitute for the natural stimulus in evoking salivation. Classical conditioning is often described as "learning by stimulus substitution": a new stimulus substitutes for an old stimulus in the evocation of a reflex response. Pavlov called the old, biologically adequate stimulus the *unconditioned stimulus* (US). He called the initially neutral stimulus, which through conditioning took on the properties of the natural stimulus, a *conditioned stimulus* (CS). This terminology is still used today. The unconditioned stimulus need not necessarily be a hereditarily given stimulus for a reflex. What is important is that it have the power to evoke a response from the subject strongly and reliably. Then, through the proper procedures, a new stimulus can be made to take on some of the same response-evoking power.

The response which comes under the control of a new stimulus in classical conditioning is rarely if ever exactly the same as the response that occurs to the natural biological stimulus. Rather, the conditioned response is usually weaker and often resembles the early or preparatory phase of the unconditioned response. It is, therefore, important to use the terms *unconditioned response* (UR) and *conditioned response* (CR) carefully to refer respectively to the reaction elicited by the unconditioned stimulus (US) and the reaction elicited by the conditioned stimulus (CS) after training.

Those events which are necessary in the experience of an animal if the typical way in which he behaves is to be altered may be said to strengthen or *reinforce* new behavior patterns. Thus such events are called *reinforcing* events. The various types and kinds of learning that we will discuss are differentiated one from another by the nature of the reinforcing event involved. Imprinting, classical conditioning, operant conditioning, and the various forms of human learning differ from one another in the events which appear to be necessary if there are to be alterations in behavioral tendencies. For example, in imprinting it is an initial exposure and reaction early in life that is crucial to the alteration of behavior. In classical conditioning it is the successive occurrence of

FIGURE 7–3
Effective order of pairing of stimuli in classical conditioning. If two stimuli, S¹ and S²,
are repeatedly paired in that order, the first comes to elicit a response like that
originally elicited by the second.

CS and US, with proper sequence and timing, which is the reinforcing
agent. As we will see later, in operant conditioning reinforcement takes
place when a special kind of event follows the performance of a particular response by the animal. We will now turn to a detailed consideration of the conditions which lead to learning by classical conditioning,
and the characteristics of the behavior patterns that are learned in this
manner.

Factors of effectiveness in classical conditioning

ORDER

It is not enough for the CS and US simply to occur close together in time;
the order and timing of their occurrence make a crucial difference in the
efficiency with which conditioning takes place.

When two stimuli occur repeatedly in the same order, the first takes
on some of the responsive-evoking properties of the second. The second
ordinarily does not take on any properties of the first. Thus we show
in Figure 7–3 a temporal sequence of stimuli. The stimulus called S^1
is whichever occurs first; S^2 is whichever occurs second. If at the outset both S^1 and S^2 could evoke responses from the animal (for example,
if the first stimulus were a metronome that evoked an attentive ear-
pricking-up response from a dog, and the second were an injection of
meat powder in the mouth, which evoked salivation), then after repeated
successive occurrences of the two stimuli in the order S^1 then S^2, S^2 would
still produce only salivation. If the order of presentation of the two
stimuli was reversed—that is, if the meat powder in the mouth became
S^1 and the metronome ticking became S^2—then what was conditioned
would also be reversed: meat powder in the mouth would come to evoke
the ear-pricking-up response as well as salivation, while the metronome
ticking would continue to produce only the ear-pricking-up response.

As a clarifying example of the problem of CS-US order in classical conditioning, a psychologist relates the following true story. His
infant daughter, Katy, was subject to ear infections that required the
administration of an evil-tasting medicine. Giving Katy the medicine
became a traumatic event, complete with spitting, screaming, and temper
tantrums. When asked by his wife for professional advice, the psychologist opined wisely that the problem would be easily solved by a little

FIGURE 7–4
How the order of pairing in classical conditioning affects behavior. If two stimuli both evoke responses and are paired repeatedly, the first acquires a response like that of the second, but the second does not change. In this example, pairings of orange juice-medicine modify (undesirably) a child's reaction to orange juice, while pairings of medicine-orange juice modify (desirably) the reaction to medicine.

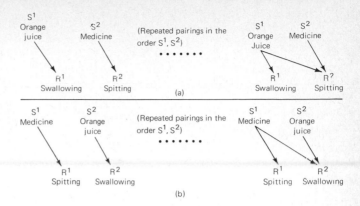

application of conditioning principles. The wife was instructed to pair the evil-tasting medicine with orange juice, which Katy loved. The next day the wife fed the infant orange juice and medicine several times during the day. But, far from being cured, the child began to refuse to accept orange juice. "Aha!" said the wise husband-psychologist, "You have been doing it wrong. You've been giving Katy the orange juice first and then the medicine, haven't you?"

"How did you know?" said the wife.

"Because [as the reader will recognize] if the orange juice took on the property of the medicine, it must have been the first of the two stimuli in the pairing. If it had been the second, the medicine would have taken on the property of the orange juice instead." See Figure 7–4 for a schematic diagram of the situation.

This is a particularly instructive example because the method Katy's mother used would be the natural one for most people. Reasoning that what one wants to do is to get the child to open his mouth, one would first give her what she likes and then quickly follow it with what she finds unpleasant. And, indeed, this might work for the first several or even dozen times. But to condition the child to open her mouth for medicine, it would be completely wrong. It would serve only to produce a new response to the orange juice which would occur along with the old response. The orange juice would come to elicit not only its natural response of swallowing, but also some of the spitting response naturally evoked by the medicine.

TIMING

It is not quite enough for the CS and US to occur in that order, CS-US. The time interval between CS and US must be just right if conditioning is to proceed reliably. In one early experiment, Spooner and Kellogg (1947) examined the relation between what is called the *CS-US interval* and the rate at which classical conditioning of a response occurred. The unconditioned response was a reflex withdrawal of the index finger on application of a painful electric shock. They conditioned this response to a buzzer by pairing buzzer and shock repeatedly. For

FIGURE 7–5

Relation between effectiveness of classical conditioning and the interval between CS and US. Shown are similar results of three different studies of finger withdrawal in which the CS was a buzzer, the US a shock. In all three studies, the optimum CS-US interval was approximately .5 second. (After Spooner & Kellogg, 1947.)

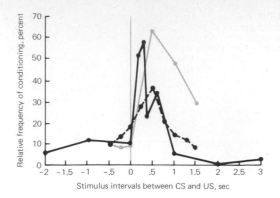

different groups of subjects in the experiment, they varied the time relations between the CS and the US. Sometimes the shock came before the buzzer; sometimes the buzzer came before the shock. They varied the intervals over a range, from US first by four seconds, to CS first by thirty seconds. The results are shown in Figure 7–5. The effectiveness of conditioning is shown on the ordinate (the vertical axis) in terms of the proportion of test trials—trials in which the CS alone was presented—on which a conditioned finger-movement occurred. As expected, no appreciable conditioning occurred when the US preceded the CS. The small number of responses on test trials for negative intervals represents what is called *sensitization*; subjects sometimes respond simply because they have been made to respond over and over again. A more surprising finding was that very little, if any, more conditioning occurred when the two stimuli were precisely simultaneous. That is, when both the shock and the buzzer came on at exactly the same instant, conditioning did not occur. This is a rather counter-intuitive fact.

As the figure shows, in this experiment the best timing for the presentation was a half-second interval. Conditioning also occurred with other intervals, ranging from near simultaneity to about ten seconds, getting less and less good as intervals either longer or shorter than a half second were used. Conditioning of this kind *can* occur with quite long intervals provided that certain aspects of the procedure, which we will not go into here, are properly arranged and, more important, provided that a very, very large number of training trials are used. However, it is always true, no matter how conditioning is effected, that the interval is important. In the case of humans learning new reflex motor responses to external stimuli, the optimum is usually about half a second.

For other kinds of conditioning, other lengths of optimal CS-US interval prevail. If a rat is fed a food with a distinctive taste and then is made sick by poisoning or x-ray treatment, he will learn to shun that food. Such conditioning will occur, however, even if the sickness is not induced until quite long after the food is eaten. Food-avoidance learning occurs very well with CS-US intervals up to 1½ hours, and less well with intervals up to 4 hours. Interestingly enough, this interval seems to correspond to the time it usually takes to get sick after eating poisonous food (Garcia, Ervin, & Koelling, 1966). Perhaps the CS-US

FIGURE 7–6

Learning curves for conditioned eyelid response with different amounts of time between successive CS-US pairings. (After Spence & Norris, 1950).

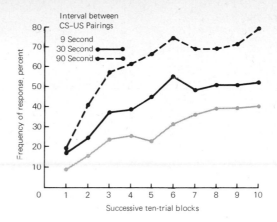

intervals that are effective in conditioning reflect the intervals that arise in natural causal sequences of the particular classes of stimuli and responses involved.

SPACING OF TRIALS

If the successive pairings occur right after one another, conditioning will be very inefficient. For example, if a dog is given a pairing of bell and meat powder once every two seconds for a total of fifty pairings, the conditioned salivary-response tendency will still be quite weak at the end of this training. On the other hand, if the pairings are separated by rest periods of one minute, conditioning will be very strong by the end of fifty reinforcements. Figure 7–6 shows data on the effect of *spacing of trials* on conditioning of the human eye-blink response. As the amount of time between one CS-US pairing and the next CS-US pairing increases, the efficiency of conditioning increases. Note carefully that this is not the same temporal variable as the CS-US interval. What we are discussing here is not the time between the beginning of the CS and the beginning of the US, but the time between one CS-US *pairing* and the next CS-US *pairing*, between one *reinforcement* and the next *reinforcement*. Later, we will meet other temporal variables of strong effect in learning and it is essential that one avoid confusing them.

STIMULUS INTENSITY

The stronger the CS and the stronger the US, the faster conditioning will occur. If a person is conditioned to blink his eye to a weak tone followed by a gentle puff of air, he will learn much more slowly than if the tone is loud and the puff of air strong. This effect of stimulus intensity holds for classical conditioning but not, apparently, for other forms of learning.

There are other variables which have some influence on classical conditioning, but they are of relatively minor importance and will not be discussed here. Let us turn now to a second process in classical conditioning—the manner in which a learned response is lost.

Conditioning and learning
173

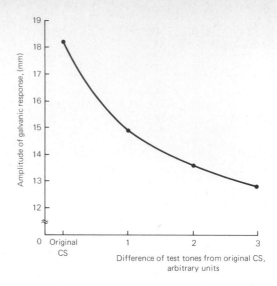

FIGURE 7–7
Generalization curve for conditioned galvanic skin response to a tone. Shown are the average reactions to the original CS after training, and to tones of different frequencies. (After Hovland, 1937.)

Amplitude of galvanic response, (mm)

19
18
17
16
15
14
13
12

0   Original
    CS

1   2   3

Difference of test tones from original CS, arbitrary units

Extinction

A response tendency acquired as a result of classical conditioning is not necessarily a permanent feature of the animal. On the one hand, if a person or animal learns a habit by classical conditioning and then is not called upon to perform the response, the tendency to do so will remain quite strong over quite long periods. If a person is trained to withdraw his finger at the sound of a buzzer, and then the same buzzer in the same situation is not presented again until several months later, the response tendency will still be there. On the other hand, if, having once been conditioned, a CS is presented over and over again without reinforcement—that is, without the properly paired presentation of the US—the response tendency will wane. The process of loss of a response tendency because of nonreinforced occurrences of the stimulus conditions for the response is called *extinction*. If a dog is conditioned to salivate to the sound of a metronome and then the sound is presented on many occasions without anything being put into the dog's mouth, he will eventually cease salivating to that sound.

Closely related to extinction is a phenomenon called *spontaneous recovery*. If a conditioned response is extinguished with closely spaced trials—e.g., a nonreinforced presentation of the stimulus every twenty seconds for an hour—the response disappears, but only temporarily. If the animal is tested a week later, the conditioned response reappears, although it is not nearly as strong as it was right after the initial training. In order to produce complete and lasting extinction the nonreinforced trials must be carried out on many successive, well-spaced occasions. Thus the spacing-of-trials effect holds for extinction as well as acquisition.

Characteristics of classically conditioned responses

There are several interesting characteristics of responses learned by classical conditioning, some of which differ from responses learned by other kinds of learning processes.

STIMULUS GENERALIZATION

If a dog is conditioned to respond with salivation to the sound of a metronome which ticks once a second, he will also salivate, although somewhat less vigorously, to a metronome ticking two or three times a second. Similarly a person who has been conditioned to blink when he hears a tone of 1,000 Hz will also blink, although less reliably, to tones of 950 Hz and 1,050 Hz. The fact that the conditioning of a response to a particular stimulus will produce a habit of responding not only to that stimulus but to ones similar to it is called *generalization*. Figure 7–7 shows a so-called *generalization gradient*, the function relating the probability of responding to a new stimulus to its similarity to the original CS. In the experiment of Figure 7–7 subjects were conditioned by presentation of a tone about half a second being given a shock to the arm. (This causes a mild emotional response which can be measured by a change in the electrical resistance of the skin which is called the *galvanic skin response*, or GSR.) Then, after conditioning was well advanced, they were tested with tones of various other frequencies; the curve shows the percentage of responses obtained. The less similar the test tone was to the trained CS, the less was the response, on the average. This general relation holds for all kinds of conditioning, although the shape of the generalization gradient varies from case to case.

DISCRIMINATION

While with simple conditioning to a single stimulus the response tendency spreads very widely to similar stimuli, it is nevertheless possible, by the use of special training sequences, to condition a response specifically to a single stimulus. After the animal or person has been conditioned to respond reliably to a particular stimulus, other stimuli to which the response would ordinarily generalize are presented without reinforcement and the generalization is thus extinguished. However, the extinction training also generalizes, thus weakening the response tendency to the original stimulus. For example, a blinking response is conditioned to a 1000 Hz tone by pairings of the tone and puffs of air to the eye. A 900 Hz tone is then repeatedly presented without the air puff. Af first, by generalization, the subject blinks. But after several unreinforced trials, response to the 900 Hz tone extinguishes. When response to the 900 Hz tone is extinguished, responding to the 1,000 Hz tone decreases somewhat as well. The response to 1,000 Hz can be brought back to strength by additional conditioning trials with reinforcement, which will in turn tend to strengthen the 900 Hz response again, and so forth. However, when series of reinforced trials with the positive stimulus are alternated with series of unreinforced trials with the negative stimulus, the distinction between the response tendency to one and the other gradually increases, until eventually the subject blinks reliably and regularly in response to the 1,000 Hz tone and almost never in response to the 900 Hz tone. This procedure is called *discrimination* training.

Applicability

In order to carry out learning by classical conditioning, it is necessary first to identify an unconditioned stimulus for which the conditioned stimulus can become a partial substitute. Most reflexes have easily identifiable natural stimuli. The knee jerk to patellar tendon deflection, the eye blink to a puff of air, finger withdrawal from pain or heat, and salivation to food are only a few examples. Most such reflexes are quite easily conditioned if the procedure is carefully arranged and enough trials are given. It is probably too early to say whether all responses for which a natural stimulus can be found are subject to classical conditioning. There are certainly wide differences in the ease with which one reflex and another can be conditioned. The eye-blink response, for example, can be conditioned quite readily in both humans and lower animals; the training sometimes requires as few as ten trials. At the other extreme, the pupillary contraction reflex which occurs in response to a rapid increase in illumination is extremely difficult to condition. Many investigators have failed altogether to produce conditioning of this reflex while others have claimed only moderate success with very large numbers of trials.

It is also possible to condition a response whose eliciting stimulus at the beginning of the experiment is itself a previously conditioned stimulus. If a knee-jerk response has been conditioned by a pairing of a mild electric shock to the thigh (CS) with a blow to the patellar tendon (US), and then the shock is paired appropriately with a bell—the blow to the patellar tendon being omitted on such trials—the tone alone may come to elicit the knee jerk. This so-called *second order conditioning* is rather hard to obtain, and requires many trials with interspersed reinforcement of the original conditioning—that is, with repetition every once in a while of the electric shock—patellar blow sequence.

In general, the kinds of behavior which are most easily modified by classical conditioning are those involving the defensive reflexes and responses which maintain the constancies of the internal environment. The latter include an amazing variety of subtle and often completely unconscious reactions. For example the heart rate, the alpha ryhthm of the brain, and the peristaltic movements of the stomach can all be conditioned by pairing an artificial stimulus appropriately with a natural biological elicitor of the reflex in question.

Classical conditioning is no respecter of species; it occurs equally in man, rabbits, and other mammals as well as in most lower animals so far studied. The effectiveness of classical conditioning can be altered by conscious, voluntary attempts by a human subject; but for the most part such control is the result of his adopting a posture or focus of attention which aids or interferes with the proper administration of conditioning stimuli.

In addition to the internal and defensive reactions, there are a number of other behaviors which are heavily influenced by classical conditioning. These include a wide range of emotional responses. Fear, an emotional response to the threat of pain, is quite easily conditioned. Shocked over and over again following a buzzer, a human will begin to respond to the buzzer with the physical signs and subjective feelings of fear.

A famous example of fear conditioning was an early experiment by Watson and Raynor (1920). They presented a furry, stuffed animal to a small boy named Albert, and immediately thereafter made a very loud noise behind him. After this procedure was repeated a few times Albert developed a fear reaction to the stuffed animal which generalized to other furry objects such as rabbits. It is also possible to cure such conditioned fears, by extinction procedures or by training an incompatible response to the same stimulus. Jones (1924) presented a feared white rabbit at a distance while the child was eating, and gradually conditioned to the rabbit the emotional responses to eating, thus counteracting the initial fear-conditioning. A similar "desensitization" technique is now being used widely in treatment of phobias and other neuroses (see Chapter 4). It is quite likely that many reactions such as anger, sexual arousal, and other emotions which are subject to changes with experience, are often modified through the process of classical conditioning.

In summary, while there is no firmly established limit on the types of behavior that can be influenced by classical conditioning, nonetheless some kinds of behavior are more readily affected by this learning process than others. The kinds of behavior which are particularly susceptible are those involving reflexes, internal defensive and environment-maintaining responses, and emotional reactions.

OPERANT CONDITIONING

A hungry rat is placed in a box which contains two pieces of apparatus—a food tray into which a small pellet of rat food can be automatically dropped, and a lever that the rat can operate with his forepaw. The rat finds food in the tray a number of times and begins to hover about it. At irregular intervals, pellets of food arrive following a distinctive click from the food delivery mechanism. Gradually the hungry rat learns to run to the food tray whenever he hears the click. Then the experimenter begins to train the rat to use the lever by a series of gradual steps. First he waits until the rat is close to the lever and then delivers a pellet of food. After this happens several times the rat begins to spend more time near the lever. Then the experimenter waits for the rat to make accidental contact with the lever before dispensing a food pellet. Eventually the rat does bump into the lever, whereupon a food pellet is dispensed. The rat makes more and more such contacts, and each time a food pellet follows. Finally the experimenter waits until the rat leans on or actually presses the lever before giving a food pellet reward. After a while, the rat does so and gets a pellet. Then he presses again and then again, at first slowly and sporadically, later smoothly and rapidly—each time getting a pellet. Thus may be described a typical sequence of events in *operant conditioning*.

The essential features of this kind of learning are: First, there is no obvious, natural stimulus that elicits the response in question; the bar press response, for example, has no known reflex-evoking stimulus. Second, the control of learning is exercised by the outcome of the behavior; the natural variations that occur are modified by a selective process emphasizing those which lead to a particular outcome. A very basic feature of behavior of all kinds and in all organisms is that it is subject to a great deal of random variation. An animal rarely makes exactly the same response twice. Operant conditioning selects from the natural variations in behavior those which are in one manner or another most adaptive for the animal. The term *operant conditioning* reflects the fact that the animal *operates* on the environment—whether natural or in a laboratory—to produce an effect. The effect produced determines whether the animal will make that response again with higher probability or will continue to behave as before.

It is the nature of the reinforcing event that differentiates operant conditioning from other kinds of learning. Whereas in classical conditioning the reinforcing event is the pairing of a new stimulus with an already effective one, in operant conditioning the event which strengthens a new behavioral tendency is the outcome of a response.

The specific events that must occur for learning to happen by operant conditioning are described in two related principles. The first, which may be called the *principle of operant reinforcement*, can be stated as follows: *When a learnable response is followed closely in time by a special event known as an operant reinforcer, the future probability of that response is thereby increased.* A reinforcing event in operant conditioning, then, is a special kind of event *following* an action on the part of the animal. It is worth noting that *response* is used in a somewhat loose way in this definition, in that the behavior referred to is not necessarily in response to any particular stimulus but is simply any action or bit of behavior on the part of the animal.

As an example of the principle of operant reinforcement, consider the following experiment which any student can perform to convince himself of the validity and usefulness of this principle. In a small class— one with, say, twelve to twenty students—the teacher ordinarily looks around from one student to another in a haphazard manner. If a student counts the number of times that the teacher's eyes meet his, he will find, usually, that this pleasant event happens something like once every minute or two. To do the experiment rigorously, a careful tally should be made of the number of eye meetings in each successive one-minute period for about ten minutes. During this time the student should maintain a more-or-less relaxed, reasonably inattentive and unresponsive demeanor. Then, at a predetermined point the student should begin to reinforce eye-meeting behavior on the part of the teacher. A good reinforcing event for the purpose is a pleasant, attentive smile—a look of approval and interest. Thus, each time the teacher's eyes meet those of the student, the student should smile and look attentive. Meanwhile the tally is continued. If the attentive smile is in fact a reinforcing event for the animal in question, the frequency of eye meetings should increase. And indeed it will. Try it.

What is necessary for operant conditioning is that an event which has reinforcing power be made to occur soon—we shall shortly discuss just how soon—after the occurrence of the behavior that is to be strengthened.

An important thing to note, however, is that the principle of operant reinforcement is nothing more than a definition. It says that when a response is followed by a reinforcing event, the future frequency of that response is thereby increased. All this actually does is to *define* a reinforcing event as an event which, if it follows a response closely in time, causes an increase in the future probability of that response. It is conceivable that having defined such a reinforcing event we could still find that no such thing existed in the world! But of course it was the empirical observation that such events do in fact exist that prompted the formulation of the principle of operant reinforcement in the first place.

But there is another problem with the principle as stated, and that is that it is very weak. How can one tell what events are reinforcing? Well, by definition, those events which lead to an increase in the probability of a response are reinforcing. Thus, to determine whether an event is a reinforcer one would have to make it follow a response and see whether the response increases in frequency. But if one had to do that every time one wanted to know whether an event was a reinforcer, what good would it do to know the principle of reinforcement? Not much. In order to apply the principle of reinforcement in any adequate way one has to know what event is going to be a reinforcer before actually using it, not simply after it has turned out to work.

What puts teeth into operant reinforcement as a training process is a second principle—*the principle of generality of reinforcers*—which can be stated as follows: *When an event is found to act as a reinforcer for any operantly conditionable response of a given animal, that same event will also act as a reinforcer for any other operantly conditionable response for that animal.* In other words, if a particular event, say the delivery of a pellet of food when the animal is hungry, has been found to increase the probability of a bar press, the principle of generality of reinforcers says that a pellet of food will also increase the frequency of any other response which the animal is capable of learning by operant conditioning. If a smile has worked to increase the frequency with which a teacher looks at a student, the frequency with which the same teacher raises his left arm, paces across the room in front of the blackboard, or says the word *cow* could also be reinforced by following its occurrence closely with a smile. The principle contains the phrase "any operantly conditionable response," because there are probably some kinds of responses that are not sensitive to operant conditioning at all.

In applying this principle it is necessary to be very careful in the description of the reinforcing event. It is not enough simply to say, for example, "a pellet of food." A pellet of food is a reinforcer only when the animal is hungry, and even then its reinforcing power will depend on his prior training to receive, accept, and swallow the pellet. It also should be noted that the principle of generality of reinforcers has not been established as an absolute law. It is not unlikely that certain reinforcers work better for some responses than others. Nevertheless, a great deal of experimental experience justifies a general faith that properly identified reinforcers will serve as such in most situations and for most responses.

Varieties of reinforcers

Another way of making the principle of operant reinforcement more useful would be to find something about reinforcing events by which they could be recognized without needing to be tested. Then one would be able to predict ahead of time what would and would not be a reinforcer for all or most animals. A great deal of experimental and theoretical effort has gone into trying to specify the nature of an operant reinforcing event, but to date no adequate general description has been obtained. There is, as yet, no single method of predicting with complete accuracy whether an event will be reinforcing or not. The only way to be sure is to test the event by its definitional criterion—that is, to make it occur shortly after a learnable response and note whether the probability of the response increases.

However, the situation is not completely bleak. It is possible to write a sizable catalog both of specifically described events and of several classes of events which usually, if not always, work as reinforcers for most animals. We shall describe some of these reinforcers below.

But first a distinction must be made between *positive* and *negative* reinforcers. A reinforcing event that commences *soon after* the response is called a *positive reinforcer*; examples are food given to a hungry animal or water given to a thirsty animal. An event that reinforces when it is present during the response but terminates soon after is called a *negative reinforcer*; examples are an electric shock or noxious noise. The important thing to remember is that a negative reinforcer is not defined as an event which decreases response probability, as one might think, but as an event which, like a positive reinforcer, increases response probability—but does so when the response serves to terminate it rather than when the response produces it. Thus, turning off a blast of air after a cat moves across a table increases his tendency to do so, and the air blast is a negative reinforcer.

DRIVE REDUCERS

Drives are generally defined in much the same way that need was described in the chapter on motivation: that is, a drive is a state which if it is not relieved leads, eventually, to a pathological condition and/or death. Drives include hunger, thirst, the need for sex, and needs for a wide variety of other goals necessary to the well-being of an animal. Alternatively one can describe a drive as a state in which occur numerous activities that usually have the effect of obtaining a certain goal. In general if one knows that an animal is low on something that is required for normal functioning, or has been deprived of some object or commodity that he is accustomed to consuming, then it can be predicted that he will ordinarily be reinforced by the provision of that object or commodity. Thus, animals do many things by which they obtain food. When an animal has not had food for a long time he may be described as having a high level of food deprivation or hunger drive. A response of an animal in such a state will almost invariably be reinforced if the level of this drive state is reduced; if the animal is given food, a response that has just occurred will be strengthened. Similarly a response of an animal deprived of water will be reinforced by water; and that of an animal deprived of sex, by sex. In fact for most known needs or drives, reduction of that drive acts as a reinforcer.

This phenomenon extends to rather subtle and sometimes unconscious need-reductions. For example it can be shown that an animal that is deprived of certain vitamins will be reinforced by provision of those vitamins. Similarly, it has been shown that an animal can be taught to make a response which leads to the injection of glucose directly into a vein (Coppock & Chambers, 1954). A goat was strapped in a restraining harness and hypodermic needles inserted into its veins so that either a control saline solution or a glucose solution could be injected. Glucose was injected whenever the goat turned its head to the right and saline whenever it turned its head to the left. The glucose acted as a reinforcer, and increased the probability of head-turning toward the right.

It is not surprising that evolution has provided animals with a means of selecting responses which are followed by drive reduction. It is not possible, however, to *equate* reinforcement with drive reduction. There appear to be numerous reinforcers that have no obvious drive-reducing properties—some will be mentioned below—and it is also quite likely that the reduction of some drives, e.g., the need for vitamin D, are not reinforcing.

INNATELY PLEASANT STIMULI

There are some stimuli which seem to be pleasant as a function of the inheritance of an animal, and which also act as reinforcers whether or not they reduce any known drive. One example is the feel of a soft object to a young animal. An infant monkey, cat, or human can often be seen rubbing its skin against a furry object such as its mother or a terry-cloth towel. If the animal is allowed contact with such an object after making a response, the future probability of that response will be increased. Thus such contact works as a reinforcer. There is no obvious way in which such an event works as a drive-reducer—it appears merely to be a naturally reinforcing stimulus. Similarly, things that taste sweet appear to act as operant reinforcers whether or not they are actually nutritive. A rat and many humans will choose saccharine-sweetened water even when not thirsty or hungry. This despite the fact that saccharine has little or no physiological effect and is not a reducer of hunger drive. A monkey can be taught to press a bar in order to be allowed to groom another monkey or the experimenter—that is, to pick at the other's skin and hair in search of fleas. This *activity* is itself a reinforcer; when it is allowed to occur immediately after some other response, that other response increases in frequency.

Allowing an animal to engage in sexual activities is a strong reinforcer. Making a male rat turn a wheel in order to get access to a receptive female will eventuate in very rapid conditioning of the wheel-turning response. That this should be so when the response leads to a complete copulation is not very surprising. However, sexual activity will act as a reinforcer even in the clear absence of sexual drive reduction. For instance, if a male rat is allowed access to a receptive female as a reward for turning a wheel, but not allowed to complete the copulatory act—he is allowed to mount but the vagina is sewn shut so that intromission is impossible—operant conditioning will still occur.

SMALL STIMULUS CHANGES

A rat in a brightly lighted box will learn to press a lever that turns the light off for a few seconds. This is no great surprise since rats, being nocturnal animals, presumably like darkness better than light. However, if a rat is placed in a dark box with a lever that turns *on* the light for a few seconds, he will also learn to press the lever! A rat can be reinforced both by a light going on and by a light going off. It seems to be a small change in the stimulus conditions which is the reinforcer rather than their absolute level.

It is likely that humans are also sometimes reinforced by small stimulus changes. And the experience of pleasantness is often correlated with such changes. If a person puts his hand in a bucket of water and gets used to its temperature for a while, and then places his hand in another bucket of water of a different temperature, he will find the new temperature pleasant if it is slightly different from the old, unpleasant if it is extremely different, and about neutral if it is the same.

If a human subject is induced to emit sequences of verbal behavior (that is, to talk) his verbal production can be altered by operant conditioning with several different kinds of reinforcers. In the original experiment of this kind by Greenspoon (1955) the experimenter said, "Mmhum," which he thought was probably a learned social reward, each time the subject uttered a plural noun. The frequency of plural nouns increased as a result. In the same way it is possible to increase self-references, length of sentence, or just about any definable aspect of conversational speech. Such results can also be obtained by using a nod of the head or the phrase "That's good" as the social reinforcer. In addition, less obviously socially meaningful stimuli can serve as reinforcers. In one experiment a small light behind the experimenter's head was turned on each time the subject said the words *I* or *me*. Frequency of such words increased. The light had no apparent drive-reducing qualities, and would probably not be reported as introspectively pleasant, but it did act as a reinforcer. Apparently animals and humans prefer a world in which there are small but nonthreatening changes over one in which everything remains constant.

ACQUIRED REINFORCERS

A pigeon is trained to peck a key to obtain grain from a dispenser. Then a light is used to illuminate the key in either red or green, and pecking of the key is followed by grain only when the green light is on. Eventually the pigeon learns to peck the key only during the green. Thus he often receives food just after he looks at the green light. According to the principles of classical conditioning, any response elicited by the food should become conditioned to the green light. And, indeed, this is precisely what happens. The reinforcing power of the food becomes conditioned to the green light, and after such training the green light will itself act as a reinforcer. If, whenever the pigeon walks to the front of the cage, the green light is turned on—with no food being given at all—the pigeon will learn to step forward more and more frequently.

By classical conditioning an initially neutral stimulus can be given the reinforcing characteristics of a natural reinforcer. This stimulus is called a *conditioned* or *acquired reinforcer*. Reinforcing power can be given in this way to virtually any stimulus.

It is hard to say to what extent human behavior is influenced by acquired reinforcers because the actual behavior of any human has a very complex history. However, there are certain events that seem to work as reinforcers for humans which are certainly not common to all humans. For example, someone saying "Yes, that's good" works as a reinforcer for a human who has learned English, but that particular expression of social approval would probably have little reinforcing value for a monolingual Laplander. The reduction of cognitive dissonance (Chapter 2) is an event which seems to increase the frequency of the kinds of behavior that lead to it, but it seems unlikely that the desire to be consistent, and the reinforcing property of so being, is an innate characteristic of humans, at least in its more sophisticated manifestations. Similarly, people appear to work for money. It is hard to say whether money works in precisely the way that an experimental operant reinforcer does, but certainly there are many gross similarities. A person given money after doing something is usually more likely to do it in the future. The reinforcing property of money is certainly not innate and does not fit into any of the other categories which we have previously described. It is, then, an acquired reinforcer. Whether it is acquired by being classically conditioned as a stimulus paired with an innately reinforcing event is impossible to say. This is one way in which such an object as money or an event like dissonance reduction could become reinforcing, but there is no reason to presume that there are not other ways in which events can become reinforcing for a human.

Factors of effectiveness in operant conditioning

Before we describe the variables and conditions that influence the effectiveness with which operant conditioning occurs, it is necessary to introduce some concepts about learning in general which we have not discussed yet. First of all we need to distinguish three stages of modification of behavioral tendencies. The first stage, which is more or less equivalent to learning or conditioning, is called *acquisition*. In this stage a behavioral tendency comes into being and becomes gradually more frequent, more complete, or more intense, until it attains its final character. The second stage is *performance*, the actual making of the learned response. The third stage, *extinction*, is the loss of the conditioned response as a result of discontinuation of reinforcement. One reason for distinguishing these stages is that in operant conditioning particularly, but in other kinds of learning as well, the variables which influence one stage often differ considerably from those which influence another. To make the distinction clearer it will help if we describe some quantitative features of the acquisition stage.

FIGURE 7–8
Schematized, idealized average
learning curve for an
uncomplicated situation,
illustrating the principle of
constant proportional gains.

PRINCIPLE OF CONSTANT PROPORTIONAL GAIN

Figure 7–8 shows a somewhat idealized graph of the average progress of learning over successive reinforcements. While no single animal would ever produce such a smooth curve—the behavior of any one individual is very erratic and unpredictable—a large number of animals learning the same task would generate an average curve much like this. While there are variations, this shape of "learning curve" represents the way learning usually progresses in uncomplicated situations.

If a behavioral tendency is measured in terms of probability of response in a given situation, then learning proceeds from an initial state in which the probability is either zero or very low, to some maximum level. Obviously, the absolute maximum would be a probability of 1.0 —that is, occurrence 100 percent of the time. However, the probability of a response rarely reaches 100 percent and sometimes may never exceed 40 percent or 80 percent. It is possible, and frequently desirable, to measure the degree of learning in terms other than probability of occurrence. For example, a rat being trained to run down a straight alley with no alternatives will start out with a response probability of 1.0. In such a case one might be more interested in, say, the speed at which the rat runs. A curve such as that in Figure 7–8 describes this situation also, if we but change the labeling of the ordinate. Generally, the gains in performance that are produced by the first few reinforcements are larger than those produced by the next few, and so forth.

Two important features of a graph of any learning process are the maximum and the rate at which the maximum is approached. The shape of the curve, for the typical learning situations being discussed, is described by what may be called the *principle of constant proportional gain*. This principle states that the amount gained in any equal period of training is a constant proportion of the amount left to be learned. The amount left to be learned is defined as the difference between the present level and the maximum which will be attained with an indefinitely large amount of training. There is always such a maximum, called mathematically an *asymptote*.

Consider Figure 7–8. Here the performance on the ordinate is in some arbitrary measure. The curve rises *toward* a level of 80, meaning

FIGURE 7-9
Two schematic learning curves
with the same maximum, but
different learning rates.

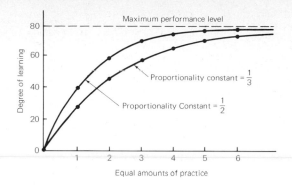

that this is the maximum performance no matter how much training is given—perhaps 80 percent correct turns in a maze or 80 feet per minute running in an alley. The abscissa is measured off in equal amounts of practice, and several different ways in which this could occur are shown: successive hours of training, or training on a certain number of days, or successive, equal numbers of reinforced responses. The reason that the labeling is so indefinite is that the principle of constant proportional gain is very general and applies to many kinds of performance and for many measures of successive equal periods of practice.

In Figure 7–8 the level of performance of the hypothetical response is assumed to start at 0. After the first period of practice it increased to 40. Since 40 is one-half of the distance between the starting place, 0, and the maximum of 80, the proportion gained in the first unit of practice was 50 percent. Now, according to the principle of constant proportional gain, the amount gained in the next equal segment of practice should be the same proportion of the amount left to be gained. The amount left to be gained is the difference between the present performance, 40, and the eventual maximum, 80, and 50 percent of the difference between 40 and 80 is 20 $(0.5 \times (80 - 40) = 20)$. Thus after the second equal unit of practice the curve rises 20 more points to 60. Similarly, after the third unit of practice the curve should again rise 50 percent of the remaining distance $(0.5 \times (80 - 60) = 10)$ and reach the level of 70. The curve continues to rise half of the remaining way towards the maximum of 80 in each additional equal segment of practice.

The proportion of the amount left to be learned which is gained in each successive unit of practice is given by a number—in the case of this first example, 0.5—known as the *proportionality constant* (or learning parameter). The proportionality constant may differ from one experiment to another, from one set of conditions of learning to another, and from one kind of animal or individual to another. In Figure 7-9 a second curve has been added to the one shown in Figure 7–8. This curve also starts at the performance level of 0 and goes to an eventual maximum of 80, but it approaches the maximum more slowly. Instead of going from 0 to 40 in the first segment of practice, it goes only to 26.7— one-third of the way from the start to the eventual maximum. In the next equal segment it again goes one-third of the remaining way, and so forth.

Conditioning
and learning
185

FIGURE 7–10
Two schematic learning curves
with equal learning rates, but
different maxima.

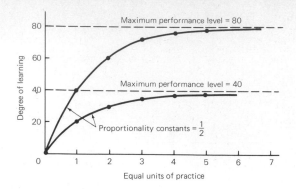

Thus for the lower curve the proportionality constant is 0.33 instead of 0.50. Note that the maximum level to which learning proceeds is the same, but the rate of learning—in terms of proportionality constant—is lower. It is this proportionality constant that is meant by the phrase *rate of learning*.

Now consider Figure 7–10. Here are shown two curves with the same proportionality constant but with different maxima. In one case the maximum toward which learning is moving is 80; in the other case, only 40. Here, however, both curves approach their maxima at the same rate: after the first segment of training they have both gone half of the way toward their eventual maxima, after the second segment three-quarters of the way, and so forth. We note that the amount of learning in absolute terms, i.e., the increase in performance level from one segment of learning to the next, is greater in the top curve than it is in the lower curve of Figure 7–10, but the *rate* of learning, as it is technically defined, does not differ since the proportionality constant is the same.

It is important to make these distinctions for at least two reasons. The first is that the variables which influence the rate of learning do not necessarily influence its maximum, and vice versa. If we were to consider only the amount learned in an absolute sense, rather than consider the rate of approach to a maximum and the maximum separately, we could not distinguish so well between the effects of various conditions of training. Secondly, the concept of constant proportional gain is of considerable theoretical interest and is a common denominator of many important theories of the learning process.

We now turn to a consideration of the substantive conditions that influence the efficiency of learning by operant conditioning. While there is not space here to go into all the factors, two or three of the most important variables for acquisition, for performance, and for extinction will be described.

VARIABLES AFFECTING ACQUISITION
Perhaps the most important determiner of the rate at which operant conditioning occurs, and of whether it occurs at all, is the delay of the potentially reinforcing event after the occurrence of the response.

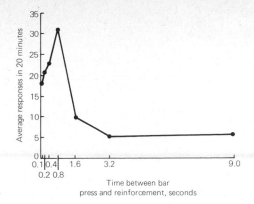

FIGURE 7–11
The effectiveness of operant conditioning as a function of the time between the response and the reinforcer. In this experiment, rats pressed a bar, then were reinforced by a secondary reinforcer—a brief signal that had previously been paired with water. (After Landauer, 1964).

Delay of reinforcement

In one study of the delay of reinforcement (Landauer, 1964) a secondary reinforcer consisting of a brief tone was used. Different groups of rats were trained with different times between a bar press and the secondary reinforcer. For some groups the reinforcement came 0.1 second after each bar press; for others, 0.2 second after; and so forth. The relation between learning and the time intervening between bar press and reinforcer is shown in Figure 7–11. The ordinate gives the number of bar presses in twenty minutes of training. When reinforcement was delayed for more than a few seconds its effectiveness for operant conditioning declined rapidly. In other studies, using a variety of different primary reinforcers and many different species, including man, the maximum time in which an operant reinforcer has an effect has rarely been found to exceed ten seconds when the situation is carefully controlled. Apparently, also, too short an interval between the response and the reinforcing event is not optimal for learning—the curve in Figure 7–11 decreases to the left of a point at about one second. The student should note that this function is not the same as the CS–US interval function previously described for classical conditioning: the relation here involves the time by which a special event follows a response; in the temporal function for CS–US pairing the relation involved the time between a neutral stimulus and an effective stimulus.

While an operant reinforcer has its strongest effects when it occurs within a few seconds after a response, this does not mean that learning cannot occur with longer delays. Some conditioning is produced by reinforcers even after very long delays. And, more important, with sufficient numbers of trials in an ordinary learning situation, a phenomenon comes into play that "bridges" the delay in reinforcement. This is the generation of new secondary reinforcers. Imagine a rat who runs down an alley, comes to a corner, turns right, runs a small additional distance through a grey passage, and then finds a pellet of food. The pellet of food is likely not to come for several seconds after the critical right turn, and consequently is of little value as a reinforcer for that response. On the other hand, the pellet of food arrives very soon after the rat sees the grey color which distinguishes the right from the left section of the maze. Eventually, the grey passage itself acquires secondary reinforcing power. Since this stimulus occurs immediately after the rat turns right, it will produce efficient conditioning of the correct response (the turn to the right).

Spacing of trials

A second factor which determines the rate of learning, or acquisition, also involves time. This is the time between one reinforcement and the next. We have already discussed this variable, which we called *spacing of trials*, in relation to classical conditioning. Its effect is similar in operant conditioning. If practice trials are massed—run one after another in quick succession—learning proceeds rather slowly. As more time—five seconds, a minute, up to at least a day—separates one reinforced response from the next, the amount of learning *per reinforcement* (that is, the proportionality constant) increases. The total number of *hours* that it may take a rat to learn a maze will probably be shorter if he has 60 trials in one hour than if he has only one trial per hour. But the number of *trials* required before he will be performing at, say, 90 percent correct, will be much smaller if the trials are given one each hour than if they are given one each minute. As in the case of classical conditioning, the biggest differences due to spacing of practice are between very short and medium intervals. If only a few seconds are allowed between one trial and the next in a maze, learning proceeds very inefficiently; while if one minute is allowed between successive trials, learning proceeds quite rapidly. However, if the interval is increased from one minute to one hour or from one hour to one day, only a little additional benefit is obtained.

PERFORMANCE

The two variables which are probably most influential in determining the characteristics and level of performance of an already learned response are motivation and arrangement or scheduling of reinforcers.

Motivation

Motivation refers to the level of the drive state under which the animal is operating. If a rat has learned to press a bar in order to receive a food pellet when hungry, he will press the bar more rapidly when he is very hungry than when he is only slightly so. The level of the maximum response to which training will lead is greatly affected by the motivational state of the animal. Motivation leads the animal to be more active and aroused, and accelerates his performance of relevant learned-response tendencies.

At this point it is worth taking a few sentences to describe the general role of motivation in learned behavior. As we have seen before (Chapter 6), motivational states include states of *arousal* and *activation*. They also include the *actuation* of reinforcers: food is a reinforcer only to a hungry animal; water, only to one that has been deprived of it, and so forth. The satiation-deprivation cycles include, along with concomitant differences in excitement and activity, variations in the efficacy of certain reinforcing events. Finally, deprivation states have stimulus properties. An animal has available stimuli which tell it that it is in a state of hunger, thirst, and so on. These stimuli can be made the conditions for performance, and a trained animal will tend to perform a response most readily under the deprivation conditions in which he was originally trained. A rat, for example, can be trained to turn to the left in a maze when he has not had food in a long time, and to turn to the right when he has been deprived of water.

To summarize, motivational states can influence learned behavior by (a) actuating the reinforcing value of certain events, (b) accelerating already learned behavior through a general activating effect on the animal, and (c) serving as stimulus conditions to which behavior can become conditioned.

Schedules of reinforcement

A second important variable in the performance of a learned task is the scheduling of the additional reinforcers which keep the response tendency going. In acquisition it is most efficient to have a reinforcer occur after each response. In fact it is hard to get learning to occur at all otherwise. But once a behavioral tendency has been acquired, its maintenance and execution are actually more reliable if a reinforcement is not given each time the response is performed, but rather on some *partial* reinforcement schedule. If a pigeon has been trained to peck a key until he is doing so smoothly, he will continue to respond quite well if, instead of each peck being followed by a reinforcer, every second one, or even every twentieth, is followed by a reinforcer. The arrangement of reinforcers with respect to responses and with respect to time is known as a *schedule of reinforcement*.

There are many kinds of schedules which can be designed to produce particular effects in the pattern of responding. For instance, a schedule can be instituted whereby the animal is reinforced only if he does not respond for a long interval; this schedule yields very slow responding. Or a schedule can be established whereby the animal is reinforced only if he responds at a high rate; such a schedule yields very rapid responding. Indeed by sufficient training and proper arrangement of a schedule, the characteristics of performance can be altered in almost unlimited ways.

EXTINCTION

We must first distinguish extinction from forgetting. Extinction is the loss of a response tendency through repeated occurrences without reinforcement. Forgetting is the loss of a response tendency with the sheer passage of time, without the occurrence of the response in the interim. If a pigeon is thoroughly taught to peck a key, as much as four years later he will, upon being returned to the experimental box, recommence pecking at a considerable rate. He will have forgotten very little. On the other hand, if a trained pigeon is allowed to stay in the experimental box and peck the key repeatedly, but no reinforcement is delivered, he will cease responding in less than an hour. This is *extinction*.

FIGURE 7-12

The cumulative recorder provides a convenient way of recording and representing a large number of responses over long periods. Left: The paper moves continuously under the recording pen, which moves a notch to the left each time the animal responds. The pen also indicates each reinforcement by a tickmark. Right: A segment of the recording, displayed horizontally. A steep line indicates rapid responding, a horizontal line no responding at all.

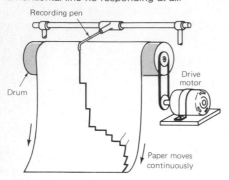

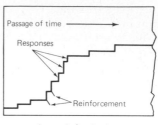

A record of extinction

As in classical conditioning, operant extinction is subject to spontaneous recovery. A pigeon whose operant pecking is extinguished one day will, when put back in the cage the next, begin pecking again, although at a slower rate. On successive days of extinction he will peck less and less. It will always, however, remain easier to train him to peck again.

Several variables influence extinction. The better an animal has been trained (the higher the maximum performance after training), the longer it will take for him to extinguish. The more the situation is arranged to induce maximum performance, the longer he will continue to perform. The higher his level of motivation, the longer it will take for his response tendency to dwindle. The most dramatic, and perhaps least expected, influence on extinction is that of the schedule of reinforcement used to maintain performance just before extinction is instituted.

Partial reinforcement

In an important early experiment, Skinner (1950) demonstrated the dramatic influence that schedules of partial reinforcement during performance can have on subsequent extinction. A pigeon was trained to peck a key, at first on a continuous reinforcement schedule in which each peck was followed by a reinforcer. Then the behavior was extinguished by inactivation of the reinforcing feed mechanism. The course of extinction is shown in Figure 7-12. This form of graph is called a *cumulative recording*. The paper moves continuously under a pen. The pen moves one notch each time the animal responds. If he responds very rapidly, the pen moves up often as the paper moves across. Thus a steep, straight line means the animal was responding at a high, regular rate. If he stops responding, the line moves only across, not up. Thus a horizontal line means he was not responding at all—that he had extinguished.

Next, Skinner thoroughly retrained the bird, this time on a partial reinforcement schedule in which the bird received a reinforcement at ir-

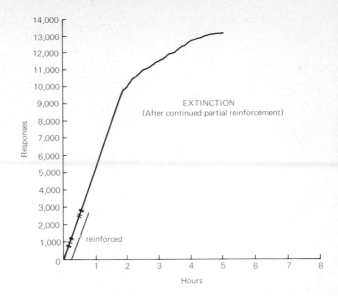

FIGURE 7–13
Extinction after partial
reinforcement. The curve is for
extinction after retraining on a
variable schedule with five
minutes as the average time
between reinforcements. (After
Skinner, 1950.)

regular intervals, averaging about a minute. Again, extinction procedures
were initiated, but this time the pigeon responded almost three thousand
times before gradually ceasing. Again Skinner reconditioned the bird,
this time on a variable schedule in which there was an average of five
minutes between reinforcements. In a subsequent extinction period there
were about ten thousand unreinforced responses before cessation. The
record is shown in Figure 7–13. Clearly, as Skinner pointed out, this
process could have been continued almost indefinitely, and almost any
number of responses obtained from the animal without reinforcement
—that is, in extinction—given only that the average interval between
reinforcements was raised to a high enough value.

No single explanation for the effect of partial reinforcement on extinction is yet agreed upon. Several plausible accounts are available.
The one offered by Skinner focused on the animal's problem in discrimi-
nating the partial reinforcement condition from the nonreinforcement
condition of extinction. When the situation has consisted of one reinforcement every ten minutes with the exact time unpredictable, it is hard
for the animal to tell that the situation has changed when reinforcement
is withdrawn altogether. Another line of explanation is that simply responding more frequently leads to a stronger response tendency, independent of whether the responses are followed by an operant reinforcing
event. In this case the animal maintained on a partial reinforcement
schedule has made many more responses than one given the same number of reinforcements on a continuous reinforcement schedule. Still another explanation rests on dissonance-reduction theory (see Chapter 2).
The theory holds that if the animal responds for a long time for very few
reinforcements he will come to value responding itself in order to pro-
mote cognitive consistency.

Although it is possible to demonstrate the partial-reinforcement

Conditioning
and learning
191

effect with humans in the laboratory, it is rather hazardous to invoke partial reinforcement as the reason for human behaviors observed "in the wild." However, remembering to be tentative and cautious, let us speculate a little on those human response tendencies that appear to go on and on and on when one might think they should extinguish. One of the most obvious examples is the compulsive gambler's attachment to a slot machine. A slot machine pays off only infrequently and unpredictably. Perhaps such behavior is maintained by a partial reinforcement schedule.

Characteristics of behavior learned by operant conditioning

In operant conditioning, unlike classical conditioning, there is no one special stimulus to which a new response is attached. The response is, to be sure, learned in the context of a particular situation, but the control which that situation exercises over the response is minimal. It is possible to change many aspects of the environment in which the response was reinforced—for example, to alter the color of the walls in an experimental box, or to illuminate in a different color the key that a pigeon pecks—without materially changing the response tendency. A response tendency strengthened by operant reinforcement tends to generalize to any situation which is similar enough for the response to be supported—that is, to almost any situation in which there is a bar, if the response is a bar press, or a key, if the response is a key peck. Only if special training procedures are carried out will the response by very much affected by changes in the stimulus conditions. The process of training an animal to respond only in the presence of a particular stimulus is called, as in classical conditioning, *discrimination training*.

DISCRIMINATION TRAINING IN OPERANT CONDITIONING

One way in which discrimination training can be carried out is by a combination of reinforcement in the presence of the positive stimulus, S^D, and extinction in the presence of a negative stimulus, $S^\triangle$. For example, a pigeon is first taught to peck a green key. Then the key color is changed to red. By generalization he will at first peck the red key almost as rapidly as the green. But if no reinforcement is given with the red key, the response will extinguish. If the key color is then turned back to green, the extinction will also generalize so that he will have to be retrained to peck at green. However, as these two conditions continue to alternate, the bird will gradually come to peck more to green and less to red, until eventually he will *discriminate* perfectly between the two stimuli.

There is another method of training operant discrimination. In this procedure, sometimes called *errorless discrimination training*, there is no extinction phase as such. The subject is trained to respond in the presence of the positive stimulus, just as before, but rather than presenting the negative stimulus and allowing responding in its presence to extinguish, the experimenter presents the negative stimulus too briefly or too weakly for any response to occur, and then switches the positive stimulus back on. For example, a pigeon is first trained to peck at a green key. After he is responding well the key color is switched from green to red for perhaps one second—too short a time for any response to occur.

The bird continues to be reinforced when he pecks the key illuminated in green. Gradually the duration of the red light is increased. If this is done very carefully and slowly, the length of the red light can be increased indefinitely without the animal ever pecking in its presence. Equally good control over the response is obtained in this way as in the first discimination training procedure described. Moreover, it is thought that the animal experiences less frustration and upset when trained in this manner.

In either case, an animal trained to respond to a particular stimulus and not to others will show a generalization gradient. He will not only respond to the positive stimulus but to ones which are very nearly like it, at least if they are more like it than like any negative training stimulus.

SHAPING

In operant conditioning the reinforcement can be arranged to be contingent upon the occurrence of not just any response, but only those responses made in just the right way. The motions, positions, and timings involved in a response are called its *topography*. The topography of a response, as well as its frequency and probability of occurrence, are subject to the selective process of operant reinforcement. This leads to a very important characteristic of learning by operant conditioning. When an experimenter sets out to train an animal in a complicated or unlikely response, he does not try to do so directly. Instead he uses a procedure of gradual approximation. For example, in being taught to press a lever, a rat would be most unlikely ever to actually raise a paw and swing it down on the lever. Ordinarily the experimenter does not just wait patiently for the rat to stumble upon the desired response. Rather, taking advantage of variations in the rat's behavior, the experimenter selectively reinforces closer and closer approximations to the desired response. When the rat comes close to the bar, it is reinforced; when it walks in the opposite direction, it is not. Once the rat is spending most of its time near the bar, the experimenter stops reinforcing it simply for being close, and waits until it raises a paw or makes some other better approximation to a bar press; then he reinforces this closer approximation. And so forth.

This process of gradually selecting the right responses from the wrong ones, moving the animal's behavior toward the desired pattern, is called *shaping*. To shape bar-pressing in a rat can take from a few minutes to a few hours depending on the proclivities of the individual animal, the skill of the trainer, and luck. Formally, shaping can be defined as *the selection of a particular response by differential reinforcement of successive approximations to a desired behavior*. Shaping requires a great deal of skill. The experimenter must reinforce just the right responses, extinguish just the wrong ones, not extinguish *everything*, and not have the animal end up staying in one place or going in circles. Very complex responses can be trained in animals as primitive as pigeons or as advanced as chimpanzees and humans, by a careful and skillful shaping process.

Let us have an example of shaping in human behavior. A child comes to his mother and says, "I'd like some candy." She says, "No." He whines. She gives him candy. The next time he asks for candy, the mother is determined to be firm and not give in to his demand. He again whines. She resists. He whines a little more. She gives him the candy. The next time the mother's resolve is stronger—she waits until he whines for a full five minutes before giving in. And so it goes until the child (whom we've all met) can whine for half a day or so in order to get candy. His behavior has been shaped: successive approximations to the eventual response of whining for a long time have been reinforced. This behavior could not have been trained in a single effort, for half-day whining would never have occurred (and therefore could not have been reinforced) at the beginning of training. But by starting with reinforcement of a distant approximation to it and then reinforcing only longer and longer periods of whining, the mother eventually shapes an initially unobtainable response.

Mixed cases

There are a number of important instances of learning that involve both classical and operant conditioning in the same training procedure. One of these we have already mentioned, *secondary reinforcement*.

SECONDARY REINFORCEMENT

An important result of acquisition of reinforcing properties is a phenomenon called *chaining*. A good example of chaining often occurs when a dog is trained to do tricks. Consider a dog that is trained first to roll over, then to sit, and finally to stand and bark. Later, when commanded to stand and bark, it stands up and barks, sits down, and rolls over! What has happened is a natural result of a very effective training technique. In teaching a sequence of responses it is best to start with the last one. If the trainer wants the dog to first stand, then sit, then roll over, and then get its reward, he should start by teaching it to roll over. Each time the dog rolls over it gets a primary reinforcement, say a scratch on the stomach. The act of turning over or the stimuli accompanying that act themselves then take on reinforcing power by being paired over and over again with stomach scratching. Subsequently, when the animal is persuaded to sit, and then is told to roll over, the command to roll over by itself acts as a reinforcer for sitting. At the next stage of training, the command to sit also becomes a secondary reinforcer, so that when the trainer then induces the animal to stand, and follows standing with the command to sit, the standing is reinforced by sitting. Thus the animal is taught the last link in the chain, in this case rolling over, first; then the next to last, and so forth. As each link is learned, it becomes the reinforcing event for the link to be added next. Rats have been taught incredibly long sequences of behavior—e.g., going through a maze, up a ladder, and across a tightrope, pulling a string to raise a bucket to pour water into a dish, swimming to the other side, and going down another ladder —by carefully working back through a chain of this sort.

A similar strategy often works well for humans learning sequences of responses. For example, to teach a child to pronounce a difficult polysyllabic word, start with the last syllable and add earlier ones—*tic*, then *lastic*, and finally *elastic*. To memorize a long part in a play, it sometimes helps to learn the last set of lines first, then the set just before that, and so forth.

Sometimes combination of operant reinforcement with classical conditioning leads to problems. One case may be called the $S^D - S^r$ *paradox*. Many events which act as secondary reinforcers (S^r) also act as discriminative stimuli (S^D), and the two effects can be in conflict. Let us outline the problem as it often arises in a training-box situation. If the magazine that dispenses food reinforcement is put at a distance from the lever, it is very hard to train the desired response. If every time the rat presses the bar the magazine clicks, both of two rather incompatible behavioral results tend to occur. The click of the magazine, because of its previous association with food, is a good secondary reinforcer and reinforces the bar press response. But, in addition, the click, being a good discriminative stimulus because of the very same prior magazine training, causes the animal to leave the bar and trot across to the magazine. Thus, the short-term effect of the stimulus is to stop bar pressing, while its long-term effect is to increase bar pressing. This is the paradox.

The same thing can happen in human behavior. A boy meets a girl for a date. She is grumpy. He smiles at her in order to cheer her up. Usually, a smile has two properties. First, it has the stimulus effect that the boy has in mind—it tends to make the girl smile back. But a smile also has a reinforcing effect for most people. As a reinforcer in this instance the smile tends to increase the future probability of grumpiness. By smiling at the grumpy girl, the boy has made her likely to smile back immediately, but also more likely to be grumpy the next time he meets her.

AVOIDANCE CONDITIONING

Another case of mixture of classical and operant conditioning is in the training method known as *avoidance conditioning*. A rat is placed in a long, thin shuttlebox that has a low hurdle across the middle and a light bulb at either end. The light in whichever end the rat is standing in goes on. Five seconds later, a painful shock is delivered through the floor under the rat. If the rat jumps over the hurdle to the other side, either during the five-second warning period or during the shock itself, he lands in a safe compartment.

As the procedure is repeated over and over again, the rat eventually learns to jump before the shock goes on. The learning proceeds in well-defined stages. At first the animal does not respond appropriately and is shocked on each trial. He runs and jumps about randomly until he happens to get over to the other side. Soon, however, he begins to respond to the shock with a fairly rapid and smooth jump to the safe compartment. At the same time he begins to show signs of anxiety during the warning signal. Since the warning signal occurs before the shock repeatedly, by classical conditioning it becomes capable of evoking some of the same fear reactions initially elicited by the shock itself. Thus when the light goes on the animal begins to crouch, defecate, and tremble.

Now, since the animal is anxious and has learned to jump, and since behavior is essentially variable, on some random trial he will jump during the warning period before the shock occurs. When he does so the light goes out, terminating the fear-arousing situation. This may be seen as operant reinforcement by termination of a secondary negative reinforcer. The light has become aversive by classical conditioning, and when it terminates it is as if a shock or any other unpleasant event had terminated.

Avoidance conditioning, then, consists of a combination of classical conditioning of the secondary negative reinforcer and operant conditioning of the jumping response, first by termination of the shock, and later by termination of the warning signal.

Aversive control of behavior

For the most part in discussing operant conditioning we have considered the control of behavior by desirable events, such as food and water reinforcers. In discussing avoidance conditioning we have introduced the first major example of the use of unpleasant or aversive situations in the control of behavior. Avoidance conditioning is one of three cases of aversive control; the other two cases are *punishment* and *escape training*. Let us begin by distinguishing between these three.

ESCAPE, PUNISHMENT, AND AVOIDANCE

Escape training is the definitional case of a negative reinforcer. Recall that negative reinforcement is defined as the strengthening of a response tendency as a result of the termination of some situation following the response. This is exactly equivalent to saying that the response is instrumental in the animal's escaping from the aversive situation. Escape training, then, consists of teaching an animal to respond in a way that will get him out of unpleasant circumstances. The initial part of a rat's training in a shuttlebox, during which he jumps from one side to the other to get away from the shock, is a case of escape training. Learning to turn down the furnace when one is too hot, or to light a fire or put on a coat when one is too cold are other examples of escape training.

What if an event that acts as a negative reinforcer starts rather than terminates after an act—as, for example, when a shock commences after an animal presses a bar? Such a procedure is known as *punishment*. Formally, punishment consists of the onset of a stimulus known to be a negative reinforcer, following an act. Punishment is thus, in terms of procedure, the opposite of negative reinforcement. The effect of punishment is to *decrease* response probability, whereas negative reinforcement increases it. But the influence of punishment on behavior is not as straightforward or simple as the effect of reinforcement. More about this shortly.

The third form of aversive control is avoidance conditioning, which we have already discussed. Avoidance conditioning may be carried out with or without a warning signal. In the example given earlier, a light appeared five seconds before the shock and served as a cue for the rat to respond before the onset of the aversive stimulus. The situation can also be arranged so that the animal has to respond every so often, without any cue, in order to prevent the occurrence of the aversive stimulus. Thus a rat may be required to press a lever at least once every fifteen seconds in order to keep a shock from occurring. Or the lever may postpone shock for twenty seconds whenever it is pressed. This kind of training is generally harder to master than avoidance with a cue, but it can nevertheless produce quite reliable performance. Avoidance conditioning may also be carried out in a discriminative manner—that is, one cue (e.g., a high-pitched noise) can be made the appropriate condition for a response which will postpone or prevent a noxious stimulus, while another cue (e.g., a low tone) requires no response.

To summarize the distinctions between these three cases of aversive control, we may state that (a) an aversive situation is one which acts as a negative reinforcer, its *termination* increasing the future probability of a response that it follows closely in time; (b) the learning of a response which in this way terminates an aversive situation is called *escape training*; (c) the application of an aversive situation, with its onset following and contingent upon an act, is called *punishment*; and (d) training in which the onset of the aversive situation can be entirely prevented by a response is called *avoidance conditioning*.

EFFECTIVENESS OF AVERSIVE CONTROL METHODS

Over the years there has been considerable controversy over the desirability of punishment and other forms of aversive control of behavior. One aspect of the question is the moral or ethical legitimacy of inflicting discomfort on another being in order to influence his behavior. Of course, this is a matter involving basic value judgments on which different societies and individuals disagree, and one in which the goals and circumstances of particular situations must be considered. A general scientific statement is difficult if not impossible.

There is, however, a second and more factual aspect to the question of the use of aversive methods, and that is whether they are effective in controlling behavior. Effectiveness varies considerably among the three techniques of escape training, punishment, and avoidance conditioning.

Escape training

In general it can be said that negative reinforcers, such as shock termination, are very effective in operant conditioning. The termination of a very painful event almost invariably acts as a strong reinforcer. Responses learned as a result are comparable or greater in resistance to extinction than those learned for strong positive reinforcement. Moreover, negative reinforcers such as pain reduction have the advantage of showing little cyclicality in their effectiveness. In a situation with food reinforcement the animal becomes satiated after many rewards; but after turning a shock off many times by pressing a lever, a rat will still press the lever to turn the shock off. Pain reduction as a reinforcer shows very little satiation. One major problem with the use of escape training, however, is that the aversive situation must be present before it can be terminated. Thus, to train a child to behave by escape training one would have to be sure that the situation was always aversive, so that when the child made a desired response the aversive situation could be terminated. It is unlikely that parents or teachers would ever wish to maintain a constant aversive situation over long periods of time. (Although perhaps the old-fashioned schoolroom in which children were kept in a state of fear and restraint at all times was very nearly such a situation.) Escape training seems to be most relevant for sporadically arising circumstances of pain or discomfort which can be effectively terminated by a particular learned response.

Punishment

The effectiveness of punishment is rather more complicated. If an animal is first trained to make a response such as bar pressing, and then this response is followed on one or more occasions by a noxious stimulus, the frequency of the response will, as you would expect, decrease. However, some experimenters have found, under some circumstances, that the decrease in response probability that results from punishment is in part a temporary supression rather than an actual unlearning of the response. Estes (1944) trained rats to press a bar, and then administered a mild punishment following a bar press. He observed that the number of responses before the animal stopped responding completely in a subsequent extinction session was very little altered by the punishment, and that the total amount of time before the animal ceased responding at all was not significantly changed. However, more recent experiments in which strong punishments have been used, and used repeatedly rather than only once or a few times, have shown that a very long-lasting decrease in response tendency can be produced by punishment (Campbell & Church, 1969). Clinical and common sense experience concerning the effects of punishment is consistent with the experimental evidence. Punishment has been used to modify behavior (particularly to get rid of unwanted response tendencies), both in animal training and in child rearing, throughout history and well-nigh universally among the thousands of known societies in the world. It seems unlikely that it would have been so widely used if it were completely ineffective. On the other hand, it is also common clinical experience to discover evidence that a completely eschewed response is still lurking beneath the surface, ready to occur when the person's environment will once more tolerate it.

There are some additional considerations that are very important in the practical use of punishment. The most significant of these is that the punishing event is, by definition, a negative reinforcer—that is, whatever response precedes its termination will be strengthened. Thus if a shock is turned on after a bar press, the bar press is weakened; but, in addition, some other response—whatever the animal does just before the shock is turned *off* (perhaps squealing, or cringing)—is strengthened.

It is essentially impossible to turn on an aversive stimulus without later turning it off. The timing of the termination relative to the behavior of the animal is just as important as the timing of the onset. Willy-nilly termination of a punishment is likely to result in the strengthening of undesirable responses, because the responses that are elicited by the stimulus properties of an aversive event are usually undesirable. For example, in the case of teaching a child to obey, the punishing stimulus of a spanking is accompanied ordinarily by crying or pouting. If the spanking terminates after a response of crying or pouting, crying or pouting is reinforced. Thus, punishment is likely to lead not only to the reduction of the undesirable behavior at which it is aimed, but also to the increase of certain responses which themselves are undesirable. This may be why children brought up in highly punitive societies or school systems often appear to be very subdued, submissive, and unhappy. Trainers have often observed that animals taught by punishment are reliable but perform with a lack of enthusiasm and vitality, while those trained by positive reinforcement methods alone are active and "happy" but may be less reliable.

Avoidance conditioning

Now let us turn from punishment to avoidance conditioning. An experiment by Solomon, Kamin, and Wynne (1953) exemplifies how effective training by avoidance conditioning can be under ideal conditions. Dogs learned to avoid an extremely intense and painful shock by jumping a hurdle to the opposite compartment in a shuttle box. The warning signal was a buzzer that went on five seconds before the shock. On the average the dogs learned in about ten trials to avoid regularly. After several more training trials, the experimenters tried to extinguish the jumping response. To begin with they simply discontinued shocking the animal for failure to jump. The dogs kept jumping to the sound of the buzzer; after 400 trials none of them had stopped jumping.

The experimenters then added a barrier between the two compartments so that when the buzzer went on and the dog jumped he was prevented from entering the safe compartment. Some animals, but only some, ceased jumping with this treatment. Others, remarkably enough, began to jump even faster. Similarly, when the experimenters added a shock in the previously safe compartment so that when the dog landed in it he was shocked, some, but only some, of the dogs ceased to jump. Again others jumped even faster. In short, the experimenters found it very difficult to extinguish behavior learned on the basis of what they called *traumatic avoidance conditioning*. They spoke of a partial irreversibility of the response tendency learned in this way.

Extremely persistent food taboos can also be taught by aversive methods. If a dog or cat is very severely punished upon touching a food, he may avoid that food forever unless very careful training is instituted to reinstate his positive reaction to it. The reason seems to be, at least partly, that the fear response conditioned to the stimulus has no opportunity to extinguish if the animal never eats the food again, and he will be unlikely to eat it again so long as the fear reaction remains strong. If the aversive condition that follows the food is nausea or other illness, the aversion is likely to be permanent unless special therapy is carried out.

It is likely that many human fear reactions which persist for long periods originate in traumatic conditioning. After a few experiences of severe pain with immunizing injections, many children develop intense and persistent fears of hypodermic syringes. One reason why these fears are often so hard to extinguish is that the child tends to avoid injections or, if he does have one, becomes emotionally upset, struggles, and creates an extremely unpleasant scene. There is thus little chance for him to discover that an injection can be received calmly and with little pain. A similar situation may exist in connection with many phobic or neurotic anxiety reactions. Indeed, the idea that such reactions may stem from and owe their permanence to traumatic avoidance learning has provided some of the rationale for modern behavior therapy (see Chapter 4).

The amazing permanence of responses learned by avoidance conditioning, as described by Solomon, Kamin, and Wynne, is, however, not a universal feature of avoidance conditioning. Under less powerful conditions, avoidance training leads to more normal response tendencies which extinguish within a reasonable number of unreinforced trials. For example, a rat will learn not to cross into a black-painted half of his experimental box if a loud noise goes on whenever he does so. But if the noise is discontinued, he will quickly discover the fact and begin to use the black side of the box again. Nonetheless, avoidance conditioning provides a very effective means of training, having the advantage of a strong reinforcing event that does not show satiation.

Like escape and punishment training, however, avoidance conditioning sometimes has undesirable side-effects. First of all, through classical conditioning, an animal or person trained by avoidance conditioning will eventually come to fear the situation in which the behavior is to be emitted. A dog trained to avoid shock in a shuttlebox will show anxiety whenever he is brought into the experimental room. An aversive stimulus evokes unpleasant kinds of reflexive responses, which will eventually become classically conditioned to the trainer and/or to the situation. Thus, a parent who uses avoidance conditioning regularly will risk becoming a secondary aversive stimulus to his child. In addition, chronic performance under an avoidance-maintained regime can sometimes lead to serious physiological results. A rat in a conflict situation, one being forced to drink from an electrified water spout, for example, will sometimes develop ulcers. So, sometimes, will a monkey or rat if required to press a lever every twenty seconds to avoid a shock. The phenomenon is not completely understood, but it appears that the essential damaging agent in such cases is long-term performance under the threat of punishment. It also appears that ulcers or other psychosomatic disorders will ordinarily develop only under special sets of training conditions; for example, if the animal is required to perform a certain number of hours per day, ulcers will result, while otherwise they may not.

Aversive conditioning versus positive reinforcement

In sum, for policy decisions regarding the training of children or animals the following considerations are relevant. When training must be exceedingly rapid and the response tendency strong and permanent, and when one is willing to risk unhappiness, surly behavior, dislike or fear of the teacher, and just possibly the development of ulcers, aversive training techniques—particularly avoidance conditioning—may be in order. On the other hand, when there is ample time for training, and when one wants the subject to be happy and friendly and to enjoy performing the trained response, positive reinforcement and shaping should be favored.

Applicability of operant reinforcement

In general, operant conditioning is most appropriate for the acquisition of modes of responding that are not part of the animal's hereditary repertoire. Classical conditioning is appropriate when there is a known stimulus which can elicit a response and it is desired to attach that response to a new stimulus. Operant conditioning is appropriate when an unconditioned stimulus does not exist, is not readily identifiable, or cannot easily be used, or when the stimulus conditions for the response are not of particular interest.

In general, although by no means without exception, the glandular and smooth-muscle responses, those controlled primarily by the autonomic nervous system, are particularly susceptible to classical conditioning; while the gross movements of the skeletal muscles and the whole-body behaviors that such muscle movements combine to form are especially susceptible to operant conditioning. Whether there are certain classes of responses which can be conditioned only by classical conditioning or only by operant conditioning is hard to say. Certainly some responses, such as the heart rate, are very easily conditioned by classical conditioning but difficult to condition by operant means. On the other hand, while it is conceivable that one could train a rat to press a lever by classical conditioning—presuming that unconditioned stimuli for just the right set of reflexes could be identified—it is certainly far easier to produce such a response by operant conditioning.

Operant conditioning can be applied to almost any response which an animal can be observed to make. A wide range of species—from cockroaches through fish, rats, cats, dogs, and monkeys, to adult humans—have been trained by operant conditioning. The range of responses which have succumbed to operant conditioning in the laboratory is also very wide: in humans, for instance, it extends from imperceptible small-muscle movements of which the subject is totally unaware, to the conscious, overt expression of opinion.

A few examples of operant conditioning of humans may be instructive. An experimenter (Hefferline, 1962) placed adult humans in a chair, attached an elaborate set of wires to various parts of their bodies, and started a loud, bothersome hissing noise. Unknown to the subject, the loud noise could be shut off by a single group of muscles in the base of the thumb, monitored by just one of the many wires. Gross movements had no effect, but a tiny movement of the thumb was followed by a reduction in the noise. This reduction in the noxious noise acted as a reinforcer (a negative reinforcer). Compared to the subjects' baseline levels of behavior (levels at which such movements of the thumb in the absence of any reinforcement were exceedingly infrequent), the number of appropriate movements increased gradually until they were made at a quite substantial rate. When asked after the experiment what response, if any, controlled the noise, subjects reported either that it was not under their control or that it was under the control of some response that they were making (for instance nodding the head to the left) which was in fact totally unrelated to the actual behavior being conditioned.

This method has helped people suffering from stuttering. In such therapy, whenever the patient emits a full sentence, free from stuttering or other defect, the noise is reduced for ten seconds. Gradually the amount of stuttering decreases. As was described in Chapter 4, the methods of operant conditioning, using both positive and negative reinforcers, have been applied with considerable success in recent years to the treatment of a variety of other behavior disorders.

Operant conditioning has also been used to good advantage in the schoolroom. For example, a shy child who speaks too softly to be heard can be taught to speak up by use of a straightforward shaping procedure. The teacher first identifies a positive reinforcer by seeing what works, and then applies it to responses more and more closely approximating the desired behavior.

The method might be as follows: The teacher suspects that her attentive smile will work as a reinforcer for the child in question. She chooses hand-raising, a response the child makes infrequently, as a test target. After tallying this response for a few days as a baseline, she begins smiling whenever the child's hand goes up. Over the next few days, hand-raising increases substantially relative to the baseline, and the teacher concludes that she has found a good positive reinforcer for this child. She then begins shaping. At first she rewards the child with a smile whenever he says anything, no matter how softly. When, and only when, the child has begun to talk frequently, the teacher makes her smile contingent on slightly louder speech—not rewarding totally inaudible utterances, but still rewarding any other. Gradually, as the loudness increases, the teacher raises her criterion, finally demanding a normal tone of voice as the condition for her smile. Notice that at the end of training the child can be treated in the same way as other children—the teacher need smile rewardingly only when the behavior is acceptable. And because of the partial reinforcement phenomenon, she need only reward proper speech occasionally to maintain it effectively.

Parents have used such training techniques effectively for teaching a variety of useful habits. One example is toilet training. A one- to two-year-old child is perfectly capable of controlling his bowels and bladder, and of using a toilet. The problem usually is to induce him to do so. A skillful shaping process, using small candies to reinforce closer approaches to the toilet at the moment of elimination, and then successful uses of that instrument of civilization, can be very effective. This method usually avoids the upset which often accompanies punitive methods (and prevents the prolonged diaper-changing that sometimes is necessary if one relies on rational persuasion). Once the child is trained, candy reinforcement can be discontinued, since elimination is its own reward.

The examples of applications of operant reinforcement that could be given are essentially endless. The important point to remember is that an almost limitless range of responses can be trained by operant conditioning, given the right conditions, appropriate reinforcers, and sufficient skill on the part of the trainer.

THEORIES OF LEARNING

A number of different theories have been put forward to explain the basic nature of learning, to give a general description of the conditions which lead to learning, and to specify in a quantitative way the course that learning will follow in one or more specific situations. Early learning theories consisted, by and large, of attempts to state in an exact manner the conditions which are required for learning and the variables that affect learning and performance. This was done by stating as few as possible basic premises, and then deriving from those premises as many of the observed phenomena as possible. One such attempt was a theory put forward by Guthrie, in which the only premise was that an animal tended most strongly to do whatever he had last done in a particular situation. Since every situation is slightly different from every other, what the subject would do in a new situation was predicted by what he had done in similar situations in the past. This very simple theory of the basic process of learning is capable of accounting for a surprising range of learning phenomena.

More recent theoretical work on learning has centered on quantitative formulations of the factors in learning and on mathematical models of limited cases of the learning process. Theorists have attempted to make a few mathematically stated assumptions about the learning process and from these derive detailed quantitative features of acquisition and performance, such as the shape of the learning curve, the average number of trials before the last error, the average number of error trials in a row, and so forth. There have been two major ways of making such derivations. One is to state a simple mathematical relation from which purely mathematical methods can be made to yield various predictive results. The other way is to make the statements in the form of instructions in a computer program, allow the computer to proceed according to these instructions, and compare the simulated behavior generated by the computer with that of live subjects.

A good example of a mathematical model is a theory originally proposed by Estes (1950) which has formed the basis of much subsequent work. The theory postulates that on each learning trial the organism is exposed to, or pays attention to, only a small part of the stimulus situation in which he is placed. On each trial he learns to make the correct response to the situation as he perceives it, that is to that portion which is actually affecting him at the time. However, on the next trial when he is placed back in the situation, he will be paying attention to a slightly different portion of the total environment and thus will be less than perfectly likely to make the same response. Formally, the theory states that the world is made up, for the animal, of a very large number of stimulus *elements*. On each trial the animal is affected only

FIGURE 7–14

Schematic illustration of main features of the Estes' stimulus sampling theory of learning.

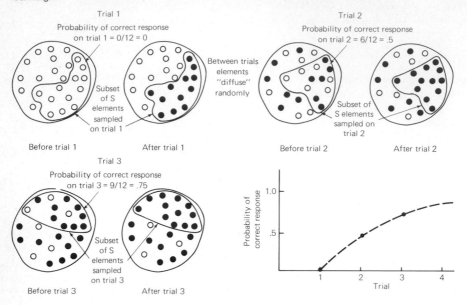

by a certain number, a subset or sample, of these elements. The correct response is assumed to be *conditioned* to all the elements in the sample present on a given trial.

The proposed situation is schematized in Figure 7–14. The black dots refer to stimulus elements which are conditioned to the correct response (let us say a rat's turn to the right in a T-maze), while the white dots are elements which have not yet been conditioned to the response. As trials progress the animal is presumed to have a constant likelihood of being affected by any one of the elements on any particular trial. Let us say that on any one trial he pays attention to—he *samples*, in the formal terminology of the theory—one-half of the possible available stimulus elements. On the very first trial his correct response is conditioned to no elements, but he samples one-half of them; these become conditioned to the correct response. On the second trial he again samples one-half of the available elements, but now, since half of those possible have already been conditioned to the response, on the average half of the ones he samples are already conditioned. Consequently, the unconditioned elements which are sampled for the *first* time on the second trial, and thus are newly conditioned to the correct response, are only half of those sampled, or half the number sampled on the first trial. Thus the amount of *new* conditioning which occurs on the second trial is less than that on the first trial.

As the figure shows, the third trial will again eventuate in the conditioning of half of the remaining elements. Notice that what happens on each trial is that half (or some other constant proportion) of the remaining stimulus elements are conditioned to the correct response. This is exactly the result required by the principle of constant proportional gain that we discussed before. The theory presumes that the probability of the animal's making a given response is directly proportional to the proportion of the elements sampled on a given trial that have already been conditioned to the correct response. Thus on trial two, at the beginning of which half of the elements were conditioned to the correct response, he had 0.5 or 50/50 probability of making the correct response.

We will not attempt to formalize this theory any further here, although we will go into somewhat more detail with respect to a related theory in the next chapter. It is worth pointing out that the very simple assumptions of the Estes model can lead to accurate predictions. Because mathematical statistics describes the expected results of sampling procedures—such as the sampling of stimulus elements underlying the Estes model—it is possible to derive from the model, in conjunction with statistical theory, a host of predictions about the details of learning. For instance one can derive the expected number of trials before the first, second, or third correct response for the median subject; or, say, the standard deviation of the number of the trial on which the fourteenth error occurs. For many situations, including T-maze learning in rats, shuttlebox avoidance-learning in dogs, and certain kinds of memorization and problem solving in humans, such predictions have been made with great accuracy. The defining, testing, and expansion of such mathematical theories is presently a very active area of research in learning.

TOPICS DISCUSSED IN CHAPTER 7

1. Three different kinds of events which change behavioral tendencies: imprinting, classical conditioning, and operant conditioning.

2. The idea of critical periods in imprinting.

3. The order, timing, and characteristics of stimulus occurrences that are effective in classical conditioning.

4. The loss and recovery of classically conditioned response tendencies.

5. The spread of conditioned response-tendencies to untrained stimuli and the prevention of such generalization by special training procedures.

6. The kinds of behavior which are especially susceptible to classical conditioning.

7. The difference between acquisition and performance; and the principle of constant proportional gain.

8. The question of what works as an operant reinforcing event.

9. Two principles of operant conditioning. The effective timing of events in operant conditioning.

10. The role of motivation in learning and learned behavior.

11. The effect of schedules of partial reinforcement.

12. How operantly conditioned behavior can be made to depend on particular stimuli.

13. The process of *shaping*.

14. Learning and performance resulting from combinations of classical and operant conditioning; acquired reinforcement, shaping, avoidance conditioning, and the $S^D - S^r$ paradox.

15. The different kinds of training based on aversive stimulation; their advantages and disadvantages relative to each other and to training by positive reinforcement.

16. The kinds of behavior to which operant conditioning is most applicable.

17. Theories of learning.

SUGGESTED READINGS

1. *There is a large number of good textbooks on the psychology of learning. Two are:*

Hall, J. F. *The psychology of learning.* Philadelphia: Lippincott, 1966; and Deese, J. F., & Hulse, S. *The psychology of learning.* New York: McGraw-Hill, 1967.

2. *Two historically important and interesting works on learning are:*

Pavlov, I. P. *Conditioned reflexes.* New York: Oxford, 1927, which described classical conditioning; and

Skinner, B. F. *The behavior of organisms.* New York: Appleton-Century-Crofts, 1938, which set out the principles of operant conditioning.

3. *A thorough review of both operant and classical conditioning can be found in:*

Kimble, G. A. *Hilgard and Marquis' Conditioning and Learning.* New York: Appleton-Century-Crofts, 1961.

4. *Theories of learning are surveyed and analyzed in:*

Hilgard, E. H., & Bower, G. *Theories of learning.* New York: Appleton-Century-Crofts, 1966.

5. *The more mathematical modern theories are introduced and treated in:*

Atkinson, R. C., Bower, G., & Crothers, E. J. *An introduction to mathematical learning theory.* New York: Wiley, 1965.

EIGHT

Language, verbal learning, memory, and thought

Humans, alone among animals, talk a great deal. No one is certain about the degree to which lower animals use sounds to communicate; almost certainly there are distress calls, sounds of contentment, and sounds which identify individuals to each other. It is quite likely that there are even some learned "symbolic" noises with special significance to particular families or pairs of animals. And it has recently been found possible to train a chimpanzee to use a large number—more than fifty at last report—of manual sign-language "words" (Gardner & Gardner, 1970). But no animal emits noises at the rate that humans do. Human noises are vastly complicated, and, most significantly, the complications are useful. They make of human language a tool for social relations, for transmission and storage of knowledge, and for solution, by abstract means, of important problems. Human language has a tremendous influence on the way adult humans learn and on the way they put their learning to work in performance.

This is not to say that the fundamental biological processes by which information is stored in the nervous system during learning that involves language are different from those operating during the kinds of learning already discussed. In fact, certain aspects of the processes of verbal learning bear striking resemblances to the factors at work in classical and operant conditioning. However, it seems clear that the understanding of verbal learning in adult humans requires consideration of a number of critical factors which can often be ignored in other kinds of learning. First and foremost, human verbal learning is pervasively influenced by past learning. The huge number of things that an adult human has already learned with and about words gives rise to the most important factors in human learning.

Language poses a requirement for a fantastic ability to learn. One aspect of this is simply the need to learn to talk—an incredibly complicated set of habits which alone requires millions of "learning trials." The other aspect is the ease with which new information can be presented through the medium of language—compare the amount of new information contained in a single bedtime story, for example, to the new things encountered in a whole day by the average hedgehog. After a person has gone to school six hours and done homework afterwards, in addition to the normal day's quota of learning to get along, every day for 15 to 20 years, it is hard to conceive of the number of individual facts he has learned, and even harder to imagine the vast and intricate ways in which these small bits of learning are interrelated.

As a result, when an adult human sets out to learn a new bit of verbal knowledge, the new learning always builds on a vast amount of previous related learning (when you learn that a new friend's name is John, you are *not* learning the name *John*, its spelling, its connotation as to gender, its ethnic or regional provenance, or its association with common sayings, jokes, songs, stories, or architectural features). Much new verbal learning has also to compete with a great deal of prior training (to learn that someone is called Njoroge—an East African Bantu name—you must be able to put aside the more familiar names of John, George, Ned, and Roger which because of your previous experience come more readily to the mind, and in addition attempt to make a new sound which is difficult because it is unlike any you have ever learned). The major factors which influence verbal learning, in both a positive and a negative way, are based on the relation of present to past learning. Similarly, thought and reasoning are clearly dependent on what has been learned before. In order to set the stage for meaningful discussion of human learning and thought, we will start by considering briefly the nature of language.

SPEECH AND LANGUAGE

Perhaps the most important single fact about language is its immense complexity. The size of the repertoire of verbal behaviors possessed by an adult speaker of any human language is staggering. Probably the average United States college student can recognize the meaning of about 200,000 different words. This reflects the fact that he has read, in some fifteen years, perhaps ten million words of print, and has listened to probably several times that many spoken words. The number of different words he actually uses in common everyday speech is much smaller but still enormous, something on the order of 10,000.

But it is not so much the number of different sounds and words which a person knows and uses that makes language complex, as it is the infinite number of ways in which these could be combined to produce phrases, sentences, and paragraphs. The way in which an individual word is used is itself, of course, anything but simple. For example, a

FIGURE 8-1

The phonemes of general American English. (From Denes & Pinson, 1963; courtesy of Bell Telephone Laboratories, Incorporated)

Vowels	Consonants	
ee as in h*ea*t	*t* as in *t*ee	*s* as in *s*ee
i as in h*i*t	*p* as in *p*ea	*sh* as in *sh*ell
e as in h*ea*d	*k* as in *k*ey	*h* as in *h*e
ae as in h*a*d	*b* as in *b*ee	*v* as in *v*iew
ah as in f*a*ther	*d* as in *d*awn	*th* as in *th*en
aw as in c*a*ll	*g* as in *g*o	*z* as in *z*oo
U as in p*u*t	*m* as in *m*e	*zh* as in gar*age*
oo as in c*oo*l	*n* as in *n*o	*l* as in *l*aw
Λ as in t*o*n	*ng* as in si*ng*	*r* as in *r*ed
uh as in th*e*	*f* as in *f*ee	*y* as in *y*ou
er as in b*ir*d	*θ* as in *th*in	*w* as in *w*e
oi as in t*oi*l		
au as in sh*ou*t		
ei as in t*a*ke		
ou as in t*o*ne		
ai as in m*i*ght		

given set of sounds can have an entirely different meaning depending on its *context*. The context of the word *it* can be the words which come before or after it, the structure of the sentence and the place of *it* therein, or the general surroundings of the speaker. The single word "Right!" without any other verbal context means quite different things when you've just said something someone agrees with, and when a traffic policeman yells at you at a corner.

In the study of language behavior by linguists and psychologists, it has proved possible to analyze speech into component parts and elements in several useful ways. (Describing the way in which these elements are combined to form meaningful utterances is a much more difficult matter.) First, speech can be analyzed into the sounds of which it is composed. The basic unit of sound in speech is called the *phoneme*. The phoneme is the minimal unit of sound which makes a difference in the comprehension of what is being spoken. For example, by a change in one phoneme the word *bat* becomes *hat*. The letters of a written language are not the same as phonemes, but are similar in function and often bear a close relation to phonemes. Often, however, more than one letter is used to indicate a single phoneme—for example, *sh* is used to stand for a single phoneme in English. Every language can be analyzed into a limited set of different phonemes, the nature and number of which vary from language to language. Figure 8–1 gives a list of phonemes for English.

The crucial differences between phonemes are primarily psychological rather than physical. Let us see what this means. A recording can be made of a speech sound showing its intensity at every frequency (see Figure 8–2). This is a complete description of the physical nature

FIGURE 8-2

A sound spectrogram of a sample of speech. The record shows the intensity—the more intense the darker—of each frequency, on the ordinate, as a function of time. (From Denes & Pinson, 1963; courtesy of Bell Telephone Laboratories, Incorporated)

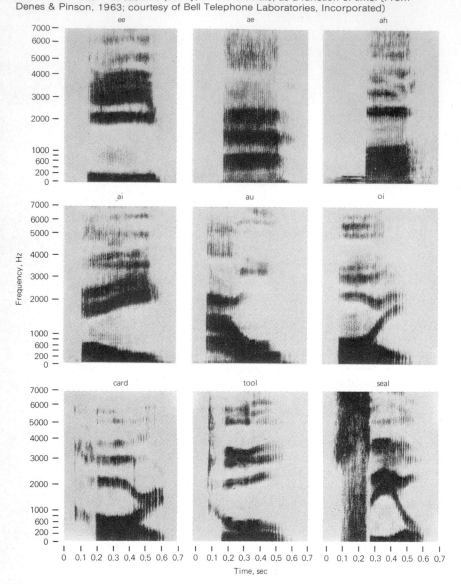

of the emitted speech sound. One might think that a 1-to-1 correspondence could be established between some aspect of the physical sound emitted by a speaker and what phoneme the listener hears. But that is not the case. Exactly the same compound of sounds is sometimes interpreted as two different phonemes on different occasions. And what is interpreted as the same phoneme, /d/ for example, may be the result of any one of several different sound patterns. Figure 8–3 shows a schema-

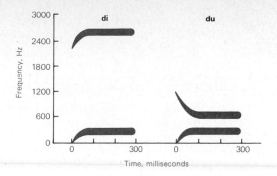

FIGURE 8–3
Schematic sound spectrograms of the English phoneme /d/ in two different words.

tic drawing of a sound spectrogram of the phoneme /d/ in two different words. The thing to notice here is that the sound patterns in these two words are different at the point where they are both heard as /d/. This illustrates that a phoneme, although perfectly identifiable as the same thing in two instances by a human listener, is not always the same thing in physical sound. Although the situation is not entirely understood as yet, one attractive theory (Liberman, Cooper, Shankweiler, & Studdert-Kennedy, 1967) is as follows: One always attempts to articulate a particular phoneme in the same way, but what comes out depends on the position of the vocal apparatus remaining from previous articulations and the position to which it is headed for following articulations. According to this theory it is not the actual *sounds* which correspond to phonemes, but rather what the listener unconsciously *infers*—from the sounds and their context—to be the intended articulation of the speaker.

The next larger unit in the analysis of language is the *morpheme*, which is described as the smallest speech segment that carries meaning. Differences between phonemes change the meaning of the sound sequence of which they are a part, but are not by themselves meaningful. A morpheme is, by and large, approximately equivalent to the common concept of "word," except that many words are compounds of a number of morphemes, and some morphemes only exist as parts of words—as prefixes or suffixes for example. In the word *bookkeeper*, there are three morphemes—BOOK, KEEP, and ER—each of which contributes its own special meaning.

The concept of a morpheme is somewhat slippery, however, since it depends on the concept of meaning, which is itself next to impossible to define in a rigorous way. About the only feasible way of deciding whether a sound sequence has meaning is to ask a human speaker if it does; obviously there will be endless debates in marginal cases. There has been a great deal said by philosophers, linguists, and psychologists about the nature of meaning, without any very adequate or universally accepted description emerging. The notion of the meaning of a speech sound includes at least the following characteristics: the referents indicated to the listener when he hears the sound—those *things* it makes him think of; the *words* it prompts him to remember or speak himself; and the information it provides about the world or the speaker.

Language, verbal learning, memory, and thought
211

Meaning clearly does not inhere simply in individual words or morphemes, but in the relation of all the words and parts of a sentence to each other and to the situation in which they are used. Not only may a single sound sequence have many different meanings depending on its context (the word *to* is an example; *two* is, too), but also the same meaning may attach to different sounds depending on their context.

The component parts of speech are put together into larger, more useful conglomerates—phonemes into morphemes, morphemes into words, words into sentences, and sentences into speeches. Some of the rules for combination of sounds and words that characterize a given language have been described by linguists.

Consider the problem of creating a sentence as straightforward as a simple command. Imagine for instance that a large audience of people is asked to formulate a sentence to be spoken to the man on the platform—a sentence that will cause the man to leave the room by a red door on one side of the stage. Presume that everyone in the audience writes down such a sentence independently. The situation is nearly identical for all the authors and they all speak the same language. But in all probability there would be almost as many different sentences as authors. One might say "Please go out the exit door to your right"; another "Leave the stage immediately by the north door"; still another "I demand that you depart through the red door," etc., etc. How is any one of these sentences produced?

Some important features of this process can be described. For example, in creating a sentence there are certain implicit rules about which kinds of words come at what part of the sentence, and which precede and which follow others. Such rules are part of grammar. In general, grammatical rules describe changes in word forms (e.g. *works* to *worked*), and in the order of occurrence of one class of words or phrases relative to another, which allow the speaker of a language to combine morphemes and words into strings with specific meanings. Thus there is a set of rules in English that allows a speaker to transform any sentence which describes an action in the present into one which describes the same action in the past. By these rules *He works* is transformed into *He worked; He does the job* is transformed into *He did the job*. The creation and comprehension of a string of words indicating a past action depends on both speaker and listener implicitly understanding the rules used to change present tense to past. Grammatical rules vary from one language to another; adjectives come before nouns in some languages, after them in others. Such rules are not just arbitrary pedantry to keep primary school teachers happy, but serve critical functions in the transmission and comprehension of speech. "He read the red book," contains phoneme sequence /red/ twice, but we have no difficulty at all in discerning that an action is meant in the one case and a color in the other. The reason is that a word's position relative to other words and phrases in the sentence often allows us to infer the intended meaning. The rules by which a speaker constructs a sentence and a listener comprehends it obviously are neither conscious nor necessarily even statable; they exist as unconscious complex habits and modes of perceptual analysis.

HUMAN VERBAL LEARNING

With this rather cursory glance at the nature of language, we will turn our attention first back to learning, which in humans occurs largely in the medium of language, and then to thought and problem solving, which in humans depend intimately on the application of language. In discussing these topics we shall have to deal with greatly simplified, highly artificial uses of words—with bits and pieces only of the processes that produce and depend on communication. Psychologists study such simple cases because natural language, and the things naturally learned in natural languages, contain far too many variables to be disentangled in any one experiment. While simplification and abstraction are often necessary scientific strategies, in using them we run the risk of losing contact with the natural processes that it is our ultimate aim to understand. Perhaps it will help if the student reminds himself from time to time of the distance between the following facts about human verbal learning and thought and the previous sketch of the intricacies and complexities of language.

We now take up that variety of learning which involves the recall and recombination of verbal (phonemic or morphemic) units by adult humans. It separates itself from the other types of learning not because its underlying mechanisms are necessarily different, but because the methods used to produce this kind of learning in the laboratory or the classroom are superficially quite different from the paradigms of imprinting, classical conditioning, and operant conditioning. In general, in human memorization, particularly of verbal materials, the learner is instructed by an experimenter, a teacher, or himself to learn something new. And the instruction (or intent) plays a large role in determining what he will or will not learn. For example, consider the double column of words in Figure 8–4. If you try to learn these as a long, so-called *serial list* beginning with 1 and ending with 8—that is, going down the first column and then down the second column and learning to repeat the words in that order—you can do so. However, you could also learn to "associate" the left-right pairs in the same rows—1 with 5, 2 with 6, and so forth—without regard to the place of each in the series. It is reasonably likely that you would go about the learning of these words in a different way depending on whether you were attempting to learn pairs or to learn the list serially, but the point which is important here is that instructions—a clearly verbal, and thus human, phenomenon—would be critical determinants of what you learned. More of this later.

Short-term memory

If one looks up a telephone number or is introduced to someone at a party, one usually "remembers" the number or the person's name immediately after it has been given, but often loses it within a few minutes. The course of forgetting after a single presentation has been plotted for several different kinds of material. Figure 8–5 shows a typical *decay* curve. In the experiment from which these data were taken, on each trial the subject was shown a single nonsense syllable, e.g., BAZ, and then required to count backward by threes from a large number until

8-4
Words as examples of materials
which might be used in studying
human verbal learning.
Depending on instruction, a
subject might learn the columns
as a serial list, or the rows as
paired associates.

(1) BIG	—	(5) SMALL
(2) RED	—	(6) YELLOW
(3) APPLES	—	(7) PEARS
(4) TURN	—	(8) SOUR

a signal for recall. The time between the nonsense-syllable and the recall signal was different on different trials. The proportion of trials on which recall was correct declined very rapidly as the time between the presentation and the recall signal increased, reaching a 50-50 level when the interval was eight seconds long. It is not certain what causes this rapid decline. The rate of short-term forgetting is greatly increased if the subject has recently learned many similar nonsense syllables (we shall see later that this is called *proactive inhibition*), or if similar nonsense syllables occur between initial presentation and attempted recall (which is called *retroactive inhibition*). The kind of item involved also makes a large difference: a single letter is retained better than a combination of six randomly chosen consonants. Similarly, a meaningful word is retained better than a nonsense syllable.

The question arises whether the rapid decline in memory soon after presentation is simply the initial part of the overall process of forgetting, a fast initial loss, or whether it represents the results of a separate short-term memory storage process which is different from the storage mechanism used by the human brain for long-term retention. One notion is that the information system requires a "buffer" storage, something that will hold information for a brief time in a readily accessible form, and from which information is easily erased when no longer needed. Long-term storage would presumably be used only for those things which are enduringly useful, for example those that are encountered repeatedly. In other words, it might be quite convenient to store everything almost perfectly for a very short time, but either impossible or inefficient to store everything permanently. The alternative view is that all memory is simply subject to very rapid decay at first, then to increasingly slow loss. While the issue is not settled yet, current evidence of many sorts points to the existence of at least two separate storage systems. For example, there are cases of brain damage in which short-term memory remains perfectly normal but the addition of new information to the patient's permanent memory store becomes impossible (Wickelgren, 1968).

Memory is not always in the form of words. People sometimes remember things they have seen, heard, smelled, and felt without necessarily converting the experience into verbal descriptions. In the case of vision, there is reason to believe that the actual visual image, or *icon*, is stored for a very brief period, perhaps partly in the eye itself, and that this briefly stored representation contains information that is not kept in a more permanent form. One kind of evidence of this comes from the following sort of experiment. A subject is shown two lines of four nu-

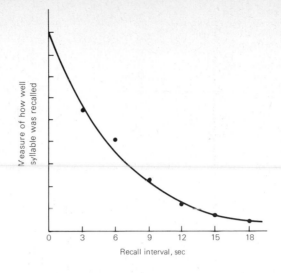

8–5
Short-term memory decay.
Subjects were shown one
nonsense syllable, then counted
backward by three from a large
number until signaled to recall.
(From Peterson & Peterson,
1959).

merals each, for one-tenth of a second. If he is asked *immediately after*
the presentation to name *either* the top or bottom four, he can do so
almost perfectly. Apparently he still has the information about all eight
numerals somewhere, waiting to be used. If asked more than about one
second after the presentation, however, the subject cannot gain access
to all eight numerals, but can remember only the four (approximately)
which constitute the usual maximum (Sperling, 1960).

Another way of studying nonverbal memory is to ask for recogni
tion judgments, e.g., "Have you seen, heard, felt, or smelled this before?"
In vision, at least, the ability to make such recognitions is remarkable.
In one experiment subjects were shown 612 illustrations taken from
magazines. When asked a week later to judge which of two pictures,
one old, one new, they had seen in the experiment, subjects were more
than 90 percent correct (Shepard, 1967). This level of accuracy far ex
ceeds levels achieved in tasks in which the learner must be able to ex
tract more from his memory than simply whether a stimulus is familiar.

While greater stress can be put on memory by requiring the learner
to draw pictures, operate levers, or perform many other nonverbal re
sponses, tasks that demand the utilization of a great deal of information
stored over long periods are most frequently encountered, both in the
laboratory and in life, when the material being learned consists of words.
We turn now to a discussion of verbal learning.

Long-term memory and verbal learning
When a human sets out to memorize something, he ordinarily does not
give himself only one chance, as in experiments on short-term memory,
but rather goes over and over the material in an attempt to master it.
Certain new features of the process of memorization are introduced by
repeated practice, and the governing principles have been studied under
the title of "human verbal learning." What exactly do we mean by *verbal*

Language,
verbal
learning,
memory, and
thought
215

learning? Most school learning, which we may describe as the changes in behavior that happen when people study, consists of some change in the way in which we use words. Although the processes of soaking up information from textbooks, newspapers, and life are of great interest, they are too variable and complicated for fruitful systematic investigation. However, there are some important aspects of the natural learning process which can be isolated for laboratory study. Three of the most thoroughly studied instances are those of paired-associate learning, serial learning, and free recall learning.

In *paired-associate* learning, the subject learns to give one of two items when presented with the other. Real-life analogs are learning French equivalents of English words or names to go with faces. In *serial* learning, the subject learns to give a long sequence of items in the proper order. Analogs are memorizing a poem verbatim or a telephone number. In *free recall* learning, the subject learns a set of separate items which he is free to recall in any order. Analogs are remembering a grocery list or set of errands. What all verbal learning tasks have in common is the use of language. In the laboratory, rather than using real words with all their connotations and prior associations, the experimenter often uses *nonsense syllables*—combinations of letters that have no conventional meanings. However, even the pronunciation of a nonsense syllable, or of the names of the letters it contains, consists of the performance of a very highly trained act. It is, thus, the new way in which old acts are put together that is being studied in all these kinds of verbal learning experiments.

For the experimenter, there are important differences between these various learning tasks. For example, one variable—the similarity of the items being learned—on the average aids free recall, hinders paired-associate learning, and is virtually irrelevant to serial learning. (You may want to see if you can figure out why after you've read the rest of this section.) Nevertheless, it is possible to illustrate most of the important phenomena and factors in verbal learning by focusing on just one task. Here we will focus on paired-associate learning, bringing the other types of task into the discussion only in reference to certain historically important experimental results.

Let us proceed, as we did in Chapter 7, by taking some examples of how verbal learning is observed in the laboratory. In a typical paired-associate experiment, the investigator prepares a list of pairs of nonsense syllables (as illustrated in Figure 8–6) and presents them to a subject by means of a *memory drum*—a roller equipped with shutters. The left-hand item of the first pair is exposed alone for four seconds, and then both items of the pair are exposed alone for four seconds. Then they both disappear and a second later the left-hand item of the next pair appears, and so forth. The first time through the list, of course, the subject can do nothing but watch the stimuli go by. However, he is instructed to try to learn which right-hand, or *response*, item goes with each left-hand, or *stimulus*, item. The list is presented over and over again, each time in a different order so that the subject must learn to associate the members of each pair rather than simply learn the responses in

FIGURE 8-6
Example of a list of paired-associate nonsense syllables. An experimental subject would try to learn to give the right-hand syllable whenever shown the left-hand member of each pair.

FIQ	–	BAP
BIP	–	NAW
ZAJ	–	MUN
PUZ	–	DEP
FOL	–	CAZ
JAQ	–	RIK
SEM	–	TOB
VOK	–	YUR

sequence. On the second and succeeding trials, the subject is asked to try to remember the response for each stimulus item. He has the initial four seconds of each presentation in which to do so, after which the response item appears telling him whether he was right or wrong and what the correct response is. Typically a subject gets only a few items correct on the first try, but gradually gets more and more of them correct until he has learned the whole list.

Now, following our usual procedure we should ask what is the critical reinforcing event in this kind of learning? Many of the features of classical and operant conditioning are present in the typical experimental procedure just described. Two stimuli are presented closely together in time, first a stimulus item (a printed syllable) and then a response item (another printed syllable). The "response" syllable is in reality a set of letters which already acts as a perfectly adequate stimulus (US) for the enunciation of the names of the letters by a literate subject. To this extent, it seems a good approximation to a CS-US pairing. Viewed differently, the situation is also analogous to that of discrimination learning in operant conditioning. When the subject makes the correct response in the presence of a particular stimulus, e.g., ZAP when he sees FAQ, he is "rewarded" by seeing the response he has just made appear. Indeed, just such interpretations have often been given to verbal learning experiments. There are, however, certain obstacles to believing that verbal learning is precisely the same as either classical or operant conditioning. In the first place there is the quite critical role of instructions that has already been mentioned. In addition, there are two much more important difficulties. First, consider the analogy to classical conditioning. The strict effect of order in CS-US pairing of classical conditioning seems to be missing in verbal learning. If care is taken that the two parts of a pair are equally familiar and easy to pronounce, it is nearly as easy, perhaps identically so, for a subject to recall the stimulus item when shown the response as vice versa. This is, of course, quite different from the situation in classical conditioning in which the US, which comes last, ordinarily gains no power to evoke a response attached to the CS. Second, consider the analogy to operant conditioning. The interpretation of verbal learning as operant conditioning rests on the assumption that the subject is rewarded by seeing the correct response matching his own after he responds. But, in fact this procedure is not necessary in verbal learning. If the subject is simply shown pairs of visually presented verbal items, without ever making the response and without ever being told whether he is right or wrong, he will learn just as fast (Battig & Brackett, 1963).

If, then, the reinforcing event in verbal learning does not appear to be either CS-US pairing or operant reward, what is it? Oddly enough, what is required to produce memorization of verbal material has not yet been specified exactly. Questions about the necessary timing of presentation of the items to be associated with each other do not have clear answers; subjects learn whether the items are presented simultaneously or successively. Similarly it is not clear what the role of the subject's response is; subjects learn whether they actually pronounce the correct response or just mutely observe the items. All that present data show clearly is that such details do not matter much. Apparently, all that is absolutely necessary in verbal learning is that the materials to be learned be presented and the subject be instructed to learn them.

IMPORTANT FACTORS IN VERBAL MEMORIZATION

The most important factors governing how well verbal memorization goes forward are primarily ones peculiar to verbal learning, in that they involve effects of huge amounts of prior verbal learning. Nonetheless there is at least one factor, the spacing of practice, which appears to have essentially the same effect as in other kinds of learning. We shall discuss this factor first.

Imagine that in a paired-associate experiment, a given pair, say ZIP-ZAP, is presented twice, and these two presentations are either immediately successive—ZIP-ZAP, ZIP-ZAP—or are separated by the presentation of other pairs. Figure 8–7 shows the results from an experiment investigating this variable. As the number of pairs intervening between the repetitions of a given pair increases, so does the rate of learning. If a pair is repeated immediately, its second presentation usually adds almost nothing to the subject's chance of recalling the pair, while if they are well separated by other activity two presentations can be almost twice as effective as one. This relation has been observed not only in paired-associate learning, but also in the recall of lists of words and of information from sentences in long texts (information from a repeated sentence is remembered better if the two occurrences are separated).

It has been known for some time that a similar phenomenon holds in motor learning. In learning to type, play a musical instrument, or shoot baskets, many short practice periods are much better than one long one of the same total duration. Thus six daily twenty-minute sessions of driving practice, of either a car or a golf ball, will produce much more gain in skill than will a single session of two or even three hours.

A related factor of considerable importance is the rate at which parts of the task are practiced. If a paired-associate list is presented repeatedly in rapid order, for example at one pair every second, it is learned much more slowly than if it is presented repeatedly at a more leisurely pace, say one pair every six seconds. Apparently the longer the verbal material is exposed to the subject (the longer he has to stare at it or think about it), on the average the better he will learn it. It is this

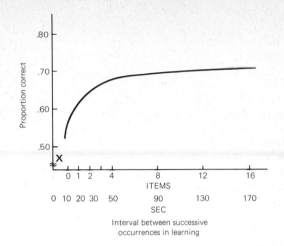

8–7
Effect of spacing of presentations in paired-associate learning. A single pair of nonsense syllables were presented either once (X) or twice. When presented twice, the two occurrences were separated by varying numbers of other pairs. When tested 20 minutes later, the well-separated pairs were remembered much better. (After Landauer, 1969)

observation, also, which in part motivates our earlier statement that the reinforcing event in verbal memorization is the subject's exposure to materials to be learned.

Previous practice

Almost all other important variables in verbal memorization reflect the interaction of prior with present learning. One very important factor of this kind is previous practice. When a subject learns several lists in succession, each successive list is mastered more easily. This improvement is not very generalized, however; for example if he has memorized nonsense syllables he will not have improved in memorizing telephone numbers or words. Just as practice in geometry does not make one more capable of doing formal logic, practice in paired nonsense-syllable learning as such does not make one better in other kinds of memorizing tasks. A few more words will be in order about the effect of practice when we take up the matter of forgetting.

The material to be learned: I—interference and transfer

Consider the two lists in Figure 8–8. List A would be harder to learn than list B, because the pairs in A are all very much alike and the learner would have considerable difficulty learning to tell them apart. The pairs in B, while of the same general kind as those in A, are very different from one another. Such distinctness between pairs greatly facilitates the learning of a list. Similarities between pairs in the same list cause *interference*, one of the most important factors in verbal learning. Note that similarity is not always detrimental to learning. If the two members of a pair are alike, e.g. ZIP-ZAP, as compared to ZIP-NAW, learning is faster. Similarly a free recall list of seven animal names is easier to remember than a list of seven words chosen at random. It is only when the similarity produces confusion between things the learner needs to keep separate that it makes remembering harder.

Language, verbal learning, memory, and thought
219

Two paired-associates lists. One
is harder to learn because the
pairs within it are confusable
with each other.

List 1			List 2		
ZIP	—	G	ZIP	—	G
ZAB	—	C	POG	—	C
ZIT	—	B	NAW	—	B
ZEP	—	F	TEM	—	F
ZAT	—	D	RUK	—	D
ZEB	—	E	MYR	—	E

Interference Interference is, definitionally, the detrimental effect of
the learning of one habit on the learning, retention, or performance of
another. It occurs in many forms. The interference in list A of Figure
8–8 is between pairs in the same list which are being learned more or
less simultaneously. The degree of intra-list similarity can be varied over
a wide range: from a list of three-letter items in which all the stimuli and
responses share at least two letters with some other item in the list, to a
list of meaningful words with nonoverlapping spelling, pronunciations,
and meaning. Different degrees of similarity have corresponding different
effects on the speed with which learning progresses.

Interference can also occur between one list and another. When
a person learns first a list containing one and then another list containing
the other of two (or more) confusable items, having learned the first
list will make learning the second harder. Responses to the list learned
first will tend to generalize and compete with responses acquired later.
The analysis of what kinds of items will cause interference with the
learning of others follows from consideration of the stimulus-generaliza-
tion properties (see Chapter 7) of the two sets of items. When stimuli
are similar, there is a maximum chance for interference because the subject will tend to give the old response to the new stimulus. When the
stimuli are very different there is much less chance for generalization,
and, therefore, less chance of competition between responses, and less
interference. Examine Figure 8–9. If list A is learned first, which of lists
B, C, and D will be easiest and which hardest to learn subsequently?

Transfer When the learning of one task, habit, or set of items influences the way a later task is learned, psychologists speak of *transfer*.
Transfer is *positive* if having learned the first task makes it easier to learn
the second (for example, having learned to snow ski transfers positively
to learning to water ski). Transfer is *negative* if having learned the first
task makes it harder to learn the second (for example, having learned
to ski improperly—e.g., with weight on the wrong ski—transfers negatively to learning to ski properly.) The interference relations we have
been discussing are, of course, cases of negative transfer; but positive
transfer, also, occurs in verbal learning. One instance is when a first and
a second paired-associated list have very different stimuli but the same
responses. See Figure 8–9. Having learned what to use as responses in
list A (BAP-FIQ) puts the subject ahead in learning list B (TIR-FIQ), so
long as there is no chance for confusion as to what is the appropriate

FIGURE 8–9
An illustration of interlist interference. Learning lists B, C and D would ordinarily be approximately equal in difficulty. However, if one had first learned List A, there would be large differences in difficulty between B, C and D.

List A	List B	List C	List D
BAP — FIQ	TIR — FIQ	BAP — TIR	TIR — DEZ
NEP — TAZ	MYR — TAZ	NEP — MYR	MYR — ZIN
BUL — KEJ	CAX — KEJ	BUL — CAX	VID — CAX

stimulus. In general, what transfers in any skill, motor or verbal, is primarily the ability or tendency to make particular responses; if they are useful in the new situation the transfer is positive.

There are interference effects in forgetting, also, as we shall see later. To keep those separate conceptually remember that the effect of prior learning on future *learning* (acquisition, as opposed to forgetting) is called *transfer*.

The material to be learned: II—What?

Next let us consider the effect of the kind of things being memorized. Read through the pairs in Figure 8–10 very carefully, trying to learn which response goes with which stimulus. Take two or three minutes to study the list, then turn the page and attempt to provide the proper responses for the stimuli listed in Figure 8–11. Which ones were easiest? Obviously the pairs in which the response was a familiar word were much easier to memorize than were those in which the response was a meaningless group of letters. In a similar way, a pair made up of very familiar, frequently encountered, or easily pronounced English words is easier to learn than one made up of rare, incomprehensible, or hard-to-say words. This variable is known as *meaningfulness*. This is a very specialized use of the word *meaning*, and refers to the degree to which the subject is familiar with the item rather than to its semantic content or grammatical context.

Why should familiarity make things easier to memorize? The answer, to the first approximation at least, is not hard to come by. It is essentially a case of positive transfer. In learning the pair 8-CRB the

8–10

Take a few minutes to memorize the pairs on this list, then turn to the test stimuli on the next page.

8 — CRB
3 — DOG
4 — BKL
1 — ZYG
6 — HAT
5 — PXM
2 — TIN
7 — MOP

8–11
Try to provide the correct responses that you learned in Figure 8–10. The ones that consist of familiar words will probably be easier than the nonsense syllables. This illustrates the pronounced effect of meaningfullness in paired-associate learning.

7 — ?
2 — ?
6 — ?
1 — ?
3 — ?
5 — ?
4 — ?
8 — ?

subject must not only learn that CRB is the appropriate response to 8, but he must also learn to put together the letters CRB. On the other hand, a pair such as 3-DOG requires much less of this kind of *response learning*, since DOG is already a well-learned, *available* sequence of letters. In short, meaningful sequences bypass a part of what must otherwise be learned. One source of evidence that this is the correct view is that in paired-associate learning the meaningfulness of the response term that the subject must learn to produce has much more effect on rate of learning than does the meaningfulness of the stimulus term, which he need only recognize.

Forgetting

Once verbal learning has taken place, *extinction* (the loss of the new response tendency as a result of the omission of reinforcement on successive presentations of the appropriate stimuli) does not appear to occur as such. Once you have learned to associate the Cardinals with St. Louis, further exposures to the word *St. Louis* without simultaneous occurrence of the associate do not seem to lead to any loss in the tendency to make the association. In fact, such practice strengthens rather than weakens the new behavioral tendency.

On the other hand, in contrast to classical and operant conditioning, *forgetting* (the loss of a new behavioral tendency over time in the absence of specific counter-training) is very important in verbal learning. A great deal of loss in newly learned verbal habits can occur if they go unpracticed. And the way in which learning is carried out, the kinds of materials involved, the nature of the relations between the material being learned and other materials learned before or after, and a host of other factors considerably influence the rate at which forgetting occurs. Let us first survey some of the facts about how forgetting takes place and what sorts of variables are important, and then consider explanations of why forgetting occurs at all and why forgetting is so much more significant in verbal memory than in other forms of learning.

The classical study of forgetting is a monumental work (1885) by the German psychologist, Hermann Ebbinghaus, the inventor of nonsense syllables. Ebbinghaus used himself as his subject, learning one or more serial lists of nonsense syllables almost every morning for many years. In one experiment he learned many lists of ten nonsense syllables, each one until he was able to go through the whole list correctly without an error. He would then put away his work, do something else for various amounts of time, and then try to recall the list. Finally, he would

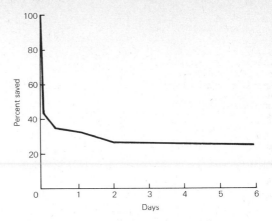

FIGURE 8–12
Forgetting over time. The data are from a classical study by Ebbinghaus (1885), who tested himself repeatedly with lists of nonsense syllables.

study the list again until he could once more get through it without a mistake. He counted the number of trials required to learn the list initially and the number of trials required to relearn it after the retention interval. The difference between these he called *savings*. He expressed retention in terms of a *percent savings score*. Percent savings is the percent fewer trials needed to relearn a list than to learn it the first time, i.e.,

$$\text{Percent savings} = 100 \times \frac{\text{no. of trials for initial learning minus no. of trials to relearn}}{\text{no. of trials for initial learning}}$$

His results are shown in Figure 8–12. These are quite famous data and have been used for years to demonstrate the purported weakness of human memory. Certainly, Ebbinghaus forgot very rapidly. On the average he lost about half the effect of the initial learning within an hour, and about two-thirds within a day. As we shall see, however, there are reasons why these results should not be taken as an indictment of human memory in general (or of Ebbinghaus's in particular).

Inhibition

Subsequently, investigators have often observed levels of retention different from and sometimes considerably greater than those in Ebbinghaus's famous curve—for example, 50 or 60 percent savings after twenty-four hours instead of the 30 percent of Ebbinghaus. In 1957 Benton Underwood noticed a feature which tied together these many apparently disparate findings. In experiments in which retention levels were much higher than Ebbinghaus's, the subjects invariably were relatively "naive," that is they had had little previous practice in memorizing nonsense syllables; however, when values like those of Ebbinghaus were obtained, it was with subjects who were very "sophisticated"—they had learned many other lists before. Ebbinghaus himself had learned literally hundreds. Putting together the results in the experimental literature, Underwood constructed the curve reproduced in Figure 8–13. Here the savings score after twenty-four hours in many different experiments is plotted as a function of the number of similar lists the subjects had previously

Language, verbal learning, memory, and thought
223

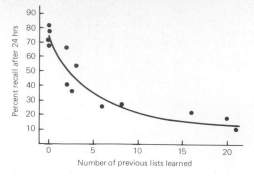

FIGURE 8–13
Effect on recall of having previously learned other lists of nonsense syllables. Each point is from a separate study in which subjects who had previously learned varying numbers of similar lists were tested 24 hours after learning (After Underwood, 1957).

learned. (Note that this is not the same function as the Ebbinghaus curve —it corresponds only to his point for twenty-four hours.) The more lists a person has learned previously, the faster he forgets a newly learned list of the same kind.

The explanation offered by Underwood is that forgetting occurs largely as a result of *proactive inhibition.* Proactive inhibition consists of confusion of newly learned materials with things learned in the past. It is an effect on the rate of *forgetting* of the new material after it has been learned, not on the learning as such. If two groups of subjects learn a set of items equally well, but one has previously learned other sets and, as a result, forgets the new set faster, proactive inhibition has occurred. You will recall that *negative transfer* is a similar effect on learning. If subjects, as a result of previous learning, learn a new list more slowly, negative transfer has occurred. Thus proactive inhibition is analogous to negative transfer, but involves the rate of forgetting of new material after it has been learned rather than the rate at which it is learned. It is important to grasp this distinction because the very same prior experience can sometimes lead both to faster learning of a new task and to more rapid forgetting once it has been learned.

One of the hoary arguments of academia is whether to "cram" or not. The foregoing observations offer an interesting possible resolution. The argument often goes on between two persons who differ widely in personality. The one who doesn't like to study very often stoutly maintains that cramming the night before an exam is a very useful device proven to him by much direct experience. The other, a conscientious booker, claims with equal conviction that studying the night before an exam does no good, because one forgets almost everything by the next day—and quotes some version of the Ebbinghaus results. It turns out that they both may be at least partly right. If one of them has never cracked a book in a particular subject (analogous to never having learned a nonsense-syllable before), whatever facts he memorizes for the first time the night before are reasonably likely to be retained the next day. On the other hand, if the other has been studying conscientiously during the whole term (analogous to having learned lots of nonsense-syllable lists before), it is likely that any new facts he memorizes will mingle during the night with what he knew already and likely be forgotten by the next day. (This is not to say that the best policy is to

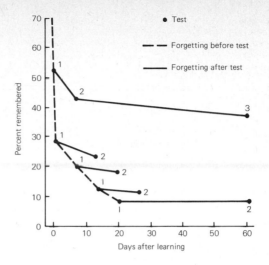

FIGURE 8–14
Beneficial effects of tests on retention. The dashed line shows a typical forgetting curve for factual material as measured by tests (1 = first test, etc.) at different intervals after initial learning. The solid lines show forgetting the same material after tests (After Spitzer, 1939).

study only the night before exams; we are discussing only the amount that is retained of the factual material newly memorized that one night, not the total amount of learning and understanding, which would clearly be greater after many hours of studying over several weeks than after a few hours of studying in one evening.)

This brings us to an important point. Even if the subject has had a large amount of previous experience with the kind of material he is to learn, and is subject to proactive inhibition, he can nevertheless prevent the rapid loss simply by being sure that he practices the new list sufficiently. It is important to keep in mind that the Ebbinghaus results were based on learning just to one perfect trial. If there is more practice, forgetting happens much more slowly.

One particularly effective way to reduce forgetting is to have tests on material after it has been learned. In a classic study of this effect, Spitzer (1939) had groups of high school students learn factual material about peanuts and bamboos. He gave tests to the different groups at various times after initial learning. The amount of forgetting by the time of each group's first test is shown by the dotted line in Figure 8–14. The usual rapid loss occurred. However, Spitzer also gave each group a second test and, in some cases, a third. The solid lines show the rate of forgetting of the material after it had been tested; the tests dramatically reduced subsequent loss. This finding has been repeated many times. It should be noted that the benefit seems to accrue only to the material that was actually tested, so that to aid retention best tests should be fairly comprehensive. The results also suggest that tests should be given early, before the material has been forgotten.

Indeed, so long as the material is still remembered well, tests are more valuable for preventing forgetting than are rereading or restudying. The reason for this may be that tests make the learner actually practice retrieving the information from memory, which more passive review activities do not.

Language, verbal learning, memory, and thought
225

FIGURE 8–15
The distinction between retroactive and proactive inhibition. In proactive inhibition
previous learning interferes with retention. In retroactive inhibition subsequent learning
interferes with retention.

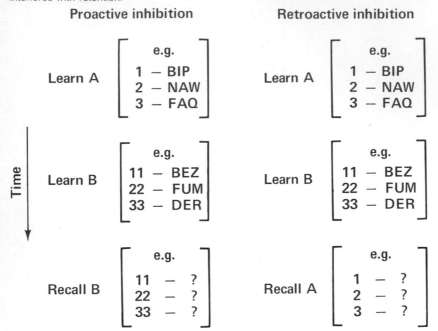

Retroactive inhibition

There is another kind of inhibition, called *retroactive inhibition*, that is
of great importance in forgetting. It occurs when a new set of materials,
B, is learned between the initial learning of A and the recall of A. The
diagram in Figure 8–15 shows the distinction between proactive and
retroactive inhibition. In both proactive and retroactive inhibition the
learning of one set of materials interferes with the retention of another.
In proactive inhibition it is the *previous* learning of another set of materials which interferes with the retention of a newly learned set; while
in retroactive inhibition it is the *subsequent* learning of another set
which interferes with retention. Not all materials will interact in the
same way.

Inhibition, like transfer, depends on the processes of stimulus
generalization and response competition. If the situation tends to
evoke two different responses from a subject at the same time, they
will interfere with each other and he will be less likely to produce either
correctly. Sometimes this kind of conflict can actually be seen in verbal
learning in the intrusion of responses from the second list into the list
being recalled. But what usually happens when a subject is presented
with a stimulus for two conflicting verbal responses is that he says
nothing. Usually he does not consciously "remember" anything either.

What sort of conditions are most likely to lead to response conflict? Well, clearly, the more similar two stimuli are, the more likely will be confusion between them. So, if a subject first learns BIP-FIQ and then learns PIP-KAW, when he tries to recall the correct response to BIP there will be confusion between BIP and PIP and, therefore, competition between FIQ and KAW and little chance of correct recall. On the other hand, if he first learns BIP-FIQ and then learns ZAG-KAW, there will be no resulting inhibition of BIP-FIQ since the two responses will not tend to be evoked simultaneously.

Why, then, does forgetting occur?

We now wish to consider whether the facts of interference and inhibition which we have just reviewed offer us an adequate explanation of why forgetting occurs. Are these factors sufficient to account for all forgetting? Current opinion, supported by the bulk of the evidence, is that they offer only a partial explanation. One major problem is the following: The number of incorrect responses imported from the interfering material should increase in proportion to the amount of forgetting that occurs, and this usually is not the case. The number of intrusions or confused responses does not increase with time as it should. There must, then, investigators now feel, be some other factor in addition to interference which contributes to forgetting.

What other factors could there be? One possibility is *autonomous decay*. The presumption here is that perhaps the memory storage system is simply imperfect, that the physiological memory trace (Chapter 10) simply weakens or loses its sharpness of definition with time. Many analogies come to mind, such as a photograph fading or a record becoming scratchy and worn. There is no reason to presume that the physical underpinnings of memory are impervious to natural degradation. But the real question is whether losses from such sources are large or trivial. We simply do not know, and there is presently no obvious way of finding out.

Another potential factor in forgetting is what psychologists have called a *generalization decrement*. The situation at the time of recall is always at least slightly different from the situation at the time of learning. If the responses learned during acquisition are discriminative reactions to the whole situation, including the array of stimuli of the internal and external environment in which the subject finds himself, then one would expect a decrement when the situation is changed, as it is later at the time of recall. Of course, the longer the time between initial learning and the attempt to recall, the greater will be the average change in the environment. The evidence from studies of animal discrimination-learning and some direct evidence from verbal learning situations support the notion that recall is better the more similar the test situation is to the learning situation. The especially beneficial effect of tests on retention is another source of evidence for this view, since tests are more similar to tests than is plain studying and should show less generalization decrement.

A related factor, or perhaps simply a different way of looking at the matter, is found in considering the problem of retrieval of stored information. Imagine that you are filing index cards bearing the names of new books acquired in a library. The file starts out small and grows with time. When you have filed a card for a given book, say *Robinson Crusoe*, the difficulty of finding it again will depend on, among other things, the number of other cards in the file. As time goes by the number of other cards in the file will increase and the chances of finding any one particular card will diminish. The difficulty is in part analogous to interference (there are more cards that are similar to the one you are looking for), and in part analogous to a generalization decrement (the situation has changed since the original filing); but it is also partly attributable to factors of a kind which we have not yet considered. These factors have to do with the way in which "coding" is accomplished. When there are only a few cards in a file, it may be sufficient to file by the author's initials only, and to ignore other information. In fact this would be much more efficient for a very small file, since it would be all that would be necessary for perfect retrieval and would save a lot of energy on the part of the person doing the filing. However, once a file gets very large such a system will fail since there will be too many authors with the same initials. With a large file, more information will be needed to uniquely identify each item. Thus, as stored data accumulate there is reason to expect changes in the filing or coding system. As a result, with time, earlier filed items may become less easy to find because they were coded for storage in a way that is no longer adequate. Such problems of storage and retrieval now appear to be involved in the course of human forgetting to a much larger extent than was realized by earlier investigators.

Several theories of memory incorporating this type of "coding" process have recently been proposed. Typically, such theories take the form of detailed sets of instructions (programs) that a computer follows, which allow it to receive, code, store, and later look up information about nonsense-syllable pairs, serial lists, or the like. It has been possible to make the learning behavior of machines operating with such programs resemble that of humans in many ways. For example, learning rate varies appropriately with variables such as similarity of items, list length, and instructions (Feigenbaum, 1967; Hintzman, 1968). This suggests, though it obviously does not prove, that similar "information processing" principles may be at work in human memory.

Theories of verbal learning

Some of the theories originally developed to describe conditioning, such as the Estes stimulus sampling theory discussed in Chapter 7, have also been applied to human verbal learning, and with considerable success. The overall feature of learning curves for conditioning summarized in the *principle of constant proportional gain* characterizes most verbal-learning situations as well (the exceptions are complex cases where more than one kind or stage of learning is required). Therefore, of course, this shape of curve is also reflected in theories of verbal learning. With respect to finer details there appear to be variations from one kind of learning to another, with corresponding differences in the goodness of fit of any one theory.

FIGURE 8–16
A gradual learning curve for averaged results does not necessarily mean that learning is gradual. For example, if each item in a 4-item list was learned suddenly, the total number correct might still appear to increase gradually.

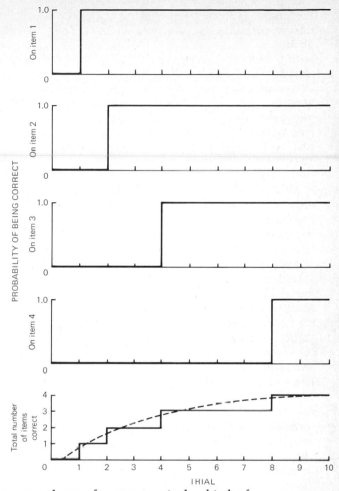

We will describe one current theory for one particular kind of task—the learning of paired-associate lists in which there is a small number of different responses, and the response units themselves do not need to be learned (e.g., BIP-1, NAW-2, FAQ-1, ZAJ-2). This is an especially interesting case, because a very simple and elegant mathematical theory can describe it with astonishing accuracy. The theory, developed by Bower (1961), assumes that for a given subject, a given stimulus-response pair is either completely known or completely unknown. There are no half-learned pairs in the postulated "all-or-none" learning process. The way learning proceeds, according to this theory, is as follows: Each time the subject sees a given pair there is a certain constant probability that he will learn it. Once he has learned the pair, he will always get it right. If he has not learned a pair yet, he will get it right only by guessing (in a two-choice situation he will be correct half of the time, and so forth). The theory has some very strong implications. For one thing, it implies that at any time before the subject makes his last error on an item, the probability of getting it right will be at the chance level, no matter how

Language, verbal learning, memory, and thought

229

TABLE 8-1
**Predictions from Bower's mathematical model and results of a
paired-associate learning experiment**

Statistic	Observed	Predicted
Total errors	2.50	2.50
Standard deviation	2.34	2.50
Trial of first correct	1.92	1.84
Standard deviation	1.20	1.12
Trial of last error	4.18	4.17
Standard deviation	4.06	4.50
Probability of error after an error	0.42	0.40
Runs of 2 errors	0.33	0.35
Runs of 3 errors	0.13	0.15
Runs of 4 errors	0.08	0.06
No. of pairs of errors:		
1 trial apart	1.06	1.03
2 trials apart	0.85	0.82
3 trials apart	0.65	0.65
4 trials apart	0.51	0.51

(After Hilgard & Bower, 1966)

long training has gone on. This seems to fly in the face of most of our experiences, and to contradict the gradual learning curves so far presented here. But these curves have been based on the learning of many different things (items, facts, pairs) at the same time, and/or on averages of many different subjects. Figure 8–16 shows how an average learning curve with all the usual smooth and gradual features can be generated by combining a large number of all-or-none, step-function, curves for individual items. In other words, if one simultaneously studies a large number of different pairs, the total number known at any point can grow in a gradual way despite the fact that each one is learned suddenly.

By application of the mathematics of probability, a large number of precise derivations can be made from this theory and these can be translated into predictions about learning. Table 8–1 shows a sample of the kinds of predictions which have been made from Bower's mathematical theory, along with some quantitative results of one experiment to which it applies. The correspondence between predictions and outcome for this particular case was quite remarkable; in fact, it has been said that this theory is one of the most accurate and detailed in all of science. Unfortunately, the range of applicability of the theory is very limited—only a few specific learning tasks conform. Other tasks, such as complex paired-associate learning in which responses as well as stimulus-response links must be learned, yield data implying a more gradual learning process than the theory postulates.[1] Nevertheless, it is possible that all learning proceeds basically by discrete, all-or-none steps; but that in some cases there are so many steps, each very small, that the overall process appears continuous. This is an unresolved issue which has received a great deal of attention in recent research.

[1] Unfortunately, no one has yet come up with a general way of describing just which tasks do and which tasks don't fit Bower's model. A few do and many don't is about all we can say so far.

THINKING AND PROBLEM SOLVING

We now turn our attention from the learning of verbal habits and their direct performance in the same form as they were learned, to problems of high-order combining and processing of words and other symbols— the processes of *thinking*. Some thinking goes on in non-linguistic terms, for example in visual and auditory images of spatial relations and melodies. But thought is primarily a matter of talking to oneself.

It is hard to exaggerate the complexity of the thinking process, or to overestimate the number and subtlety of the components that go into talking to oneself effectively. To think requires having previously learned thousands of symbolic components, being able to retrieve them in a useful form and then manipulate them according to rules in ways that represent grammar, logic, inference, extrapolation, and recombination, and finally being able to recognize a good product when it occurs.

Solving intellectual problems

To achieve a desired result, whether it is a new series of steps in a mathematical proof or a readjustment on a screw setting in a television circuit, it may be necessary to invent a new way of behaving. In finding the best action to suit the situation, people often go through a process of experimental trial and error, either actual (with real movements in space and feedback from the world) or *vicarious* (with evaluation of the success of a new idea accomplished by thinking).

The way in which a person goes about searching for a solution can be important. Let's take a few examples. Faced with a television set that does not work, the repairman must first diagnose the ailment and then correct it. There are a number of different principles on which he might proceed, all of them having some value but also some drawbacks. He might hark back to his prior experience with fixing television sets and choose whichever was the most frequent problem. The difficulty with this method is of course that the repairman will often end up treating nonexistent problems. Perhaps because of the effects of partial-reinforcement schedules, too many repairmen have a tendency to do just this—always look for pet malfunctions. A second procedure would be to devise a system whereby all the possible malfunctions could first be divided into two equal-sized sets and a test made to determine which set the present failure falls in. Then the possibilities would be further subdivided into equal subsets, and so on until that part or function which was truly at fault was found. This is a neat and logical system which would always work, could it be implemented. Its inefficiency lies in the fact that certain malfunctions really do occur much more often than others, and it doesn't make sense to ignore this fact. A third technique would be to develop a set of correspondences between diagnostic signs and specific ills: if it could be found that a certain kind of weird flickering on the upper left-hand corner of the screen always corresponded to a failure in a particular part, then this sign could be used as a direct path to the proper treatment. The problem here, of course, is that frequently no such 1-to-1 correspondence exists but, rather, that a particular symptom may have many different causes.

Language, verbal learning, memory, and thought

231

Obviously, the optimal method of solution is some combination of these three techniques, using a logical narrowing-of-alternatives search strategy, but giving priority to the failures which are most probable on the basis of present symptoms and general experience.

Next consider solving a chess problem. The pieces are arranged on the board in some stage of a game, and the player is required to choose one of the many available moves in a way that maximizes his chance of winning. One *logically* possible method of solution would be to examine all the possible moves one at a time, and for each one trace all possible responses on the part of the opponent, and for each of these to trace all possible rejoinders, and so on to the end of the game. Obviously this would lead to an astronomical number of moves to be considered (about 10^{125}). The first three moves alone would require considering several *million* possibilities. Even high-speed computers, which have been programmed to solve chess problems, find this method prohibitively time consuming. An alternative strategy would be to recognize some particularly important features of the situation as related to past experience with the game, in much the same way the TV repairman uses the symptoms of failure, and thereby reduce tremendously the number of moves to be considered. The player might say to himself, "In situations like this, when I attacked my opponent's queen I usually won the game." In addition, rather than try to evaluate the move in terms of the final outcome of the game, one might evaluate it instead by reference to general principles about the kinds of positions that are good to hold on the chessboard. In other words, intermediate goals, whose attainment is more manageable, would be set up.

In some problems it is not even obvious what kinds of alternatives are open—what is to be tried or even considered next. In such cases one of the requirements for a good problem-solver is that he have available a wide variety of things to try and a great deal of experience on which to base an intuitive guess about what might work. This is the case with difficult mathematical problems in which the solution frequently hinges on applying a particular manipulation of the components. Mathematicians often refer to the techniques of manipulating problems as "tricks." A large and well-used bag of mathematical tricks is very important to the creative mathematician.

We have seen several ways in which prior experience is important in problem solving. Let us consider its role in more detail. On the one hand it is quite obvious that to solve difficult problems one requires information. The medical researcher looking for a new painkiller that will not be addictive will be ahead if he knows what compounds have been previously tried and found wanting. And the creative artist or poet must know what forms, styles, techniques, and subject matters have been so overworked that they have become clichés. On the other hand, prior experience can also be very detrimental to problem solving. If a person is too used to solving a certain kind of problem in a specific way, he may be inhibited in trying new attacks when they are needed. This effect has been demonstrated in studies of what is called *functional fixedness* or *habitual set*. In one type of experiment some of the subjects are given

FIGURE 8–17
Example of some problems used
in studying the bad effects of
set on solution of logical
problems (After Luchins, 1942).

Problem	Given the following empty jars as measures			Obtain the required amount of water
1	21	127	3	100
2	14	163	25	99
3	18	43	10	5
4	9	42	6	21
5	20	59	4	31
6	23	49	3	20

a series of mathematical or logical problems for which a certain method of solution works (see the sample in Figure 8–17), and then suddenly are shown another problem that apparently has the same form but which can be solved much more easily by a new method. These subjects do much worse than others who are given only the last problem. Thus, to approach a problem in the wrong way can inhibit its optimal solution.

Creativity in problem solving

Perhaps one of the abilities which characterize creative people is that they are somehow able to overcome the bad effect of prior successes in problem solving! What does it take to be creative? For one thing, it obviously requires the right kind of background of information and experience to produce something which is new (unlike anything achieved before) and also good (meeting carefully constructed criteria). But a person who knows all the relevant facts and has experience with all the methods of solution apparently available might be all the more likely to try to use old answers and familiar approaches. Perhaps this is one reason why a period of *incubation* has often been thought to be important in the creative problem-solving process. Many scientists, and others, have reported that insights often come after a period away from a problem. It is known that the effect of habitual set dissipates somewhat with time, as shown in Figure 8–18. If the methods being used to approach a problem are not yielding results, perhaps a time away from the problem allows the thinker to start afresh.

EPILOGUE ON SOME APPLICATIONS TO EDUCATION

Before we conclude this discussion of human memory and problem solving, it seems reasonable to discuss the bearing of what we know scientifically of such things on some issues of belief, value, and strategy in education and learning. This discussion will perforce include some speculation and some controversial opinions. The reader of this section is therefore urged to be careful not to accept the conclusions as facts, but rather to use the observations and arguments presented as foils for his own thoughts on the issues raised.

What should be the goals of education? What should a student expect and strive to get? What should a teacher attempt to impart? Of course, answers to such questions depend largely on the motivation of the

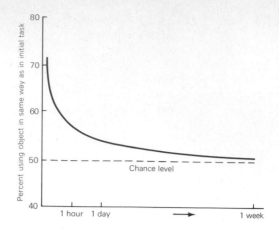

FIGURE 8–18
The dissipation of functional fixedness over time. Subjects were required to use a tool for something other than its normal use—such as pliers as the legs of a small table. If they first used the object in its normal way, the novel use tended to be inhibited. However, the longer the time between normal use and test, the more inhibition was reduced. (After Adamson & Taylor, 1954)

scholars involved and in turn on the needs and values of the society around them, of which they are part. Nevertheless, decisions on such matters are strongly rooted in assumptions about the nature and capability of the animal doing the learning, and about the processes of learning, thinking, and forgetting, and their limitations.

One particularly pertinent issue involves the learning of facts. Educationists, students, and liberal board of education members alike increasingly decry "rote memorization," and the teaching of "facts." They espouse instead "understanding," "thinking," and learning by "doing," "discovery," or "involvement." While there is obviously much wisdom in these pronouncements and attitudes, it is worthwhile examining their relation to what is known about the human information-processor and storer, if only as an exercise in relating academic psychology to real-life problems. There are two major charges lodged against what is derogatorily called "rote learning": the first is that the things that are learned by rote are forgotten rapidly; the second is that rote is an inferior method of learning (which implies that there are better ways). The question of forgetting, as we have seen, is somewhat more complex than this. Certainly, under ideally *bad* conditions things memorized are indeed forgotten very quickly: if the things learned are meaningless, learned in the context of a large amount of interference from previous learning of similar things, practiced only to a low level, and not over-learned, reviewed, or tested, then there may be a 60 percent or more loss in a day. On the other hand if "rote" learning occurs under ideal circumstances, forgetting can be almost negligible: if the materials are arranged and learned in a way which differentiates them clearly from other things previously learned, if their practice is well-spaced and carried well beyond apparent mastery, and if they are practiced, reviewed, and tested at optimal intervals, the amount of loss can be kept almost as low as desired.

There are two apparent alternatives to deliberate memorization in learning. One is learning without apparent direct effort, by participation, or by reading or talking about a subject. The other is by learning principles or general laws in place of facts. With the latter procedure there can be no quarrel. It is clearly better to learn the law of gravity than to learn a table of the times required for every conceivable object in the world to fall to the earth from every possible height. Whenever a set of complex facts or relations can be effectively reduced to a simple, general, and accurate principle, it is a tremendous saving in energy to use the reduced form. Unfortunately, a very large part of man's useful knowledge can't be so reduced. The names, shapes, and functions of parts of the body learned in anatomy, the meanings and conjugations of words in foreign languages, the events of history, the arbitrary names and rules of arithmetic combinations, cannot, as yet at least, be reduced to simpler statements. In these cases it would obviously be foolish to reject sheer memorization, since without it one would also reject very useful knowledge.

Students often claim that some courses require only rote memorization of facts, while others require only understanding. Remarkably often the courses accused differ from one student to another; while one says that biology is all facts, and physics all understanding, another will say that physics is all memorization, and biology just "came naturally." A part of this phenomenon may depend on the interests of the student. If you are very interested in the subject matter, and find reading and thinking about it a pleasant activity, you will spend a lot of time on it and expose yourself to the facts of which it consists without thinking of it as work. When you are done you will think you have not "memorized" but simply "absorbed." For another person, exactly the same materials and exactly the same activities of reading and thinking may be onerous, in which case he will report that he has suffered through rote memorization.

It is also said that all too often students memorize instead of think, and that people accept facts by authority instead of principles by cogitation. The educational system is accused of encouraging this evil. It may well be that people could, on the average, be better at thinking than they are, and every effort should be bent toward inventing ways of teaching better understanding and information processing. On the other hand, the utility of sheer memorization in even the most esoteric, creative thought-processes should not be underestimated. It seems to me that it would be a mistake to adopt a posture of refusal to memorize. As was previously pointed out, all good thinking, all truly creative thinking in which real solutions are sought and found, depends critically on the thinker's command of a vast number of relevant facts. Thinking in the absence of fact is frivolous, because the solutions reached may either be based on totally incorrect premises and therefore useless or be ones already arrived at before and therefore superfluous.

It is interesting and relevant to examine the peculiar abilities of the human as an information-processing system, compared with those of his most obvious competitors, electronic computers. What the modern electronic computer does extremely well is perform logical operations at lightning speeds—many can perform literally hundreds of thousands of operations per second. These operations can be anything in the realm of rigorous logic or arithmetic, e.g., adding two fifteen-place numbers or deriving a logical conclusion such as $A > B$, $B > C$, therefore $A > C$.

The human, by contrast, can perform easy operations (like adding single digits) at a rate of *at most* five per second, with a rather high probability of error. The computer seems, in this regard, to be at least several thousand times as good as a human. What should one call this aspect of information processing? Certainly if you asked a human who was hard at work mentally solving arithmetic or logic problems, he would tell you he was thinking.

Luckily, there is another aspect of information processing in which humans stack up much better against computers. Ask a human to recall an associative fact (the name that goes with a face, the meaning that goes with a word, the category in which the word should be placed—noun, name of an animal, real word, or nonsense) and he will give you an answer within about one second. The average adult human probably could answer in the neighborhood of a million such questions (this is a very rough estimate, not to be taken too seriously, based on the fact that college students can correctly classify about 200,000 words, and might be assumed to know five or ten times that many facts of other kinds). It is not just the number of facts which is so impressive, but the way in which they are stored for access. Given the word *horse*, literally dozens of implications and associations become available almost instantaneously and for the asking. To create a file of this kind in a computer would be a gargantuan and presently impossible task. The immediately available memories of even very large computers are too small by a factor of hundreds.

It is reasonably clear, then, that the single most outstanding capability of the human, as compared to a computer, is his talent for storing and retrieving facts. Indeed, a very strong case can be made for this ability being the feature which makes creative thought in a human possible, and which makes him able to perform the apparently complex feats of cognitive activity that computers so far cannot match. For example, language translation by computer is not yet feasible, largely because it requires a fantastic amount of knowledge of the meanings of words and the changes in their meaning that are occasioned by differences in context, sentence structure, and the like, which cannot be represented in the limited memory of a computer, and cannot be generated (at least as yet) by the logical processes at which the computer is so good. It appears then, although it can't be proved, that the superiority of the human in those kinds of thinking in which he is in fact superior lies primarily in his ability to easily and quickly gain access to huge amounts of relevant materials, that is, to utilize an astonishingly powerful memory system. If this is truly the case, it would be a sad mistake to reorganize education so as to downgrade the use of this capability in a misdirected attempt to make the human use his manipulatory facilities more and his memory less. If the view presented here is correct, the information-manipulating system of the human is a strictly limited and low-power affair, while his information *storage* and *retrieval* system is an incredibly good one. This natural characteristic of the human probably should be taken advantage of rather than struggled against.

TOPICS DISCUSSED IN CHAPTER 8

1. The requirements and opportunities for learning posed by the possession of language.

2. The nature and components of speech; phonemes, morphemes, grammar.

3. The rapid loss of verbal material if it is not practiced; and some contrasts with recognition memory.

4. The reinforcing events in human verbal learning that lead to long-term retention.

5. The factors of spacing and rate of practice.

6. Factors of kind of material to be learned.

7. Various effects, good and bad, of learning many similar things at once or in succession; interference, transfer, inhibition.

8. The rapidity, causes, and prevention of forgetting.

9. One mathematical theory of verbal learning.

10. Some aspects of thinking; strategies in solution of intellectual problems.

11. The good and bad effects of prior experience on creative thinking.

12. Some speculations and opinions relating the special talents and limitations of man to the role of memorization in education.

SUGGESTED READINGS

1. *A general textbook on learning that deals with both human and animal learning is:*

Deese, J. E., & Hulse, S. *Psychology of learning,* 3rd ed. New York: McGraw Hill, 1967.

2. *Two good books on language are:*

Brown, R. *Words and things.* New York: Free Press, 1959; and

Carroll, J. B. *Language and thought.* Englewood Cliffs, New Jersey: Prentice-Hall, 1964.

3. *A classic monograph on human learning is:*

Ebbinghaus, H. *Memory: a contribution to experimental psychology.* New York: Dover, 1964 (paperback; originally published in 1885).

4. *A good collection of important and interesting papers on human learning can be found in:*

Slamecka, N. J. *Human learning and memory.* New York: Oxford, 1967.

5. *Some original papers on thinking are reprinted in:*

Duncan, C. P. *Thinking: current experimental studies.* New York: Lippincott, 1967.

NINE
Developmental psychology

We are now ready to consider how people get that way. An adult has a rich variety of well-established behavioral tendencies: abilities, personality characteristics, social habits, attitudes and values, modes of feeling and perceiving. He has at hand huge stores of facts, and any number of idiosyncracies and peccadillos. Infants are much more restricted in their behavioral repertoires. This is certainly not to imply that a newborn infant is a piece of unmarked, infinitely pliable clay— there are wide differences in activity and reactivity between one infant and another from the first breath. And as we have already noted, there is ample evidence of important contributions of heredity to the basic predispositions and capabilities of individuals. Nonetheless, the major portion of the intricate and sophisticated behavior of the adult develops after birth. This fact is particularly important for human beings because, compared to many other animals, the human infant is born very immature. Contrast with humans, for example, the golden hamster who comes from the womb prepared to walk, eat the foods normal for adults of his kind and, with some success, avoid his natural enemies.

It is worth a short digression to sketch the probable reasons for the delayed maturing of human infants. A much simplified and somewhat speculative account of the factors that have interacted in the evolution of this characteristic goes as follows: The greatest single adaptive advantage of humans lies in their large brains. The evolution of large human brains was probably intimately related to the advent of upright posture that freed the hands to use tools, an activity that demands large brains and can put to use great information-processing capabilities. Large brains in turn require large heads. But walking upright requires a strong, peculiarly oriented pelvis, which accommodates only a rather small hole in its middle. Unfortunately, this is the hole through which an infant, with its large head, must be born. These two facts, a large head and a small pelvic opening, pose a distinct problem. The evolutionary "solution" appears to be the ejection of the infant from the womb at a very immature stage. Immaturity at birth has, of course, many implications for human development and human society. For example, the immature infant cannot walk for many months. Fortunately but probably not fortuitously, he has a human mother who walks upright and thus has free two arms in which to hold the infant. With her arms full, however, the mother becomes unusually dependent on her mate for food and protection during child-bearing years. This has probably encouraged the evolution of a number of female characteristics which are apparently especially suited to attracting males and are seldom found in the animal kingdom, notably: protuberant breasts, lack of body hair, constant sexual receptivity, and a sexual cycle in which drive is largely uncorrelated with fertility. At the same time, the sedentary life required of a human mother ideally suits her to use (and perhaps also to have invented) language, with which she can communicate with other females in the same plight around the home-fire. Luckily, the prolonged dependence of the human infant provides time during which he can learn the fantastic intricacies of speech and language which, like tool use, require not only a large brain, but also a lot of experience. And round and round it goes.

In sum, no other animal needs to learn so much to get along in its normal environment as does the human and no other has such a long time in which there is little else it *can* do!

To return to our main theme, we wish to find out how and when the various behavioral tendencies of an individual develop. We may simply want to describe average, or "normative," development. For example, we might want to know the normal rate at which vocabulary increases with age. Answers to such questions not only satisfy our curiosity, but also are of practical significance in problems of education and social relations.

Further, we would like to know why and how a certain development occurs and why it occurs when it does—how children start to walk, and why they usually don't until they are over a year old, for example. Still another kind of question is how normal development can be accelerated or modified, and how failures which lead to abnormal development—such as retardation, or mental illness—occur, and how they can be avoided.

Where shall we look for causes of development, either normal or awry? On the purely descriptive level, it is quite easy to discern in almost all development a general progress. Most children get a little better every day in every way! Although there are some exceptions to this rule, it does seem to describe in at least a gross way almost all research findings to date in child development. On the other hand such a principle doesn't help us very much in understanding what is going on in development or in making it happen better.[1]

The interesting reasons why development proceeds the way it does can be divided into three groups. The first is *maturation*, the genetically guided development of the body, its organs, nervous system, muscles, glands, and behavior. Many of the changes in the behavior of a growing animal are obviously and closely related to the changes taking place in its body.

The second major factor in development comprises the situations presented to each individual by his *environment*. Every culture provides an array of experiences, different to some degree from those provided by other cultures, which shape the people who grow up in it. Every family has ways of doing things which it imposes on its members, traditions about daily routines and schedules, conventions of mealtime, dress, and clothing. Each parent, each sibling, and each peer provide to a growing child yet another set of stimuli, sensations, reactions, reinforcements, punishments, facts, influences, and models which mold his behavior. Thus, every child is exposed to a multitude of influences. Some he shares with all human children, some with all children in his culture, some with other children in his family, and some are his alone.

The third group of causes or principles might be called *natural* or *logical sequencing*. Many skills can be acquired only after other, more basic ones have appeared, either through maturation or through learning. For example, it is unlikely that a child could stand before he could sit up, learn to run before he had learned to walk, speak sentences before he could speak words, or learn to read English words before he had learned to recognize letters.

In what follows we will be concerned with the development of several aspects of behavior: perceptual abilities, physical growth and motor skills, language and intelligence, social relations, and personality. In each of these there are developmental influences corresponding to each of the three factors just described—maturation, differences in experience, and natural sequencing. A few of the influences on development are well established and can be neatly described; most are still in the realm of guesswork. In all cases, however, it is certain that development depends on not one, but all three of these factors, operating in endless and intricate concert.

It is not easy to tease out the relative importance of each of these factors. Note especially that how complex a behavior is tells us nothing about its developmental roots; it is no more nor less difficult to imagine how the nervous system could acquire new complex capabilities through experience than to imagine how the same capabilities could arise through the unfolding of hereditary influences. Careful investigation and inference are needed anew in every case to trace the actual contributions

[1] When value words like "better" are used here, they should not be taken to imply that anyone need accept criteria set by psychology. Indeed, psychology has no criteria of good development. But what psychological understanding should, one day, make possible, is development in ways that are "better" according to the values of society, parents, and children.

of the many determiners of behavior. As we will see, even characteristics such as physical size, which might seem to depend only on genetics and physical factors, turn out to be influenced by experience and by the order in which events happen. And even behaviors such as the ability to speak, which might seem to depend only on experience, also have roots in physical maturation, and demonstrate an internal logic in their stages of acquisition.

PERCEPTUAL DEVELOPMENT

What is the world like to an infant? When a baby lies in its crib, what does it see, feel, and hear? Obviously, its perceptions cannot be the same as those that an adult in the same position would have. Objects, sounds, and feelings have no associations with past experience for a newborn infant. They have only the meanings inherent in the rudimentary organization of the nervous system at birth. Just how good this organization is, just how much detail it can process, or how much significance it can assign to events in the world is difficult to guess. The neural development of the human infant is quite incomplete at birth. Over much of their length many important nerve fibers are not yet completely formed, and many of the hormonal systems are not yet functioning fully. Thus, the infant lacks more than just experience.

Psychologists and philosophers have speculated on what life must be like in one's first days. Such speculations usually start with the observation that when an adult encounters a brand-new environment — as when one moves to a new city — things are at first a rather undifferentiated and confusing blend, and only gradually take on discreteness and differentiation. Extrapolating, one would guess that the world of the newborn in a pretty homogeneous, unintelligible place. William James put it this way: "The baby, assailed by eyes, ears, nose, skin and entrails all at once, feels it all as one great blooming, buzzing confusion."

It is tempting to assume that the newborn infant recognizes nothing, is responsive to nothing, and has no thoughts. Since the infant has almost no way of showing that he is perceiving or thinking, it is easy to assume that he is not. But the infant does show a startle reaction to a loud noise as soon as he is born, and responds to the sound of a rattle by ten days. And in recent years a number of rather clever experiments have shown that even the youngest infants engage in surprisingly sophisticated perception. Casually observed, the newborn's eyes appear to wander aimlessly, but in fact a young infant can focus, provided only that the object that it is attending to is about a foot from his eyes (about the usual distance of his mother's face). If a vertical line is placed in front of an infant, his eyes will move so as to make the line cross the sensitive fovea. Evidently, there is a wired-in response mechanism for "homing in" on regions of high contrast, which, of course, usually mark the edges of objects. A week-old infant will stare at a patterned surface longer than at a plain one. Infants only a few months old can be taught to show even more impressive perceptual abilities and preferences. A three- or four-day-old infant will learn to turn his head to one side if he is reinforced with a dextrose solution (Lipsitt, 1966). Slightly older

children have been taught to make such head turns only when they see
a particular object. Moreover, an infant will show certain perceptual
constancies. Taught to respond to a square object held in view so that
its retinal image is actually square, he will continue to respond to it when
it is presented at another angle, at which its retinal image (Chapter 5)
is actually trapezoidal (Bower, 1966). A two-month-old infant, provided
with two different visual patterns over his crib, will ordinarily stare at
one more than the other (even if their positions are frequently switched),
thus showing not only that he can see and likes to look at such patterns,
but also that he prefers some over others. The patterns can be quite
complicated and quite small, e.g., $\frac{1}{64}$ inch wide stripes are preferred to
plain surfaces by many six-month-olds.

At four months one of a baby's favorite activities is to look at
his own hands. By six months he can use visual information to help

him avoid falling off high places. Placed on a table with an edge discernible only by vision—a piece of glass level with the table top prevents both falling and the use of tactile cues—most infants will avoid the deep side (Figure 9–1). Many other terrestrial animals, like humans, perform this life-sustaining avoidance of "perceptual cliffs" on their first trial without prior experience (Gibson & Walk, 1960).

Later, during the early years of development, perceptual abilities develop in rather expectable ways. Young children apparently need more information about common objects in the visual display in order to be able to identify them. For example, they sometimes have trouble recognizing sketchy line drawings of familiar objects. The various *constancies*, such as color constancy and size constancy, become somewhat better with age. There are, however, some exceptions with interesting implications. Some constancies, rather than simply becoming stronger as the child gets older, appear to go through a stage in which they are *too* good. When a child has first learned to recognize letters, he seems to immediately recognize them in many altered forms or transformations. Having learned that a certain shape is a *T* by seeing it in large boldface type, a child will recognize it in very small type, or when it is rotated 90 degrees, or when it is made sloppily, with the angles slightly wrong or the lines weaving. This is well and good. But the early reader often mistakes *b*s for *d*s or *p*s for *g*s, fails to discriminate *3* from *E*, and so forth—all cases of different patterns being perceived as *same* beyond conventional limits of allowable variation.

What lies behind developments in perceptual ability? As we have said, the nervous system of the infant is still incomplete at birth and gets nearer to its final form as he grows older. But new perceptual abilities also take advantage of experience. For example, learning the correspondence between letter combinations and meanings depends on experience. One way of separating the effects of experience from those of physical maturation in perceptual processes is to investigate what happens to an organism when its perceptual experiences are restricted. This matter has been explored quite extensively in lower animals. Monkeys have been deprived of pattern vision by having their eyes covered with translucent goggles (if there is no light at all the nerves degenerate) for the first several months of life. When normal vision is restored, such animals are capable of seeing to some extent, but have to be trained to make many discriminations normal for nondeprived monkeys of the same age (Riesen, 1961). Similarly, humans who have been blind from infancy but have their vision surgically restored can see some things but are incapable of certain other perceptual tasks: they can tell an object from its background immediately, but cannot identify specific shapes such as triangles without training (Senden, 1932).

In general, early deprivation of visual experience seems to cause deficits in pattern perception of the kind necessary for object identification, or object constancy, but leaves locus perception of the kind needed for locomotion and grasping virtually unaffected.

Dogs raised in severely restricted environments—small enclosed cages—in which they see little patterned light, hear few varieties of sounds, and get little opportunity to play or explore have considerable trouble in dealing with the world. For example, such a dog will respond to a match held in front of his nose in a most peculiar way: he sniffs it, burns his nose, and then sniffs it again and again with the same result. Apparently he fails to identify the sameness in meaning of the two stimulus events which he encounters (Melzack & Scott, 1957).

These examples illustrate quite nicely the interaction of physical maturation factors and experience. In all known cases of restricted perceptual experience the animal or person has been left not with a complete lack of perceptual ability, but rather with a peculiar set of incapacities, most of which appear to be related to what might best be called *meaning*. The chimpanzee with restricted early visual input can get around in the world and avoid objects, but he has to learn to tell one object from another; the human who suddenly can see can tell that an object is present but has to learn to tell a square from a triangle; the dog raised in a restricted environment can walk around, respond, and feel pain, but is deficient in his ability to infer that a particular object is dangerous.

Are there also perceptual developments which illustrate our third factor of development, natural or logical sequencing? Probably yes. Learning to recognize letters before words may be such a case. Although certainly a child can learn to identify a word as a whole image without ever having learned letters, this is not the usual progression. The recognition of letters seems to proceed by a process of first recognizing the critical features which distinguish one letter from another, then overgeneralizing a letter—as in the *d-b* example given above—and finally by noting particular features which allow him to avoid the overgeneralizations. However, whether this is a *necessary* sequence is not presently known.

PHYSICAL GROWTH AND MOTOR SKILLS

The infant human spends his first months lying down, with only an occasional smile, blink, kick, or scream to show his worldly ambition. Only slowly do the basic motor skills of grasping objects, walking, etc., emerge. The first movements of a neonate are almost entirely uncoordinated and undifferentiated. Poke him sharply and he responds, with no particular muscle or limb and in no particular direction, but rather with his whole body: legs, arms, and head flail, twitch, and wiggle without obvious order. The first well-formed, coordinated actions are usually head and eye movements—turning to bring the mother's face into view, and moving the eyes to focus on objects. Next comes the use of the hands in purposeful, guided ways. Later come coordinated movements of the lower limbs. In general the parts of the body near the head develop coordinated actions earlier than those towards the feet. This is often referred to as a *cephalo-caudal*, or head-tail, trend in development. Similar trends in development are quite common in many biological systems. In embryos, organs and structures at the head end differentiate first.

Much of the early motor development of an infant is, of course, correlated with changes in his body. Muscles are becoming stronger, limbs bigger, and the nervous system more nearly ready to assume its full duties.

Physical growth

Physical growth is one of the clearest cases of a maturational development based on the unfolding of a genetically determined biological process. That genetics is of prime importance in physical growth is doubted by no one. As an example of the evidence, the correlation between parental stature and the adult stature of their children is very high, and that between identical twins almost perfect. On the other hand, differences in environment can be important even here. Certain drugs, notably the steroid hormones such as cortisone, have a side effect of slowing growth. Stress, either from disease or from psychological sources, stimulates secretion of similar hormones, and also seems to slow down growth. Again, while growth in height is usually very regular and predictable, adiposity (amount of fatty tissue) is obviously affected

TABLE 9-1

Adult male height in inches as related to infant stress

	Piercing or molding stress during first 24 months of life	
	Present	Absent
First sample	65.2 (N = 17)	62.7 (N = 18)
Second sample	66.1 (N = 19)	63.4 (N = 11)
Combined sample	65.7 (N = 36)	63.0 (N = 29)

Significance of difference between combined means, by *t*-test, $p < .001$.

(After Landauer & Whiting, 1964)

by learned habits.[2] But even more striking an example of the claim that all development is a joint function of heredity and environment, is some recent evidence that early experience may affect eventual adult stature. Laboratory experiments with rats and other lower animals have shown that certain kinds of "stressful" experiences during the first few weeks of life (which is probably a critical period) are followed by lasting changes in endocrine responses to novel situations. At the same time, and probably as a result of the changes in hormonal responses, early stress apparently causes other differences in development. Rats who have been roughly handled, shocked electrically, exposed to cold, or subjected to any number of other untoward experiences usually grow *faster* and attain a greater weight and length at any age than animals not so treated. They also usually react differently to stressful experiences later in life, and in ways that are generally beneficial and adaptive, including having greater resistance to psychosomatic diseases such as ulcers. What appears to happen in these experiments is that the early stress "immunizes" the animal against later stress.

In looking for evidence of a similar effect of early stress in humans, Landauer and Whiting (1964) studied correlates of early stress in samples of societies from all over the world. Some societies inflict quite drastic procedures on young infants. For example, there are people who painfully tattoo or scarify the skins of infants, others who knock out several teeth, and still others who plunge the infant into scalding water every day. Ordinarily these procedures are rationalized as a benefit to the health, strength, or beauty of the infant. Some other societies, by contrast, are careful to protect the infant from any distress, and keep him wrapped up, isolated, and carefully guarded at all times. Societies in which infants are apparently subjected to stress (presumably in the

[2] Most of us have experimentally demonstrated the effect of diet on weight to our own satisfaction (or dissatisfaction). Surprisingly, the effect of variations in diet on height, excepting cases of severe malnutrition, has never been directly ascertained. While many scientists believe that diet influences human stature, this conclusion is based almost entirely on inference from the fact that people in different social classes, cultural groups, or historical time periods often differ in stature. There are, however, any number of other environmental and genetic differences between such groups, in addition to diet, which may be at work.

FIGURE 9–2
The age at which children first acquire certain important motor skills. Ninety-five percent of a sample of 215 American children learned these skills sometime during the age range indicated by the dashed lines. (After Aldrich & Norval, 1946)

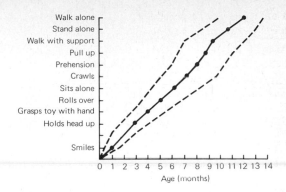

physiological sense of producing hormone response) were compared with those which have no such regular customs of stressing infants. A correlation was found between stature of adult males that corresponds to the differences observed in the laboratory with lower animals. The results of this study are shown in Table 9–1. The males in societies with stressful early infant-care practices averaged over two inches taller.[3] Here, then, is a case in which a developmental trend that seems thoroughly maturational appears nevertheless to show strong effects of the particular experiences which the person undergoes.

Motor skills and readiness

The opposite lesson seems to follow from some facts about motor abilities. In its first few years a child learns to crawl, to walk, to grasp objects, to manipulate tools such as eating utensils, scissors, and crayons, to run, to climb stairs, and to perform many other fine and gross muscular coordinations. Some norms are shown in Figure 9–2. Notice carefully the *range* of ages at which children are first able to perform these skills; there is great variation from one normal child to the next.

To what should we attribute the large differences between one child and another in the time of appearance of particular motor abilities? Such skills are temptingly open to interpretations in terms of experience. Certainly, some children are encouraged to walk at a very early age, while others, usually those with older brothers and sisters, are left more to their own devices. Surprisingly, research shows that coaxing and training don't help much. Apparently, a child walks when he is ready, and not before. Perhaps the most dramatic evidence comes from studies by Dennis & Dennis (1940) in which they observed Hopi Indian children

---

[3] In these studies, differences in racial stock, diet, and various factors of geography were also studied. Diet was not related to adult stature in the societies examined. Race and amount of rainfall (the less rain, the taller, for unknown reasons) were, but their effect was independent of the early stress relation. That is, early stress was associated with tallness in every racial group, and in every different geographical condition. The student should note, however, that the relation between stress and human stature is a correlation, not necessarily a causal connection. We will have more to say about the problem of inferring cause from correlation in later parts of this chapter and in Chapter 11.

who were raised with almost no opportunity to touch the ground with their feet for the first eight to twelve months. Hopi infants are almost constantly lodged in a cradle-board hanging from their mothers' backs or a tree limb, or leaned against a building. Yet they learn to walk, and at the same age as other children.

The limited effectiveness of early training has also been noted with several other motor skills. In one experiment on stair climbing (Gesell & Thompson, 1941), two identical twins, T and C, were given different training schedules at different times. T was given six weeks of intensive training starting at the 46th week, which is younger than the usual time to learn stair climbing. His stair-climbing ability improved quite dramatically. Then C's training was begun. The important difference was that C was six weeks older than T, and at about the age at which children normally begin stair-climbing, when he began to learn this task. Within two weeks C was performing as well as T. This same principle has been found to hold for a variety of early skills, including the use of scissors and the memorizing of digits. An older child who is more physically mature or more "ready" for some other reason, e.g., having had other relevant experiences, will often learn the same task much more rapidly than a younger child. It often appears that earlier training does not give the child any long-term advantage over a child who learns the same thing later and more quickly. Certainly if stair climbing (or any other skill) can be learned in two weeks at one point in development and requires six weeks at another point, the efficient choice may be to postpone training until later. This principle should not be overly stressed, however. There is only a certain amount of time available for a child to learn all the thousands of things we might like him to, so it may make sense to teach some of them earlier, even if it is somewhat harder to do so. Besides, skills such as stair climbing and using scissors are not entirely representative. Compared to some skills they are relatively discrete, and once well learned they do not improve very much. For other skills which continue to improve over many years, like reading and skiing, it may well be that an initial head start provided by early training can be maintained as long as training continues. It is also possible that there are some skills which are learned *more* rapidly early than late. If a child were to learn a skill that requires motor actions which conflict with those of normal walking, as may be the case in roller-skating for instance, he might find it easier to learn before he had too much experience in walking. There are swimming instructors who believe that infants can be taught more easily than toddlers; in this case the theory is that the muscular potentialities for swimming exist before the fear of water develops. It has similarly been proposed that language learning is more rapid and easier if it occurs very early, perhaps before the age of seven. It is not, then, a valid general principle that training should be done later rather than earlier. Perhaps the strongest statement that should be made is that some skills, particularly those in which there is just one particular thing to be learned, can often be learned more quickly if training is postponed rather than carried out as soon as possible.

It is never entirely clear in any one instance whether readiness to learn is based simply on physical maturation, or on the accretion of many related learned behavioral abilities, or on both. "Both" is usually the best guess. Certainly, in addition, readiness patterns frequently display the natural sequencing typical of growth processes; e.g., a child must acquire the ability to oppose thumb and forefinger before he can learn to write. There are many other examples of the principle that what is done first and what later often depends on certain building blocks being necessary for the later tasks, rather than simply on an otherwise unordered unfolding of the genetic pattern or on idiosyncratically ordered experiences of the child.

LANGUAGE

Perhaps the most significant accomplishment in a human's life is learning to talk. A person without some kind of language is doomed to an existence something less than human. In our society such an individual usually is institutionalized. In certain primitive societies a child is not considered fully human and is not given a name or legal protection until he has learned to speak.

Language acquisition presents a particularly instructive case of the "nature-nurture" problem. Humans are almost certainly the only truly language-using animals. Thus language use is a species-specific characteristic. One might be tempted to infer, therefore, that language is completely genetically determined. But it is also true that a human learns the language which his parents speak, whatever it may be. And this appears to prove that language is entirely a matter of learning. Thus, language is completely a matter of genetics, and also completely a matter of learning! Actually this last sentence, preposterous as it sounds, is probably the best description of the situation. Language acquisition depends completely on proper genetic endowment (that is, on being a normal human) and cannot occur without proper sets of experiences.

Language acquisition has a high degree of internal logic. The first words learned in most languages are ones beginning with bilabial sounds—such as m or p as in *mama* or *papa*—which are naturally made by a babbling infant, and usually stand for the most important and frequently present objects in his young life.[4]

Isolated words come first, and then combinations of two or three words without, however, the interstitial modifiers and other machinery of normal speech, such as *the, and,* and *but.* The child moves on next to longer phrases, then to sentences, and finally to grammatically organized passages or utterances. The entries in Table 9–2 show some *norms* or averages for development of language skills in young children.

[4] Although we stress here acquisition of the ability to produce speech, it is clear that before a child says his first word, he has learned a lot about language. A child listens to speech from the time of birth, and shows clear signs of being able to discriminate many of its sounds and understand many words—e.g., by following directions—long before he knows how to talk. Indeed, throughout life the number of words and the complexity of syntax that a person can readily understand far exceeds that which he can spontaneously produce.

TABLE 9–2
Some norms for speech development

Language behavior	Average age, months after birth
Cries and grunts	0
Makes vowel sounds like "ah," "uh," "ay"	1–2
Looks toward sound of human voice	2–4
Babbles and coos	3–4
Talks to self, using sounds like "ma," "mu," "do," "na"	4–6
Puts sounds together and repeats them over and over, e.g., "mamama-mama," "booboo," "dadada"	6–9
Imitates sounds made by others	9–10
Understands gestures (waves and sometimes says "bye-bye")	9–12
Understands and responds to simple commands ("Hold the spoon," "Look at the doll")	11–15
Imitates syllables and single words	11–15
Says two or more different words	12–13
Says at least three to five different words	13–18
Understands and responds to prohibitions ("Don't touch that")	16–20
Names one object or picture in book (cup, ball, baby, etc.)	17–24
Combines words into phrases ("Go out," "Give milk," "Where ball")	18–24
Identifies three to five familiar objects or pictures	24
Uses phrases and simple sentences	23–24

(After McCarthy, 1946)

These are subject to the usual qualification that normal children sometimes develop at very different rates.

There is an interesting parallel between physical growth and the development of language. A human infant ordinarily does not begin to use words until about one year of age (see Table 9–2), which is also about the age at which his brain has grown larger than that of any adult ape. It is at this time, too, that the ordinary infant adopts the human bipedal gait. Thus, the age of slightly over a year is the point when the infant attains most of the important characteristics that distinguish humans from other species.

One way of defining language is to equate it with the use of arbitrary symbols. For the most part, the words of human language consist of sounds which bear no necessary or logical relation to the things they stand for. The sounds of the word *book* have no more physical or logical relation to the shape, use, or nature of the thing than do the sounds in *livre*, or any other string of phonemes which might be used for the purpose. The symbols of language are quite arbitrarily made to stand for objects in the world, relations between objects and the world, or relations with other words or other abstract ideas, simply on the basis of tacit agreements between speakers. It is this arbitrariness of symbols which distinguishes them from simply communicative (but usually nonlanguage) acts such as crying or laughing.

Many animals, including humans, have certain innate reactions to important situations or to emotional states which serve to express and communicate the existence of special circumstances to a fellow member of the species. When an infant cries, it "means" he is uncomfortable, hungry, or in pain—and in this case "means" implies that the response is innately tied to his psychological state (although the cues which elicit crying or laughing can be and are altered through learning). A baby's cry, in turn, may evoke a response in his mother. A monkey's mother will run in the direction of the cry, help him if something is wrong and cuff him if all is well; a human mother will behave similarly. Spoken language, by contrast, requires taking an arbitrary sound and somehow attaching to it a meaning and a set of rules for its proper use.

The noises made by an infant include ones roughly corresponding to most of the phonemes heard anywhere in the world. The infant gradually begins to make more and more noises that are discrete, and his babblings begin to resemble the sounds made by his attendants. The point at which he makes noise that is clearly speech is, as we have said, a little over one year, on the average. Some of the things we have said earlier (about brain size for instance) might lead one to believe that the important developments that come about at this age are by physical growth only and not at all by experience. But this is not the whole story by any means. Experience plays a large role—it not only determines what language the child will speak, but also influences when he will begin to talk and how well. If the language which he hears around him is consistent and frequent, he will learn to speak more easily and earlier than if he is exposed to inconsistent talkers or none. For example, a child brought up in a bilingual household usually learns to speak later than does a child who has but one language to learn; and children brought up in environments lacking in adult company tend to be retarded in speech development (Dennis & Najarian, 1957). Children with several older siblings learn to speak later than do first children, probably because the "vocal" time of the parent is divided among more consumers. For some unexplained reason girls begin to speak earlier, on the average, than do boys. In fact, many verbal abilities, e.g. those measured on aptitude tests, remain higher for females than for males throughout the lifespan.

Once the child begins to speak, his use of language increases at a galloping rate. The number of words which a child uses day-to-day, and the far greater number that he can recognize, grow very rapidly in the second and third years and then ever more slowly for the rest of his life.

Language is not just vocabulary, of course. Both speaking and comprehending language depend on proper application of the implicit laws of syntax which are part of the unconscious language-skills of every normal adult. How do these apparently complex abilities develop?

The first sequences of words that are produced by the child learning to speak English usually contain two words, e.g., "Bad kitty," or "Go bye-bye." But even these earliest two-word utterances often show some grammatical structure. The child reporting a rivalrous attack from his older sibling says, "Johnny bite," not "Bite Johnny." He already uses the order of words to create a special meaning in the utterance as a whole. It is thought (Brown, 1965) that the child may first acquire proper word-orders by condensing the speech of adults. If you say to a child, "The dog bites the man," and ask him to repeat the phrase, he will often say, "Dog bites man." If you say, "The dog will bite you," he may mimic with "Dog bite." *Functor* words such as *to, and, with,* and *my* are dropped in favor of words with more information content. Possibly the child, having a shorter memory span than the adult, can remember only part of what the adult says and chooses to remember those words on which the adult places most vocal emphasis.

But the child does more than simply memorize the order of important words and sentences that he hears. He learns general properties of words and of ways to modify words and word orders, to make them communicate what he intends. Witness the common errors young children make: "I digged a hole," or "I see some sheeps." This was demonstrated systematically by Berko (1958), who showed children pictures such as the one in Figure 9–3 and said, "This is a wug. Now there are two of them. There are two _____." To answer correctly a child had to be able to apply a rule rather than simply remember a specific instance (he had never heard of a "wug" before). Possessive endings on nouns and the third person indicative inflectional formulas are also properly executed by four-year-olds.

How a child acquires the various skills of language is not yet really understood. On the evidence that language acquisition is extraordinarily difficult for individuals who, because of early deafness or isolation, are not exposed to language until eight years of age or more, some investigators (e.g., Lenneberg, 1964) have suggested that human language may depend heavily on genetically determined neural organizations. According to this view, only the special features of a particular language, and not the deeper principles of syntactic speech construction and comprehension common to all languages, need be imposed by experience. The specific forms of the particular language are then thought to be added to the inherited structure by an imprinting-like process.

Another hypothesis concerning the learning of language is based on a common interactive pattern of adults with children. The child utters a short unembellished sequence of words such as "Want cookie," which the adult interprets and then expands and repeats back to the child as a full grammatical sentence, "I want a cookie."

Exactly how the child uses this expanded information or, for that matter, any other information to arrive at his ability to generalize and apply the sound-forming, word-forming, and phrase- and sentence-forming regularities of his language is not known. What is clear is that the ordinary child receives a tremendous amount of training in language. He is talked at, around, in front of, and for; prodded, rewarded, cudgeled,

FIGURE 9–3
Example of test used to study the use of grammatical rules by young children. Four-year-olds, for example, can correctly make plurals of completely novel nouns. (From Berko, 1958)

This is a WUG.

Now there is another one.
There are two of them.
There are two_____.

and bribed to make noises, words, sentences, and paragraphs virtually all day long, every day for years.

Logic and reasoning

One of the most interesting and useful purposes to which language is put is, of course, the solution of problems by thinking and reasoning. A child's ability to think logically increases as he gets older; its early formation closely follows his increasing language ability. Consider the following experiment. A three-year-old child is presented with a black and a white panel, and taught always to press the black one. The shape of the panel (square or circle) is varied from trial to trial but is irrelevant. Once he has learned the relevant discrimination, the child is given, without warning, one of two new problems: now he has either (1) to press the white panel rather than the black—a "reversal shift"—or (2) to press the square and not the circle, with the black-white dimension now irrelevant—a "nonreversal shift." For the young child the shift from black-white to circle-square is easier than reversing from black-white to white-black. By contrast, people about seven years or older find the reversal shift, choosing white instead of black, easier than the non-reversal shift. One explanation is that the preschool-age child does not verbalize the situation, but simply learns an operantly conditioned discriminative response to whichever panel leads to reward. Thus, in the reversal shift he has learned a mechanical habit, which he has to unlearn before he can learn the opposite habit. The nonreversal shift is easier for him because he has nothing to unlearn; he has simply to learn a new and easy response. By contrast, the seven-year-old child, whose verbal skills are much better developed, presumably describes the situation to himself in words. In the first part of the training he says something like, "Color is important and white is right," and then finds it easy to change his description to "White isn't right any more." The ability to manipulate symbols in the place of actions allows the older child to behave in a qualitatively different way.

There are a host of other *cognitive* tasks which also show a dramatic shift between the ages of five and seven. Most of the changes are related to his burgeoning sophistication with language. This is at least in part a sequential development, one thing building on another, for the more language a child knows, the more he can learn and the more he can do with what he knows. However, the fact that so many "cognitive," language-based changes occur between five and seven raises the as yet untested possibility that they may be largely due to the beginning of schooling. (Or has the beginning of school been pegged to these changes by a wise cultural invention?)

LOGICAL REASONING

The development of logical reasoning in children has been traced in some detail. The most extensive and influential work in this area has been that of the Swiss psychologist Jean Piaget and his followers. Piaget observed his own children and a number of others in nursery schools and other settings, and described what he believes to be regular stages in the development of a child's logical world.

According to Piaget (1968), the child begins life without such rudimentary concepts as an action causing a result, objects being closer or farther away, or one event occurring before another. However, he acquires many of these concepts by maturation and by interactions with the environment—even before he learns to talk. The infant's first task is to distinguish himself from other objects. At first he has no way of knowing that his arm, his crib, and his mother are not one and the same. By watching them move separately, by noting the sensory changes that do and don't occur when he makes voluntary movements, he gradually constructs a knowledge of reality in which he is a separate entity. This knowledge is built of direct relations between sensation and motor activity, not on abstractions or symbols. Piaget calls the kind of thinking that emerges during this early period, which lasts from birth to about a year or a year and a half, *sensorimotor* intelligence. During this stage of development the child performs thousands of practical "experiments." He watches his hand while he moves it; he manipulates objects in play; he drops things to the floor and watches them fall, etc. From such experiments he learns a great deal: that his hand is part of him, not the crib; that the cereal bowl falls after he pushes it; that the cereal bowl on the floor is the same object as the cereal bowl that used to be on the tray, etc.

Piaget inferred the existence of these processes in the developing child's thinking from ingenious observations. For example, the concept of *object permanence* was tested by concealing a block that the child had just been playing with beneath a cover to see whether the child would search for the hidden object. Very young children act as if the block has evaporated.

The next stage of intellectual development described by Piaget spans the ages of about two to seven. During this time the child is learning to think in words and symbols, to represent objects and actions in thought rather than in actual sensations and movements. This is a difficult ability to master. It is not until the child has used language for several years that he is able to carry out such mental operations. For example, the four- or five-year-old children observed by Piaget knew their way to school perfectly well, but they were unable to represent the route in a sandbox. Piaget called the kind of thinking typical of this period—in which the child uses symbols verbally but cannot operate on them in an abstract logical manner—*preoperational thought*.

An important aspect of logical thinking is the ability to take a variety of views of the same facts. A boy in the preoperational stage can say that he has two brothers, but also tell you that each of them has only one brother—because he doesn't consider himself a brother. Similarly, children during this stage are often unable to appreciate that things can change in some ways and still be the same. They do not have the concept of *reversibility*—the idea that one can get the original thing back after it has been transformed. To illustrate, if a quantity of liquid is poured from a tall thin glass into a short fat one, a child under about five will think the quantity has changed. He apparently equates quantity with height; he does not possess the concept of *conservation* of quantity. He doesn't realize that the water can regain its previous appearance by being poured back into the tall glass. Piaget has studied a number of such conservation concepts. Some of them are not mastered until quite late. Until the age of eleven or twelve most children think that a round lump of clay will take up less room in a cup—will displace less water— if it is reshaped like a sausage.

At around seven or eight years—about the time of several other cognitive changes mentioned earlier—the average child has begun to make certain kinds of mental manipulations: he classes objects together, deals with relations between symbols, and counts and orders abstracted entities (like "six fruits" when they are all different). As one manifestation of the increasing power of his thought processes during this period, the child begins to master the various conservation concepts. However, according to Piaget, thinking at this stage still concerns only representations of concrete objects. He calls this kind of thinking *concrete operations* and distinguishes it from the final form of logical thought, *formal* or *hypothetico-deductive operations*, in which the person reasons about verbal hypotheses. This last development is marked by the ability to reason with purely verbal materials, and to create theories. It is said that most children begin to think in this way by about the twelfth year.

To what extent the various stages must occur exactly as Piaget has described them, in exactly the same order, and at the same age is still somewhat unsettled. Some, but not all, of the results have been found to hold at least roughly in several different cultures. It is sometimes possible to speed up progress within a stage or from one stage to another by special training, but it appears to be difficult to devise training which will allow a child to skip a stage or phase. This would seem to indicate that these stages may represent a necessary progression—either the unfolding of a genetic growth pattern, or a logical sequence in which learning one thing is requisite for learning the next.

Intelligence

Intelligence, broadly defined, is not a constant quantity. The mental age (MA) of a child is usually measured by the kinds of problems he can solve, the common knowledge that he has, the size of his vocabulary, the number of digits he can repeat back, and other factors, all of which increase continually in the early years. Intelligence, as we have already observed (Chapter 3), is greatly influenced by heredity. Various estimates attribute from 60 to 90 percent of the variability in intelligence to genetic factors. However, there are certain deficiencies in all the studies on which such estimates are made—most notably that the environments from which the subjects have come have been quite homogeneous, at least as compared to the full range of potential conditions of human life. As a result we know little about effects on intelligence which *could* be produced by unusually large differences of environment. For example, if we studied the IQ of twins raised in different parts of England, we would be likely to find only small differences. But this would hardly imply that the intelligence of one identical twin raised in Oxford as the only child of a don would not differ considerably from the intelligence of the other twin raised in Mexico as one of ten children of an impoverished migrant laborer. Evidence, as summarized by Hunt (1961), indicates that adult intelligence can be influenced by childhood environment *at least* to the extent of ten IQ points.

What kinds of early experiences influence intelligence? For the most part, probably, the same factors that influence language acquisition. There is a close relation between language ability and intelligence. Correlations are very high between vocabulary size, reading comprehension, and any number of other verbal skills on the one hand and IQ on the other. (Indeed, verbal skills are a large part of what is measured in IQ tests.) Children raised in restricted early environments—in foundling homes or other institutions where there is a minimum interaction of infants with adults—are often seriously retarded in mental development. But there are flaws in many of these observations, in that children who are left to institutional care in the first place, and particularly those who remain there for lack of any one who wants to adopt them, are likely to be subnormal.

Recent work (Hess & Shipman, 1965) has established a more direct correlation between the way mothers interact with their children and the children's rate of cognitive growth. Mothers who encourage questions and other conversation, and who explain things with reasons, logic, and comparatively complex language, have children who do better in school and on tests of cognitive ability.

SOCIAL RELATIONS

The earliest social relations of an infant are normally with its mother. As we have already mentioned, an infant does not give any sign that it recognizes its mother for some time after birth. There is, however, evidence that as soon as a child is able to smile it tends to smile more at a human face than at most other visual patterns. Fantz (1961) and Kagan (1970) have studied the reactions of infants to masks that either resemble human faces or are in some way altered. Some of the masks used in these studies are shown in Figure 9–4. In general, infants look and smile most at faces that are neither scrambled nor upside down. By about six months most infants reach a smiling "peak"—they smile at any and all human faces, and do so at virtually every opportunity. Not much later, however, the average child becomes more selective and starts to show fear of strangers. At eight months the face of a pediatrician on whose knee the infant is placed no longer evokes a smile, but begins instead to elicit crying or struggling. By a year friends and family are strongly differentiated from other people. This *pattern* of development is reasonably constant from one child to another, although the ages of the various peaks differ by as much as several months from one child to the next. While the similarity of stages in all children implies a large role for autonomous physical developments, the fact that it is his own mother at whom the infant smiles shows clearly that learning is involved. It is known that social reactions can be influenced by training procedures, e.g., smiles can be operantly reinforced by an experimenter or parent who picks the child up after he smiles. It is quite likely that parents, through the contingencies of their attention to a child, greatly modify the frequency and objects of smiling and fussing.

Studies of institutionalized infants have often found that the most grievously abnormal aspect of their development is in the area of social relations and *attachments* to "mother-figures" and other adults. In one foundling home studied by Spitz (1945), interactions of children with adults were severely limited by cribs with high sides and a minimal number of caretakers. By one year, about one in every six infants developed a severe withdrawal response, becoming almost completely unresponsive to adults or to stimulation of any kind. In another investigation (Goldfarb, 1943) children who were originally placed in an institution were studied later, after they had been placed in foster homes. The social responsiveness of these children remained quite subnormal. They had difficulty fitting into their new families, often were withdrawn or hostile, frequently got into difficulties at school, and were unable to get along with their peers. There were certain methodological inadequacies in these studies too—notably again the problem of just what kind of children were left to institutional care in the first place—and

FIGURE 9-4
Masks used to study reactions of infants to human faces. From a very early age, infants look and smile at normal-looking faces more than at distorted ones. (From Kagan, 1970)

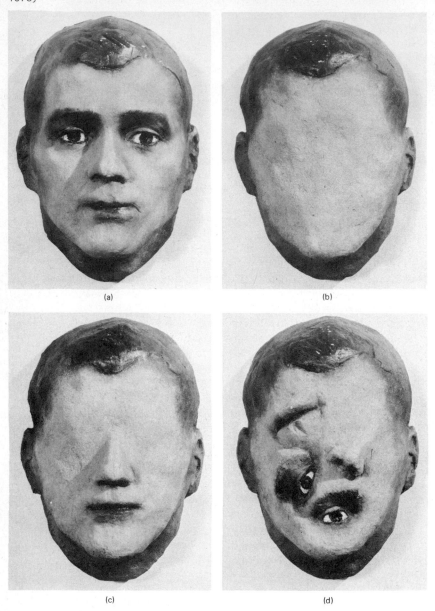

(a)

(b)

(c)

(d)

a good deal of reservation should mark one's acceptance of the conclusions from them.

However, there have been a number of experimental studies of sub-human primates that show severe effects on later social relations in infants deprived of normal companionship during their earlier life. These studies are not open to the same criticisms as the human studies, since the differences in early environment were assigned randomly and were therefore not correlated with initial differences in the infants themselves.

Harlow (Harlow, 1958; Harlow & Harlow, 1966) has extensively investigated the effect on the development of infant monkeys of separation from their mothers and peers. In one set of experiments infant monkeys were raised either with their natural mothers or with several kinds of "surrogate" mothers: chicken-wire models with various attachments, such as artificial feeding nipples, papier-mâché heads and faces, and terrycloth "skin" to mimic the feel of a mother (see Figure 1–2). One of the first objectives of these studies was to try to discover what features of a mother led to the usual strong infant-mother attachments in primates. The results were fairly clear-cut. Young infants developed strong attachments (love?) for surrogate mothers if and only if the models were covered with a soft material to which the infant could cling. Whether the mother gave food or not was almost entirely irrelevant, as were the shape and features on the head. Apparently the primary way a primate becomes fond of his mother is by clinging to her and comforting himself by body contact. Harlow called this "contact comfort." If put into a frightening environment—for example into a bare room with a loud mechanical toy—a young monkey will throw himself on a cloth-covered model mother for comfort, even if he has been raised from birth with only a wire-covered mother, and even if one of these is also present. There appears to be something inherently calming about the soft, textured skin. (One might speculate that the security blankets so popular among toddlers and Peanuts characters derive some of their comfort value from the same source.)

When Harlow's motherless infant monkeys got older they experienced grave difficulties in establishing proper social relations with their fellows. Both males and females were incapable of normal sexual activities. The males failed to perform the usual stereotyped behaviors by which copulation is brought about. The females were almost entirely incapable of and unwilling to be mounted even by normally aggressive and experienced males. When such females were forcefully impregnated, they were extremely pathological in their behavior toward their infants. Sometimes they would try to kill an infant by stepping on him or biting him or pushing him through the wire mesh of the cage floor. Usually the infants of these "motherless mothers" had to be rescued and brought up elsewhere. Much, but not all, of the social inadequacy of mother-separated infant monkeys could be overcome by allowing the infants in their early months of life to play freely with peers. Apparently some normal monkey developmental patterns are not dependent on interacting with a "mother" as such, but are quite dependent on interacting with *some* member of the same species. It seems likely that normal give-and-take social relations are learned early or not at all.

Morals, values, and attitudes

An important basis of human social relationships, and in turn a direct outcome of them, is a set of beliefs and practices of each individual concerning what is proper behavior and what is not. To judge from the conduct of our close cousins in the animal world, the various species of apes, the "natural" behavior of animals of our kind includes a goodly amount that is either immoral or indecent according to the conventions of most human societies. Most apes are able and enthusiastically willing to eat whatever food is available without sharing (a mother gorilla will sometimes snatch away a piece of particularly juicy food from her own infant), to copulate with any other member of the troop who is handy and appealing, irrespective of who else's mate or even what sex the individual may be, and to scream, defecate, and masturbate in public. (This is not to say that there is no cooperation or restraint among apes. Apes pair off to groom each other, they possess innate patterns of behavior to warn each other of enemies and to keep the troop together for protection, and so forth. Most notably, they seem to possess some inborn mechanism by which violent aggression between members of the same species—anything resembling war—is prevented.) The principal line of social regulation and prerogative among most non-human primates is established through a system of dominance hierarchies. Each individual knows which other individuals are above or below him in a "pecking order." These dominance hierarchies are established by one or more bouts of blustering, screaming, and threatening; usually the dominant animal is the larger and more aggressive. The dominance relations stay stable until something causes one of the animals to lose or gain power. For example, if one ape breaks a limb or becomes sick, he will slip quickly in the ratings; and a female ape will rise temporarily during the sexually receptive period of her estrus cycle.

While dominance relations are probably discernible throughout human interactions, they are certainly not the sole basis for regulation of social relationships, nor are they by any means the most important ones. The new varieties of behavior evolved by humankind seem to have buried the basic primate social patterns of dominance (and the innate mechanisms against warfare as well) under a massive accumulation of cultural rules and regulations for individual conduct. Humans in all known societies have strict rules about which piece of food or decorated shell or iron scrap belongs to whom; who can talk to whom, and with what words, and, for that matter, which sounds are "proper" to say and which are not; who may sleep with whom; under what circumstances one may urinate; which parts of the body must be kept covered and from whom and when; and on, and on, and on. Perhaps the most impressive thing about these sets of rules by which humans live is the fact that they are obeyed so uniformly. A human obeys most rules even when he is alone and unobserved. Apparently there is something about man that makes him prone to and capable of designing, perpetuating, and living by such precepts. A good guess would be that it is the use of language that lies behind this peculiar human trait. Certainly, one of the primary features of moral and ethical behavior is the fact that the rules are usually, if not always, stated verbally. It may be this very quality of abstractness that allows moral rules to be followed with such independence of situation.

Piaget (1932) has described a set of stages through which a child's moral judgments proceed. He outlines the manner in which a child acquires first very rudimentary notions of right and wrong, and then gradually more logical and sophisticated ones. Piaget told children pairs of stories and asked them which of the two represented the "naughtier" behavior. One of the stories might be about a girl who accidentally cut a hole in her dress; the other would add that the girl had disobediently taken the scissors from her mother's sewing basket. From such questioning Piaget inferred that children under about eight years understand morality chiefly in terms of distinct rules supported and sanctioned by the authority of a parent. What is *wrong* to a child of this age, according to Piaget, is just and only what his parents say is wrong. Duty is seen as obedience to authority, wrongdoing as violation of absolute universal rules given by authority; the intent of the actor or the welfare of the people involved is irrelevant. At a later stage, usually beginning around eight years, the child begins to see rules as principles agreed upon between people for their mutual benefit. Justice is seen as concerned with the welfare of other people, consistency with one's own laws becomes important, and the intent of the wrongdoer and other relativistic features of the situation are taken into account.

A change with age from objective, absolute, authority-based morality to a more subjective, relativistic, and society-based morality has been found to occur in many different societies. It has also frequently been noted that there is usually a second, perhaps more gradual, liberalization of moral values as a person moves out of adolescence into adulthood. Adolescents often possess a very severe and unbending conscience—expressed as "right is right, and it is absolutely necessary to follow one's principles at all times and damn the consequences." Adults—that is, the very same people five or ten years later—manifest a greater degree of flexibility in the application of moral principles, perhaps because they have discovered that they cannot formulate a completely consistent set of principles which always seem just, or which always eventuate in a greater sum total of good or justice.

PERSONALITY

Since the beginning, philosophers, theologians, psychologists, psychoanalysts, and mothers have believed that a person's character is formed in his early relationship to his parents. The aphorism "As the twig is bent, so grows the tree" expresses an idea that has stimulated considerable research and more speculation.

We will consider two topics relative to this issue. First, we will describe one aspect of personality—sex-role learning, or sex identification—about which there is evidence suggesting that gross variations in early experiences may have lasting effects. Then we will discuss differences in child-rearing practices within the essentially normal range of variation, where strong effects have proved hard to find.

Early experience and sex identification

Wide variations in early environment can result from differences in membership of the household in which a child grows up; consider the difference between having and not having a father.

L. Carlsmith (1964) studied boys who were born during the second world war, some of whose fathers were absent for long periods. She compared these boys at college age in terms of some convenient indices of the thoroughness of their masculine and feminine identification. For example, one measure was the extent to which a boy showed the normal male pattern of a higher mathematical than verbal ability score on college board exams. Paper-and-pencil tests of preference for typical masculine versus feminine activities were also used. Boys who had no father in the home during their first three years of life appeared to be less strongly "masculine" than boys from homes with a man around. Another correlation which suggests the same conclusion comes from cross-cultural studies. Where there is polygyny (one man having more than one wife), the mother usually lives in her own house from which her husband is barred when there are infants living there. Consequently young boys spend their early years in the absence of consistent adult male companionship. Such societies more frequently than others have customs which can be interpreted as showing a failure of strong masculine identification. For example, male initiation ceremonies at puberty, with hazing and painful circumcision rites avowedly intended to "masculinize" the initiates, are found very frequently in such societies but almost never in cultures where families always include a salient adult male.

Additional plausibility is lent to the hypothesis that the early years can be important to sex-identification by evidence about children with congenitally disordered sexual characteristics. A child who is born with sex organs inappropriate to his true, or genotypic, sex is called a pseudohermaphrodite. Often the condition can be rectified by surgery. Apparently no personality adjustment difficulties result from this early sexual confusion, even if a boy has always been treated as a girl, so long as the change of sex is accomplished before the child is about two years old. But if the change is made after the age of three, sex-role difficulties almost always ensue (Money, Hampson, & Hampson, 1957).

Child-rearing practices

It has been a very attractive, nay almost irresistible, idea that the ways in which children are raised (harshly or gently, restrictively or permissively, with or without corporal punishment, coldly or with warmth and love) shape their characters in broad ways to make them honest or psychopathic, aggressive or passive, dominant or submissive. There can be no doubt that parents influence their children's personality development. The training by intentional and unintentional conditioning, the models of behavior that are set, the information transmitted, the attitudes communicated, and the opportunities provided by parents must play a very important part in shaping a child's beliefs, attitudes, and behavior. However, there is another and separate question: whether specific techniques, modes, or styles of child rearing have consistent and generalized effects on the way children develop. To put this another way, one can imagine the logical possibility that a child could be brought up to have a particular personality trait—say being very submissive—in a multitude of different ways. He might be shaped by operant reinforcement while an infant, bullied by traumatic avoidance procedures as a toddler, gently persuaded by example as an adolescent, etc., etc. It could, then, be only the content conveyed by a child-training method, rather than the method itself, that matters. However, many psychologists have sought evidence for the belief that child-training methods as such, including their timing with regard to the child's maturation, have pervasive effects on personality development.

The most popular mode of inquiry into such matters has been to interview mothers about the way they treat children and attempt to correlate rearing techniques with results. Various investigations have focused on methods and time of toilet training or weaning, on discipline, on frequency and warmth of child-parent interactions, and on many other potentially influential variations in how parents act toward their children. The effects on the child have been measured in many ways: by what the mother herself reports, by ratings of teachers or observers in the school, by personality tests, or by reactions in laboratory situations. A rather large number of such studies, some of them very ambitious, have been made. The results can be summed up quite simply: almost no strong correlations that hold up from one study to the next have been found.

Why have such studies been unable to establish clear and consistent relations? There are several possible reasons. For one thing, the research methods are not entirely adequate. Mothers' reports of child-rearing methods are known to be unreliable, particularly when the mother must remember what she did several years before. Even when asked about current practices, parents have a strong tendency to report what they think they should do rather than what they actually do. In addition, the art of measuring personality is presently a crude one, as we have seen. Given two crude ways of measuring different things, it is hardly surprising to discover no close correspondences between them. However, in some experts' judgment, these inadequacies in method are not sufficient explanation; the problem may lie deeper. As was outlined in chapter 4, a case can be made that personality is more fluid and fragmented than has been believed—that it is largely a shifting combination of specific and changeable traits rather than a tightly integrated structure of strong and enduring factors. Most research on antecedents of personality has focused on the experiences which would make a child more "aggressive" or more "dependent." But if there are really no such things as generalized tendencies to be aggressive in all situations, or dependent, or honest, then such research is doomed from the outset. Much of personality may develop by the slow accumulation of detailed habits—ways of behaving in particular situations with particular people. Some of the ways in which such habits are learned have been described in the chapters on learning (Chapters 7 and 8). Moreover, in a child's acquisition of the behavior which makes up his personality there is an additional process, that of learning from adult models by imitation, that is probably particularly important. It has been shown in laboratory experiments that children between four and six years old will copy the behavior of adults whom they see as important (Bandura, 1962). The behaviors copied have ranged from aggressive attacks on dummies to petting feared animals. Learning by copying adult and peer models in parent-child interactions and in play, and even from television, may actually be more frequent and of more importance than almost any other source of new ways of behaving for the growing child. The apparently strong effect of having or not having an adult male around in early childhood could be explained by the important influence of learning from models.

If detailed training and model-setting are the principal modes by which parents teach detailed behaviors to their children, the number of observations which would be needed to trace the development of any one individual personality would be very large. And the focus of observation would have to be quite different from what it has been in past research. Knowing that a mother frequently used praise would be unlikely in itself to tell us what the child would be like. We would have to know exactly when, for what, and how—with what method and skill—she used praise, in order to predict its effects. Whether present understanding would allow us to predict the results even with detailed information is doubtful. In any event, it does not seem to be possible to predict how a child will turn out by asking his mother about her child-rearing methods.

Unfortunately, popular psychology of the ladies-magazine variety has promulgated a number of beliefs about child rearing that come from largely speculative theories or from "hints" in early research reports which have subsequently failed the test of repeated observation. Consequently it is worth a few lines to specify some things we *don't* know. Among these is the effect of various forms of toilet training on personality. Certain extrapolations from Freudian theory (Chapter 3) led people at one time to believe that strict toilet training would produce either compulsively neat behavior or its opposite. There is no acceptable evidence to support this belief and there are some negative results that deny it. Another thing we *don't* know is that thwarting a child's expressions of anger or hostility leads to neurosis. This popular hypothesis has the scientific standing of an interesting idea, and nothing more. A much more tragic unfounded belief is that childhood schizophrenia or *autism* is caused by an unloving or rejecting mother. Many authorities on the subject now believe that such abnormalities are often hereditarily or physiologically based and have little or nothing to do with the care given the infant. The tragedy is that for many years, in the absence of real knowledge, "experts" told mothers of autistic children that they had caused this horrible state.

Consider another example: one of the more (but not entirely) consistent findings in research on correlates between child-rearing methods and personality is a *positive* correlation between punishment for aggression toward the parents and the amount of such aggression the child displays; in other words, children whose parents report punishing them for aggressive behavior are the same ones who often behave aggressively. The problem is to interpret this relation. It may be, as some theories have suggested, that punishing a child for aggression backfires and makes him more aggressive instead of less—perhaps through copying of the aggressive behavior of the parent. But it could also be that the more aggressive the child, the more likely his behavior is to anger the parent to the point of punishment. It might even be the case that parents who are aggressive, as indicated by the fact that they physically punish their children, pass on genes for aggressiveness to their children. Still another possibility is that parents who are willing to *report* physical punishment may be those who are also willing to *report* aggression on the part of their children—that is, they are parents who are not ashamed of their own or their children's aggressive behavior. The fact that the correlations reported for this association are very small makes this kind of suspicion more telling, since it would require only a fairly weak spurious factor to produce the kind of results observed. These and similar kinds of problems exist for many other correlations, no matter how many times they may have been observed.[5] An often-reported relation between disrupted home environments and delinquency is another case. We can never be sure that the same factors which cause disruption of the home, such as antisocial attitudes, lack of social responsibility, or simple poverty, might not lead to both broken homes and delinquent children. Again, early independence training is correlated with achievement motivation, but it is possible that parents who stress early independence training are those who most want their children to achieve and who tend to use every means at every age to instill achievement strivings. It is even possible, for all we know, that such parents harbor the genetic seeds of ambition in their germ-plasm.

In sum, while there are many suggestive findings, there are as yet no established causal relations between child-rearing techniques and broad personality traits. The results to date provide important leads for further research, but do not yet explain individual differences in personality or tell us anything specific about how to raise or how not to raise children. Perhaps by default, however, they suggest that the content and skill of parents' interactions with children may be more important than general rearing-practices.

Enculturation

An important feature of development is acquisition of the skills, attitudes, and behaviors required by the roles a person will play in his community or culture. We have already discussed one important example, the acquisition of culturally sex-typed behavior. There are others. Societies often require of an individual that he fill certain task or employment roles and certain social or family positions. Different societies with different organizations and different kinds of economic activities demand different individual traits. Within any single society, different individuals develop traits peculiar to their own specialized

[5] The correlational findings mentioned earlier, e.g., the relation between early stress and stature, the effect of social deprivation, and the relation between father absence and sex identity are not exempt from this criticism. However, in these cases there are factors which make interpretations slightly less dangerous. In each of these cases more than one kind of evidence has led to the same conclusion. In each, some of the evidence is experimental (see Chapter 11) or at least quasi-experimental, rather than only correlational, e.g., there are parallel experimental results from laboratory animals for the effects of stress and social deprivation, and the study of pseudohermaphrodites comes close to true experiment in the case of sex identity.

status. Sometimes it is easier to see the dynamics of enculturation by looking to less familiar cultures. In many East African tribes the roles of boys and girls are differentiated markedly at a very young age. Among the Kikuyu a seven- or eight-year-old girl, especially if she is the oldest girl in her family, is expected to stay home and take charge of her younger siblings and of the household, including the fire and the boiling food pot, while her mother works in the field all day. Her brother of the same age is already, in many cases, spending his day herding a flock of sheep. At this age an American or European child is usually considered to be too young for any task except that of learner.

Some of the most significant roles into which a person is placed by a society, and for which he must acquire appropriate behaviors, are those regarding his social relations. We have mentioned the hypothesis that many adolescent problems in our society may stem from the fact that the roles assigned to pre-adults are dramatically different from those of adults and there is insufficient provision for a gradual transition between the roles.

At least one theoretical description of the course of personality development throughout life, and of its critical problems, places considerable stress on problems of role assignment, role learning, and role satisfactions. Drawing upon his clinical experience, Erik Erikson, a famous modern psychoanalyst, has proposed a number of stages of development through which a person is said to progress if he is normal. One way of characterizing these stages is in terms of the predominant concerns of a person during different periods of his life. Table 9–3 lists the stages proposed by Erikson. While these are only one wise man's opinion, and should be treated more or less as literary descriptions, they do present an interesting pattern worth considering in conjunction with the present discussion. Each stage may be seen as closely related to the task assignment or social role of the person in our society. The child in the fourth stage is going to school, and his concerns and problems are very closely related to that task. Similarly, the adolescent's main concern, according to Erikson, is with identity, and this may be closely related to the fact that adolescents in our society are in the later stages of going to school, and are in the process of setting long-term goals. Young adults are already enmeshed in careers—they have been assigned or have assigned themselves a work task and other personal goals— and now their psychological crises and concerns typically involve productivity, or doing a job effectively.

Whether the same stages would be proposed by a Samoan or Eskimo psychoanalyst is at best problematical. It seems more likely that the concerns seen by Erikson reflect the problems of adjustment associated with at different ages in this particular society.

CLOSING COMMENTS

At this point, a few words are in order on the problems of adjustment typically encountered in college years. Be warned that these are informal observations, speculations, and opinions, not scientific fact. Much has

TABLE 9–3
Stages of development proposed by Erikson

	Psychosocial crises	Radius of significant relations	Psychosocial modalities
First year	Trust vs. Mistrust	Maternal Person	To get To give in return
Second year	Autonomy vs. Shame, Doubt	Parental Persons	To hold (on) To let (go)
Three to five	Initiative vs. Guilt	Basic Family	To make (= going after) To "make like" (= playing)
Six to puberty	Industry vs. Inferiority	"Neighborhood," School	To make things (= completing) To make things together
Adolescence	Identity and Repudiation vs. Identity Diffusion	Peer Groups and Outgroups; Models of Leadership	To be oneself (or not to be) To share being oneself
Early adult	Intimacy and Solidarity vs. Isolation	Partners in friendship, sex, competition, cooperation	To lose and find oneself in another
Young and middle adult	Generativity vs. Self-absorption	Divided labor and shared household	To make be To take care of
Later adult	Integrity vs. Despair	"Mankind" "My Kind"	To be, through having been To face not being

(After Erikson, 1959)

been written and said of late about the so-called *identity crisis*, the term and concept originating in the works of Erikson and certain other philosophically oriented psychologists. Modern Western man lives in a very fluid society, in which the roles and tasks open to a person are very wide and heterogeneous compared to those of an earlier and presumably simpler day in which each person's niche in life was defined by his birth, family, religion, and circumstances. Moreover, for most of us the basic needs and biological problems of existence, such as getting enough to eat, no longer occupy all our time or mental energy. As a result, it is proposed, modern Western man is freed to worry about just what it is that he is doing here. He asks himself "What am I?" "What is the meaning of my life?" and a number of other such questions. These worries are most prevalent and severe among adolescents and young adults.[6] Often the identity crisis is very much bound up with a problem of deciding "what to be." The person worries about what he "really" is, and what he should do with his life. While it would be a mistake to make

[6] It is probably not the case, as often supposed, that adolescents are especially emotional, hard to get along with, or unhappy; scores on emotionality tests are generally lower during adolescence than either before or after, the incidence of problem behavior in the classroom declines from early grades to later, and old people remember adolescence as a relatively happy time of life (Eichorn, 1968).

light of these very real personal problems, a few factors do tend to mitigate the usual seriousness of these issues. First, it is a natural feature of the role-assignment structure of our society that people in the late stages of schooling are unsure of "what they are" or what they are going to be. In going to college one intentionally exposes oneself to a variety of new influences, a cafeteria of ideas and potential life-styles. Rather than a cause for alarm this could be viewed as a fortunate state of freedom. Second, the very notion that there is a "true self" which is to be exposed by lengthy introspection, or any other process, may often be a false presumption. As has been pointed out in the chapters on social psychology and personality, the consistency of a person's traits, their interrelatedness and association with deep underlying structure, is a somewhat tenuous concept. People change often and dramatically in their interests, abilities, and goals. Development may consist largely of gradual accretion, such that each year changes a person about a year's worth. While each new year's worth is less of his total personality, since he has accumulated more before, it is still clear that at no point in a person's life is he anything like a settled and determined entity. Most people no longer hold the notion that there is any one individual of the opposite sex "made in heaven" who is the only one to marry. Similarly, there is probably no one "calling" or career, no one way of life or set of interests which uniquely suits an individual. Rather there is a vast range of possibilities open, any one of which might be as satisfying to a particular person as any other.

There is a very real sense in which a person of college age does not and probably *should not* have a really firm identity. He is usually not committed to a career or a way of life as yet, and the roles and behaviors associated with a life style are a very large part of what a person is. Attaining an identity is not primarily accomplished by searching within one's self, but by committing oneself to a way of life, a job, or other consistent role. A person's life style five years after college often bears little resemblance to his life-style during college. (We know that most juvenile delinquents grow up, marry, and become perfectly normal, law-abiding citizens.) Through the processes of dissonance reduction, social influence, and acquisition of skills and tastes, one is almost certain to come to identify with whatever role in life one jumps into (including the role of college student). Since a college student will by necessity soon change roles in a somewhat unpredictable way, it is not surprising if he has a rather unsettled identity. But this should, ordinarily, be no cause for alarm since it is a normal state which will be naturally rectified in the course of time. Perhaps rather than being spent in search of a chimerical "real self," the college years are better spent in the acquisition of a broad and deep range of skills, knowledge, interests, commitments, experiences, likes, and tastes which will make life richer and more rewarding.

Summary

What generalizations can one make about development? Primarily that it is gradual. Development proceeds partly from the slow unfolding of genetically guided maturation, partly from the step-by-step building of one skill, ability, and accomplishment on another, and partly from the gradual accretion of large numbers of individual habits. The notion sometimes found in myths, psychological novels, and folk stories that a person's total character may be set for all time by one dramatic event in his early life is probably, by and large, a false picture. Certainly it is possible that some specific fears, which may come to be of wider significance in a person's life, may be conditioned by one or a few traumatic events. But most of the important influences on a person's nature are small, accumulative, and gradual. For the most part, then, such factors as how the child is weaned, how and when he is toilet-trained, and whether his parents are stern or gentle are probably of less consequence than the details of the millions of small experiences that he has, in conjunction with the unfolding genetic endowment with which he comes into the world and the irresistible logic of development.

A last word. Does our knowledge of development add up to any prescriptions concerning the best way to be a parent? By and large, prescriptions for general ways of dealing with children are unlikely to be of great value. Techniques for teaching particular skills, for shaping behavior at the point that it needs modification, coupled with knowledge of the normal progressions of development, may be as important as *overall* attitudes or techniques. In the chapters on learning and social psychology we discussed many of the methods by which attitudes and behavior can be shaped. Modeling is a natural technique for most parents (and one often inadvertently used to shape undesired behavior). In general, it is safe to say that positive reinforcement is also a very good way to shape new behaviors without bringing with them bad side-effects. For example, positive reinforcement with M & M's has often been used for toilet training, and its proponents claim that the method works well. It was also pointed out that dissonance theory suggests that in teaching a taboo—such as not to touch the ashtrays—the best technique is to use a threat or punishment which is just sufficient (but *must* be sufficient) to achieve the desired change in behavior, but not to overdo it. To teach important habits—like not running in front of buses—more inherently dangerous methods such as avoidance conditioning may be in order. It is also important for a parent to understand the roles of maturation and sequencing. For example, since walking is so strongly maturational, a parent might well choose to plan to teach behaviors that depend on walking—like using the toilet independently —at an appropriate age. Likewise, knowing about normal sequences of intellectual development should help a parent to introduce tasks and concepts only when the prerequisite skills have been acquired. Rather than be exasperated by a four-year-old who can't understand that one nickel is worth more than two pennies, a sophisticated parent realizes that this is a more complex problem to the child than it appears, and, perhaps, concentrates first on providing the child with more experience in simple counting.

In general the views put forward here suggest that the important role of a parent is to afford his child the opportunity to acquire a large number of skills which will fit him for a number of different courses in life. To build verbal and other intellectual skills, the parent should provide opportunities for the child to talk, solve problems, and make decisions, thus giving him, in essence, a chance to practice, with a parent as tutor and model, those behaviors of which intelligence consists. To

TOPICS DISCUSSED IN CHAPTER 9

1. The immaturity of the human infant and its probable evolutionary reasons.

2. The three factors of psychological development: genetically guided maturation, experience, and logical sequences. All of these in relation to the following topics:

3. What the world is like to a newborn; what he senses and how he responds as he gets older.

4. The early development of motor abilities.

5. Some determinants of physical stature.

6. The relation of experience and maturation in the acquisition of motor skills; "readiness."

7. The development of language; phonemes, vocabulary, syntax, and grammar.

8. The development of thought; Piaget's description of the development of logical reasoning.

9. The beginnings of social relations; smiling, reactions to mothers and strangers, and the effects of social isolation.

10. The basis and development of moral values.

11. The effects and non-effects of early environment and child-training practices on personality.

12. Learning of social roles.

13. The relations of what is known to problems of early adulthood and child rearing.

SUGGESTED READINGS

1. *A very good general textbook on child development is:*

Mussen, P. H., Conger, J. J., & Kagan, J. *Child development and personality,* 3rd ed. New York: Harper & Row, 1969.

2. *For treatments of development during later portions of life, see:*

Hurlock, E. *Adolescent development,* 3rd ed. New York: McGraw-Hill, 1966.

Williams, R. H., Tibbits, C., & Donohue, W. *Processes of aging*. New York: Atherton, 1963.

3. *Interesting descriptions of child-rearing practices around the world are presented in:*

Whiting, B. B. (Ed.) *Six cultures: studies of child rearing*. New York: Wiley, 1963.

TEN
Physiological psychology

At this point, we have a fairly good picture of the way animals and men behave and of the psychological processes by which behavior is generated: perception, motivation, learning, and development. Now that we know the things the animal does, we are ready to take a look at how it does them. While it cannot be said that the physiological basis of mind is yet understood, there are clear signs that we have entered the era in which these great scientific problems will see their first significant solutions. In this chapter we will describe what is known now and try to convey some of the exciting flavor of current work.[1]

To see how any system for processing and storing information works, we must be concerned with the way it acquires information (its input), its memory and information-processing facilities, and how it affects the world (its output). The first step is to transform or transduce information from its raw physical form into a form that is usable within the system. This is accomplished by the sense organs, which translate various kinds of physical energy into nerve impulses. Once this transduction is accomplished, the information must be transmitted to the brain. There, information from various sources is integrated in the making of decisions. Information must then be transmitted to the muscles and glands—and from these back to

[1] We have omitted discussion of the physiological basis of behavior, notably the systems involved in attention and arousal (Chapter 6) and some of the mechanisms (Chapter 5).

the brain. Between the input and output are extensive storage and processing capabilities, corresponding to motivation, attention, learning, memory, and thought. In this chapter we will consider first the physiological bases of input and output processes, perception, and movement. Next we will turn to the more primitive and fixed forms of central control: reflexes, instincts, emotions, and motives. Finally, we will consider the higher mental processes of learning, memory, and consciousness.

The modern study of the physical basis of behavior draws on a large number of different fields of science. The description of the machine's parts is given by anatomy, and the analysis of their function by physiology. But this is not all. Direct observation of the activities of the nervous system depends heavily on sophisticated measurement and data-analysis techniques drawn from the fields of physics, electronics, and engineering. Relevant data come not only from laboratory experimentation, but also from clinical, pathological, and pharmacological studies in the medical sciences. It is obviously not feasible here to provide the student with a thorough grounding in all these disciplines. But it is possible to provide enough background to allow him to understand the major questions and results.

RUDIMENTARY NEUROPHYSIOLOGY AND NEUROANATOMY

Behavior is a function of the whole body—of all its organ systems, including the muscles, circulation, hormone (or endocrine) and other glandular systems, as well as of the nervous system. To understand the physical basis of any behavior, one would have to be able to trace the intricate interrelations among all the individual functions of these component systems. However, a little background in the nature and workings of the nervous system is what is most important for present purposes. We will introduce facts about other organ systems as we need them.

Neurons and action potentials

The first thing to consider is the *neuron*, the type of cell that makes up most of the nervous system and accounts for most of its functional properties. Figure 10–1 shows an idealized, diagrammatic neuron. It consists of a cell body, where most of the life-sustaining machinery of the neuron is located and where genetic material resides, and, emanating from the cell body, a number of long strands or fibers. These fibers are of two types: the dendrites, which are usually short, many-branched configurations, and the axon, which is a single, sometimes very long fiber. In some parts of the nervous system fibers may be as long as a yard or so. These long fibers connect the receptors to the spinal cord and thence to the brain, and carry most of the information utilized by the nervous system.

These fibers act like the long lines in telephone systems, or the cables in computers. However, unlike those of telephones and computers, the signals sent over these fibers are not electrical, at least not strictly so. Rather, the neural signal is an *electrochemical* impulse. The neural fiber is, of course, a part of a living cell. As shown in Figure 10–1, it has

FIGURE 10–1
Idealized neuron.

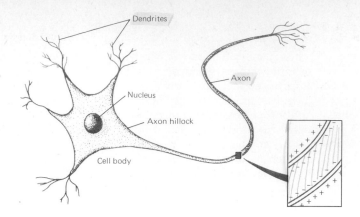

a thin (two billionths of a cm) outer covering. The ability of neural fibers to transmit information depends on some remarkable properties of this membrane. The protoplasm inside the membrane is a watery substance containing many large protein molecules and very large numbers of simple ions, preponderantly potassium (K^+), sodium (Na^+), and chlorine (Cl^-). It is possible with very delicate instruments to record the electrical potential (the number of volts of difference in electrical energy) between the inside and outside of the membrane. This turns out to be about 70 millivolts (a millivolt is one-thousandth of a volt), with the negative pole being on the inside of the membrane. This inside-outside charge difference is known as the *resting potential*, and is a property of most living cells. The resting potential is a result of an uneven distribution of positively and negatively charged molecules, or ions, on the inside and outside surfaces of the membrane. Put very simply, the reason for the resting potential is that large protein molecules, which are negatively charged, cannot pass out through the membrane. This disturbs the electrical neutrality that would otherwise be produced by the free back-and-forth movement of small positively and negatively charged ions.

So far we have described the state of electrical charges around the membrane of a nerve cell at rest. In a living animal, nerve cells do not remain at rest long. Whenever the animal engages in any activity, receives any information from his receptors, or simply makes adjustments in his internal economy, the networks of nerve fibers throughout the body are hard at work. Even when a nerve fiber is not actively involved in any behavior it nevertheless breaks away from its resting state every now and again. Like the resting state, the active condition of a neuronal fiber is characterized by the electrochemical events around its membrane. If a sensitive measuring instrument is applied to the surface of an active neuron, sudden, brief changes in electrical voltage can be observed from time to time. A recording of the electrical activity on a nerve fiber is shown in Figure 10–2. This rise and fall in electrical potential (voltage) is known as an *action potential*. The action potential in most nerve fibers lasts—if recorded at a single point—for about one or two milliseconds. Because of its shape, as recorded, this phenomenon is sometimes called

FIGURE 10–2

Diagram of a spike potential: the change in voltage between the inside and outside as an impulse passes a point on a neural fiber.

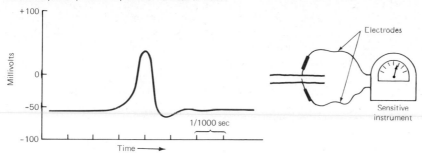

a spike. The spike or action potential travels down the nerve fiber from its point of origin. It is such "propagated" or traveling spike potentials which form the messages used in the nervous system for long distance communication. They are the analogs of the electrical pulses sent down the wire by telephone or telegraph.

What gives rise to this brief, traveling change in potential? There is another special property of the membrane which we have not mentioned yet, namely that it keeps positively charged sodium ions out of the cell during the resting state. During an action potential, this feature of the membrane changes for a short time. Temporarily, the membrane allows large numbers of positively charged sodium ions to rush in. In fact, so many positive charges come in, that for a little while there are more positive charges along the inside of the membrane than along its outside, and the potential is reversed. This short period, during which the inside is positive with respect to the outside of the membrane, is called the "overshoot" of the spike potential. This can be seen in Figure 10–2—it is that portion of the spike which is above zero on the ordinate. At the same time, other more complex changes in the equilibria of ions inside and outside the membrane are also effected—for example, the potassium ions undergo transient redistribution. We need not bother with these complexities for present purposes, but simply note the resulting changes in electrical charge across the membrane over time as depicted in Figure 10–2. The potential wobbles around for a bit and then (in about one-hundredth of a second) comes back to its resting state.

Now we must consider two last questions: how does the temporary breakdown of the resting state and the initiation of the action potential occur? and how does the start of an action potential at one point in a fiber cause a wave of activity to travel down the rest of the fiber?[2] It turns out that several different influences can momentarily disrupt the membrane's ability to keep sodium out. One such influence is a change in the potential of the resting state. If the difference between inside and

---

[2] There are several other questions we will have to leave unanswered, e.g., why is the change in Na^+ permeability only temporary, and how does the Na^+ that comes in during a spike get back out? Satisfactory answers to these questions are not presently available.

outside is lowered from the usual 70 millivolts to around 50 millivolts or less, the membrane becomes temporarily permeable to sodium and a spike results. At certain parts of some neural membranes, the sodium permeability switch can also be triggered by certain biochemicals that are secreted by the ends of other neurons.

Once the potential has been altered in one place on the fiber, it will affect the neighboring area. The action potential has some width. At its edge its potential will disturb the potential of the membrane in the region just beyond, reducing it to less than the critical voltage of about 50 millivolts, and in turn causing that region of the membrane to undergo a spike discharge. This will in turn trigger off the next region and so forth, much as a burning fuse ignites gradually, the burning point moving slowly along the string. The rate of transmission of impulses along a nerve fiber ranges from about 10 to 100 yards per second, varying with the size of the fiber; the larger the diameter of the fiber, the faster the transmission. (These rates are much slower than conduction of messages in telephone wires—which go at about the speed of light.) After the spike potential has run its course, the neural membrane comes back to its initial resting state. This process takes a little while—several milliseconds—and there is a time during which a new spike potential cannot easily be initiated. This short time of inexcitability on the part of the fiber is called the *refractory period*.

A traveling spike potential can go in either direction down a fiber if it is started in the middle. However, in nature potentials normally start, not in the middle of a fiber, but, rather, near the cell body at the axon hillock. The discharge can be triggered either by a receptor organ or by another neuron which acts on the receiving neuron at a special juncture called a *synapse*.

Synaptic transmission

Figure 10–3 shows, semischematically, a synapse, the juncture where information is passed between one nerve fiber and the next. The transmission of impulses—electrochemical messages—across synapses is not a straightforward event. The action potential does not, as such, cross the gap between one fiber and another. Instead, the traveling action potential comes to a halt at the end of one fiber, and then a separate impulse is initiated in the next fiber. Between the two fibers there is in fact a space, although a very, very minute one. One of the ways in which we know that electrochemical impulses do not cross synapses is by the fact that the time between the arrival of an impulse at the end of one fiber and the time when an impulse can be observed in the succeeding fiber is very much longer than would be required for an impulse to travel down a single fiber for a similar distance. In addition, impulses can cross synapses in only one direction. A traveling spike moving up one fiber toward the synapse will cause a spike to be produced in the second fiber, but one moving down the second fiber to the same juncture usually will not give rise to an action potential in the first fiber.

Transmission across a synapse, as we have already hinted, is brought about by a process involving a biochemical transmitter. The

FIGURE 10–3
Diagram of a neural synapse,
the juncture between one
neuron and another. (After
Eccles, 1964)

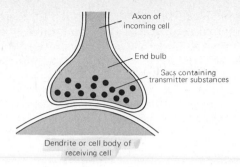

Axon of
incoming cell

End bulb

Sacs containing
transmitter substances

Dendrite or cell body of
receiving cell

impulse arriving at the end of one fiber causes secretion of one of several special chemicals, the most common being *acetylcholine* and *epinephrine*. These substances are apparently stored in small sacs located in the end of the incoming fiber. On contacting the membrane of the next fiber, at another specialized region, sufficient quantities of these chemicals will cause the initiation of a spike potential. After having served their function, the transmitter substances diffuse and are broken down by specific enzymes. If they were not broken down, the next neuron might eventually go into a prolonged siege of discharge.

Another property of the spike potential is important to note. A given nerve fiber always gives rise to the same size and shape of action potential. At a synapse an action potential is either initiated or it is not. Thus we speak of "all-or-none" activity in neural information transmission. This all-or-none mode of impulse transmission is the normal mode in the nerves connecting the muscles and receptors with the spinal cord and the brain (the *peripheral nervous system*) and in most of the activities of the brain itself. It is not the only kind of information transfer in the nervous system, however. The dendrites in many parts of the spinal cord and brain (the *central nervous system*) are very small and closely packed together. The electrical events going on in one are not insulated from those in another, and there is a great deal of interaction. Electrical influences from one cell spread to others. Changes in the charge along one dendrite, even if they are not big enough to trigger a spike potential, are nonetheless capable of modifying similar "graded," sub-spike-level potentials in other dendrites. It is believed that these low level interactions, which do not involve transmission over long distances, may nonetheless have important (but not clearly understood) roles in the processing of information in the brain.

The nervous system: anatomy

The individual neuron, with its dendrites and axon, is the basic building unit of the nervous system. But, by and large, neurons are found in large groups, in bundles of fibers known as *nerves*. Nerves of varying size branch out to all the receptors on all surfaces of the body, into the internal organs, and to all the muscles and organs that are controlled by the nervous system. Incoming information from the receptors goes to the spinal cord and to the brain over afferent (sensory) pathways. Control messages go out to the muscles and organs over efferent (motor) pathways. For long distance transmission, as in the nerves running from the hand to the spinal cord, the axon fibers are covered with a special insulating substance, a fatty material called *myelin*. Conduction of impulses over myelinated fibers is much more rapid than over unmyelinated fibers, and there is much less interaction between one strand of a cable and another when they are separated by this substance. The cell bodies of neurons are also found gathered together in large groups called *nuclei* or *ganglia*. These ganglia are not found in the long parts of the nerves, but in and near the spinal cord, the brain, or the organs being controlled.

In general, the nervous system is divided, for purposes of anatomical discussion, into the central and peripheral systems and their subparts, as follows:

Central Nervous System
  brain
  spinal cord
Peripheral Nervous System
  somatic system
    spinal nerves
    cranial nerves
  autonomic system
    sympathetic division
    parasympathetic division

Figure 10–4 gives an overall view of the human central nervous system, which consists of the brain and spinal cord. The peripheral nervous system consists of the nerves leading from the brain and spinal cord to the outlying areas of the body. The peripheral nervous system is usually further subdivided into the *somatic* and *autonomic* systems. The somatic system consists of nerves which control the muscles of the limbs and receive information from the surface, muscles, and various sense receptors. The autonomic system is concerned with receiving information from and controlling certain activities of the internal environment—of the heart and lungs, stomach and intestines, sweat glands, blood vessels, hair follicles, sphincter muscles, tear ducts, and others.

The autonomic nervous system, is further subdivided into the *sympathetic* and *parasympathetic* systems, which work in different and complementary ways in controlling the internal environment. Some of the functions of the sympathetic and parasympathetic systems are listed in Figure 10–5. It seems unnecessary for a new psychology student to memorize these lists of functions, but it is worth noting that the functions of the nervous system are divided up in a systematic way, with certain sets of nerves devoted to one or another set of duties. The subsystems of the nervous system are distinguished not only by their functions but also by correlated differences in where the nerves come out of the spinal cord, and in some other features, such as location of the ganglia, which differentiate them anatomically.

FIGURE 10–4
The central nervous system of
man: brain and spinal cord.

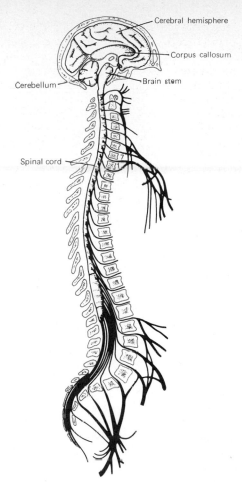

THE CENTRAL NERVOUS SYSTEM

The spinal cord consists primarily of bundles of nerve fibers running
from the various parts of the body to and from the brain. These bundles
of fibers are located within the protective sheath of the bony spine. Down
the middle of the spinal cord itself is a small fluid-filled space that is
continuous with similar fluid-filled cavities in the brain. The *cerebrospinal fluids* serve to absorb shock, to provide a nutritive solution for
the neural cells and, in the brain, have some additional functions which
we will describe later.

The spinal cord acts as more than a simple pathway. It contains
within it a large number of nuclei—collections of cell bodies—and a
very large number of synapses—connections between one neuron and
the next. These synapses serve as relay stations, passing information
along from one neuron to another. They are also involved in certain
control functions: many stimulus-response sequences that are vital
to life and behavioral adaptation are carried out within the spinal cord.

FIGURE 10–5
The autonomic nervous system of
man (very schematic).

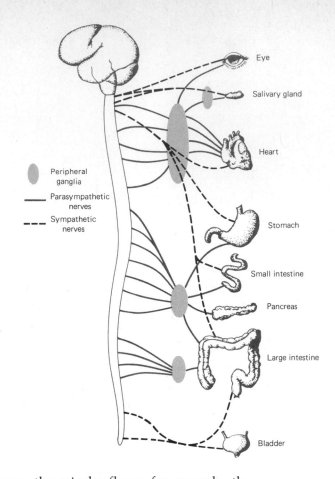

Peripheral
ganglia
Parasympathetic
nerves
Sympathetic
nerves

Eye

Salivary gland

Heart

Stomach

Small intestine

Pancreas

Large intestine

Bladder

Among the simplest of these are the spinal reflexes, for example, the
knee-jerk response. (The natural function of this reflex is to cause an
extension of the leg when the knee is bent by the force of gravity, thus
keeping the animal standing.) When the patellar tendon is struck a sharp
blow, the knee flexes. A message from the muscle attached to the patellar
tendon indicating that it has been stretched is transmitted to the spinal
cord where it passes through just one synapse and back out on an
efferent nerve fiber to the same muscle, which extends the leg at the knee.
This reflex is processed completely within the spinal cord. There are a
large number of such reflex arcs. A schematic diagram of how the simplest kind of reflex arc works is shown in Figure 10–6. Here only six
neurons are represented: three afferent neurons which synapse with
three efferent neurons which lead to the muscle. In reality, this reflex
would be mediated by not three but hundreds of such pairs of neurons
working in parallel. And in most reflexes, the incoming afferent neurons do not synapse directly on the outgoing efferent neurons, but
instead connect to intermediary neurons, of which there may be a chain
of several, which in turn connect with the efferent neurons. In addition,

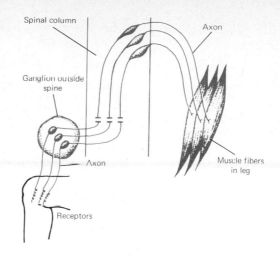

FIGURE 10–6
Schematic diagram of a simple single synapse reflex arc. Any actual reflex would involve a large number of neurons connected in this way "in parallel," rather than just the three shown here. (Similarly, any actual muscle would be composed of a great number of muscle fibers.) Most reflexes also have more than one synapse—there are intermediate neurons between input and output. The one shown here represents only the simplest case.

Spinal column

Axon

Ganglion outside spine

Axon

Muscle fibers in leg

Receptors

such reflex arcs ordinarily are not completely isolated from the rest of the nervous system. There are probably few, if any, completely independent reflex units going about their own business without giving information about their activities to the higher centers or without being influenced by the higher centers. For example, in the knee-jerk reflex, you can easily dampen the response by trying not to move the leg when the hammer hits, or facilitate it by clenching your fist. Therefore, there must be some additional efferent fibers coming from the brain through the spinal cord that make connection with those neuronal circuits underlying the knee-jerk reflex and are capable of modifying them.

The brain

At the top end of the spinal cord the nervous tissue undergoes, during embryological development, a large increase in mass and a complex folding and differentiation. This overgrown end of the neural tube is the brain. The brain, like the spinal cord, consists of a dense collection of billions of neurons, their fibers interwoven and leading this way and that in an immensely intricate and complicated organization. In the central nervous system in general, and in the brain in particular, there is a large number of nerve cells that are not neurons at all but similar cells, lacking dendrites and axons, which are called *glia* or *neuro-glia*. In the human brain, glial cells account for more than half the total number of cells. Their function is not well understood as yet, but it is clear that they have important roles in the nutrition and physical support of the neurons, and it is possible that they may have more exciting functional roles as well.

There are areas in the brain that consist mostly of cell bodies and unmyelinated fibers. These areas appear gray in the preserved brain. There are other areas that consist mostly of tracts of fibers covered with white, fatty myelin. These areas appear white. This gives rise to the description of the brain as being made of gray matter and white matter, respectively. The white matter, as one might expect, since it contains the

FIGURE 10–7
The human brain. (a) A
photograph of the lateral
surface of the human cerebral
hemisphere. It is facing left, and
the covering tissues have been
removed. (b) Outline sketch of
the lateral surface of the cerebral
hemisphere. Some structures and
landmarks are labeled. (From
Gardner, E. *Fundamentals of
Neurology.* Philadelphia: W. B.
Saunders, 1968)

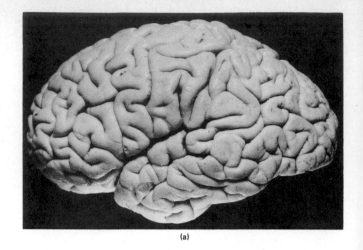

(a)

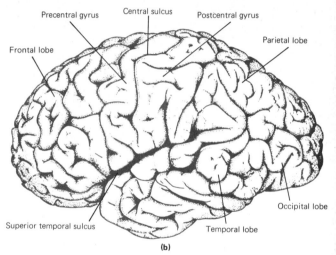

Precentral gyrus   Central sulcus   Postcentral gyrus

Frontal lobe   Parietal lobe

Superior temporal sulcus   Temporal lobe   Occipital lobe

(b)

insulated nerve fibers, is generally concerned with the conduction of
impulses from one part of the brain to another, while the gray matter
is primarily concerned with the processing or storage of information—
although generalizations of this kind are quite dangerous in the light
of our present ignorance of brain function. (The living brain as a whole
is neither gray nor white, but is given a pinkish color by its extensive
blood supply; and the tissue is rather soft, resembling the consistency of
Jell-O more than that of muscle.)

The brain contains a very large number of cells, on the order of
ten billion. These cells are extremely highly organized; the brain can be
differentiated under the dissecting scalpel or microscope into literally
thousands of named parts, each of which has a different set of systematic
connections with other parts, and in all likelihood some specialized
function. For our present purposes, luckily, all we need to become

Psychology:
an overview
282

FIGURE 10-8
(a) A photograph of the medial
surface of the brain. (b) Outline
sketch of the medial surface of
the brain. (From Gardner, E.
Fundamentals of Neurology.
Philadelphia: W. B. Saunders,
1968)

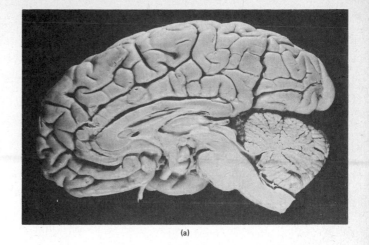

(a)

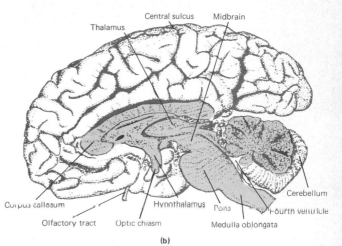

Thalamus   Central sulcus   Midbrain

Cerebellum

Corpus callosum   Hypothalamus   Pons   Fourth ventricle

Olfactory tract   Optic chiasm   Medulla oblongata

(b)

acquainted with are some of the major landmarks and some of the
structures that are important for behavior. Let us start by examining a
picture of the outside of the brain. Figure 10–7 shows the brain, much
as it might look soon after removal from a skull. The brain is facing in
a normal heads-up manner; the nose would have been to the left. As you
can see, the whole surface of the brain is covered with a thick, folded
and corrugated covering. As Figure 10–8 shows, this covering is exactly
that, an outer layer over an inner core which sits on the top of the spinal
cord. The inside part of the brain is roughly analogous to a stem, as in
a stalk of broccoli, the outside layer to a bark or covering. Indeed, this
covering layer is called the *cortex,* which is Greek for *bark.* It consists
of cell bodies and unmyelinated fibers, and is thus "gray matter." The
front and top portion of the brain, as shown in Figure 10–7, is called
the *cerebrum,* and its covering is called the *cerebral cortex.* In the outside

view of the brain shown in Figure 10–7, all one can see is the cerebral cortex. The cerebral cortex has names assigned to its various parts. Listed in Figure 10–7 are its major subdivisions, the so-called *lobes*, with arrows running to the regions specified. To go a little deeper into our subject, Figure 10–8 shows a view of the brain sliced in half along a line running front to back over the top of the head. The structures labeled in this figure are those seen on the inside of the brain that are of more than passing interest for our purposes. The student would be well-advised to familiarize himself with the geography and spelling of these few names. Of these structures, the most important for the discussions which follow are the *corpus callosum*, the *thalamus*, and the *hypothalamus*.

The right half of the body is primarily controlled from the left hemisphere of the cortex, and the left half of the body from the right hemisphere. In order, almost literally, for the left hand to know what the right hand is doing it is necessary to have communication paths between the hemispheres. The principal link is the corpus callosum, a wide, dense band of myelinated fiber tracts. The thalamus is a large, two-sided, roughly dumbbell-shaped body. The thalamus lies between the fiber tracks coming up from the spinal cord and the cortex, and serves as a way station for sensory input. Sensory messages of all sorts, with the exception of smell and possibly pain, pass through the thalamus on their way to the cortex. The hypothalamus, as its name implies, is the structure below *(hypo-)* the thalamus. If one thinks of the thalamus as the ice cream, then the hypothalamus is the cone, a roughly triangular region lying below the thalamus. The hypothalamus is richly connected with other parts of the brain, including the cerebral cortex and the spinal cord, and with the pituitary gland—the master gland of the body, which is intimately involved in the control of moods, emotions, and emergency reactions. In addition to all these neural connections, the hypothalamus is bordered by the major fluid-filled cavity of the brain, where it is in contact with the cerebrospinal fluid.

The *reticular formation*, whose function in attention and arousal we discussed at some length in Chapter 6, runs through the middle of the stem of the brain from about the level of the hypothalamus down to the spinal cord. Sitting above the spinal cord just behind the cerebral cortex is the *cerebellum*, which has connections both with the brain stem region, and between its two bilateral hemispheres over a bridge, the *pons*, which goes underneath the brain stem. The cerebellum is a primitive structure, one of whose important functions is the coordination and smoothing of muscular activity.

It would be a good idea to refer to these figures from time to time, as descriptions of functions mean more when you have some idea of where the functions dwell.

Information processing in the nervous system

What goes on in the structures we have been describing is the processing of information. A system that processes information must first have a means of representing or coding it. Most computers, for example, represent and operate on information coded as yes-no pulses of electricity. We have already seen that the nervous system has an analogous coding in its all-or-none spike conduction. An information-processing system also needs means for combining such representations so that it can give different outputs depending on different patterns of input. In computers, information is combined by electronic circuits called "gates," which do or do not output an electric pulse, depending on whether they have received an appropriate combination of inputs. One way in which such combination of information is accomplished in the nervous system is by means of the mechanisms of synaptic transmission.[3]

Let us, therefore, consider further the nature of transmission at synapses. The main thing is that this transmission sometimes happens and sometimes does not. Several factors can determine whether it does or does not. First, never (or at least hardly ever) does any one neuron receive input from only a single ending of one other fiber. Typically hundreds or thousands of incoming axonal fibers synapse on the cell body of a single receiving neuron. Thus, virtually every neuron in the brain is subject to the influence of many other neurons, and these influences can add and interact in many significant ways. The three most important interactions between synaptic influences are described by the terms *excitation, inhibition,* and *summation.* Since we have already discussed excitation, let us start with inhibition. Some fiber terminations (synapses), rather than inducing the recipient cell to produce an action potential, have the opposite effect. They tend to prevent it from firing under conditions in which it ordinarily would. If excitatory and inhibitory influences impinge on different regions of the same cell at the same time, its tendency to fire will depend (but not necessarily in a simple way) on their combination. This is summation. Summation of incoming impulses can occur even if they do not arrive at exactly the same time; there is a small interval—measured in milliseconds—over which the effects of two inputs can still combine to give a greater (or different) effect than they would if further separated in time.

Before going on to describe the interaction of synapses in a more precise and formal way, we need one more concept. This is the notion of a threshold for neural firing. The sensitivity of neurons to incoming impulses, that is the number of impulses required within some small interval of time in order to induce an action potential, can and does vary quite widely. Some cells may fire under the influence of only one or a few incoming impulses, as we have suggested would be the case in the reflex arc shown in Figure 10–6; others require ten, hundreds, or perhaps thousands before they fire. The amount of excitation required in a given time to induce an action potential in a given neuron is the neuron's threshold. Whether the threshold of a cell is reached is roughly determined by adding together the excitatory influences and subtracting

[3] There may be more than one mode of information-combining in the nervous system. What is outlined here is the best understood and probably most common mode, the interaction of all-or-none impulses at synapses. Graded, nonimpulse interactions in the retina and brain may also be important, as was hinted earlier, but too little is known about such processes to justify a description here of how they might work.

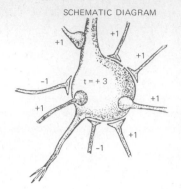
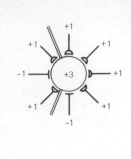

SCHEMATIC DIAGRAM   SYMBOLIC REPRESENTATION

FIGURE 10–9
Diagram of a neuron with (a) a schematic and (b) a symbolic representation of multiple inputs and a threshold value for stimulation. Each input represents a neural fiber that has either an excitatory or inhibitory synapse with the cell. Note the representation of excitatory and inhibitory synapses. The cell fires if the threshold (t) is exceeded by the sum of inputs.

the inhibitory influences concurrently acting on a cell.[4] One can represent the conditions for firing of a particular neuron (doing only small injustice to reality) by presuming that each excitatory synapse contributes a value of $+1$ and each inhibitory synapse a value of -1, assigning a threshold-value number to the neuron, and presuming that the neuron fires whenever its threshold is exceeded. Figure 10–9 illustrates this principle. The neuron shown here is assumed to have a threshold value of $+3$. This means that it would fire whenever any three of the excitatory input synapses were active, provided that neither of the two inhibitory synapses were active. If one or more inhibitory synapses were active, four, five, or more excitatory impulses would be required to exceed threshold. It can be seen that this combinative facility could be very useful to the nervous system in processing and analyzing both incoming and outgoing information. We will see how the nervous system might make use of these kinds of analyses in the discussions that follow. We will make extensive use of symbols such as those used in Figure 10–9 and the notions of excitation, inhibition, summation, and threshold.

SENSATION AND PERCEPTION: THE INPUT AND ANALYSIS OF NEURAL INFORMATION

We begin our description of the physiological bases of behavior by considering the way in which information is transformed into neural messages at the receptors, then combined, transmitted, recombined, and analyzed to produce perception. The first stage of this process is the transformation, or *transduction*, of physical energies into neural signals. Each of the various sense organs has a different physical mechanism underlying its particular job of transduction, and there is neither space nor need here to trace each one in detail. However, we do want a general understanding of what such a system is like. To this end, we will closely examine aspects of two examples, the auditory and visual systems.

---

[4] The actual situation is, of course, much more complicated in detail than the schematic representations presented here, but the principles are the same.

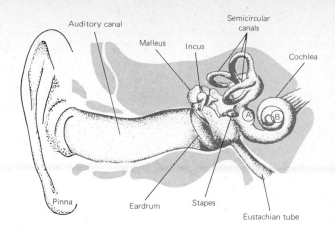

FIGURE 10–10
Diagram showing general
structure of the ear.

Auditory canal

Malleus

Incus

Semicircular
canals

Cochlea

A   B

Pinna

Eardrum

Stapes

Eustachian tube

Transduction in the auditory system

Sound enters the outer ear as rarefactions and compactions in the atmosphere. Information about sound leaves the inner ear over the auditory
nerve as electrochemical impulses traveling along nerve fibers. In between are the remarkable mechanisms diagrammed in Figures 10–10
and 10–11. Sound-pressure variations produce corresponding motions
in, first, a membrane, then a series of delicate bones, acting on each
other as successive levers, and finally a small flat piece of bone that
pushes against a curved tube of fluid. The fluid in the tube is thus set
into vibration. Already one level of transduction has taken place, from
motion in air to motion in a much more viscous fluid. But this is still
a long way from a nerve impulse. The next step involves a long membrane—the basilar membrane—which runs the length of the curved
tube of the inner ear. This membrane picks up the vibrations of the
fluid. But since this membrane is thick and resilient compared with the
fluid, and is attached to the bony structure surrounding the ear, its
vibrations do not follow exactly those of the sound. Rather it moves
in wave-like fluctuations similar to the ones produced in a jump-rope
when one end is moved up and down very rapidly while the other end
is fixed. The shape of these waves varies with the frequency of vibrations in the fluid. The faster the vibrations, the greater the movement
in the end of the membrane near the stapes where the membrane is stiffest
(label A in Figures 10–10 and 10–11), and the less the motion, relatively,
at the other end (label B) where it is least stiff. The transduction, so far,
has been the conversion of sound into the vibration of a membrane,
accomplished in such a manner that which part of the membrane vibrates
most strongly depends on the frequency of the sound waves coming in.
The next stage in the transduction depends on neural sense-organs lying
along the cochlear membrane. These are *hair cells* of the *organs of Corti*,
a dense row of structures with hairlike projections that reach down to
contact the vibrating basilar membrane, and which are thus stimulated.
At frequencies produced by low tones, under about 500 Hertz, the

FIGURE 10–11
Section through the cochlea, and diagram of the cochlea, shown uncoiled for
clarity's sake, showing the basilar membrane.

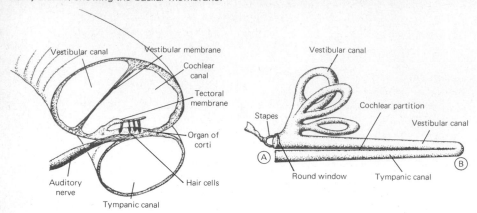

receptor cells at the far end of the cochlea respond in direct relation to
the frequency, that is, every time the membrane bends back and forth
as it vibrates an impulse is sent out along the fiber. For low tones, this
completes the transduction of sound energy into nerve impulses, and in
a very simple way. For each rarefaction and compaction in the air, an
impulse is sent down the nerve fiber, the frequency of impulses in the
fiber thus matching the frequency of impulses in the sound. This simple,
straightforward system unfortunately cannot work for very high
frequencies because nerve fibers cannot respond more than 500 or 1,000
times per second. However, while no single fiber can follow the frequency
of higher pitches, there is still a representation in the ear that can be
used, namely, the region of the cochlear membrane which is in greatest
fluctuation. The higher the frequency, as we have said, the closer to the
stapes does the maximum motion occur. The receptor cells along the
membrane respond accordingly: those cells located at the point on the
membrane where the vibrations are the largest respond at the highest
frequency. To transduce and transmit information about what frequencies are being received, these cells do not need to respond at a rate
equal to the frequency; instead, the brain gets the information in terms
of *which* fibers are firing. The firing of one fiber "means" to the brain
that the major frequency being heard is 1,000 Hertz, while the firing of
another fiber "means" a frequency of 10,000 Hertz.

Actually, the vibrations of the membrane do not differ enough
from point to point to produce the specificity shown in the fibers of the
auditory nerve. The membrane vibrates over its whole length, and the
amplitude of vibration at the maximum point for any frequency is only
slightly greater than at nearby points. Yet only the fibers serving the
maximum point respond; the neighboring cells, at places where the
vibration is almost as wide, do not. Something about the neurons coming
from the organ of Corti must markedly increase the differentiation of
frequencies. One hypothesis is that there is some sort of competition,
with the maximally stimulated neurons suppressing the slightly less

stimulated neurons next to them. At any rate, we know that the response of the neural fibers is quite specific; by the time the auditory input gets to the cortex, each fiber is signaling the presence of only a very narrow range of frequencies. We will not follow auditory perception any farther; instead, we turn to the visual system, where higher levels of processing have been more clearly worked out.

Perceptual analysis in the visual system

In Chapter 5 we made much of the point that perception consists of inference—of the analysis of information in order to construct the nature of the world, rather than a simple reporting of physical energies. We are ready now to examine the machinery by which some of these analyses are accomplished. We will be concerned primarily with understanding how such a system might work, rather than with tracing its details. The perceptual-analysis mechanisms to be described in what follows are largely hypothetical. We do not yet know how visual or any other perceptual analysis really works. Nevertheless, most of the available facts are consistent with an elegant yet simple and plausible theory of the underlying processes. Outlining these hypothetical mechanisms should have the virtue of showing the reader that it is possible to reduce complicated and mysterious functions to simple, understandable mechanisms. Whether or not these are the true mechanisms, they will illustrate the spirit of the explanations we are seeking. This discussion will rely on a set of facts about the ways in which individual cells in the visual system behave when various patterns of stimulation are applied to the retina. These facts, which constitute a real breakthrough in physiological psychology, have been discovered over the last few decades through the work of a number of investigators (e.g., Hartline, 1940; Hubel & Wiesel, 1959, 1962; Kuffler, 1953; Lettvin, Maturana, McCulloch, & Pitts, 1959).

Before we begin, let us set ourselves a problem to keep in mind as we examine the various stages of processing of information from eye to brain. Move a pencil back and forth across your span of sight. You see it as a single, straight, moving object. This is a common enough experience, and seems a simple act. It is, in fact, anything but simple. Consider whether and how you could build a machine which could do this—which could continue to recognize a line as the same line after it had moved or while it was moving. It is no mean task. Indeed, the mechanism of object perception is a mystery that has troubled science for many years, and for which many elaborate and often mystical explanations have been proposed. A potential solution that is emerging from current research is dramatically simple and straightforward. In fact, once you know this explanation, it will appear so simple and obvious that it may not seem interesting or exciting. You are urged, once more, therefore, to spend a few minutes trying to imagine a system that would perform the pencil-recognizing feat. Be warned that it will not solve the problem to postulate the existence of a tiny little man (homunculus) somewhere in the head. Some great thinkers have made this mistake in a disguised fashion. They have postulated that each point on the retina connects to a corresponding point in the brain (which it does), such that a mosaic picture is created there corresponding exactly to the mosaic on the surface of the retina. This is fine as a first step but does not in the least explain the ability to see an object as the same object while it moves, or for that matter to see an object at all. It only moves the "picture" from the eye to the brain, but does not get it perceived or understood. Thus, if one proposes a point-to-point projection of this kind as a complete explanation of perception, one has, in effect, tacitly assumed that there must be a little man sitting in the head looking at the new picture projected there. The problem, of course, is that even if there were a homunculus, we would still be left with understanding how *he* sees, how he manages to make equivalences of a line seen in two different places on that television screen in our heads. No, we have to do better than that, and that is where the difficulty comes in.

Because it is so important to understand, let us have one more illustration of the nature of the problem we face. The image projected on the retina is upside-down. Must we find some way in which the image of the world is turned upright again as it is passed back to the brain? For many years philosophers worried about how they could see things upright when the retinal image was inverted. But if one is worried about this problem, one has not yet grasped the nature of the real mystery. If one thought that anything would be solved by turning the image over once more before it reached the cortex he would implicitly be assuming not only a homunculus, but one who could not stand on his head! The problem is not to get the world reflected, but to get it understood. It is not the mechanisms by which an image is transferred intact that are important, but those which change it, modify it, reduce it, and make sense out of it.

We begin at the retina, and try to find out what sort of information is passed from the retina to the optic nerve. A good way to do this is to monitor the optic nerve with a sensitive microelectrode that can detect single nerve impulses in single fibers as they travel from the eye to the brain. Examine Figure 10–12 and you will see that the retina consists of three layers of cells: first, the receptor cells themselves; then, so-called *bipolar* cells; and, finally, ganglion cells whose axons, as fibers of the optic nerve, reach from the eye to the brain. The receptor cells are concerned with transduction. The bipolar cells are responsible for a first stage of processing in which information is collected from several different receptor cells and combined. There are still other types of cells which allow lateral interaction among the bipolar cells. The ganglion cells in turn pick up information from one or more bipolar cells and transmit it to the brain. Thus, by recording from the axon of a ganglion cell in the optic nerve one can find out what processing has occurred between the light falling on the retina and a message about it being sent to the brain.

An experiment like this proceeds as follows: An animal, usually a cat or a monkey, is put in a restraining harness and appropriate muscles are anesthetized so that its eyes stay fixated on a point on a projection screen. The experimenter displays dots, lines, or other patterns on this screen, and thus controls the pattern of light on the retina. Next, the

FIGURE 10–12
Layers of cells in the retina. Only a few representative cells have been indicated; in reality the retina is densely packed with cells and connecting dendrites. (After Polyak, 1941)

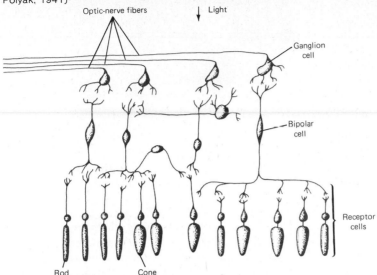

Optic-nerve fibers   ↓ Light

Ganglion cell

Bipolar cell

Receptor cells

Rod   Cone

experimenter puts an electrode, usually a tungsten wire only a few millionths of an inch thick at its tip, into some part of the nervous system. With proper electronic amplification, activity emanating from a single neuron located near the tip of the electrode can be displayed on an oscilloscope (a television-like screen) or heard through headphones. The experimenter tries one pattern after another, in one place on the projection screen after another, in a painstaking and systematic fashion. For example, he might start with a very small spot of bright light on an otherwise black screen, and move it to all possible positions on the screen. Now, imagine that when the spot is at ten o'clock and ten degrees from the fovea (the sensitive center of the retina) of the animal's left eye, the right one being covered, the cell whose activity is being recorded suddenly starts to give forth bursts of activity. When the spot of light is moved one way or the other, the activity ceases. From this, the experimenter concludes that this particular cell is stimulated to fire when there is a spot of light in a certain place in the visual field. This is summarized by saying that the cell has a *receptive field* so characterized. By receptive field we mean simply that pattern of stimulation which will influence—activate or suppress—a particular cell, or a particular group of cells.

Let us see what kind of receptive fields are found as we work upward from the retina. The first place we will consider is the optic nerve, the data consisting of observations of impulses in the axonal fibers of ganglion cells of the retina as they travel toward the brain. What pattern of light on the retina will give rise to activity in a ganglion cell? Two types of receptive fields commonly found for these cells are shown

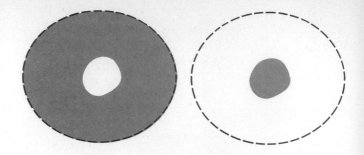

FIGURE 10–13
Two patterns of illumination which cause retinal ganglion (and lateral geniculate) cells to fire. An "on-center" cell responds when the retina is illuminated with a spot of light in a dark surround (left). "Off-center" cells respond when there is a dark patch in a light surround (right).

in Figure 10–13. The maximally stimulating visual pattern for some of them (called *on-center cells*) is a spot of light surrounded by dark; for some others (called *off-center cells*) it is a dark spot surrounded by light. Light over the whole area within the dotted circles in Figure 10–13 leads to much less activity on the part of such cells than does the appropriate pattern of stimulation.

In actuality, many different types of receptive fields have been observed for ganglion cells. There is even some evidence that the same cell may respond well to more than one visual pattern, perhaps even changing its receptive field as the requirements of the situation change (Weingarten & Spinelli, 1966). In many animals quite complex visual analysis takes place at this level; frogs, for instance, have ganglion cells that respond only to small curved moving spots—bug-like patterns. In cats, monkeys, and probably humans, the more complex analysis tasks seem to have been moved to the cortex. However, what is never found at any level is a simple point-by-point correspondence of the activity of one fiber to that of one retinal receptor. By the time information is passed to the brain, it has already been extensively processed.

Now let us ask how on-center and off-center ganglion cells could respond the way they do to the input they receive from receptor cells in the retina. What we want is a hypothetical "wiring diagram" showing how the neurons could be hooked up to give the observed results. Figures 10–14 and 10–15 show such hypothetical wiring diagrams. Consider the on-center cell first. A group of retinal receptor cells clustered together all connect to a single ganglion cell through excitatory synapses. Another set of retinal cells occupying the doughnut-like ring of projection area surrounding the center of the field also connect with the same "analyzer" cell, but through inhibitory synapses.[5] Consider the receptive field of the analyzer cell. First, what happens if a diffuse light shines on this whole region of the retina? All the cells in the diagram would be stimulated and send impulses to the analyzer. The four center cells would tend to excite the analyzer but, at the same time, the four outer cells would inhibit it. The two effects would, therefore, cancel out and the analyzer cell would fail to fire.

What if, instead, there were light in the middle of the circle, but

---

[5] These connections presumably are by way of the bipolar and various lateral cells, but for our purposes we can represent them as if they were direct links.

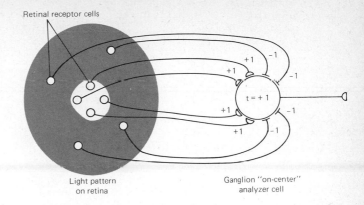

FIGURE 10–14
Hypothetical wiring diagram for an "on-center" analyzer cell—one that responds when the retina is stimulated by a pattern of light like that on the left in Figure 10–15.

Light pattern
on retina

Ganglion "on-center"
analyzer cell

none in the outer ring? The middle receptors would excite the analyzer cell and, without any offsetting inhibition from the outer cells, it would respond. Thus this hypothetical cell fires when, and only when, the retina is exposed to a spot of light in a dark surround. The student should be able to follow the diagram in Figure 10–15 of a hypothesized off-center cell, whose dynamics are the opposite of those for the on-center cell. The cells in the middle here are inhibitory, while those in the ring around the middle are excitatory, and the summation and threshold arrangements make this cell's receptive field one of a dark center in a light surround.

Ganglion cells connect to cells in the lateral geniculate, a part of the thalamus. Because receptive fields in the lateral geniculate are very similar to those of ganglion cells, we shall skip them and move on to the next major stage of processing. Lateral geniculate cells synapse with cells whose fibers go to the cerebral cortex. Let us follow them with our fine electrodes and see what cells in the occipital cortex get excited about. There are several stages here, one cell synapsing with another. At what is probably the first stop, cells are stimulated by fibers coming directly from the lateral geniculate. Most of these cells respond to neither spots of light nor doughnut-shaped bright fields, although some still do. Rather, there is a predominance of cells whose receptive fields are much

FIGURE 10–15
Hypothetical wiring diagram for an "off-center" cell.

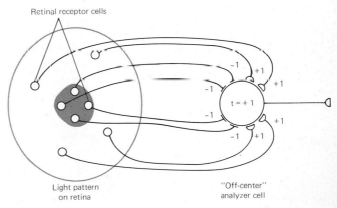

Light pattern
on retina

"Off-center"
analyzer cell

FIGURE 10–16
Patterns of light that cause firing
of "simple cells" in the cerebral
cortex.

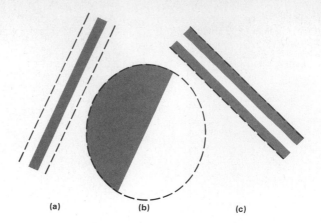

(a) (b) (c)

more sophisticated. Some cells, called *simple cells*, respond to patterns
like those shown in Figure 10–16, which may be described as bars, lines,
or edges. The effective stimuli consist of regions of contrast: a dark bar
in a light surround, a light bar in a dark surround, or a line where dark
meets light. Such a cell will usually respond to its effective stimulus, e.g.,
a line, so long as it is in the right general area of the retina (within say
three degrees) and at the right orientation, e g., pointing from ten o'clock
to seven o'clock, or from eleven o'clock to five o'clock. The orientation
is fairly critical—rotate the line 10 to 15 degrees and the cell no longer
responds.

Given the on-center and off-center field cells of optic nerve (and
lateral geniculate) as components, how could one wire up an analyzer
cell in the cortex to respond as a simple cell does? We extend the wiring
diagrams of Figures 10–14 and 10–15 to a new stage shown in Figure
10–17. A group of on-center cells whose receptive fields lie in a line
across the retina are all assumed to synapse on a single analyzer cell in
the cortex. They all have excitatory influences on this cell, and if enough
of them fire they exceed its threshold of +4, giving rise to activity in that
cell. If a diffuse light falls over this whole area, so that both the center and
the surround of each on-center cell's receptive field are stimulated, then
neither the on-center cells nor the simple cell into which they feed will

FIGURE 10–17
Hypothetical wiring diagram of
line detector cell. Receptive
fields of five "on-center" cells are
shown schematically; they would
be connected to retinal receptor
cells as shown in Figure 10–14.

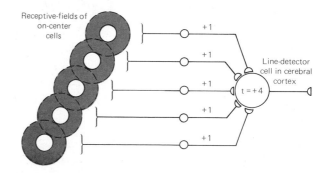

Receptive-fields of
on-center
cells

+1

+1

+1

Line-detector
cell in cerebral
cortex

t = +4

+1

+1

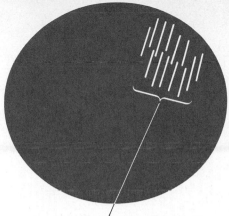

Any of these lines cause one complex cell to fire

fire. If a small spot of light in a dark surround falls in this region, it will fire one of the on-center cells which will in turn send impulses to the simple cell. But excitation from one input is insufficient to excite this simple cell; it requires four or more at once for its threshold. So, nothing happens. However, if a single, long line of light is placed down the middle of all the receptive fields at once, aligned with their centers and thus failing to stimulate much of their surrounds, then all these on-center cells will fire, and the sum will exceed the threshold of the analyzer cell. This analyzer cell, then, fires when and only when exposed to a line in a particular place and orientation on the retina. Notice that in this model, a line in the seen world is not represented at the cortex by a line of activity but by the activity of a single cell.

Other cells with other kinds of receptive fields can also be located in the cortex. For example, a somewhat more elaborate level of analysis is found in what are called *complex cells*. One kind of complex cell,

FIGURE 10-19
Hypothetical wiring diagram for
"complex-cell" that responds
when the retina is stimulated as
in Figure 10-18.

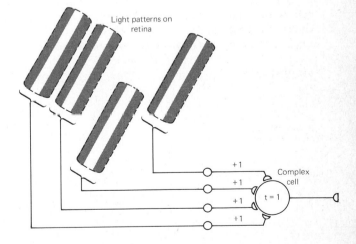

FIGURE 10-20
Patterns for demonstrating line-width specific adaptation effects. First note that the two left-hand patterns are identical. Then place the figure five to six feet away in good light. Stare fixedly at the horizontal line between the two right-hand patterns for at least a full minute. Then quickly shift your fixation to the square between the two left-hand patterns. Do the line widths still look the same? (From Blakemore and Sutton, 1969; copyright 1969 by the American Association for the Advancement of Science)

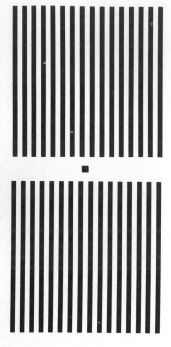

perhaps the easiest to understand, is one that also responds to a line on an angle, but will respond to any line on that angle, no matter where, over a limited range, it is located on the retina. Figure 10–18 shows the patterns of light on the retina that will cause one type of complex cell to fire. A possible wiring diagram for this is easy to construct (see Figure 10–19). We wire an output from each of a large number of simple cells so that they converge on one complex cell, which has a threshold of +1. Then when any one of the line-detecting simple cells fires, so also does the complex cell.

Notice that such a cell fires for any line with the right width and the right orientation, so long as it is within the same general region of the visual field. Might it not, then, fire even better for several nearby parallel lines? Cortical cells have been observed that do, indeed, respond maximally to patterns of stripes like those in Figure 10–20. Such cells are sometimes quite particular about the width of stripe they will respond to — four-per-inch stripes, say, activating one cell; eight-per-inch stripes activating another (Campbell, Cooper, & Enroth-Cugell, 1969). Thus, the stripes in the upper and lower left of Figure 10–20, if placed at the correct viewing distance, would activate different cells in the cerebral cortex of a cat.

Although the human cortex has not been studied directly, human vision does act as if it contains line-detector cells. One demonstration of this makes use of the phenomenon of adaptation, the pervasive tendency for neural structures to become temporarily less excitable after prolonged stimulation. (In Chapter 5 we discussed the fact that the nervous system responds primarily to changes in stimulation and stops responding when stimulation remains steady; and we presented several demonstrations of visual afterimages that are due to adaptation phenomena.)

If cortical cells that respond to lines of a certain width were stimulated for a prolonged period they would adapt; and the person would become temporarily less sensitive to stripes of that width presented in the adapted portion of his visual field. But cells that respond to sufficiently wider or narrower lines would not have adapted. As a result the perception of lines might be somewhat distorted: given a line of ambiguous or intermediate (between adapted and not-adapted) width, the non-adapted cells would be more prone to respond than the adapted ones, and the person might tend to see lines as wider or narrower than they actually were.

This prediction is borne out provided that the stripe widths and viewing distances are carefully controlled (Blakemore & Sutton, 1969). The caption on Figure 10–20 tells you how to perform this demonstration on yourself. The demonstration takes time, but most people find the effect sufficiently surprising and instructive to be worth the effort.

We have now seen that the brains of cats and monkeys contain single cells that would respond when the eye was presented with a line of a particular width, and would continue to respond as the line was moved across the field of view. We have been able to draw relatively simple neural wiring diagrams to account for the existence of such cells. And we have seen suggestive evidence that the human visual system may contain similar cells. We have, thus, outlined a hypothetical system that performs many of the functions needed to solve our pencil-perception problem. From the complex patterns of light falling on the retina, the system could abstract the fact that there was a continuous line of dark (or light) out there, and represent this abstraction as the activity of just one cortical cell, even when the line moved.

This is obviously still a long way from a real pencil-perceiver, however. For example, we can still see a pencil as the same thing when it is rotated, which our line-detector cell would not. And we can tell that the pencil is not a pen, which our cell could not. In principle, such higher-order percepts could be generated by continuing the hypothetical wiring process we have begun. A "rotating line" cell could be made by connecting line-detector cells of several different orientations, for instance. Such a process could be continued up to "mother-in-law" cells, if there were sufficient cells and connections available. At present we don't know how far this kind of analysis goes in the brain. Cortical cells have been found that appear to respond optimally when the retina is exposed to corners, particular oblique or obtuse angles, edges moving in one direction only, or in either of two directions, and even to a view of a monkey hand (Gross, Bender, & Rocha-Miranda, 1969). But whether this is the whole story remains to be determined. Some investigators believe that the astronomical number of connections that this straightforward analysis system requires is unreasonable, and that for higher-order perceptions, like mother-in-law recognition, more sophisticated processes must come into play.

Nevertheless, the lesson learned here should not be forgotten. What seemed at first to be a mysterious, even mystical or supernatural mental event (or, worse yet, a natural thing that just happens and needs no explanation)—the perception of a line as a line despite movement on the retina—turns out to be explainable in terms of very simple neural circuitry. The fact that we do not yet understand what happens next does not mean that it will not appear equally simple once we understand it.

MOTIVATION AND EMOTION

There is evidence that the perceptual-analysis systems we have been discussing are "wired in."' For example, visual detector cells can be found in infant cats. Thus, the first steps of input processing are probably largely primitive, in the sense that they do not depend in great measure on prior experience. In the final section of this chapter we will be concerned with how the nervous system alters itself through experience. Here we will consider another aspect of relatively primitive physiological organization in behavior, that involved in decision and action related to maintenance of homeostatic balance (equilibrium of life-sustaining processes; see Chapter 6). We will sketch the way in which the nervous and hormonal systems produce some of the emotional responses, appetites, rewards, and other motivational phenomena described in Chapter 6.

Most of what follows will concern goings-on in the deeply buried, subcortical regions of the brain. There are a number of methods available for studying these structures. First, the electrode recording method, whose use we encountered in exploration of the visual analysis system, can also be used in deep parts of the brain, and at times has yielded important clues. A second method is to stimulate a given area of the brain and see what the animal does. This is usually accomplished by implanting one or more electrodes (much larger than the microelectrodes used for recording) permanently in the animal's brain. A third method is to destroy or remove a small bit of brain tissue. This is often done by passing a strong electric current through an electrode until the tissue around it is heated and killed.

We have already seen (Chapter 6) that the center of the lower brain stem, the reticular formation, is intimately involved in arousal and excitation. But other parts of the brain also play a part in emotional reactions, and the methods just described have been used systematically to find out which parts are involved in which aspects of emotion. If its cortex is removed, an animal, rather than showing a decrease in emotional reactions, shows quite a dramatic increase. The animal becomes enraged and fearful, and shows greatly increased curiosity and sexuality. The behaviors used to express emotions are often awkward and poorly integrated. It appears that the cortex, in the normal state, serves to suppress and regulate emotional reactions. When it is removed, lower centers are freed to respond emotionally in cruder ways to lesser provocation. These lower centers are found in the hypothalamus. If the upper and lower parts of the brain are separated below the hypothalamus, a very different picture emerges. The small components of emotional responses are still present: biting, spitting, scratching, partial postures of attack and threat (such as baring the claws or the fangs) still occur, although the eliciting stimuli may have to be more intense than normal. But integrated, instinctual emotional sequences are gone—a cat will no longer pounce on and kill a mouse, for example. The triggering and integration of overall emotional responses is apparently a function of the hypothalamus. Other evidence exists that this is the case. Stimulating or removing certain parts of the hypothalamus itself, while leaving the rest of the brain alone, affects emotional responses such as rage, fear, and sex, increasing or abolishing them depending on the treatment and the particular place involved.

Emotions are intimately related to homeostasis, particularly to the mobilization of the energies and response patterns needed to deal with emergencies. Also closely involved in homeostasis are the control of

FIGURE 10–21
A rat with a lesion in the ventro-medial hypothalamus. (From Miller, 1958; photograph by J. F. Stevenson)

appetites in the consumption of food, water, and other necessities, the setting of goals for activity, and the selection of habits by their outcomes in reinforcement. These are the matters usually covered by the term *motivation* (Chapters 6 and 7). It should come as no surprise that, like the organization of emotional reactions, motivational processes are largely controlled by structures in and around the hypothalamus. To illustrate this assertion, let us consider the regulation of food intake and the way in which the consumption of food acts as a reinforcer. When a certain part of the hypothalamus, the *ventromedial* (which means toward the underside of the brain, in the middle) *nucleus* is destroyed, a rat will overeat to the point of obesity (Figure 10–21). This overeating *(hyperphagia)* is of a particular kind. The rat can still discriminate foods he likes from foods he does not like—if quinine, which has a very bitter taste, is added to his food he will stop eating—but what no longer stops him eating is having had enough. If a closely adjacent area, the *ventrolateral* (under, on the side) *nucleus* is destroyed, there is an essentially opposite result: the animal stops eating and may starve unless force-fed or enticed with a particularly preferred food. If, instead of being destroyed, these areas are stimulated with a mild electric current, other interesting things happen. If a rat has just pressed a bar when the ventrolateral "hunger" center is stimulated, he will soon repeat the bar press response; in other words, stimulation here acts as a strong operant reinforcer. He will also, frequently, begin to eat. The strength of the reinforcement depends on the animal being deprived of food at the time. A rat who has just eaten will not be reinforced by stimulation of the lateral hypothalamus, whereas a hungry animal will be greatly reinforced by the same stimulus. By contrast, stimulation of the ventromedial hypothalamus (whose descruction leads to overeating) is aversive, and also causes cessation of consummatory responses like eating.

An integrated picture of motivational control emerges from all these facts. The ventral region of the hypothalamus appears to be involved in the regulation of food intake, in detecting when food is needed, in organizing responses for its consumption, in deciding when enough food has been consumed, and in making the receipt of food a reinforcer that stamps in new behavior patterns which lead to food. The lateral centers apparently are responsible for detecting when the animal needs food and getting him to start eating, while the medial centers are responsible for detecting when he has had enough and getting him to stop. The two centers are reciprocally related. Ordinarily, the satiety center works by shutting off the eating center; when the satiety center is gone the eating center keeps blithely on until the animal is obese. This kind of reciprocal relation between two adjoining centers in the nervous system is quite common.

Other structures in the hypothalamus perform similar functions with regard to water consumption and many of the other homeostatic activities of an animal, including defecation and urination, fighting, fleeing, and sexual activity. Areas in which stimulation is reinforcing are also usually involved in one of the homeostatic balance processes.

Brain-stimulation that is reinforcing usually also produces the reflex responses of consummatory behavior: eating, ejaculation, sweating, or resting, depending on the control system involved. Whether stimulation acts as a reinforcer is in turn ordinarily modulated by the related need-state of the animal: we have seen that only when the animal is hungry does ventrolateral hypothalamus stimulation—which produces eating behavior—work as a reinforcer. Similar relations often hold for other centers and the need systems they regulate.

We see here, then, the makings of a general homeostasis-maintaining principle. A particular center in the brain is responsible for detecting when a particular need-system is out of balance, and for initiating and organizing responses which will bring that system into equilibrium. A reciprocally related center is responsible for shutting off the system when it has attained its goal. Recognition that the goal is being attained forms the occasion for strengthening responses that led to this biologically desirable result. All of these features and functions of motivational regulation are intimately interrelated and are carried out primarily by the hypothalamus and neighboring deep parts of the brain.

We have made the situation seem quite simple. It most certainly is much more complicated. For one thing, some motivational functions are carried on outside of the hypothalamus. We have already noted that the cerebral cortex exercises important control over emotional reactions; it almost certainly also serves to modulate the functions of the hypothalamus in setting and seeking goals. And there are other structures in the brain, most of them located deep beneath the cortex, that are involved in motivation. For example, there is a structure called the *amygdaloid nucleus*, the destruction of which—in monkeys—also leads to excessive eating. However, it is a different kind of overeating from that caused by damage to the hypothalamus. The animal is not insatiable, but instead is simply very bad at telling which things are food and which aren't. (The monkey without his amygdala may eat first the popcorn, then the bag. He is also bad at telling which things are appropriate sexual objects.) We add this example merely to point out the fact that there are other structures and other complications in motivation. Nonetheless, the hypothalamus and the kinds of mechanisms sketched above occupy the center of the stage in the story of the physiology of motivational control.

LEARNING AND MEMORY

The fact that animals can learn implies that the nervous system can change as a result of experience. Just where and how these changes come about and what they consist of is the question we will consider next.

Where is memory stored?

Perhaps by examining the brains of various animals we could find some structure that intelligent species have and less intelligent species lack. The first attempts along this line produced a clear answer. As the phylogenetic scale progresses, the size of the cerebral cortex gets cor-

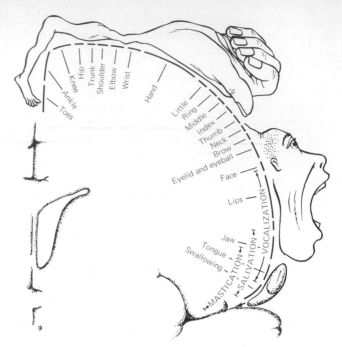

FIGURE 10–22
Motor homunculus, showing regions of the cortex stimulation of which produces movements in various body parts. The relative size of the parts of the body indicate the relative amounts of cortex devoted to them. (After Penfield and Rasmussen, 1952)

respondingly larger and larger. The cortex is almost lacking in primitive vertebrates like alligators. Cats, rats, and dogs have somewhat more cortex, and monkeys, apes, and man a great deal more. The cortex also changes shape, and becomes a much more complicated-looking structure. In man it has become hugely enlarged and occupies a quantitatively preeminent space in the skull. Perhaps, then, the cerebral cortex is the storehouse where memories are kept.

But the role of the cortex in behavior can be studied more directly by experimental stimulation, recording, and ablation, and as we shall see, the picture that emerges is not quite so simple. When the area just in front of the middle of the cortex, the *precentral gyrus* (shown in Figure 10–8), is stimulated, motor movements are often observed. It is possible to map the motor functions of this area by carefully stimulating one point after another and noting which part of the body responds. This has been done in animals. It has also been done in humans, usually as a concomitant of operations to remove diseased parts of the brain; the surgeon needs to verify the function of each part before he begins to remove it. The results are illustrated in Figure 10–22, which shows approximately the part of the body that moves when the corresponding part of the surface of the cerebral cortex is stimulated. If the region of the cortex just behind the central fissure is stimulated in an awake human, a similar diagram can be constructed of the parts of the body in which sensation is felt.

We have already seen that the occipital cortex is involved in the receipt of visual information. There is good spatial correspondence between the location of light-stimulation on the retina and resulting activity on the surface of the brain; stimulation in a certain region of the retina causes activity in a corresponding region of the occipital cortex.

There are a few other cortical regions whose activity is correlated with either actions or sensations, e.g., in the temporal lobes there is a projection area for sounds. But there are also very large "silent" regions where no simple connection to motor or sensory effects can be established. In the human brain these silent areas make up the greater portion of the cortex. The silent areas, like the cortex as a whole, are much larger in the more advanced and more intelligent animals. Since they are so big and seemingly do nothing else, perhaps *these* areas—in particular—are the centers of learning, memory, and thinking. A popular idea has been that these regions might form links between the sensory projection areas and the motor projection areas. Indeed, illustrations in medical texts, some quite recent, often have these regions labeled as "association areas." Unfortunately, however, phylogenetic comparisons and lack of other obvious functions are about the only evidence in favor of this view.

It is now time for the story of Phineas Gage. In 1848, a railroad man by that name made a grievous error in the manipulation of a dynamite charge with a tamping rod. The tamping rod was blasted out of the drill hole and into his head. It left a fairly clean hole through the front of his skull and forehead, taking with it a rather large chunk of frontal "associative" cortex. It is not so miraculous as you might think at first, but Phineas did recover from this insult to his brain tissue. The question of present interest is what this loss of tissue did to the memory and thinking prowess of Phineas Gage. The answer is, very little. He was still able to remember all of the things he had known before and to learn new things. Although there is no evidence that he was ever a great intellect, neither is there evidence of a great change in his capacities. Apparently he became irritable and hard to get along with—but it would be rash to attribute this to more than an understandable displeasure with fate and the railroad company.

Phineas Gage's story is not unique. Many people have lost large portions of cortex through surgery or disease. Pasteur, for example, is said to have had much of the cortex of one hemisphere destroyed by an infection, but he still functioned at quite a high intellectual level. What do such data do to the notion that these tissues are responsible for the highest qualities of human and intelligent activity? They raise some doubts at least.

A more systematic attempt to study the functions of the cortex by removing it was launched by the psychologist, Karl Lashley. Lashley (1950) taught rats to run mazes or make visual discriminations, both before and after removing parts of their brains. He carried out an extensive series of such studies over almost a quarter of a century. The results can be summarized quite clearly. He was never able to find any particular place that was essential to learning or memory; he was never able, having first taught an animal a habit, to find any discrete, small area of the brain whose removal would abolish just that particular habit; and he had to destroy large areas of the cortex before he could obtain any reliable effects at all on either the rat's ability to remember things he had learned prior to the operation, or his ability to learn new things afterward. Lashley formulated a general principle which he called the "law of mass action." This stated that the chance that the removal of cortex would interfere with a previously learned habit depended on the amount of cortex removed, and not where it was removed from. If the whole cortex was removed, habits were usually lost—although there were certain exceptions. If only a small portion of the cortex was removed, there was a correspondingly small chance that the habit would be lost.

Since Lashley, many other investigators have done similar experiments. Brain areas have been found whose presence are essential to certain kinds of behavior, somewhat modifying Lashley's conclusions. But by and large, parts of the cortex appear to be responsible for general functions or duties rather than specific habits or memories. For example, the occipital cortex is necessary for learning discrimination of visual patterns, such as vertical and horizontal stripes. An animal cannot learn such a discrimination after the occipital cortex is removed. But it seems to be the general mechanisms for the analysis of patterns, rather than particular habits, that are localized there.

The major implication of Lashley's work, that particular memories are not stored in particular parts of the cortex, thus remains largely unchallenged. If it is true, what can it mean for our question of where memory is stored? There are several possible answers. First, it may be that memory is not stored in the cortex at all, but in some lower centers, for example the reticular formation. In that case one would look to the cortex for performance of other functions—for example, initial analysis and simplification of information input, putting it into a condensed or abstract form for memory storage. Another possibility is that memory is stored in very small places, and that these places can be anywhere at all in the cortex (or anywhere in the brain for that matter). If this were the case, it would be impossible to destroy a memory by removing brain tissue unless one was either very lucky or removed a large enough area —just what Lashley observed. A third alternative is that the information about a given habit or memory is not stored in just one place but rather in a very large number of different places, as if one were to scatter many different cards for a particular book in various places in a card catalogue. A fourth possibility is that any memory requires the cooperation of the whole cortex. Which, if any, of these alternatives is correct remains to be determined.

Although we do not know where memory is actually stored, we do know something about certain parts of the brain—parts of the cerebral cortex in particular—that perform functions essential to learning and memory. We have already mentioned the analysis of information by the visual system. This analysis is equivalent to "coding" the information, putting it into a storable form. Similar analysis is carried out in other input modalities. And there are more direct memory-forming functions that can be assigned to specific parts of the cortex. The most dramatic example involves the temporal lobes. Studies of many people whose temporal lobes have been removed show that there is invariably a striking deficit following surgery. While such people remember everything they knew before the operation, they may be totally unable to learn anything new for more than short-term retention. They can repeat a newly met person's name, or a newly encountered short series of digits, and they are able to carry on conversations. But having been first introduced to Dr. Smith two minutes ago, provided Dr. Smith has left the room in the meantime, they are totally unable to remember having ever seen him. Similarly, a string of digits, although repeated back perfectly, is not remembered a minute later if attention has shifted in the interim. No new phone numbers, new names of people, or new anything can be committed to long-term memory by a person who lacks temporal lobes.

Another piece of evidence suggests localized functions related to memory in the temporal lobes. Some cases of epilepsy are caused by scar tissue in the cortex. Often it is possible to alleviate the symptoms by removing the affected parts. In performing such operations, it is standard practice to first map the cortex by the electrical stimulation methods described above. This is done to find out where various functions are located so as to be sure not to remove them, and also, frequently, to pinpoint the offending region by actually inducing an epileptic discharge from it. During such mappings (e.g., by Penfield, 1954), a most remarkable thing sometimes occurs. When the stimulating electrode is applied to the surface of the temporal lobe, the patient reports vivid memory-like experiences; sights and sounds run through his head. The experience reportedly has all the qualities of a clear and distinct recollection. When the electrode is reapplied to the same spot, exactly the same "memory" may be evoked again. These findings do not show that memory is stored in the temporal lobe; we know that it certainly is not because the temporal lobes can be removed without old memories being lost. But they do suggest that the temporal lobe is somehow in contact with old memories, at least in the case of long-term epileptic patients. This last remark should be emphasized; in normal individuals no such pehnomenon is observed.

In how many different places can the same memory be stored? No one knows, but there are data to show that the same memory may be stored in at least *two* different places, the two cerebral hemispheres. These data come from studies of animals and men whose brains have been "split" in such a way as to sever the connections between the left and right portions of the cerebral cortex.

In experiments with monkeys (Sperry, 1961), the corpus callosum (the large band of fibers connecting left and right hemispheres of cortex) and most of the other, smaller connecting links were severed. In some such experiments animals were taught habits in which both stimulus and response were restricted to a single hemisphere. One way of doing this is as follows: While both eyes normally send fibers to both the left and the right hemisphere, the optic nerve can be separated at the optic chiasm (see Figure 10–23) so that the left eye communicates only with the left hemisphere and the right eye only with the right hemisphere.

FIGURE 10–23

Representation of monkey brain
surgically split to enable study of
memory storage in one
hemisphere. (After Sperry, 1961;
copyright 1961 by the American
Association for the Advancement
of Science)

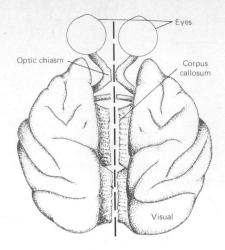

Animals prepared in such a way were first taught to press a panel bearing
a particular visual stimulus—say a triangle as compared to a square—
in order to obtain a raisin. With one eye covered the information went
to only one hemisphere. The response was made by the limb controlled
by that same hemisphere (the right arm if the left hemisphere). When
the animals were tested with the trained eye covered, and the untrained
eye open, they acted as if they had never learned. This shows that the
operation successfully prevents communication between the two hemispheres, and that a single hemisphere is capable of learning and performing the task. Indeed, with the connections between them cut, the two
cerebral hemispheres can learn different things independently; there
are two functional brains in one skull.

In other experiments, animals were first trained with the optic
chiasm cut and one eye covered, but the corpus callosum intact. The
visual information went into just one hemisphere, but connections to
the other were available. After training, the two halves of the brain were
separated surgically, and the animal was tested to see what it could do.
The question: is information put into one side of the brain also stored in
the other side? After the operation, when tested with the eye which
communicates only with the "untrained" hemisphere, will the animal
act as if he has learned or not? The answer is that he acts as if he has
learned—he responds just as well as he would if the corpus callosum and
other communicating fibers had been left intact. It follows that during
the original learning, the same memories were laid down in both sides
of the brain.

What is memory made of and how?

If we cannot pin down exactly where memories are stored in the brain,
perhaps we can at least get some idea of what they are—that is, whether
they are stored in chemical, electrical, or some other form. Some progress
has been made along this line, and we will review the highlights of current intelligence. (We will again introduce some unproven hypotheses as

Psychology:
an overview
306

FIGURE 10–24
Recurrent neural circuit. Once
neural fiber (A) has stimulated
fiber (B), (B) and (C) might
continue to fire indefinitely. (After
Lorente de Nó, 1938)

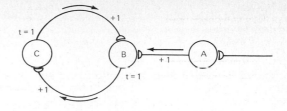

illustrations of the spirit of sought answers.) Before proceeding, let us think briefly about what we are looking for. Essentially, memory must depend on some change in the nervous system that is of a more or less permanent nature. Therefore, we want to find a way in which the nervous system is different long after an experience from the way it was before that experience. The change must be inducible by the kinds of events that are to be remembered, and it must be such that is could actually give rise to different kinds of performance. It is not enough to store information; we must be able to retrieve and use it later.

An analogy may help to clarify the issue. Sound can be recorded as bumps along a groove in a record or as variations of magnetization on a tape. In both cases there is a physical mechanism which does the recording—puts bumps on the record or magnetizes the tape—and another mechanism that later turns these stored representations into music. The recording function is analogous to learning, the playing function to retrieval of memories. The bumps or magnetic variations are the medium of information storage. We wish to know what is the medium of information storage in the brain.

One natural hypothesis is that perhaps the same form in which neural information is transmitted along neurons is also used for its storage. Look at the neural circuit diagram in Figure 10–24. Here we see one fiber making a synapse with a second fiber which in turn makes a synapse with the first. With all thresholds properly arranged as they are in the figure, once one of them fires, the two will continue to excite each other in a never-ending, nose-to-tail cycle.

Self-perpetuating or recurrent circuits like this have been used in some computers to act as memory stores. The fact that such a circuit is active means that it has at some time in the animal's or machine's past received an input; if that input were the result of a complex processing of information, the activity would then stand for the fact that the animal had experienced some important event. The microscope has actually revealed arrangements of neurons in such feedback loop patterns in animals (Lorente de Nó, 1938).

The great appeal of the idea of recurrent circuits as the storage medium for the nervous system is that it does not require any new properties to be discovered; it relies only on what we already know about impulses, transmission, and synapses. However, there is quite good evidence that this is not the medium used by the nervous system. One can interfere with the electrical activity of the brain in a number of different ways without altering long-held memories. The impulse activity of the cortex, and of most of the lower centers as well, can be reduced to a very low level by certain drugs, and can be almost abolished by cooling the brain to very low temperatures; or it can be greatly disorganized by still other drugs, or by the application of massive electrical influences, as in shock therapy. None of these rather drastic changes in neural activity has ever been found to have appreciable effects on the memory of old, well-learned habits (although, as we will see below, most of them can have detrimental effects on recently acquired memories). If memories were stored as recirculating neural impulses, one or another, if not all, of these manipulations would certainly disrupt them.

Such evidence leads us to infer that memories are probably stored in a more permanent, physical representation. Several possibilities for the nature of this change in the structure of the nervous system have been proposed. It could be that neural activity during a learning experience could stimulate actual growth of nerve fibers. The points at which synapses occur are marked by swellings or knobs on the fine endings of the axons. Enlargement at this region might bring the axons and dendrites closer together and thus make it easier thereafter for an impulse coming down an axon to initiate an impulse in the next dendrite.

This is one form of a more general hypothesis that memory is represented by a lasting change in "synaptic resistance," the difficulty of transmission across synapses. Change in synaptic resistance could, of course, come about in other ways, which gives rise to other theories of the nature of the memory trace. Some recent proposals have involved the biochemistry of the cells involved. The transmission of an impulse across the synapse, as we have already noted, depends on the release of a transmitter substance by one cell and the substance's action on the next cell. Either of these two processes could be altered by changing something that goes on in the space between the two cells. For instance, if the concentration of the enzyme that breaks down the transmitter substance after it has been released into the juncture between the two cells were increased, then the time between one impulse and the next could be changed. Or the chemical reaction by which the recipient cell generates its spike potential could be made more sensitive by a change in the concentration of enzymes there.

There are a large number of such possibilities which depend on some sort of lasting change in chemical synthesizing machinery within cells. The synthesis of all biochemicals is controlled by the genetic material of a cell, the large molecules of nucleic acids found primarily in the nucleus. These large molecules are known to act as the blueprints and messengers which guide the formation of proteins (including enzymes) and other components. It is likely (though not necessary), therefore, that any very long-lasting change in the sensitivity of a cell would have to be related to changes in the structure of these nucleic acid molecules. For this reason a great deal of attention has been focused on their possible role in the storage of memory.

These ideas as to just how a change in biochemistry could be responsible for memory have so far been merely conjectural, and quite far from substantiation by data. But there are some related findings that make the case at least somewhat plausible. There are large changes in the concentration of RNA in neurons that are stimulated in the course of learning, and in their surrounding glial cells as well (Hydén & Egyházi, 1963). In the experiment of Hydén and Egyházi, rats were trained to climb a rope to get food. There was an increase and a change in the average type of RNA in certain special cells known to be involved in the performance of this habit. Other experiments have shown that drugs that can inhibit the synthesis of RNA or of proteins sometimes inhibit learning. What such experiments suggest, but do not prove, is that changes in RNA are related to the laying down of memory traces. However, it must be kept in mind that RNA is involved in some way or another in almost all important metabolic processes within cells, and its specific role in learning is yet to be established.

This summarizes current knowledge of what substance, on a cellular, biochemical, or mechanical level, memory consists of. Essentially, we have some promising leads and ideas about what kinds of structures and processes may be involved.

The next question we may ask is what processes, on a neurological level, are necessary and sufficient to induce the unknown changes in cells which form the record of memory. Is it necessary to stimulate some kinds of cells in some special way in order to make the permanent changes happen? We have already mentioned a few facts related to this matter. Reinforcement can be mimicked by direct electrical stimulation of certain parts of the brain. In all probability these same areas, the hypothalamus and neighboring points, are involved in natural reinforcement as well. Reinforcement is, of course, intimately related to many kinds of learning, and structures that give rise to reinforcement are very likely involved somehow in the laying down or activation of memory. It has been hypothesized (Landauer, 1969; Pfaff, 1969) that changes initiated by reinforcement cause the brain to repeat the critical series of neural events which were the result of a just-prior experience, and thus make a firmer trace.

Another interesting aspect of the process of memory formation concerns the relation between the form in which information comes into the nervous system and the form in which it is stored. We have already shown why long-term storage must be in structural changes. But we also know that information comes into the brain as evanescent electrochemical impulses along nerve fibers. There must be some transition between these two forms of information. A popular notion of the nature of this transition was described early and well by Hebb (1949). Hebb postulated that information coming into the nervous system is first stored in an active form, in reverberating circuits such as that shown in Figure 10–24. These circuits presumably remain active for a certain amount of time after an experience and constitute a first, active form of memory trace. This very activity of impulses running round and round was supposed to stimulate changes in synapses (Hebb proposed that there might be a swelling of synaptic end bulbs). Such a theory implies that there is a time after an experience during which memory is being "consolidated." Evidence in favor of the consolidation hypothesis has come from experiments in which a disruptive influence is applied to the nervous system after a learning trial. There appears to be a short period during which memory is unusually easy to disrupt. The disruptive influences that have been used include electroconvulsive shock, which makes a muddle of normal brain activity; the application of drugs that cause convulsions, or of others that slow brain function; and cooling to temperatures inconsistent with normal neural activity. All of these have been shown to decrease learning if they are applied within about five to ten seconds after a learning trial, but have little or no effect on old memories. These findings suggest that the changes in nervous tissue which constitute learning take some time to be accomplished after the to-be-remembered experience is over.

In summary, while we are still far from real understanding of what happens in the brain when learning occurs, there are a lot of things about the process which we do know and which are providing direction for future research.

CONSCIOUSNESS AND SPEECH

It is very difficult to study the role of brain structures in speech and consciousness, since speech and introspective reports are special to humans and their living brains are not available for experimental study. Nonetheless, some interesting facts are known, primarily from the results of pathology and from observation of the effects of medical interventions. For example, if the activity of the whole cortex is seriously depressed by the use of drugs or cooling, consciousness is lost. In the same way, consciousness can be localized within the cortex to some extent. For most people, if only the right side of the cortex is put to sleep by an anesthetic, conscious awareness remains, while it is lost if only the left side is depressed. The left cortex controls the dominant hand in right-handed people, and also contains centers required for comprehension and production of speech. The region required for speech production is called Broca's area. If this region is removed or damaged, speech is impossible. It may not be a coincidence that speech and control of the dominant hand have their centers in the side of the cortex that is required for consciousness.

From time to time it has become desirable to separate the two halves of a human brain, as, for example, in some cases of severe epilepsy. A number of such cases have been studied. The same localizations of memory are observed in humans as in experimental animals; after the split, things learned on one side are not transferred to the other. An interesting sidelight on these cases concerns conscious awareness and speech mechanisms. The nonspeech side of the cortex in such individuals is extremely limited in its ability to interpret and act on signals that are coded in terms of language, while the side in which the person's speech center is located can still function normally in this way. The nonspeech side of the cortex is still perfectly capable of learning new habits and of carrying out quite complicated responses. It can even subserve responses based on simple language-like signals; for example, if the word *spoon* is presented to the part of the eye which connects to the nonspeech hemisphere, and the person is required to point to the object named with the hand controlled by the same hemisphere, he can do so perfectly well. But he cannot *say* the word *spoon;* and if one later asks, by presenting the object or the word to the part of the eye that connects with the other hemisphere, whether he has seen it before or not, he will respond that he has not. In a split-brain human, the side of the cortex which contains the speech center can perform mental arithmetic and other conscious thought processes, but the other side cannot. Such findings point to the conclusion that, for any one person, speech and related conscious symbolic activities are, in fact, carried out primarily in one of the two cortical hemispheres (Sperry, 1961; Gazzaniga, Bogen, & Sperry, 1965).

This completes our survey of how the nervous system works in the production of behavior. Obviously, much is still unknown. But understanding such questions does now appear to be a possible goal; within the next few decades it will, one hopes, be possible to outline the function of the brain in visual perception or in control of eating, much as we can now outline the function of the heart in blood circulation.

TOPICS DISCUSSED IN CHAPTER 10

1. The anatomy of a neuron, and the nature of resting and action potentials.

2. Transfer and combination of information at synapses.

3. The divisions and parts of the nervous system: the central and peripheral systems, the autonomic systems.

4. The structure and parts of the brain: the lobes of the cerebral cortex, the thalamus, hypothalamus, corpus callosum, and optic chiasm.

5. Transduction in the auditory system: the representation of sound energy as nerve impulses.

6. Perceptual processing and analysis in the visual system, extracting information from receptor messages—line detectors and other "analyzer cells."

7. The locus of control of motivational behavior, activity, consumption, satiation, and reinforcement.

8. The determinants, nature, and locus of changes in the nervous system during learning.

9. The locus of functions underlying speech and consciousness.

SUGGESTED READINGS

1. *There are several reasonably up-to-date textbooks on physiological psychology. A good one is:*

Thompson, R. F. *Foundations of physiological psychology.* New York: Harper & Row, 1967.

2. *An interesting, short paperback is:*

Woolridge, D. E. *The machinery of the brain.* New York: McGraw-Hill, 1963.

3. *And a collection of original journal articles covering much of the material presented here is:*

Landauer, T. K. (Ed.) *Readings in physiological psychology: the bodily basis of behavior.* New York: McGraw-Hill, 1967.

ELEVEN

Psychological research: an appendix on experimental method and statistics

EXPERIMENTAL METHOD

EXPERIMENTAL DESIGN
Equalizing
Counterbalancing
Randomizing

STATISTICS
Descriptive statistics
Inferential statistics
The experimental attitude

For the most part, this book presents psychological knowledge as established fact. It does so primarily by leaving out topics on which no scientific agreement has been reached, partly by omitting topics of less than central importance, and partly by ignoring minority opinions. This has the virtue among others, of keeping the book short, but also the disadvantage of underrepresenting the degree of doubt and controversy in the field. More important, it fails to give an adequate picture of ways in which questions of psychological fact are answered. The book's approach is predicated on the assumption that it will usually be supplemented by other reading or classwork in which one or more topics are examined in greater depth, and that deep study of a limited area is a more appropriate context in which to encounter details of scientific argument. Nonetheless, there are certain general principles of enquiry in psychology which (1) lie behind the knowledge presented here, (2) will help the student to read in the field with greater understanding, and (3) should be interesting in their own right to anyone who is curious about behavior.

This section of the book presents certain rudiments of the logic and methods of psychological research. It may be read either as the last chapter of the book—as a prologue to further work in the field—or at any other point when the student needs to know something about the technical tools of the trade. It presents only as much about experimental design, experimental method, and statistics as should be needed to understand original research reports.

EXPERIMENTAL METHOD

Psychologists frequently claim that their research is particularly hard to do. Psychological research *is* difficult, for at least two sets of reasons. The first set of reasons contains the unavoidable *objective* difficulties in the materials to be studied. For one thing, most of the important practical problems of psychology involve behavior that is complexly determined. The causes of schizophrenia, for example, or the determinants of superior creativity will probably not be found in a single event in a person's life, but rather will turn out to involve many complexly interrelated factors. Another objective difficulty stems from the fact that behavior is intrinsically and necessarily variable. Variation is not just an accident in behavior; it is one of its most important and useful features. In this chapter we shall consider some of the ways in which the complexity, and more especially the perverse instability, of behavior can be dealt with in research.

But a second set of problems in psychological research has proved to be much harder to overcome, because these problems are more *subjective*. The crux of this second kind of problem is that people don't realize how difficult it is to discover psychological truth. Psychology, we are all tempted to reason, is just the study of the way people behave, and since we're people ourselves, we must know a great deal about it already. This may be called the "personal wisdom fallacy." It results in our all having extraordinarily firm intuitions about things psychological —about how thought proceeds, about what events in a person's life change his character, about what is the best way to study, and so on. Even if such intuitions were accurate, which most of them are not, they would make the business of studying behavior harder, not easier. Psychology, as a scientific endeavor, needs answers that are dependable on the basis of an objective, unbiased reading of the evidence.

When a researcher has strong beliefs about the truth before he looks at the evidence, it is terribly easy for him to fool himself. In several experiments college students have been asked to administer electric shocks to other human beings. When college students are asked to predict what they would do in such an experiment, they are close to unanimous in saying that they would not give painful or dangerous shocks. Yet research has shown over and over again that when they are actually placed in such a situation almost all college students *do* administer shocks they believe to be painful and dangerous.

Our intuitions and insights about our own behavior and that of others, no matter how strongly felt, are objectively quite unreliable. If one needs witness to this fact, the dismal failure of people to cure their personal and social ills over the millennia should make the point. We do *not* understand one another, we do *not* understand ourselves, we do *not* know how best to think, learn, teach, or persuade; we know next to nothing about how to cure mental disorders or set the social world in order.

One cause of the personal wisdom fallacy is that almost every kind of behavior is familiar to us, if only because behavior is so variable.

We've done this and we've seen that. Therefore, when an experimenter tells us his results, we are rarely very surprised. Since we are not too surprised, we can easily forget that we would not have been too surprised by the opposite result either, and we can say "I knew that all along."

The danger of the fallacy of personal wisdom, then, is that it leads to sloppy thinking about matters psychological. It leads us to substitute intuition for research. It tempts us into accepting data that are inconclusive. It beguiles us into relying on impression rather than on accurately recorded and clearly analyzed observations. If a man is asked whether his wife is more miserable on Mondays than on other days of the week, he is likely to simply mull over his recent experience and think "Hmmm, yes, she is unhappy on Mondays." But it is almost certain that such an impression is based on the recollection of only a few isolated events, and is unreliable to the point of sheer silliness. When asking psychological questions it is essential to be tough-minded. If you really want to know whether your wife is sad on Mondays, then on every day of the week you must ask her in a standardized way whether she is sad or happy, and you must continue to do so for many many weeks.

How do we overcome difficulties that inevitably confront us in studying behavior, and how do we force ourselves to stay tough-minded and skeptical about the subject matter? The answers, of course, are as varied as the ingenuity of investigators. But there are a few general principles.

In dealing with the problem of the complexity and multiplicity of causes (the determinants of schizophrenia or the mechanisms of memory, for example) the first and most important remedy is an old and honored scientific strategy—to simplify. It has almost never proved possible in science to study important problems whole and raw. Real, relevant problems are almost always impossibly difficult, impossibly large in scope, and impossibly complicated in nature. To circumvent this difficulty, the scientist doesn't study "real" problems. Instead he picks some small part of a problem that he thinks he can manage, even though it seems to those about him (and sometimes to himself) that he is studying near-trivia. The hope, sometimes the success, of the method is that by learning a little more about one part and then a little more about another part, either the original problem or some related problem will become soluble.

Thus in studying memory the greatest advances have come from attacking only a tiny corner of the problem. For example, the most advanced knowledge we have in this field concerns not memory as a whole or anything approaching "how to remember better," but rather the process by which one can recall whether a single digit is or is not a member of a set of one to six digits previously memorized. (For example, in the set 7, 2, 1, 6, 3, 4 is there a 6?). This would seem to be an intuitively obvious process; introspection tells most people that they say the numbers to themselves until they find the one they are searching for, and then stop. To find out more about the process might seem superfluous, but nothing could be farther from the truth. First of all the process is nothing like what introspection tells us. In fact, a particular digit is found in a memorized set by a process that always involves a search through all the remembered digits, no matter what the position of the target digit, at a rate at least five times faster than that at which a person can consciously think digits to himself. A very clear and conclusive exposition of how this process works has in turn led to great strides in understanding how the recognition of digits and letters occurs (Sternberg, 1966, 1967).

To overcome the "personal wisdom fallacy" we need objectification in research. Objectification takes different forms, some more obvious than others. An obvious form involves the keeping of careful records, the immediate recording of observations; uniform and unambiguous, reliable and valid quantification techniques; checks, replications, and constant caution. Psychological variables can often be quantified by such simple procedures as interview schedules that make sure that the same questions are always asked; by standardized tests, some of which we have discussed and some of which the reader has taken; and by observations which are made in a systematic fashion that leads to reliability and validity. As we saw in Chapter 1, no datum is of any use to us if it isn't reliable—if it can't be observed the same way twice. It is sometimes surprisingly hard to get reliable data in psychological observations. If you were to have three people independently decide whether a common friend were happy or sad each morning at ten o'clock for a week, you would be appalled at the lack of agreement.

It is remarkable how much can be learned about behavior by simply writing down things carefully and then counting results. What this usually does is rob us of our pet ideas, but that is often a great advance toward understanding. A favorite trick of psychologists is to apply this technique to people's claims of taste sensitivity. The author of this book tried for many years to persuade his wife to buy an expensive brand of coffee. She had heard him talk about the need for tough-mindedness in psychology so often that she decided to turn the breakfast tables on him. She used a random-digit table to decide which coffee to use on what morning, the expensive brand or whatever happened to be on sale at the supermarket. After several months of this unfeeling treatment, I was convinced that my fancy-coffee money was better off in the bank, since the recorded data did not support my strong belief that I could tell the difference.

Another matter of great importance in getting tough with psychological data concerns *experimenter bias*. It has been demonstrated beyond any reasonable doubt that the outcome of an experiment can be and usually is influenced by the bias of the person who conducts it or analyzes the data. In one study (Rosenthal, 1964), members of a psychology class were given rats to train in a standard laboratory performance. Some of them were told that their rats were bright, others that their rats were dull. In reality all the rats were drawn randomly from the same batch of littermates. Nevertheless, the "smart" rats outperformed the "dumb" rats.

The same kind of experiment has been repeated over and over again in almost every context of psychological investigation, with similar results. One reason, among many, is that when a person counts or tabulates results, errors always creep in—and they are predominantly in favor of the hypothesis held by the person doing the data analysis. This is not usually outright cheating; it is simply what happens. One way it can happen is exemplified as follows. You are trying to find out whether a certain drug has a particular effect on peoples' perception of the loudness of music. From your own experience you are absolutely sure that the drug makes music sound louder. You administer it to ten people and give another ten a placebo (something which, when taken, is indistinguishable from the drug but is inactive). You have each person record his judgment of the loudness of the same musical performance. If, in analyzing the data, the average of the judgments is higher for the drugged group, you heave a sigh of gratification and write up your report. But if it turns out that the average of the judgments of those who took placebos is louder, you will think you have made a mistake. You will check to see if you got the two groups mixed up, to see if you made any mistakes in adding, and so forth. Now this doesn't mean you have cheated, but it does mean that if you happen to make errors—and who doesn't?—the chances of your assiduously tracking them down are greater if the outcome contradicts your prior belief than if it confirms it. Therefore, in all research it is essential to use procedures that preclude the possibility of *any* errors in tabulation or adding.

To escape the possibility of bias earlier in an experiment it is important to use features that keep the experimenter and subject "blind" to what is going on. For example, in our drug experiment, it is essential that neither the person administering the drug nor the subjects themselves know whether they are getting the drug or the placebo. If the experimenter knew, he might unconsciously communicate in some subtle way to the subject what he wanted him to do. If a subject knew, he would be strongly tempted (consciously or otherwise) to behave in a way consistent with how he thought the drug should act. Neither of these things is what we want to study. We want to find out what the drug actually does, not what the experimenter or the subject thinks it should do. The goal of "double blindness" is sometimes very hard to accomplish in psychological experiments. But the trustworthiness of data derived from double-blind procedures is so much greater than that derived in any less rigorously controlled way that it is worth a tremendous amount of bother.

EXPERIMENTAL DESIGN

Now we turn to the matter of dealing with variability in behavior. There are two ways in which psychologists cope with it. One is by the way they set up their experiments; the other is by the way they analyze their data. In this section we discuss experimental design; in the next, data analysis. The important thing in designing an experiment is to make sure that every outcome of interest has a fair and equal chance of occurring. There are several techniques that can help, the most common and useful being *equalizing*, *counterbalancing*, and *randomizing*.

Equalizing

If you want to find out whether it is better to study French vocabulary words by reciting them out loud or silently, you do not want to have the best students in the class do it one way and the worst students do it the other way. You don't want to have students learning by one method study in a hot uncomfortable room late in the day, and the others study in a comfortable room early in the day. Rather, you want the test made fair by having everything but the difference to be compared as nearly equal as possible.

Counterbalancing

Say you want to find out whether drinking coffee or tea is best before driving. You have one driving-simulator apparatus in which you can test two subjects a day, one in the morning and one in the afternoon. But it is just possible that the time of day may affect driving ability. Therefore, it is critically important to avoid testing all the tea subjects in the morning and all the coffee subjects in the afternoon. Otherwise you won't be able to tell whether it is the difference between morning and afternoon or the difference between coffee and tea that causes your results. This problem can be solved easily by testing half the tea subjects in the morning and half in the afternoon, and doing likewise with the coffee drinkers. The time when the test is given may still influence performance, but it can't affect the *average* difference between the coffee and tea groups. Such a design feature is called *counterbalancing*. The general principle is as follows: Try to make sure that the things which must vary in an experiment vary as often in favor of any one of the experimental conditions being studied as they do in favor of any other.

Randomization

A still more important principle and technique is that of *randomization*. If you want to discover which of two methods leads to the most rapid learning, you are faced with the obvious fact that different people learn at different rates, and that even the same person learns at different rates at different times depending on his mood, his motivation, how tired he is, and so on. What is worse, you have no way of knowing at any given moment which of such factors are affecting a particular person. You don't know if he is more alert than usual, whether he has a headache, whether you picked something for him to learn that he finds unusually hard or easy. Furthermore, any number of uncontrolled or uncontrollable things can happen during an experimental session—someone may cough, the sun may go behind a cloud, a pencil may break. You can't possibly equalize or counterbalance for every influence on learning, if only because most of them are unknown. The only way around this problem of bias from unknown or uncontrollable factors is to randomly assign subjects and sessions to the various experimental conditions being studied. Which experimental condition (for instance which of three methods of study) is tried with which subject, during which hour, and so forth must be made to be only a matter of chance.

Randomization, then, means the use of some method that ensures that any particular subject (or other factor) has an equal chance of falling into one experimental group or another. We want the assignment of subjects to conditions to be determined by nothing but the laws of chance. We might do this by flipping a coin; heads the subject is in one group, tails in the other. Or we could get a computer to generate random numbers, and assign a subject to one group if his number is odd, to the other if even. The great advantage of randomization is that the subjects are assigned to the tea group or the coffee group (or to whatever groups are necessary for the comparison you are interested in) in a way that couldn't possibly be correlated with anything that would make them perform better or worse. Therefore, if you found that people in one group performed better than those in the other, the only difference between the two groups that could be other than a chance difference would be the one that you imposed—in this case, the drinking of coffee or tea before performing on the simulated driving test.

Note that there will always be differences between two randomly constituted groups. But the amount of difference is determined solely by irrelevant chance. And since there are good ways of estimating how much difference to expect from chance events, we can compare the outcome of a randomized experiment with these estimates and get a good idea of whether an experimental variable is or is not adding anything to the outcome.

The principle of randomization is extremely important in psychological research. The essential problem with which randomization deals is that of inferring causation from correlation. That two things, A and B, always occur together does not prove that one causes the other. You may have noticed that subway trains (B) usually come soon if there are a lot of people on the platform (A). You would not conclude that bringing a crowd into the station would cause the train to appear. Yet, we are often guilty of this hoary logical fallacy (it's been around so long it even has a Latin name, *post hoc ergo propter hoc*), particularly when we draw conclusions about behavior. The fact that almost all heroin users have previously used marijuana is frequently offered as proof that one leads to the other. To get around this problem, a way is needed to ensure that the reason why variable A occurs in the first place is totally unrelated to variable B. Then if B always follows A, A must have caused B. This is where randomization comes in.

Let us take one more example. You want to find out whether massed or spaced practice helps most in studying lists of French words. Say you go to a classroom and find those students who did all of their studying in one sitting and those who spread their practice out, and give them a test. If you found that one group did better, would this allow you to conclude that one kind of practice was better than the other? The answer is a resounding *No*. The reason is that you could not be sure that the method of study was the only relevant variable. It might be that massed studying was used by students who were busiest with extracurricular activities, and that such students are on the average more talented. Anyone can think of other ways in which students who study one way or another might differ. You could conclude essentially nothing about the effectiveness of study methods by finding people who used one or another and comparing their results. To demonstrate a causal relation, you would have to be sure that the study method each subject used had been assigned in an arbitrary way that could not be connected to anything else about him. The only way one can really be sure of such a thing is to use a random process to arbitrarily assign experimental treatments—in this case, to arbitrarily decide which students would use which study method.

It cannot be stressed too heavily that there is no way of assessing causation except through an experiment in which the presumably causative conditions are assigned randomly. Causation simply cannot be inferred unless one knows exactly what was different between two groups. Random assignment has the beauty that the experimenter knows exactly how likely it is that *anything* other than the variable in question has occurred in conjunction with it. Let us pursue this assertion a little further. Suppose that in your experiment on the learning of French words you assign subjects to massed and spaced practice groups by flipping a fair coin: heads massed, tails spaced. What is the chance that a subject of above-average intelligence will get into the massed group? It is just the probability that when a person with greater than average intelligence comes along the coin comes up heads. Since we know that the chance of a head occurring is 0.5, then we know that the chance of a person of more than average intelligence getting into the massed practice group is also 0.5. Similar logic will hold for *any* other attribute of a person being assigned to the experiment. The chance of any attribute's going into one group rather than the other is 0.5. Thus, using a fair coin ensures that, at least on the average, the two groups will be equivalent not just in the few traits that one could think of and equalize, but in *all* the relevant characteristics that could possibly exist.

Moreover, the randomization procedure has an extra benefit. Of course we won't be so lucky as to have all the people with above-average intelligence perfectly evenly divided between our massed-practice and our spaced-practice groups. (When you flip a coin 100 times you rarely get exactly 50 heads and 50 tails. Sometimes you get 48 heads and 52 tails, sometimes 57 heads and 43 tails, and so forth.) But statistical theory tells us exactly how much departure from "ideal chance" we should expect on any difference between people in the two groups. If we measure people after the experiment and see how different the two groups are, and how spread out each group is, the statistical methods outlined in the next section allow us to compare our results with what was likely to have happened by chance. This is a powerful method, and one that is an absolutely necessary part of any valid psychological investigation.

STATISTICS

In some kinds of data, the variation between two measurements of the same thing is so small that it can safely be ignored. One careful measurement of the distance from Philadelphia to Hoboken should produce a sufficiently trustworthy result for many purposes. But there are other kinds of data in which measurement errors are much larger. Some of the classic examples come from agriculture. You want to know whether one fertilizer is better than another, so you do an experiment: twenty plots of kale are covered with cow manure, while another twenty are spread with fertilizer X. You would not expect all the former to grow exactly 112 bushels of kale apiece, and each of the latter to grow exactly 100. What you would expect and find is that one plot would yield, say, 100 bushels, another would yield 140, another 110, and so on. What in the world would you do with such data? The art of counting, summarizing, and making sense out of information about things that are countable but variable and otherwise confusing is called *statistics*.

There are two major branches of statistics with which we will be concerned here. One has to do with the description and summary of variable data, the other with analyzing and making inferences about what they mean. We encounter the first kind, *descriptive* statistics, in many places in this book: in such notions as the "average person"; in the frequency distribution used to describe the various levels of intelligence in the population; and in indexes of association between two variables, such as the correlation coefficient used to describe the association between different personality traits. (The frequency distribution and the correlation coefficient will be discussed below.)

We have less occasion to use *inferential* statistics in this book, although discovery of the knowledge summarized here depended heavily on it. If one wants to read original reports of those discoveries, some understanding of the statistics of inference is indispensable.

Descriptive statistics

Behavior is *intrinsically* variable; it is not just measurement error that causes psychologists to encounter variable data so often. To be adaptive, behavior must change continually. New forms must occur so that better ways to meet the demands of the environment can be selected by reinforcement. Nature—for which read evolution—has made variability one of the fundamental characteristics of behavior. Therefore, if we want to see the effect of any factor which might be influencing behavior, we must have methods that allow us to see through the variability all behavior exhibits. Statistics provides such methods.

We shall not attempt anything like a thoroughgoing introduction to statistics in this book. The subject is too important for a cursory treatment, which is all that could be accomplished here. Rather, what follows is a short lesson in what might best be called "statistical literacy." It should enable the student to comprehend the special symbols and notations found in journal articles and give him some understanding of the ideas behind the methods, without teaching him how to work many formulas or solve many problems.

Let us begin by considering a set of numbers that might have come from a study that has to do with behavior. Say we want to study love among men of the (fictional) Mbongo-Mbongo tribe. The first thing we decide is that we can't study all the Mbongo-Mbongo men; there are

TABLE 11–1 (a)
Love-life of the men of Mbongo-Mbongo

Name	Number of cows	Number of wives
Mwangi	1	0
Maruga	4	3
Kamau	6	1
Okoko	2	1.5
Kariuki	8	7

too many of them. So we decide to study only five, whom we randomly select. Figuring that love is most clearly represented in the relationship between a man and his wife and cows, we count for each man the number of each. Table 11–1(a) shows the data. Now, what can we say about these data? How many wives and how many cows do Mbongo-Mbongo men have? Do they have more cows than wives? Do men with more cows have more wives than men with fewer cows?

Let us take these questions one at a time. How many cows do Mbongo-Mbongo men have: To start with, how many cows do the five men in our *sample* have? One answer is that they have 1, 4, 6, 2, and 8 cows, but this isn't very satisfactory because it takes too long to say. It would be better to find a single number that represents all five men fairly well. Such a number is called an *average*. An average is something that tells us the *central tendency* of a set of numbers, that is, some center around which one can imagine all of the rest of the numbers falling. One kind of average would be the number of cows that divides the group in such a manner that we could say "Half the Mbongo-Mbongo men have fewer than x cows and half have more." In Table 11–1 that number would be 4. Half the men have fewer than 4 cows, and half have more. This number is called the *median*. What is the median number of wives that the Mbongo-Mbongo men have? Another average is the common average, or arithmetic mean (see Chapter 1); the mean number of cows owned by Mbongo-Mgongo men is 4.2. What is the mean number of wives?

We can be a little more sophisticated about the meaning of *median* and *mean*. The median is that number which minimizes the sum of the absolute differences between it and all the numbers in our set. The absolute differences between 4 and the five numbers in the set are 3, 2, 2, and 4, respectively, the sum of which is 11. There is no other number that would give a lower sum. The mean does something similar, but what it minimizes is not the sum of the absolute numbers but the sum of the squared differences between the mean and all the numbers. The differences between 4.2 and the numbers of cows are -3.2, -0.2, $+1.8$, -2.2, and $+3.8$. These differences squared are 10.24, 0.4, 3.24, 4.84, and 14.44, of which the sum is 32.80. [Look at Table 11-1(b)]. You could not find any other number which would yield a lower sum of squared differences.

Our confidence in the accuracy of the mean (or other measure of

TABLE 11-1 (b)
Love-life of the men of Mbongo-Mbongo (with some
numbers related to statistical manipulations described
in the text)

Name	Number of cows	Deviations from mean (cows)	Squared deviations (cows)
Mwangi	1	−3.2	10.24
Maruga	4	−0.2	.04
Kamau	6	+1.8	3.24
Okoko	2	−2.2	4.84
Kariuki	8	+3.8	14.44
Σ X (sum)	21	0	32.80
Median	4		
x (mean = $\frac{\Sigma X}{N}$)	4.2		6.56
Range	7		
S.D. (standard deviation)	2.56		

central tendency) of a sample as a reflection of what is going on in the population from which that sample was drawn depends on how big the sample is. If we want to know the average income in California, we would place more faith in the results obtained by polling 1,000 people than in the results obtained by polling only 10. To understand just why this is, we must consider another notion, the *variability of means.* Any set of numbers has a measurable amount of variability. If we take six successive random samples of 10 and find the mean of each, we get a set of six new numbers, and we can then consider the variation in them. It turns out that the expected variation of the means (as measured by an index called a *standard deviation,* which will be described below) is inversely proportional to the square root of the size of the samples. This is an important relation. If you want to increase by a certain amount the accuracy of an estimate from a sample, you have to increase the size of the sample by more than a proportional amount. For example, to double the accuracy—that is, to halve the variability of the means—you need to quadruple the size of the sample (the square root of 4 is 2, the square root of 16 is 4, etc.).

Even more important than sample size in getting an accurate estimate of a population value is the way in which the sample is drawn. A sample properly represents the population from which it is drawn if and only if any datum in it *could with equal likelihood have been* any datum in the whole population. If, in estimating the average income of people in California, we choose a sample that happens to take in a higher proportion of people from rural areas than there are proportionately in the population at large, the sample will be inaccurate, and our estimate of the statewide average income will likewise be inaccurate. The only way to ensure against this kind of error is to be certain that the sample is truly random, that any member of the population has an equal chance of appearing in the sample. Statistical tests, that is, methods of making inferences from variable data, are based on theories of chance which assume absolute randomness; they are of no help to us if we compromise on randomization.

These are good methods for describing the central tendency of a set of data. But there are other things of interest to be described. For example, as we have already noted in Chapter 1, an interesting aspect of a set of numbers is its *spread*, or variability. In Chapter 1 we used one measure of this variability, the *range*, which is the difference between the largest and the smallest measurement. Another, somewhat better description of variability is based on the notion of squared deviations, which we have just met. While we could simply add up the difference from the mean of each observation and call the sum an index of the amount of spread in the sample, there are several reasons why squaring these differences before adding them gives a better index. One reason is that the sum of the squared deviations from the average is the number that is minimized by the common average or arithmetic mean, as we have just seen. We get a mutually consistent set of numbers if, along with the mean, we use an index of spread that is also based on squared deviations, i.e., a measure of just what that minimum sum of squared deviations is. The other reasons have to do with variables that are important in many theories of how numbers disport themselves by chance. In order to compare actual data with expectations from these theories we need to describe sets of numbers in the same way these theories do.

The most commonly employed measure of variation, the standard deviation, is not simply the sum of the squared deviations, although the two measures are directly related. Such a sum would vary with the number of observations in the sample, in the same way that the sum of all the numbers of cows would vary with the number of Mbongo-Mbongo men. We usually want to express such numbers in a way that takes into account the number of cases. Just as we divide by the number of cases to get the mean, so with the index of variability we divide the sum of the squared deviations by the number of cases. The resulting number is the mean squared deviation (also called the *variance*). The mean squared deviation of cows in Table 11–1 is obtained as follows: the sum of the squared deviations, 32.80, which was obtained earlier, is divided by 5, the number of cases, yielding 6.56.

But most of us don't find it very natural to think about squared numbers. So, finally, to get back to numbers like the ones we started with, we take the square root ($= 2.56$). The square root of the mean squared deviation is called the *standard deviation* (SD, or σ). This measure is calculated by the formula:

$$SD = \sqrt{\frac{\Sigma \ (x - \bar{x})^2}{N}}$$

Σ = sum of

x = each individual number or score

$\bar{x}$ = arithmetic mean

N = number of cases

from which the meaning of *standard deviation* ought to be clear enough: The deviation is the difference between an observation and the mean. An average deviation would be a simple average, or mean, of all of these deviations. A standard deviation is simply a standard way of getting a somewhat better number to represent the same thing; it is obtained by first squaring the numbers representing the deviations, then averaging them, and finally taking the square root of the result.

Related to the standard deviation is a way of transforming data. Recall now our discussion of measurement problems in Chapter 1, in particular the way in which numbers that started out on different scales were brought into line for comparison. There, you will remember, we used a transformation in which we divided each deviation score by the range of all the scores. We used the range as a base by which to adjust for the differing variability or different measurements. A similar, and for most purposes better, transformation is achieved by using a better measure of the variability, namely the standard deviation. If each deviation score is divided by the standard deviation of the set of scores, we get a new number, a transformed number, which is called a *z score*. The *z* scores for the numbers in Table 11–1 are shown in Table 11–2. This kind of transformed score, which is sometimes also called a *normal score* or *normal deviate*, is widely used in statistics and often met in psychological research.

TABLE 11–2
Love-life (number of cows) in Mbongo-Mbongo transformed to normal deviates (z scores)

Name	Raw score	Deviation from mean	z score $= \dfrac{\text{Deviation}}{\text{SD} = 2.56}$
Mwangi	1	−3.2	−1.25
Maruga	4	−0.2	−0.08
Kamau	6	+1.8	+0.70
Okoko	2	−2.2	−0.86
Kariuki	8	+3.8	+1.49
ΣX	21		0.00
$\bar{X}$ (Mean)	4,2		0.00
SD	2.56		1.00

A somewhat more complete way of describing a set of numbers that is often used in statistics and psychology is the *frequency distribution*. A frequency distribution is a tabulation of how often numbers of various sizes occur in a given set. A very large group of observations can be summarized conveniently and accurately in a frequency-distribution graph. For example, the following set of numbers—5, 7, 2, 2, 1, 3, 7, 6, 6, 1, 7, 6, 6, 3, 6, 6, 8, 4, 5, 4, 5, 5, 3, 2, 6, 7, 8, 1, 5, 6, 4, 4, 2—is represented much more simply in the frequency-distribution graph given in Figure 11–1. The height of the curve at each point represents the number of numbers in the set of the size given on the abscissa at that point.

Figure 11–2 is a slightly more sophisticated frequency distribution; here the frequency is that of successive groups of numbers, rather than

FIGURE 11–1
An example of a frequency
distribution graph for a set of
numbers listed in the text. The
interpretation of the graph is that
the set contained three 1's, four
2's, three 3's, four 4's, five 5's,
eight 6's, four 7's, two 8's, and
no 0's, 9's or 10's.

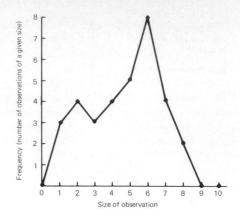

Frequency (number of observations of a given size)

Size of observation

of single numbers. The student should be sure he can interpret such a graph. (The particular distribution shown here is of some interest; it represents the so-called *normal distribution*. The normal distribution is generated by a mathematical theory that describes expected variations in the values of certain classes of chance events. Variables which are determined by a large number of unrelated influences—as are human stature and many psychological traits—often have frequency distributions like this.)

There are other aspects of sets of data that one might want to describe. Looking at Table 11–1 and thinking about our original questions, we might wonder if there is some way to describe the relation between the number of wives and the number of cows. Just by staring at the numbers one certainly gets the impression that the more cows a man has, the more wives he has (perhaps a man who loves cows also loves women, or perhaps there is some crass economic explanation). How can we describe this relation between the two sets of numbers? The extent to which they vary together is called a *correlation*. There are available several different quantitative indices of the degree of correlation between two sets of numbers. The one that is most commonly used, and which is most closely related to the mean and the standard deviations, is the *product-moment correlation coefficient*. This method of measuring correlation is based on the following idea: If the members of one set of numbers are multiplied by the corresponding numbers in the other set, the sum of these products will depend on how they vary together. To see this, consider the three sets of paired numbers below. In set 1, when one number is high so is the other. This is a *positive correlation*. In set 2,

(1)		(2)		(3)	
Pairs	Product	Pairs	Product	Pairs	Product
6,5	30	2,5	10	2,5	10
2,3	6	6,3	18	6,3	18
4,4	16	4,4	16	4,1	4
1,1	1	1,1	1	1,4	4
Sum 53		Sum 45		Sum 36	

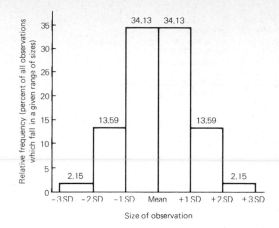

FIGURE 11–2
Another example of a frequency distribution for a set of numbers distributed according to the theoretical "normal probability function" which approximates the distribution of many psychological traits.

there is no relation between members of a pair; highs are paired with lows, lows with lows, etc. In set 3, highs always go with lows; there is an inverse, or *negative, correlation*. The same numbers are involved in all three sets, but in the first set the products add up to 53, in the second to 45, and in the third to 36. The sets of numbers have the same means and the same standard deviations—as indeed they must, since they are the same. But the relation within the pairs is different. This relation is reflected in the sum of the products. In general, the biggest products are obtained when the numbers are of the same size as each other, i.e. when each pair has deviations from the mean in both measures which are identical; of course, this is exactly what we would want to mean by "having the greatest correlation." So the product-moment correlation coefficient, as its name implies, is based on the products of one set of numbers and another.

The first step in computing the product-moment correlation coefficient is to multiply each pair of numbers. Next one finds the sum of these products. But this total product will depend on two things: the amount of correlation between the two, of course, but also the variability of the two sets of numbers. If they vary from 1000 to −2012, the sum of the products is going to be much larger than if they vary from 1 to 4. The formula for computing the correlation coefficient, shown in Table 11–3(a), takes this into account. Essentially, it subtracts from the observed sum of products the sum that would occur if the same set of numbers were rearranged to have no correlation, then divides by the greatest value that this subtraction could yield. The result, the *product-moment correlation coefficient*, is an index number which can vary from −1.0, when the two variables always go in opposite directions—when one goes up, the other goes down proportionally—to +1.0, when they are perfectly correlated in the same direction. Both −1.0 and +1.0 represent "perfect correlation," but one of them is an inverse, or negative, relation while the other is a positive relation between two things. No correlation at all is represented by a coefficient of 0.0. See Table 11–3(a) for a cow-wife example.

TABLE 11–3(a)
Mbongo-Mbongo cows and wives correlated by product-moment method

Name	Cows (X)	X²	Wives (Y)	Y²	XY
Mwangi	1	1	0	0	0
Maruga	4	16	3	9	12
Kamau	6	36	1	1	6
Okoko	2	4	1.5	2.25	3
Kariuki	8	64	7	49	56
	$\Sigma X = 21$	$\Sigma X^2 = 121$	$\Sigma Y = 12.5$	$\Sigma Y^2 = 61.25$	$\Sigma XY = 77$

$$r = \frac{\Sigma XY - (\Sigma X)(\Sigma Y)/N}{\sqrt{[\Sigma X^2 - (\Sigma X)^2/N][\Sigma Y^2 - (\Sigma Y)^2/N]}} = \frac{77 - (21)(12.5)/5}{\sqrt{[(121) - (21)^2/5][61.25 - (12.5)^2/5]}}$$

$$\frac{24.5}{\sqrt{(32.8)(30)}} = \frac{24.5}{31.4}$$

$= .\underline{78}$, the product-moment correlation coefficient

TABLE 11–3(b)
Mbongo-Mbongo cows and wives correlated by ranks method

Name	Cows (x)	Rank	Wives (Y)	Rank	D	D²
Mwangi	1	5	0	5	0	0
Maruga	4	3	3	2	1	1
Kamau	6	2	1	4	2	4
Okoko	2	4	1.5	3	1	1
Kariuki	8	1	7	1	0	0

$$\rho = 1 - \frac{6\Sigma D^2}{N(N^2 - 1)} = 1 - \frac{6(6)}{5(5^2 - 1)} = 1 - \frac{36}{120} = .70$$

There is a shortcut way of calculating a correlation coefficient. This method makes use of ranks in place of the original data. Data from cows and wives translated to ranks are shown in Table 11–3(b). The advantage of ranks is that any set of ranks of the first n numbers always has the same standard deviation, and if we took two sets of ranks of this kind, the sum of the products would always have the same maximum. This greatly simplifies the calculation of the correlation coefficient. All we do, after assigning the ranks, is to find the difference between corresponding ranks D, pair-wise, as has been done in Table 11–3(b). Then we take the squares of these differences, D^2, find their sum, ΣD^2, and enter it in the formula shown below:

$$\rho = 1 - \frac{6\Sigma D^2}{N(N^2 + 1)}$$

The result is the rank-order correlation coefficient, *rho*. It can be interpreted in essentially the same way as the product-moment correlation coefficient, although the two do not, of course, always have the same numerical value.

There are other descriptive statistics, but the ones we have described—the mean, standard deviation, frequency distribution, and correlation coefficient—represent those most often encountered in psychological research.

Inferential statistics

The second major use of statistics is to decide, when one's data are variable, whether some aspect of the data—a difference between two central tendencies, the size of a correlation between two variables, or the like—is to be trusted or is merely a quirk of chance. Deal yourself two hands of cards. Do you expect the total number of spots on the cards in each of the two hands to be exactly equal? Hardly. You would not be in the least surprised to find that one hand had more spots than another. You would attribute such a difference to something you might call "merely chance." The problem is very similar in most research. The number of cows owned by our sample of Mbongo-Mbongo men is greater than the number of wives, but perhaps if we had asked some other men they would have had more wives than cows. Thus, perhaps the difference observed in this sample is "merely the result of chance." Inferential statistics enables us to deal with this kind of problem.

In a moment we shall return to the question of whether Mbongo-Mbongo men really do have more cows than wives. First let us try to creep up on the basic method by studying an example in which the assumptions and theory are pretty obvious. I reach into my pocket and pull forth a penny. I declare that I have strong magic and am able to make pennies come up heads each time that I toss them. I proceed to toss the penny in the air, catch it, and examine it—without, however, letting you see it. I state that it was a head. Am I cheating? (I might have cheated in two ways; by having a two-headed coin, or by lying.) I toss the coin again, and once again I say it was a head. Am I cheating? I toss the coin again and say heads again. Am I cheating? Clearly, if I toss the coin and say heads enough times you will eventually become suspicious. You will be suspicious because you believe than an ordinary "fair" coin will, on the average, come up heads about half the time and tails about half of the time. If there are many too many heads or tails there must be something other than chance operating.

We want to make some quantitative expression of such suspicions —to state just how likely it is that I was or was not cheating. To do this we start with a theory of what the chance outcome should be in the situation. In this case the theory is rather simple: We assume that on any one toss of the coin there is an equal chance that it will come up heads or tails. This is a theory about probability; stated in the usual mathematical terms, it says that each event, heads or tails, had a probability of 0.5. Total probability always adds to 1.0; in this case $p = 0.5$ for heads and $p = 0.5$ for tails; the two ps sum to 1.0. What is the probability of one toss coming up heads with a "fair" coin and no hanky-panky? Obviously, you expect that to happen by chance about half the time, so the probability is 0.5. With the second toss, things have changed. What are the chances that a "fair" coin fairly tossed will come up heads twice in a row?

Psychological research: an appendix on experimental method and statistics
329

TABLE 11-4

Some binomial probabilities (values are the probability p of at least as many observations in one direction for given numbers of paired observations, like head or tail coin tosses, where chance probability is assumed to be .5)

Number of pairs (coin tosses) observed (N)															Number of differences in one direction (heads)	
>15	>14	>13	>12	>11	>10	>9	>8	>7	>6	>5	>4	>3	>2	>1	>0	
5											.03	.19	.50	.81	.97	1.00
6										.02	.11	.34	.66	.89	.98	1.00
7									.01	.06	.23	.50	.77	.94	.99	1.00
8								.00	.04	.14	.36	.64	.86	.96	1.00	1.00
9							.00	.02	.09	.25	.50	.75	.91	.98	1.00	1.00
10						.00	.01	.05	.17	.38	.62	.83	.95	.99	1.00	1.00
11					.00	.01	.03	.11	.27	.50	.73	.89	.97	.99	1.00	1.00
12				.00	.00	.02	.07	.19	.39	.61	.81	.93	.98	1.00	1.00	1.00
13			.00	.00	.01	.05	.13	.29	.50	.71	.87	.95	.99	1.00	1.00	1.00
14		.00	.00	.01	.03	.09	.21	.40	.60	.79	.91	.97	.99	1.00	1.00	1.00
15	.00	.00	.00	.02	.06	.15	.30	.50	.70	.85	.94	.98	1.00	1.00	1.00	1.00

Well, the chance is one-half that it will come up heads the first time, and on the second toss the chance is again one-half that it will come up heads. (The fact that it is called "the second toss" in no way changes the probabilities involved—it is an event independent of the preceding toss and of any following tosses, insofar as the probabilities are concerned.) Thus, it should come up heads both the first *and* second time one-half of one-half, or one-fourth, of the times one tries two tosses. In general, the chances of heads n times in a row are $\frac{1}{2} \times \frac{1}{2} \times \frac{1}{2} \ldots$ for n times, or $(\frac{1}{2})^n$. Table 11-4 shows the probabilities for certain combinations of coin tosses (or other events in which there are just two possibilities, each with a probability of 0.5 on each separate occasion).

To return to our example, as the number of times in a row that I claim to have tossed heads gets greater and greater, your suspicion that this could not have happened by chance becomes greater and greater.

It is just this kind of thing that underlies the use of statistics in making decisions about variable data. One begins by trying to establish what can be expected from chance. If something happens that would be extremely unlikely to occur by chance, one tends to reject the notion that there is nothing but chance involved.

Now let us return to the Mbongo-Mbongo men. What kind of ideal theory of chance might we apply here? One possibility is to use the same notions that applied in the case of coin tossing. If we know nothing else about the situation, we might assume that there is no reason to expect a man to have more wives than cows or cows than wives. We then observe whether each man has more cows or wives. In Table 11-5 we list the outcome. We can treat these pluses and minuses exactly as if they were coin tosses, assuming for each a fifty-fifty chance of more cows or more wives. If this assumption is correct, then about half should be pluses and half minuses (excluding ties). In fact, it turns out that each man has more cows than he has wives. Since there are five men, we need only turn to the theory of chance for such kinds of binary events with equal probability. If the probabilities are really equal, the probability is $\frac{1}{2}$ that one man has more cows than wives, $\frac{1}{4}$ that two out of two have more cows,

TABLE 11–5
Mbongo-Mbongo cows and wives: testing the difference

Name	Cows	Wives	More cows (+) or more wives (−)
Mwangi	1	0	+
Maruga	4	3	+
Kamau	6	1	+
Okoko	2	1.5	+
Kariuki	8	7	+

$\frac{1}{8}$ that three out of three do, $\frac{1}{16}$ that 4 out of 4 do, and $\frac{1}{32}$ that five out of five do (listed as .03 in Table 11–4). From this we can conclude that had there been nothing favoring having more cows than wives the observed result would have happened, on the average, in only 1 out of 32 studies of this kind. That is, if we had gone out repeatedly and randomly picked groups of five Mbongo-Mbongo men (rejecting, however, those who had exactly the same number of wives and cows, since they would provide no information on our question), and if chance alone had been operating, and there really were equal wives and cows on the average, then only 1 time in 32 would we have observed that every man in a sample of five had more cows than wives. We would express this, conventionally, by saying that the probability of the observed result by the binomial theory of chance was .031 (one in thirty-two).

Notice the term *binomial theory* in the last sentence. That is the name of the theory of chance that applies when an event can be one of two things (heads or tails, more cows or wives) and there is a constant probability of it being one or the other. This is only one theory of chance; there are a number of others that correspond to different ways in which events can happen and be distributed. In inferential statistics there are ordinarily two things involved in the computation of a probability level. The first is a theory of what chance should be like for the situation under consideration. The second is some index about the sample that we can compare with the theory. In the coin-toss example, the theory is called the *binomial probability distribution theory* (we won't go into its mathematical details here), and what we need to know about our data is simply the proportion of heads and tails. Indices computed from data are called *statistics;* the proportion of heads is a *statistic* describing the sample of observations made, as is the proportion of men having more cows than wives. In other kinds of statistical tests other statistics are used. In reports of experiments noting a difference between groups or some other feature of the data, one often reads a statement of the form "$t = 4.36$, $df = 18$, $p < .01$," or "$S = 27.2$, $df = 87$, $p < .01$." The first letter symbol (sometimes a word or name is used instead) refers to the theory of chance that is assumed to apply to the case, and this symbol is also the name of the statistic that was calculated from the data. The statement about p tells how likely it is, according to the theory of chance employed, that the observed result or one even more

Psychological research: an appendix on experimental method and statistics
331

extreme, would have occurred. For example, $p < .01$ means that there is less than one chance in a hundred of observing as large a difference between two means, as large a correlation coefficient, or the like, as was actually found in the data. Ordinarily in psychological research a chance probability of 5 percent ($p < .05$) or less—or, better, 1 percent ($p < .01$) or less—is considered low enough that a result may be considered *significant*—that is, probably not due to chance. Results that are likely to occur by chance more than 1 to 5 times in a hundred are viewed with proportionally greater caution. The lower the probability level associated with an experiment, the more confidence one has that the results were not a fluke.

The other number in the statement about the statistical results of an experiment is related to the number of observations; *df* stands for *degrees of freedom*, which is essentially the number of different, independent facts which are calculated from the data. We will not go into this matter further except to say that the *df* for a statistic is usually less than the number of data observations. A statement of *df* is needed because most theories of chance require that one have both a statistic computed from the data and a statement of the number of independent observations on which it was based in order to calculate the chance probability. For example, a complete statement of the results of the coin-tossing or Mbongo-Mbongo observations would be $x = 1.0$, $df = 5$, $p < .03$, because there were five independent facts about cow-wife differences on which the statistic was computed.

Without knowing anything more about statistics, the student should be able to read most psychological journal reports with understanding. Whenever you see a mysterious message claiming that some Greek or English letter equals something, and p equals something, you should translate as follows: "According to a theory of chance for which the appropriate statistic is named by that letter, the probability of the result having occurred by chance was less than the stated value for p."

This completes our discussion of statistics. We have not given you many real tools of statistics to use; there are good sources available from which to get these tools when you need them. But now you have the wherewithal *to understand how conclusions based on statistics are reached*, and so the science that you are now learning need not be taken completely on faith.

The experimental attitude

Perhaps oddly for a textbook, this treatise has a moral. It follows from what we have said earlier—that learning about behavior is difficult, but can be done if the right methods are used. The moral is: When faced with a question about behavior, don't settle for just an intuitively appealing or reasonable answer. Rather, go out and collect good reliable data, tabulate and count them, analyze them, and subject them to statistical inference. It is possible to get valid information about behavior and to draw solid inferences, but one needs to be tough-minded and to go about it right.

Social problems and personal problems are crying for solutions.

But the old methods of simply looking at the problems and "feeling" their answers have not availed. The methods of applying one's best intuitions, noblest motives, most sensitive perceptions, best common sense, and distilled personal experience are sincere and gratifying, but they don't work very well. The thousands of years of failure to end war, poverty, and unhappiness attest to the fact that solutions arrived at in this manner are grossly untrustworthy. One earnest and wise person's common-sensical solution is often the opposite of another's. This alone proves conclusively that desire, good intentions, personal experience, deep thought, and even wisdom are not enough.

We have outlined here the sufficient method for asking and answering a question about behavior. It consists of doing an experiment: of setting up two or more conditions, assigning the conditions to subjects equally and randomly, carefully avoiding any chance of bias, collecting objective and countable data, and analyzing the results so as to compare them to what might have happened by chance. These methods are strict, rigorous, and demanding. But before we can hope to make real progress, before we can build solution on solution, we must stop accepting answers about behavior on the basis of what feels good or seems right. Otherwise we will just continue the long human history of enthusiastic failures. To make progress we must make it piecemeal, by finding out one small thing upon which we can rely, and then another.

In the eventual solution of problems of behavior, the most important ingredient may be an initial attitude that combines humble ignorance with a confidence that our ignorance can be overcome. We must realize that we now know precious little on which to base plans of action. And we must realize that for every psychological problem relevant data can be collected. The attitude of wanting empirical, experimental evidence on which to make decisions about behavior could, if it became popular, make a big difference to the world.

SUGGESTED READINGS

1. *Two good books giving a little more detail on experimental design and statistics, are:*

Hammond, K. R., & Householder, J. E. *Introduction to statistics.* New York: Knopf, 1962.

Spence, J. T., Underwood, B. J., Duncan, C. P., & Cotton, J. W. *Elementary statistics.* New York: Appleton-Century-Crofts, 1968.

References

Adamson, R. E., & Taylor, D. W. Functional fixedness as related to elapsed time and set. *Journal of Experimental Psychology*, 1954, **47**, 122–126.

Adorno, T. W., Frenkel-Brunswik, E., Levinson, D. J., & Sanford, R. N. *The authoritarian personality*. New York: Harper & Row, 1950.

Aldrich, C. A., & Norval, M. A. A developmental graph for the first year of life. *Journal of Pediatrics*, 1946, **29**, 304–308.

Allport, G. W. *Becoming*. New Haven, Conn.: Yale, 1955.

Allport, G. W. *Pattern and growth in personality*. New York: Holt, 1961.

Allport, G. W., & Pettigrew, T. F. Cultural influence on the perception of movement: The trapezoidal illusion among Zulus. *Journal of Abnormal and Social Psychology*, 1957, **55**, 104–113.

Allport, G. W., Vernon, P. E., & Lindzey, G. *A study of values: A scale for measuring the dominent interests in personality*. (3d ed.) Boston: Houghton Mifflin, 1960.

Anderson, N. H. Likableness ratings of 555 personality-trait words. *Journal of Personality and Social Psychology*, 1968, **9**, 272–279.

Aronson, E., & Carlsmith, J. M. Effect of the severity of threat on the devaluation of forbidden behavior. *Journal of Abnormal and Social Psychology*, 1963, **66**, 584–588.

Asch, S. E. Opinions and social pressure. *Scientific American*, 1955, 193(5), 31–35.

Asch, S. E. Studies of independence and submission to group pressure: 1. A minority of one against a unanimous majority. *Psychological Monographs,* 1956, **70**(9, Whole No. 416).

Astin, A. W. "Productivity" of undergraduate institutions. *Science,* 1962, **136,** 129–135.

Astin, A. W. Undergraduate achievement and institutional "excellence." *Science,* 1968, **161,** 661–668.

Bandura, A., Grusec, J. E., & Menlove, F. L. Vicarious extinction of avoidance behavior. *Journal of Personality and Social Psychology,* 1967, **5,** 16–23.

Battig, W. F., & Brackett, H. R. Transfer from verbal-discrimination to paired-associate learning: II. Effects of intralist similarity, method, and percentage occurrence of response members. *Journal of Experimental Psychology,* 1963, **65,** 507–514.

Benham, T. W. Polling for a presidential candidate: Some observations of the 1964 campaign. *Public Opinion Quarterly,* 1965, **29,** 185–199.

Bennett, E. L., Diamond, M. C., Krech, D., & Rosenzweig, M. R. Chemical and anatomical plasticity of brain. *Science,* 1964, **146,** 610–619.

Berelson, B. R., Lazarsfeld, P. F., & McPhee, W. N. *Voting: A study of opinion formation in a presidential election.* Chicago: University of Chicago Press, 1954.

Berko, J. The child's learning of English morphology. *Word,* 1958, **14,** 150–157.

Blakemore, C., & Sutton, P. Size adaptation: A new aftereffect. *Science,* 1969, **166,** 245–247.

Bower, G. H. Application of a model to paired-associate learning. *Psychometrika,* 1961, **26,** 255–280.

Bower, T. G. R. Slant perception and shape constancy in infants. *Science,* 1966, **151,** 832–834.

Brayfield, A. H. Testimony before the senate subcommittee on constitutional rights of the committee on the judiciary. *American Psychologist,* 1965, **20,** 888–954.

Brehm, J. W. Post-decision changes in desirability of alternatives. *Journal of Abnormal and Social Psychology,* 1956, **52,** 384–389.

Brown, R. *Social Psychology.* New York: Free Press, 1965.

Brown, R. W., & Berko, J. Word association and the acquisition of grammar. *Child Development,* 1960, **31,** 1–14.

Bruner, J. S., Shapiro, D., & Tagiuri, R. The meaning of traits in isolation and combination. In R. Tagiuri & L. Petrullo (Eds.), *Person perception and interpersonal behavior.* Stanford, Calif.: Stanford, 1958. Pp. 277–288.

Bustanoby, J. H. *Principles of color and color mixing.* New York: McGraw-Hill, 1947.

Campbell, A. B., & Church, R. M. *Punishment and aversive behavior.* New York: Appleton-Century-Crofts, 1969.

Campbell, F. W., Cooper, G. F., & Enroth-Cugell, C. The spatial selectivity of the visual cells of the cat. *Journal of Physiology,* 1969, **203,** 223–235.

Carlsmith, L. Effect of early father absence on scholastic aptitude. *Harvard Educational Review,* 1964, **34**(1), 3–21.

Cattell, R. B. *Personality*. New York: McGraw-Hill, 1950.

Chapanis, A., Garner, W. R., & Morgan, C. T. *Applied experimental psychology*. New York: Wiley-Interscience, 1949.

Church, R. M. The varied effects of punishment on behavior. *Psychological Reveiw*, 1963, **70**, 369–402.

Coleman, J. S., and others. *Equality of educational opportunity*. Government Printing Office, 1966.

Coppock, H. W., & Chambers, R. M. Reinforcement of position preference by automatic intravenous injections of glucose. *Journal of Comparative and Physiological Psychology*, 1954, **47**, 355–357.

Cornsweet, T. *Visual perception*. New York: Academic Press, 1970.

Crowne, D. P., & Marlowe, D. *The approval motive*. New York: Wiley, 1964.

Dahlstrom, W. G., & Welsh, G. S. *An MMPI handbook: A guide to use in clinical practice and research*. Minneapolis, Minn.: University of Minnesota Press, 1960.

Darwin, C. *Expression of the emotions in man and animals*. Chicago: University of Chicago Press, 1965 (originally published in 1872).

Dement, W. The effect of dream deprivation. *Science*, 1960, **131**, 1705–1707.

Dement, W., & Kleitman, N. The relation of eye movements during sleep to dream activity: An objective method for the study of dreaming. *Journal of Experimental Psychology*, 1957, **53**, 339–346.

Denes, P. B., & Pinson, E. N. *The speech chain*. Murray Hill, N.J.: Bell Telephone Laboratories, Inc., 1963.

Dennis, W., & Dennis, M. G. The effect of cradling practices upon the onset of walking in Hopi children. *Journal of Genetic Psychology*, 1940, **56**, 77–86.

Dennis, W., & Najarian, P. Infant development under environmental handicap. *Psychological Monographs*, 1957, **71**(7, Whole No. 436).

Dingman, H. R., & Tarjan, G. Mental retardation and the normal distribution curve. *American Journal of Mental Deficiency*, 1960, **64**, 991–994.

DuBois, R. H. (Ed.) The classification program. *Army Air Force Aviation Psychology, Program Research Report*, 1947, No. 2.

Durkheim, E. *Suicide*. Chicago: Free Press, 1958 (originally published in 1897).

Ebbinghaus, H. *Memory: A contribution to experimental psychology* (trans. H. A. Ruger & Clara E. Bussenius). New York: Teachers' College, Columbia University, 1913 (originally published in 1885).

Eccles, J. C. *The physiology of synapses*. New York: Academic, 1964.

Eichorn, D. Adolescence. In D. Sills (Ed.), *International Encyclopedia of the Social Sciences*, Vol. 1. New York: Macmillan, 1968. Pp. 84–96.

Epstein, S., & Fenz, W. D. Steepness of approach and avoidance gradients in humans as a function of experience: Theory and experiment. *Journal of Experimental Psychology*, 1965, **70**, 1–12.

Erikson, E. H. Identity and the life cycle. *Psychological Issues*, 1959, 1(No. 1).

Estes, W. K. An experimental study of punishment. *Psychological Monographs*, 1944, **57**(No. 263).

Estes, W. K. Toward a statistical theory of learning. *Psychological Review*, 1950, **57**, 94–107.

Fantz, R. The origin of form perception. *Scientific American*, 1961, **204**(5), 66–72.

Feigenbaum, E. A. Elements of an information processing theory of memory. In D. P. Kimble (Ed.), *Proceedings of the third conference on learning, remembering and forgetting*. New York: New York Academy of Science, 1967.

Festinger, L. *A theory of cognitive dissonance*. Evanston, Ill.: Row, Peterson, 1957.

Festinger, L., & Carlsmith, J. M. Cognitive consequences of forced compliance. *Journal of Abnormal and Social Psychology*, 1959, **58**, 203–210.

Festinger, L., Schachter, S., & Back, K. *Social pressures in informal groups: A study of human factors in housing*. Stanford, Calif.: Stanford, 1963.

Franks, C. M. (Ed.) *Behavior therapy: Appraisal and status*. New York: McGraw-Hill, 1969.

Freedman, J. L., Carlsmith, J. M., & Sears, D. O. *Social Psychology*. Englewood Cliffs, N.J.: Prentice-Hall, 1970.

Frenkel-Brunswik, E., & Sanford, R. N. Some personality factors in anti-semitism. *Journal of Psychology*, 1945, **20**, 271–291.

Fromm, E. *Escape from freedom*. New York: Holt, 1941.

Fuster, J. M. Effects of stimulation of brain stem on tachistoscopic perception. *Science*, 1958, **127**, 150.

Galanter, E. Contemporary psychophysics. In R. Brown and others (Eds.), *New directions in psychology*. New York: Holt, 1962. Pp. 89–156.

Garcia, J., Ervin, F., & Koelling, R. Learning with prolonged delay of reinforcement. *Psychonomic Science*, 1966, **5**, 121–122.

Gardner, E. *Fundamentals of neurology*. (5th ed.) Philadelphia: Saunders, 1968.

Gazzaniga, M. S., Bogen, J. E., & Sperry, R. W. Observations on visual perception after disconnexion of the cerebral hemispheres in man. *Brain*, 1965, **88**, 221–236.

Gesell, A., & Thompson, H. Twins T and C from infancy to adolescence: A biogenetic study of individual differences by the method of co-twin control. *Genetic Psychology Monographs*, 1941, **24**, 3–122.

Gibson, E. J., & Walk, R. D. The "visual cliff." *Scientific American*, 1960, **202**(4), 64–71.

Goldfarb, W. Infant rearing and problem behavior. *American Journal of Orthopsychiatry*, 1943, **13**, 249–265.

Gould, G. L., Henery, M., & MacLeod, M. C. Communication of direction by the honey bee. *Science*, 1970, **169**, 544–554.

Greenspoon, J. The reinforcing effect of two spoken sounds on the frequency of two responses. *American Journal of Psychology*, 1955, **68**, 409–416.

Gregory, R. I. *Eye and brain*. New York: McGraw-Hill, 1966.

Gross, C. G., Bender, D. B., & Rocha-Miranda, C. E. Visual receptive fields of neurons in inferotemporal cortex of the monkey. *Science*, 1969, **166**, 1303–1305.

Hall, C. S., & Lindzey, G. *Theories of personality*. New York: Wiley, 1957.

Harlow, H. F. The nature of love. *American Psychologist*, 1958, **13**, 673–685.

Harlow, H. F., & Harlow, M. K. Learning to love. *American Scientist*, 1966, **54**, 244–272.

Harlow, H. F., & Zimmerman, R. R. Affectional responses in the infant monkey. *Science*, 1959, **130**, 421–432.

Hartline, H. K. The receptive field of the optic nerve fibers. *American Journal of Physiology*, 1940, **130**, 690–699.

Hastorf, A. H., Osgood, C. E., & Ono, H. The semantics of facial expressions and the prediction of the meanings of stereoscopically fused facial expressions. *Scandinavian Journal of Psychology*, 1966, **7**, 179–188.

Hebb, D. O. *The organization of behavior.* New York: Wiley-Interscience, 1949.

Heber, R. Modifications in the manual on terminology and classification in mental retardation. *American Journal of Mental Deficiency*, 1961, **65**, 499–500.

Hefferline, R. F. Learning theory in clinical psychology—an eventual symbiosis? In A. J. Bachrach (Ed.), *Experimental foundations of clinical psychology.* New York: Basic Books, 1962. Pp. 97–138.

Heist, R., McConnell, T. R., Matsler, F., & Williams, P. Personality and scholarship. *Science*, 1961, **133**, 362–367.

Hernández-Peón, R., Scherrer, H., & Jouvet, M. Modification of electric activity in cochlear nucleus during "attention" in unanesthetized cats. *Science*, 1956, **123**, 331–332.

Hess, F. H. Imprinting. *Science*, 1959, **130**, 133–141.

Hess, R. D., & Shipman, V. C. Early experience and the socialization of cognitive modes in children. *Child Development*, 1965, **36**, 869–886.

Hewes, G. W. The anthropology of posture. *Scientific American*, 1957, **196**(2), 122–132.

Hilgard, E. R., & Bower, G. H. *Theories of learning.* (3rd ed.) New York: Appleton-Century-Crofts, 1966.

Hilgard, J. R. Personality and hypnotizability: Inferences from case studies. In E. R. Hilgard (Ed.), *Hypnotic susceptibility.* New York: Harcourt, Brace & World, 1965. Pp. 343–374.

Hintzman, D. L. Explorations with a discrimination net model for paired-associate learning. *Journal of Mathematical Psychology*, 1968, 5(1), 123–162.

Hirsch, J., & Boudreau, J. C. Studies in experimental behavior genetics: I. The heritability of phototaxis in a population of *Drosophila melanogaster. Journal of Comparative and Psyiological Psychology*, 1958, **51**, 646–651.

Hovland, C. I. The generalization of conditioned responses: I. The sensory generalization of conditioned responses with varying frequencies of tone. *Journal of General Psychology*, 1937, **17**, 125–148.

Hubel, D. H., & Wiesel, T. N. Receptive fields of single neurones in the cat's striate cortex. *Journal of Physiology*, 1959, **148**, 574–591.

Hubel, D. H., & Wiesel, T. N. Receptive fields, binocular interaction and functional architecture in the cat's visual cortex. *Journal of Physiology*, 1962, **160**, 106–154.

Hunt, J. McV. *Intelligence and experience.* New York: Ronald, 1961.

Hydén, H. & Egyházi, E. Glial RNA changes during a learning experiment in rats. *Proceedings of the National Academy of Science of the United States*, 1963, **49**, 618–624.

Jones, M. C. The elimination of children's fears. *Journal of Experimental Psychology*, 1924, **7**, 382–390.

Jost, H. Die Assoziations Festigkeit in ihrer Abhäng Keit von der Verteilung der Wiederholungen. *Zeitschrift für Psychologie*, 1897, **14**, 436–472.

Jung, C. G. *Psychological types*. New York: Harcourt, Brace & World, 1923.

Kagan, J. The distribution of attention in infancy. In *Perception and its disorders*. The Association for Research in Nervous and Mental Disease, 1970, Vol. XLVIII, 214–237.

Kanfer, F. H., & Saslow, G. Behavioral diagnosis. In C. M. Franks (Ed.), *Behavior therapy: Appraisal and status*. New York: McGraw-Hill, 1969. Pp. 417–444.

Kety, S. S. Biochemical theories of schizophrenia, Part II. *Science*, 1959, **129**, 1590–1596.

Kohler, O. Über den Gruppenwirkungsgrad der Menschen Korperarbeit und die Bedingum optimal kollectiv Kraftreaktion. *Indus. Psychotechn.*, 1927, **4**, 209–226.

Krech, D., Rosenzweig, M. R., Bennett, E. C., & Krueckel, B. Enzyme concentrations in the brain and adjustive behavior patterns. *Science*, 1954, **120**, 994–996.

Krogh, A. The language of the bees. *Scientific American*, 1948, 179(2), 18–21.

Kuffler, S. W. Discharge patterns and functional organization of mammalian retina. *Journal of Neurophysiology*, 1953, **16**, 37–68.

Landauer, T. K. Delay of an acquired reinforcer. *Journal of Comparative and Physiological Psychology*, 1964, **58**, 374–379.

Landauer, T. K. Reinforcement as consolidation. *Psychological Review*, 1969, **76**, 92–96.

Landauer, T. K., & Whiting, J. W. M. Infantile stimulation and adult stature of human males. *American Anthropologist*, 1964, **66**, 1007–1028.

Lashley, K. In search of the engram. In Symposium of the Society of Experimental Biology, No. 4: *Physiological Mechanisms in Animal Behavior*. New York: Cambridge, 1950. Pp. 478–505.

Latané, B., & Darley, J. M. Bystander "apathy." *American Scientist*, 1969, **57**, 244–268.

Lazarsfeld, P. F., Berelson, B., & Gaudet, H. *The people's choice.* (2nd ed.) New York: Columbia, 1948.

Lenneberg, E. H. (Ed.) *New directions in the study of language*. Cambridge, Mass.: M.I.T., 1964.

Lettvin, J. Y., Maturana, H. R., McCulloch, W. S., & Pitts, W. H. What the frog's eye tells the frog's brain. *Proceedings of the Institute of Radio Engineers*, 1959, **47**, 1940–1951.

Lewin, K. *A dynamic theory of personality*. New York: McGraw-Hill, 1935.

Liberman, A. M., Cooper, F. S., Shankweiler, D. P., & Studdert-Kennedy, M. Perception of the speech code. *Psychological Review*, 1967, **74**, 431–461.

Lipsitt, L. P. Learning processes of newborns. *Merrill-Palmer Quarterly*, 1966, **12**, 45–77.

Long, G. E. The effect of duration of onset and cessation of light flash on the intensity-time relation in the peripheral retina. *Journal of the Optical Society of America*, 1951, 41(11), 743–747.

Lorente de Nó, R. Analysis of the activity of the chains of internuncial neurons. *Journal of Neurophysiology*, 1938, **1**, 207–244.

Lorenz, K. Über die Bildung des Instinktbegriffes. *Naturwisserschaften*, 1937, 25, 289–300, 307–318, 324–331.

Luchins, A. S. Mechanization in problem solving: The effect of *einstellung*. *Psychological Monographs*, 1942, 54(No. 248).

Maddi, S. R. *Personality theories: A comparative analysis*. Homewood, Ill.: Dorsey, 1968.

Marks, I. M., & Gelder, M. G. Clinical and psychological changes during faradic aversion. *British Journal of Psychiatry*, 1967, **119**, 711–730.

Maslow, A. H. *Toward a psychology of becoming*. Princeton, N. J.: Van Nostrand, 1962.

McCarthy, D. A. Language development in children. In L. Carmichael (Ed.), *Manual of child psychology*. New York: Wiley, 1946. Pp. 476–581.

McClelland, D. C. *The achieving society*. Princeton, N.J.: Van Nostrand, 1961.

McClelland, D. C., Atkinson, J. W., Clark, R. A., & Lowell, E. L. *The achievement motive*. New York: Appleton-Century-Crofts, 1953.

McClosky, H. Conservativism and personality. *American Political Science Review*, 1958, **52**, 27–45.

Melzack, R., & Scott, T. H. The effects of early experience on the response to pain. *Journal of Comparative and Physiological Psychology*, 1957, **50**, 155–161.

Miller, N. E. Experimental studies of conflict. In J. McV. Hunt (Ed.), *Personality and the behavior disorders*. New York: Ronald, 1944. Pp. 431–465.

Miller, N. E. Central stimulation and other new approaches to motivation and reward. *American Psychologist*, 1958, **13**, 100–108.

Mitchell, P. H. *General Physiology*. (5th ed.) New York: McGraw-Hill, 1956.

Money, J., Hampson, J. G., & Hampson, J. L. *Archives of Neurological Psychiatry*, 1957, **77**, 333.

Morrell, F. Effect of anodal polarization on the firing pattern of single cortical cells. *Annals of the New York Academy of Science*, 1961, **92**, 860–876.

Mueller, C. G. *Sensory psychology*. Englewood Cliffs, N.J.: Prentice-Hall, 1965.

Murray, H. A. and others. *Explorations in personality*. New York: Oxford University Press, 1938.

Myrdal, G., with the assistance of R. Sterner & A. M. Rose. *An American dilemma*. New York: Harper and Row, 1944.

Olds, J. Self-stimulation of the brain. *Science*, 1958, **127**, 315–323.

Osgood, C. E. The nature and measurement of meaning. *Psychological Bulletin*, 1952, **49**, 197–237.

Page, J. D. & Page, D. S. Criteria for mental hospitalization. *Journal of Abnormal and Social Psychology*, 1941, **36**, 433–435.

Paul, G. L. *Insight vs. desensitization in psychotherapy: An experiment in anxiety reduction.* Stanford, Calif.: Stanford, 1966.

Pavlov, I. P. *Conditioned reflexes.* New York: Oxford University Press, 1927.

Penfield, W. The permanent record of the stream of consciousness. *Proceedings of the 14th International Congress of Psychologists,* 1954, **4,** 47–69.

Penfield, W., & Rasmussen, T. *The cerebral cortex of man.* New York: Macmillan, 1952.

Peterson, L. R., & Peterson, M. J. Short-term retention of individual verbal items. *Journal of Experimental Psychology,* 1959, **58,** 193–198.

Pettigrew, T. F. Personality and sociocultural factors in intergroup attitudes, a cross-national comparison. *Journal of Conflict Resolution,* 1958, **2,** 29–42.

Pfaff, D. Parsimonious biological models of memory and reinforcement. *Psychological Review,* 1969, **76,** 70–81.

Piaget, J. *The moral judgment of the child.* Glencoe, Ill.: Free Press, 1948 (originally published in 1932).

Piaget, J. A theory of development. In D. Sills (Ed.), *International encyclopedia of the social sciences,* Vol. 4. New York: Macmillan, 1968, Pp. 140–147.

Polyak, S. L. *The retina.* Chicago: University of Chicago Press, 1941.

Rachman, S. The treatment of anxiety and phobic reactions by systematic desensitization psychotherapy. *Journal of Abnormal and Social Psychology,* 1959, **58,** 259–263.

Richards, C. B., & Dobyns, H. F. Topography and culture: The case of the changing cage. *Human Organization,* 1957, **16,** 16–20.

Riesen, A. H. Stimulation as a requirement for growth and function in behavioral development. In D. W. Fiske & S. R. Maddi (Eds.), *Functions of varied experience.* Homewood, Ill.: Dorsey, 1961. Pp. 57–80.

Riggs, L. A., Ratliff, F., Cornsweet, J. C., & Cornsweet, T. N. The disappearance of steadily fixated visual test objects. *Journal of the Optical Society of America,* 1953, **43,** 495–501

Rock, I., & Harris, C. S. Vision and touch. *Scientific American,* 1967, **216**(5), 96–104.

Rogers, C. R. *On becoming a person.* Boston: Houghton Mifflin, 1961.

Rosen, B. C., & d'Andrade, R. The psychosocial origins of achievement motivation. *Sociometry,* 1959, **22,** 185–218.

Rosenthal, R. Experimenter outcome-orientation and the results of the psychological experiment. *Psychological Bulletin,* 1964, **61,** 405–412.

Rozin, P. Specific aversions as a component of specific hungers. *Journal of Comparative and Physiological Psychology,* 1967, **64,** 237–242.

Schachter, S. *The psychology of affiliation.* Stanford, Calif.: Stanford, 1959.

Schachter, S., & Singer, J. E. Cognitive, social and physiological determinants of emotional state. *Psychological Review,* 1962, **69,** 379–399.

Senden, M. V. *Raum-und Gestaltauffassung bei Operierten Blindgeborenen vor und nach Operation.* Leipzig, Germany: Barth, 1932.

Selye, H. *The stress of life.* New York: McGraw-Hill, 1956.

Shaw, M. E. Some effects of problem complexity upon problem solution efficiency in different communication nets. *Journal of Experimental Psychology*, 1954, **48**, 211–217.

Shepard, R. N. Recognition memory for words, sentences and pictures. *Journal of Verbal Learning and Verbal Behavior*, 1967, **6**, 156–163.

Skinner, B. F. Are theories of learning necessary? *Psychological Review*, 1950, **57**, 193–216.

Solomon, R. L., Kamin, L., & Wynne, L. C. Traumatic avoidance learning: Acquisition in normal dogs. *Psychological Monographs*, 1953, **67**(No. 354).

Spence, J. T. A personality scale of manifest anxiety. *Journal of Abnormal and Social Psychology*, 1953, **48**, 285–290.

Spence, K. W., & Norris, E. B. Eyelid conditioning as a function of the inter-trial interval. *Journal of Experimental Psychology*, 1950, **40**, 716–720.

Sperling, G. Information available in brief visual presentations. *Psychological Monographs*, 1960, **74**(No. 11).

Sperry, R. W. Cerebral organization and behavior. *Science*, 1961, **133**, 1749–1757.

Sperry, R. W. The great cerebral commissure. *Scientific American*, 1964, **210**(1), 42–52.

Spitz, R. A. Hospitalism: An inquiry into the genesis of psychiatric conditions in early childhood, Part I. *Psychoanalytic Study of the Child*, 1945, **1**, 53–74.

Spitzer, H. F. Studies in retention. *Journal of Educational Psychology*, 1939, **30**, 641–657.

Spooner, A., & Kellogg, W. N. The backward conditioning curve. *American Journal of Psychology*, 1947, **60**, 321–334.

Stephan, F. F., & Mishler, E. G. The distribution of participation in small groups: An exponential approximation. *American Sociological Review*, 1952, **17**, 598–608.

Sternberg, S. High-speed scanning in human memory. *Science*, 1966, **153**, 652–654.

Sternberg, S. Two operations in character-recognition: Some evidence from reaction-time measurements. *Perception and Psychophysics*, 1967, **2**, 45–53.

Stevens, S. S. The psychophysics of sensory function. In W. A. Rosenblith (Ed.), *Sensory communication*. New York: Wiley, 1961. Pp. 1–33.

Stevens, S. S. To honor Fechner and repeal his law. *Science*, 1961, **133**, 80–87.

Stromeyer, C. F., & Psotko, J. The detailed texture of eidetic images. *Nature*, 1970, **225**, 346–349.

Taylor, D. W., Berry, P. C., & Block, C. H. Does group participation when using brainstorming facilitate or inhibit creative thinking? *Administrative Science Quarterly*, 1958, **3**, 23–47.

Taylor, J. T. A personality scale of manifest anxiety. *Journal of Abnormal and Social Psychology*, 1953, **48**, 285–290.

Terman, L. M., & Merrill, M. A. *Stanford-Binet Intelligence Scale: Manual for the third revision form L-M*. Boston: Houghton Mifflin, 1960.

Triplett, N. The dynamogenic factors in pacemaking and competition. *American Journal of Psychology*, 1897, **9**, 507–533.

Underwood, B. J. Interference and forgetting. *Psychological Review*, 1957, **64,** 49–60.

von Frisch, K. *The dancing bees.* London: Methuen, 1954.

Wallach, M. A., Kogan, N., & Bem, D. J. Group influence on individual risk taking. *Journal of Abnormal and Social Psychology*, 1962, **65,** 75–87.

Warren, J. R., & Heist, P. A. Personality attributes of gifted college students. *Science*, 1960, **132,** 330–337.

Watson, J., & Rayner, R. Conditioned emotional reactions. *Journal of Experimental Psychology*, 1920, **3,** 1–14.

Weickart, D. P. Preliminary results from a longitudinal study of disadvantaged school children. *Selected Convention Papers*, Convention of the Council for Exceptional Children, Washington, 1969.

Weingarten, M., & Spinelli, D. N. Retinal receptive field changes produced by auditory and somatic stimulation. *Experimental Neurology*, 1966, **15,** 363–376.

White, R. W. Motivation reconsidered: The concept of competence. *Psychological Review*, 1959, **66,** 297–333.

Whiting, J. W. M., & Child, I. L. *Child training and personality: A cross-cultural study.* New Haven, Conn.: Yale, 1953.

Whiting, J. W. M., & Whiting, B. B., in collaboration with R. Longabaugh. *Children of six cultures: Part I.* New York: Wiley, 1971, in press.

Wickelgren, W. A. Sparing of short-term memory in an amnesic patient: Implications for strength theory of memory. *Neuropsychologia*, 1968, **6,** 235–244.

Wohlwill, J. F. Developmental studies of perception. *Psychological Bulletin*, 1960, **57,** 249–289.

Wolpe, J., & Lazarus, A. A. *Behavior therapy techniques: A guide to the treatment of neuroses.* London: Pergamon, 1966.

Zelman, A., Kabat, L., Jacobson, R., & McConnell, J. V. Transfer of training through injection of "conditioned" RNA into untrained planarians. *Worm Runner's Digest*, 1963, **5,** 14–21.

Index

Cochlea, 288
Cocktail party phenomenon, described, 123
Cognition, defined, 8
Cognitive consistency:
  attitude changes and, 46–48
  need for, defined, 44
Cognitive dissonance, theory of, 47
Cognitive factors, relations between personality traits and, 65–66
Cognitive tasks in language development, 254
Collaterals of sensory pathways, 145
Color contrast effects, 121, 122
Communication inside groups, 35–36
Complex cells of cortex, 295–297
Complexity of language, 208–209
Computers:
  human memory compared with, 236
  information processing by, 284
Concrete operations stage of development (hypothetico-deductive operations stage of development), 255–256
Conditioned reinforcers (acquired reinforcers), 182–183
Conditioned responses (CR), 174–176
Conditioned stimulus (CS), 169–173
  intensity of, 173
  sequence and timing of, 169–172
Conditioned stimulus-unconditioned stimulus intervals (CS-US intervals), 171–173, 187
Conditioning:
  classical, 169–177
    applications of, 176–177
    factors of effectiveness in, 170–174
    forgetting in, 222
    paired-associate learning compared with, 217
    responses to, 174–175
    workings of, 169–170
  generalized anxiety and, 163
  imprinting as, 166–168
  mixed cases of, 194–196
  operant, 177–203
    applicability of, 201–203
    aversive control of behavior and, 196–200
    characteristics of, 192–194
    described, 177–178
    factors of effectiveness in, 183–192

Conditioning:
  operant: forgetting compared with, 222
    paired-associate learning compared with, 217
    principles underlying, 178–179
    reinforcers of, 180–183
  phobias produced by, 93
Conflict:
  adjustment and, 76–80
  intergroup hostility, 29–30
Conformity, generalized, 26–28
Congenital anomalies as sources of mental retardation, 90–91
Consciousness, speech and, 310–311
Conservation of quantity, concept of, 255
Conservatives, characteristics of, 44
Consistency:
  of attitudes, 43–44
  cognitive: attitude changes and, 46–48
    need for, 44
  intra-cultural, 24
  in personality testing, 62–63
Consistency theories of adjustment, 80–81
Consolidation of memory hypothesis, 309–310
Consonants of English language, 209
Constancy:
  of perception, 125–126, 242, 243
  of shape, defined, 125
Constant proportional gain, principle of, 184–186, 228
Constant stimuli, method of, 107
Contact comfort:
  defined, 259
  mother-infant relationship and, 3, 5
Context of words, defined, 209
Contrasts in perception, 123
Conventions, teaching of, 25–26
Cooper, F. S., 211, 295
Coppock, H. W., 181
Corpus callosum, 284, 305
Cortex, 283, 301–305
  destroyed regions of, 303–304
  effects of removing parts of, 298–299
  left and right, 310–311
  storage of memory and, 302–305
Cortical cells in visual system, 295–297
Counseling psychology, defined, 9

Counterbalancing as technique of experimental research, 317, 318
Counterconditioning (systematic desensitization), 97–98
CR (conditioned responses), 174–176
Creativity:
generalized conformity and, 27
in problem solving, 233
Critical flicker frequence (CFF), 115
Critical period of imprinting, 166
Crowne, D. P., 57, 161
CS (see Conditioned stimulus)
CS-US intervals (conditioned stimulus-unconditioned stimulus intervals), 171–173, 187
Cultural-familial sources of mental retardation, 92
Culture, 22–28
defined, 22–23
mechanisms of maintenance of, 24–28
personality traits and, 64–65
Cumulative recording, defined, 190
Curiosity, defined, 156
Cycles affecting behavior, 145–146

D'Andrade, R., 163
Dark-adaptation curve, 114, 115
Darley, J. M., 31
Darwin, Charles, 148
Decay curve of short-term memory, 216
Decibel, defined, 130
Defense mechanisms, functions of, 66, 78–80
Degrees of freedom (df), 332
Deindividuation (responsibility diffusion), 31
Delinquency as character disorder, 86
Dement, W., 149
Dennis, M. G., 251
Dennis, W., 247
Deprivation:
of REM sleep, 149
satiation-deprivation cycles, 188–189
of visual experience, 244
Depth perception, 123–124, 242–243
of infants, 242–243
Descartes, René, 9
Descriptive statistics, 321–329
Desensitization, systematic, 97–98

Desiderata:
in adjustment, 73–74
defined, 72
Development, 238–271
brain and, 238–239
determiners of, 240–241
Erikson's stages of, 267
language, 249–257
intelligence and, 256–257
logic and reasoning, 253–256
perceptual, 241–245
personality, 261–266
child-rearing practices and, 262–265
early experience and sex identification in, 261–262
enculturation and, 265–266
physical, 245–250
motor skills and, 245–249
psychosexual, 68–70
of social relations, 257–261
morals, values, attitudes and, 259–261
Developmental psychology, defined, 8
Devil effect (halo effect), 43
df (degrees of freedom), 332
Diamond, M., 3
Difference threshold of sensitivity, 107
Differential diagnoses of behavior disorders, 84
Discrimination training:
in classical conditioning, 175
in operant conditioning, 192–193
Discussion groups, small, participation in, 33
Diseases:
causing mental retardation, 91
physical, defined, 83
Dislikable persons, words describing, 39
Disorders (see Behavior disorders)
Distance, texture density as cue for, 124
Diurnal cycle, behavior affected by, 144–145
Dobyns, H. F., 34
Dominance hierarchies, 260
Double blindness, 317
Doubling (fractionation), defined, 130
Downe's Syndrome (mongolism), 65, 90–91
Dreaming, 149–150
Drive reducers as reinforcers, 180–181

Homeostatic balance, defined, 297
Homosexuality, aversion therapy for, 98
Hormones, state-determined behavior and, 150–152
Hostility, intergroup, 29–30
Hubel, D. N., 289
Human factors engineering:
  defined, 9
  examples of, 10
Human infants (see Infants)
Hunger, factors producing, 138
Hunt, J. McV., 65, 256
Hydén, H., 309
Hydrocephaly, 90
Hyperphagia, defined, 299
Hypnosis, state-determined behavior and, 153–154
Hypothalamus, 284
  emotion and, 299–301
Hypothetico-deductive operations stage of development (concrete operations stage of development), 255–256
Hz (hertz), defined, 116

Idealized neurons, 274
Identity crisis, 267–268
Illusions of perception, 126
Imagery, edeitic, 6–7
Images received by the eye, 110–111
Imprinting as mode of learning, 166–168
Incubation period of problems, 233
Individual behavior, effects of group on, 30–32
Individual expression, generalized conformity and, 27
Industrial psychology, defined, 9
Infants:
  delayed maturing of, 238–239
  mother infant relationship: contact comfort and, 3, 5
    effects on social relations, 257–259
  nervous system of newborns, 244
  smiling, 168, 257, 258
  stress, growth and, 246–247
  visual perception of, 241–244
Inferences of perception, 120–128
Inferential statistics, 329–332
Information:
  attitudes and, 45–48
  input and analysis of, 286–287
Information processing in nervous system, 284–286

Inherited anomalies as sources of mental retardation, 90–91
Inhibition:
  forgetting and, 223–227
  proactive, 214, 224
  of synapses, 285
Innate behavior patterns, 138–143
Innately pleasant stimuli as reinforcer, 181–182
Insight therapy, 96–97
Instinctive reactions, 157
Instinctual drives, 67
Intellectual inquiries, stages of development of, 11
Intelligence:
  assessment of, 51–54
  language development and, 256–257
Interaction (see Interpersonal interaction)
Interests, values and, 57–59
Interference, transfer and, in verbal learning, 219–221
Intergroup hostility, 29–30
Interlist interference, 221
Interpersonal interaction, 37–48
  conformity influenced by, 28
  defined, 23
  determinants of, 37–40
  outcomes of, 43–48
  processes of, 40–43
Interposition, defined, 124
Interviews, 60
Intra-cultural consistency, language as expression of, 24
Introversion-extroversion, characteristics of, 59
IQ (intelligence quotient), hypothetical distribution of, 83
IQ tests, 51–54
Isolation, defined, 78–79

Jacobson, R., 3
James, William, 10
Jost's law, 167, 168
Judgment:
  choice, recognition and, 128–135
  developing moral, 260–261
Jung, Carl, 59

Kabat, L., 3
Kagan, J., 271
Kamin, L., 199, 200

Nature-nurture problem, language acquisition as, 249
Nearsighted eyes, 114
Need states (drive states), 156–157
Needs:
  list of personal, 74
  satiation of, 156
Negative correlations, defined, 326
Negative fixation, defined, 69
Negative reinforcers, 180
Negative transfer, 220, 224
Nerves, functions of, 277–278
Nervous system:
  anatomy of, 277–284
  at birth, 244
  information processing in, 284–286
Neural circuits, recurrent, 307–308
Neural information, input and analysis of, 286–297
Neural organization, language development and, 252
Neuro-glia (glia) of brain, 281
Neurons, action potentials of, 273–276
Neuroses (psychoneuroses):
  causes of, 92–93
  classical conditioning in treatment of, 177
  defined, 84
  treatment of, 95–100
  types of, 85–86
Nicotine, 153
Noise, signal detection and, 133
Nondirective counseling therapy, 96–97
Non-rapid eye movement sleep (non-REM sleep), 149
Nonsense syllables:
  forgetting, 222, 223
  recalling, 6
  verbal learning and use of, 216
Normal scores (normal deviates), defined, 325
Normalized scores (transformed scores), 17
Norms of groups, 36–37
Nuclei (ganglia), 278
Nucleic acids, nature of memory and, 308–309

Object permanence, concept of, 255
Objective difficulties of research, 314
Objective tests, 57

Observation, knowledge and, 11–12
Obsessive-compulsive reactions, defined, 86
Oedipal stage of psychosexual development, 68
Off-center cells of retina, 292, 294
On-center cells of retina, 292, 294, 295
Operant conditioning, 177–203
  applicability of, 201–203
  aversive control of behavior and, 196–200
  characteristics of, 192–194
  described, 177–178
  factors of effectiveness in, 183–192
  forgetting compared with, 222
  mixed cases of, 194–196
  paired-associate learning compared with, 217
  principles underlying, 178–179
  reinforcers of, 180–183
Operant reinforcement, principle of, 178–179
Optic nerve, cells of, 293–294
Oral stage of psychosexual development, 68
Order of stimuli in classical conditioning, 170–171
Organic psychoses, 88, 93
Organization:
  of perception, 126–128
  of personality, 63–70
Organs of Corti, 287, 288
Osgood, C. E., 42

Pain, sensitivity to, 118–119
Paired-associate learning:
  effects of spacing of presentation in, 219
  experiments with, 216–217
  lists of pairs, 220–222
Paradoxical sleep [rapid eye movement (REM) sleep], 149
Parallax, defined, 123
Paranoia, defined, 88
Parasympathetic nervous system, functions of, 278
Partial reinforcement, 190–192
Party preferences, changes in, during election campaign, 45
Patience, adjustment and, 75
Paul, G. L. A., 100–101
Pavlov, Ivan, 5, 11, 169
Penfield, W., 305

Percent savings score, formula of, 223
Perception, 105–135
  analysis and inferences of, 120–128
  constancies of, 125–126, 242, 243
  defined, 8, 40, 105–107
  judgment, recognition and, 128–135
  organization and reorganization of,
    126–128
  person, 40–43
  sensation and, 286–287
    auditory, 287–289
    visual, 289–297
  sensitivity and, 107–120
    to heat, pressure, and pain,
      118–119
    to light, 108–116, 121
    measures of, 107–108
    to sound, 116–117
Percepts, high-order characteristics
  of, 123–125
Perceptual constancies, 125–126,
  242, 243
Perceptual development, 241–245
Perceptual performance, factors
  describing, 134
Performance:
  as factor in operant conditioning,
    188–189
  perceptual, 134
Performance stage of operant conditioning, 183
Peripheral nervous system, components of, 277, 278
Perseverance, adjustment and, 75
Person perception, difficulties of,
  40–43
Personal vs. social adjustment, 72
Personal needs, listed, 74
Personal wisdom fallacy, overcoming,
  314–316
Personality:
  consistency of attitudes and, 44
  defined, 49–50
  organization and dynamics of,
    63–70
    psychoanalytic theory and,
      66–70
Personality development, 261–266
  child-rearing practices and, 262–
    265
  early experience and sex identifica-
    tion in, 261–262
  enculturation and, 265–266
Personality inventories, 59–60
Personality psychology, defined, 8

Personality traits:
  assessment of, 50–63
  cognitive factors and, 65–66
  origins and interrelation of, 64, 70
Peterson, L., 6
Peterson, M., 6
Pettigrew, T. F., 44
Pfaff, D., 309
Phenylketonuria (PKU), 91, 95
Phobias:
  classical conditioning in treatment
    of, 177
  defined, 5–6, 85
Phonemes of English language,
  209–211
Physical diseases, defined, 83
Physical disorders, conflict-caused,
  78
Physical growth, 245–250
  motor skills and, 245–249
Physiological psychology, defined,
  8
Piaget, Jean, 254–256, 260
Pitts, W. H., 289
PKU (phenylketonuria), 91, 95
Pleasure, 157–159
  sensations yielding, 159
Political values, 57
Pons of brain, 284
Positive affective states, laughter as,
  148
Positive correlations, defined, 326
Positive fixation, defined, 69
Positive reinforcement vs. aversion
  conditioning, 200–201
Positive reinforcers, 180
Positive transfer, 220
Power function, defined, 130
Prejudice:
  authoritarianism and, 44
  education and, 30
  persistence of, 39
  sources of, 29
Preoperational thought stage of
  development, 255
Pressure, sensitivity to, 118–119
Primitive societies:
  child-rearing in, 4–5
  duration of socialization period in,
    28
Proactive inhibition, 214, 224
Probability distribution, binomial,
  330, 331
Problem solving, thinking and,
  231–233